A Shining Thread of Hope

A Shining Thread of Hope

THE HISTORY OF BLACK WOMEN IN AMERICA

DARLENE CLARK HINE *and*
KATHLEEN THOMPSON

Broadway Books

NEW YORK

BROADWAY

Broadway Books titles may be purchased for business or promotional use or for special sales. For information, please write to: Special Markets Department, Bantam Doubleday Dell Publishing Group, Inc., 1540 Broadway, New York, NY 10036.

BROADWAY BOOKS and its logo, a letter B bisected on the diagonal, are trademarks of Broadway Books, a division of Bantam Doubleday Dell Publishing Group, Inc.

Library of Congress Cataloging-in-Publication Data
Hine, Darlene Clark.
A shining thread of hope : the history of Black women in America /
Darlene Clark Hine and Kathleen Thompson. — 1st ed.
p.   cm.
Includes bibliographical references (p. 333) and index.
ISBN 0-7679-0110-X (hc)
1. Afro-American women—History.   I. Thompson, Kathleen.   II. Title.
E185.86.H68   1998
305.48'896'073—dc21   97-34578
                                                                CIP

FIRST EDITION

Designed by Vertigo Design, NYC

98 99 00 01 02 10 9 8 7 6 5 4 3 2 1

To

BARBARA ANN CLARK

and

ALMA (BRENDA) CLARK MACINTOSH

and to

CLARA LUPER

Black women are a prism through which

the searing rays of race, class and sex are

first focused, then refracted. The creative

among us transform these rays into a

spectrum of brilliant colors, a rainbow

which illuminates the experience of

all mankind.

MARGARET B. WILKERSON

Contents

Prologue

EVERY SMALL TOWN has its honored citizens. You can find their names on plaques in the library and in the history of the town, bound in leather and getting dusty on the shelves. Parks are created in tribute to them, and streets are named after them, and the people of the town remember them, even if they don't always know why.

Deerfield, Massachusetts, remembers Lucy Terry Prince. She came to the town when she was only about five years old. Ebenezer Wells bought her off a slave ship to help him with his housework. She was baptized in the First Church of Deerfield on June 15, 1735. The town history remembers that, when she was grown up, "she was noted for her wit and shrewdness" and the boys of the town flocked to her house "to hear her talk," so we can assume that she learned her new language quickly and was a sociable child. When she was fourteen, she was admitted to "the fellowship of the church." When she was sixteen, nearby Indians attacked that part of Deerfield known as "The Bars," and teenaged Lucy wrote a poem commemorating the event. We don't know whether it was her first effort, but it was the first and only poem of hers that was preserved.

BARS FIGHT

August, 'twas the twenty-fifth,
Seventeen hundred forty-six,
The Indians did in ambush lay
Some very valient men to slay,
Samuel Allen like a hero fout,
And though he was so brave and bold,
His face no more shall we behold.

Eleazer Hawks was killed outright,
Before he had time to fight—
Before he did the Indians see,
Was shot and killed immediately.

Oliver Amsden he was slain,
Which caused his friends much grief and pain
Simeon Amsden they found dead
Not many rods distant from his head.

Adonijah Gillett, we do hear,
Did lose his life which was so dear.
John Sadler fled across the water,
And thus escaped the dreadful slaughter.

Eunice Allen see the Indians coming,
And hopes to save herself by running;
And had not her petticoats stopped her,
The awful creatures had not catched her,
Nor tommy hawked her on the head.
Young Samuel Allen, Oh, lack–a–day!
Was taken and carried to Canada.

The adolescent Lucy Terry's feelings for her neighbors were clearly not tainted with a sense of racial inferiority or even self-consciousness. The tone of the poem makes it obvious that young Lucy Terry considered the white people she described to be friends and neighbors. In fact, probably the most appealing quality of the poem is the evident affection the poet feels for her subjects. And the poem itself was treasured in Deerfield. Handed down from generation to generation, it was published in 1855 in *History of Western Massachusetts* by Josiah Gilbert Holland.

In 1756, when she was about twenty-six, Lucy Terry married Abijah Prince. At this time, she was free, although it is not certain by what means. Wells may have freed her, or Prince may have bought her freedom. He was an established man, having served four years in the militia during the French and Indian Wars and, perhaps because of his service, having acquired his freedom and three parcels of land in Northfield, Massachusetts. He was older than his new wife by about twenty-five years. Sometime during the 1760s, he and Lucy acquired a farm near Guilford, Vermont, and moved their family there. Later, Abijah Prince was one of the founders of the town of Sunderland, Vermont. The Princes seemed to fit in well at Guilford, a town of culture and learning, with a library and musical societies. However, in 1785, the Noyse family—white neighbors of the Princes—threatened them with violence. Lucy and Abijah appealed to Governor Thomas Chittenden for protection, and he ordered the selectmen of the town to see to it that the Princes were bothered no more.

The Princes had seven children. Lucy applied for the admission of one of her sons, Abijah, Jr., to Williams College. George Sheldon, historian of Deerfield, writes, "He was rejected on account of his race. The indignant mother pressed her claim before the trustees in an earnest and eloquent speech of three hours, quoting an abundance of law and Gospel, chapter and verse, in support of it, but all in vain. The name of no son of Lucy Prince graces the catalogue of Williams College." In a later case, Lucy Prince won the day. A Colonel Eli Bronson tried to steal a lot belonging to the Princes in Sunderland, near the home of Ethan Allen. The case ended up in the Supreme Court of the United States. According to Sheldon, "our Lucy argued the case at length before the court. Justice Chase said that Lucy made a better argument than he had heard from any lawyer at the Vermont bar."

Lucy Terry Prince died in 1821. Her obituary in the *Franklin Herald* stated, "In this remarkable woman there was an assemblage of qualities rarely to be found among her sex. Her volubility was exceeded by none, and in general the fluency of her speech captivated all around her, and was not destitute of instruction and edification. She was much respected among her acquaintance, who treated her with a degree of deference." The obituary writer, please note, considered Prince's wisdom and eloquence extraordinary *for a woman,* not for an African American.

Why have we told the story of Lucy Terry Prince at such length and in such detail? Because the meaning is *in* the details, in the respect she was given by her neighbors, in the affection she held for them, in her expectation that her son would be admitted to Williams College. Lucy Terry Prince was a citizen. Like many white citizens of the colonies, she had come to these shores as an unfree laborer, but she had passed into freedom and earned a place of prominence in her community. There is meaning also, though of a different kind, in the threat of violence from white neighbors in 1785 and the fact that Williams College rejected Abijah, Jr.

This remarkable woman lived for close to a century. During her lifetime, America changed. *Race* changed in America. By the year of Prince's death, slavery had been abolished in the North, and in the South it had become an institution of horrifying cruelty. If Lucy Terry Prince had been brought to this country and sold to a southern plantation owner in 1800, she would have occupied a status little higher than livestock. She would have entered into a world where beating a woman until she bled was considered routine labor management and selling away a child was good business practice. She would probably have married, but her marriage would not have been legal, and her husband might well have been sold. In that case, she would doubtless have been required to accept another man in her bed. She would almost certainly never have learned to read or write. She would almost certainly never have known freedom.

Slavery is slavery. The lack of freedom in itself, regardless of conditions, is an offense to human dignity. And conditions could sometimes be intolerable, even in the North and even in colonial days. Still, the possibility existed in the early years of this land for those who came here as slaves to become simply another part of the patchwork. White America destroyed that possibility. Slavery became not just unfree labor but one of the two great stains, along with the destruction of Native American culture, on this nation's honor.

Most Americans, when they think of the history of black women, think of that terrible stain. They do not think of Lucy Terry Prince. Or Phillis Wheatley, the second woman to publish a book in America, in 1773. Or Elizabeth Freeman, who sued for her freedom in 1781 and won, basing her case on the new constitution of Massachusetts. Or Elleanor Eldridge, who owned a wallpaper business and sold the best cheese in the town of Warwick, Rhode Island. These women make what happened in the antebellum years not just a disgrace but an American tragedy. They also make the rest of the history of black women understandable. The extraordinary achievements of black women in the nineteenth and twentieth centuries did not grow out of degradation but out of a legacy of courage, resourcefulness, initiative, and dignity that goes back to 1619.

In the last two decades, the history of these women has been, and is being, uncovered in a completely unprecedented way. Historians are digging into the records of towns like Deerfield, Massachusetts, into court records and slave inventories and long-lost narratives. Much of the history of black women was lost forever because it was considered by almost everyone to be unimportant, but a great deal still remains and is being brought to light. We can see now that the courage, strength, and resourcefulness contemporary readers have come to expect from characters in the novels of Toni Morrison and Alice Walker and in the poetry of Maya Angelou, Gwendolyn Brooks, and Rita Dove are genuine. They existed in the characters and lives of thousands of black women from colonial America through the American Revolution to the terrible years of antebellum slavery. They are revealed in stories of Civil War spies and of resistance during the Jim Crow years, stories that move black women from the fringes of American history. A new look at the Civil Rights movement and an examination of the triumphs of recent years show what black women have to teach all Americans about survival. The history of black women in America is a remarkable story, covering almost four centuries, but there are themes that run through it from beginning to end.

The emphasis by black women on community developed in the slave quarters where they taught their children—and especially their daughters—different codes of conduct for their fellow slaves and for the white masters. It grew in the mutual benefit societies formed by free African Americans, especially women, in the eighteenth century. It continued through the abolitionist societies and black churches of the late eighteenth and early nineteenth centuries. Then, out of the churches, mutual benefit societies, and literary societies came the black women's club movement of the late nineteenth century and early twentieth century. Faced with a total lack of services from the U.S. government, black women in the clubs raised money to build hospitals, fund college scholarships, and take care of the aged and the children of the community. Because of this emphasis on community and the skills learned in these organizations, black women became the foundation of the Civil Rights movement in the 1950s and 1960s. For the first time in history, a political movement relied on the organizing skills of women.

Interwoven with the theme of community is the priority placed on education. Again, the story begins in the slave quarters, where black women formed underground schools to teach reading and writing. It was illegal in most places in the South to teach a black person to read, but they managed it. That story goes on through the academies for free black children founded by young black women, some of them only teenagers. Then, after the Civil War, there were the floods of northern black women moving into the South to teach former slaves. There were the thousands of black women who functioned as leaders of their communities and who, during school desegregation and the combining of black and white schools, were the first to be fired. Today there are the forty or more black women who are college presidents and the black washerwoman who recently used her life savings to endow a scholarship at a southern university.

Against this background the third major theme glows with truth, especially in today's world. Black women's history teaches us that, as important as the community is, each individual's sense of worth and dignity must live inside that person. It must be nurtured and made strong, apart from the valuation of the world.

These are all themes that will shape our chronological narrative. And, oddly enough, given the tremendous sufferings of black women, another primary theme is triumph. Quite simply, the way black women approach life works. It cannot overcome all obstacles, but it has enabled black women to shape the raw materials of their lives into an extraordinary succession of victories, small and large. From the beginning, they have done more than find ways to feed a family with little or nothing in the house. They have found ways to educate children, resist the oppressions of slavery, support their churches, build hospitals, register voters, and get elected to the United States Senate. Theirs is more than a story of oppression and struggle. It is a story of hope.

The heart of a woman falls back with the night

and enters some alien cage in its plight,

And tries to forget it has dreamed of the stars,

While it breaks, breaks, breaks on the sheltering bars.

GEORGIA DOUGLAS JOHNSON

A NEW AND
ALIEN WORLD

CHAPTER ONE

A Y O U N G W O M A N stood on the shores of the New World. The place was Jamestown, Virginia. The year was 1619, the year before the arrival of the *Mayflower* at Plymouth Rock. We do not know this woman's name, but we will call her Oni. She will be, for us, not a number—one of twenty slaves who were the first to be brought to North America—but the real woman she was. Oni may have been born in a town in West Africa, not far from the coast where European slave traders came to shop. Most of the women brought from Africa to the New World were from West Africa.

She had been playing with her niece in the trees behind the village while her sister took laundry to the river to wash. She was hoping that Nnamdi, the chief's son, would find her there. He had taken to flirting with her lately, and she thought he was very handsome. Her niece, Abiona, looked up at her and laughed. She smiled and nuzzled the child's soft, dark hair.

She may have been taken as the spoils of war or in payment for a debt. It is possible she was captured by a neighboring tribe.

Suddenly, as she turned to lift Abiona into a rope swing, hands grabbed her roughly from behind. Swiftly, she was dragged through the trees and to a waiting boat. Her head banged heavily against the side of the boat as she was thrown in. When she came back to consciousness, she was being pulled to her feet and stood on a box. Dried blood stained her foot. Strangers surrounded her.

We know that she was sold to slave traders and sent across the Atlantic Ocean in a Spanish frigate. A Dutch man-of-war raided the frigate and took over its human cargo off the coast of the New World. The Dutch ship then ran into bad weather. Supplies gave out. Disease and starvation ran rampant. Of the one hundred Africans on the ship, eighty starved to death. Their bodies were thrown overboard.

She trembled now as she remembered the pale faces, the hands that pushed and pulled at her, the cold eyes that examined her. One of the traders had breathed in her face, and she had almost gagged from the smell. And then someone pushed her toward another boat, a large one this time. In it there were others who looked as frightened as she felt, but she couldn't understand what they said to her.

Whatever else we do or do not know about Oni, we can be certain that she was horribly, terrifyingly alone. The traders took her past. They robbed her of all that made life understandable—family, home, language, native land.

Now, after months at sea, she was in a place strange beyond her imagination. She recognized a tree here and a plant there, but these were achingly vague similarities. It was difficult, almost, to believe that she was still herself. She reached out to the woman next to her, seeking comfort as she had on the boat. Although they spoke different languages, they had found a way to speak—with their eyes first, then with a few words here, a sign there. But the woman was gone. Oni saw her being pulled away by a tall man with skin as white as a snake's belly, whiter even than the men on the boat. And then hands began to grab her again.

Oni and the other women in that first ship were the first of thousands, tens of thousands, of black women who would be brought to labor in America. They would live lives of sorrow and toil, separation and loss, and often desperate humiliation. They would also create a new culture in this new land. Weaving fragments of their African past with rags and threads from a new, alien world, they would dress themselves in dignity, love, and even joy.

Their story is history. There are few kings or military campaigns in it, but it is history in the purest and deepest sense, the record of what has happened to us—all of us—as a people. At its greatest moments and in its cruelest times, black women have been a crucial part of this country's history. In 1624, just seventeen years after the first permanent settlement in North America was founded, 2 percent of the population of Virginia was black. In that same year, a woman known to us only as Isabel, wife of Antoney, gave birth to the first black child born in English North America. There were free African Americans in this country more than a hundred years before it *was* a country, and these black Americans were able to achieve property and status. By 1630, only eleven years after Oni landed in Jamestown, there was at least one black landowner in New Amsterdam. In 1644, a significant part of what is now Greenwich Village in New York City was owned by a group of African Americans. In 1651, Anthony Johnson founded a black settlement in Virginia which eventually included twelve homesteads, and he imported white indentured servants for use there.

In these early years, some black women came to identify with their new country and to participate in its economic, cultural, and political reality in a way that would become impossible in later years. Others resisted fiercely their new condition in life. Still others died from the shock of their transplantation and the heartache of losing everything they knew and held dear. All of these women are part of the story, and that story begins back in Africa, where Oni should have lived out her life.

O, Ye Daughters of Africa

The second largest continent in the world, Africa is a huge, complex land mass occupied by thousands of tribes and nations. Generalizations about it should be made with considerable caution. Even West Africa, from which most slaves came, contained tremendous differences in culture, language, and political and economic structure. Nevertheless, there are some things we can surmise about Oni and her past, some experiences that were shared by *most* of the women who came to America from Africa.

Like women the world over, Oni grew up expecting to get married and have children. She might have looked forward to being the one wife of her husband or she might have thought she would be one of several, but she looked at the young men in her village and wondered whom she would marry. There were also some expectations she shared specifically with other African women. Almost certainly she could have expected to participate in the economic life of the community outside her own home. Along the coast of West Africa, in particular, women were often traders, an especially important role in an area where the economy was still primarily mercantile rather than industrial. Oni could also have expected to own and control some of her own property after marriage without having to get permission from her husband. In many areas, women could buy and sell land or goods.

In Africa, Oni probably would have participated in a separate women's community which, at times, influenced the political actions of the larger community. Of course, women in all parts of the world had an effect through their husbands and sons, but African women often had formal structures through which to work, making decisions and effecting changes that had an impact on the entire tribe or nation. In these ways, African women had somewhat more power and autonomy than women in European countries. But how far did their power reach? Was Oni a matriarch in the making?

Hardly. Women in Africa could trade, own property, and sometimes collectively influence political decisions, but they did not exercise power over men. In most places, for example, women, girls, and young children were not allowed to eat until the men and boys had finished, and they were forbidden to eat certain highly nutritious foods. Most tribes showed all the signs of a patriarchal culture, including the branding of women as "other." As historian Claire Robertson put it, "[We] have no historical record anywhere of a matriarchal society in a sense equivalent to patriarchal, that is, *where women held most positions of power and authority and dominated the society's economic and ideological structure."* (Italics ours)

Oni wasn't a matriarch, then, but she was accustomed to being resourceful, determined, and somewhat independent economically. She probably had all of these qualities to a greater degree than the average young woman her age in, say, Belgium or France. To that degree, the enslaved African woman had a cultural advantage, a background that would help her survive in the New World—if she brought it with her. A great many writers and scholars, however, have argued that the horrors of the Middle Passage—the brutal ocean voyage between Africa and America—as well as isolation from members of the same language group, virtually wiped out all memories of culture and upbringing in African Americans. In their view, slavery was a great eraser, and enslaved Africans came to northern farms and southern plantations as blank slates on which their masters could write.

Pointing out that most arriving slaves couldn't even talk to each other, scholars have asked how they could share a culture. The answer, of course, is that they didn't. They did, however, *create* a culture. And in doing that, they used what they had, what they had brought with them from Africa. Africanists have pointed out dozens of bits of evidence—the equipment African women made to process rice in the Georgia Sea Islands, the way they carried water on their heads, the images on appliquéd quilts and clothing, and so forth. And, of course, there are folktales, music, and dance.

We can conjecture, then, that Oni brought from Africa traits that ranged from resourcefulness to the ability to weave baskets using the patterns of her grandmother. They must have seemed frail supports as she faced the loneliness and confusion of her new life, but they were all she had, and she used them, sometimes in amazing ways. She also brought an experience of slavery that was very different from the conception most people have of it today. One of the reasons slave traders went to Africa to do their buying is that slaves were available for sale. Slavery was an important part of most African cultures. But it differed in almost every possible way from the chattel slavery that would develop in the American South.

"Unfree labor" has taken many different forms over history. It has included serfdom in Europe and forced labor on the Great Wall of China. The great philosophers of ancient Greece were waited on by slaves at dinner, and the pharaohs of Egypt used slaves to build their pyramidal monuments to themselves. Wherever labor has been in demand, some form of unfree labor has usually been found. Sometimes the word "slavery" is used when referring to unfree labor. Sometimes—usually when talking about forced labor in the history of Europe—less loaded words such as "vassalage" or "serfdom" are employed.

In West Africa, there were many ways for a woman to pass into slavery. Enslavement of those defeated in war was a relatively common practice. It was a way of adding to the workforce of the community and to the wealth of the conqueror. Slaves were also obtained through kidnapping or in payment of debts. In most cases, these slaves were women, simply because most agricultural workers were women and because, in areas where polygyny was practiced, slave wives were greatly in demand. This may be one reason that fewer women than men were brought to the Americas; Africans simply outbid the Europeans for valuable female slaves.

However, in most African societies an enslaved woman could usually look forward to passing *out* of slavery and into the status of citizen in the new community. Usually, the children of enslaved women attained freedom when their free fathers acknowledged paternity, and even those who remained slaves could rise in status. Male slaves could sometimes become patriarchs of free families, and both men and women who were enslaved themselves could, and did, own others. There were few second-generation slaves.

This sort of slavery was far from benign, but it was also far from the condition that would develop in the United States in which, as the Supreme Court stated in the Dred Scott case, "a slave has no rights that a white man need recognize." The chattel slavery that evolved in the American South in the late eighteenth and early nineteenth centuries was complete and often brutal. It was also virtually unprecedented. Until the development of the "peculiar institution" during the reign of King Cotton, the slave was almost always recognized as a person as well as an item of property. The American South changed all that, but it took about a century and a half for American slavery to become the cruelly vicious institution we remember today.

Slaves and Pilgrims

In many history texts, slavery is scarcely mentioned until a few decades before the Civil War and then it is dealt with only in terms of the abolitionist movement. In *The New York Public Library's Book of Chronologies*, for example, the first mention of slavery in the North American time line comes in 1820, with the Missouri Compromise. Slavery itself is not history, only the battle against it. We are thus led to believe that there were no black faces in the colonies, that the good Pilgrims never held anyone in bondage, except in the stocks. But there were, and they did.

In fact, there were slaves in the colonies before there were Africans. About a quarter of a million poor, white indentured servants came to the colonies in the early years to find themselves in servitude that differed in no significant way from slavery, and not all of them came of their own accord. Convicts, women accused of prostitution, paupers, and orphans were taken off the streets of English cities and shipped to the colonies, where they were sold. Sometimes their capture and sale was legal. Sometimes they were kidnapped. All of this would change drastically in the decades to come, but when Oni was brought to these shores, her status was parallel to that of a white indentured servant in the colonies.

There were differences from one place to another and from one owner to another, but it is likely that she was given a new name, put to work on a farm, called a servant, and encouraged, or required, to go to church. (In 1641, there were at least forty black members of Bouweire Chapel in New Amsterdam.) She might even, after a number of years, have been given her freedom. At that point, she could have continued to work for wages for her former owner or have married, bought a piece of property with her husband, and spent her life as part of a farming community. This is absolutely the best that could have happened, but it was possible.

In the early colonies most black women were agricultural workers on farms or domestic servants in cities, often working alongside white indentured servants. Sometimes a farmer would use a slave or free family along with his own for work in the field and in the house. A free family would usually own only one or two slaves and, in the northern colonies, these slaves lived closely with the family. They attended the same churches and sang the same hymns. They received religious instruction and, so that they could participate in the church music, lessons in singing.

Enslaved Africans brought with them to America a great many skills, and they also quickly learned European methods in many fields, from weaving to playing a musical instrument. Black men became highly skilled at working in iron, building boats, and playing the banjo or violin for colonial dances, as well as serving on board ships and working next to their masters in a variety of other businesses. Women, especially, were skilled agricultural workers and proficient in all kinds of textile work, from spinning and weaving to dressmaking. They made soap and candles, wove baskets, cooked, prepared medicines, and planted gardens. They also worked as midwives, delivering both black and white children. With their knowledge of herbal medicines and traditional African healing arts, they were often the only source of care in slave quarters and free black communities. They also nursed white families in their roles as domestic servants. In some areas, the entire population, black and white, depended on the services of a black nurse and midwife.

Sometimes when a slave had completed her daily work for her owner, she was allowed to sell her labors. Or she made an arrangement with her owner to hire out her services for a certain amount, and if she could get more, she could keep it. In this way, ambitious workers could sometimes save enough money to buy their own freedom or that of the people they loved. This was not common, but it happened. These were the earliest black entrepreneurs.

All laborers in the colony, whatever their ethnicity, were denied rights and privileges that landowners took for granted. For good or ill, their lives were in the hands of their employers. Whether they were overworked, physically punished, sexually exploited—all these were a matter of luck, depending on the character of the boss. However—and this is a big however—in the early days of the colonies, people could escape from this labor pool. Indentures ran out. Enslaved Africans earned their freedom. Once people owned land or set up in business, they moved onto a different level of society. This shift was so significant that extending the vote—the symbol of citizenship—to those men who *did not own land* was a major political issue. The legalization of slavery and the development of chattel slavery, however, changed everything. A family could be trapped in the laboring class not for a single lifetime but for generations. Movement out of it would be virtually impossible.

It took many decades for the colonists to recognize slavery as a legal institution and to define it. However, between 1641 and 1717, every colony except Georgia legalized slavery. Georgia held out, even passing a law in 1735 banning the importation and use of slaves. That law was repealed fourteen years later, and in 1750, Georgia joined the other colonies in recognizing the "peculiar institution."

To Be a Slave

Defining slavery was not an easy task in a democracy, or rather, a group of democracies. And it is not easy for patriotic Americans to accept the fact that it was going on at the very time that colonists were chafing under the oppression of British rule and talking in lofty terms about freedom and the rights of man. Essentially, slavery, as a legal category, defined certain people as part people and part property. In the half century or so following 1641, hundreds of laws would be passed clarifying the position of these "part-people" socially and economically. But the most significant laws were those that defined exactly who could be classified as a slave and who could not. The white men in power decided right from the start that white people—with a very few exceptions—could not be enslaved. They could enter indentured servitude, which we have seen was a form of slavery, but they could not legally be slaves. For a number of reasons, Native Americans were seldom held as slaves in the colonies. For one thing, it was too easy for them to run away. They were also susceptible to European diseases and, when they lived around whites, their mortality rate was high. Besides, enslaving whole tribes was beyond the capability of most groups of colonists, so enslaving individual tribe members could lead to reprisals. And so, for slave labor, that left Africans and African Americans—black people.

However, the issue was soon complicated. Children were born who were black *and* white. Or black and Native American. This was a completely natural result of the living conditions at the time, as enslaved Africans and indentured white servants often worked side by side. They relaxed together, rebelled against their situation together, became friends, and created families. This mixed population was problematic to the lawmakers. Could they be enslaved? Did their white blood protect them or did their black blood condemn them?

It took a while to answer these questions, and different colonies answered them differently for a time. Then, in 1662 in Virginia, the fateful—and fatal—law was passed. In most places, at most times in history, children have been blessed or cursed by the social positions of their fathers. The son of a gentleman was a gentleman. The son of a serf was a serf. The mother's status, while it might be a spot of tarnish on the family crest or a source of curdled pride to her déclassé children, was essentially irrelevant. But in the early 1660s—beginning with the 1662 Virginia law—the American colonies without exception passed laws stating that "all children borne in this country shall be held bond or free only according to the condition of the mother." Children born to free women would be free, but children born to slave women would be slaves and, of course, the property of the woman's owner.

The 1662 law and its successors in other colonies settled the issue of who could be enslaved. At the same time, it altered the status of black women in the most profound way, by redefining their position as women. From then on, black motherhood was, at least for slaves, a legal curse. Henceforth, black women would be valued not only for their work, but for their ability to produce more workers. In later years, in the plantation South, this legal justification would undergird the horrifying sexual abuses of black women. In the North, it meant that slavery was not, as in Africa, a one-generation condition. Slavery would be inherited, and through the mother.

The full implications for black women of the 1662 law were not immediately apparent, however, because in the second half of the 1600s and the first half of the 1700s, the African slave trade was thriving. In fact, it became easier and easier to buy slaves. In 1700, there were about 26,000 Africans and African Americans living in the colonies. By 1730, that number had grown to over 70,000. And then between 1740 and 1780, according to one estimate, *210,000 enslaved black people were imported into the colonies.* So long as it was possible to buy slaves easily and fairly cheaply, black women were not pressured to produce children. In fact, one of the earliest torments black women faced in the colonies was completely contrary to the image of "breeder" that would one day be promulgated by southern slaveholders. In the beginning, they were often not *allowed* to become wives and mothers. Because the masters valued their productive labor more than their reproductive capacities, women workers seldom experienced love and family life as we understand it. The significance of this should not be underestimated. It was one of the most serious early oppressions of enslaved American women.

To Be a Woman

In both the African cultures from which black women came and the American culture into which they were transplanted, a woman's identity was bound up in and even defined by her familial roles. Her sense of self depended on fulfilling those roles, and many of the early enslaved black women were robbed of the opportunity to do so. This was particularly terrible in a society where limitations on women *outside* the family were so severe. In the 1600s and 1700s, there were few places in Western civilization where women enjoyed any significant degree of equality with men. In the colonies, Puritanism exacerbated the problem. Being "the cause of sin in the world" did not help women in their struggle against patriarchy.

In the early years of settlement, the behavior of women was rigidly restricted in order to minimize their alleged tendencies to emulate Eve, tempting men away from righteousness. White women's rights and resources belonged to their fathers or husbands, following the Christian religious precept that God is the head of the church and man is the head of woman. Women—black or white—could not vote, of course, or hold public office. Married women could not bring suit in court. They had no rights over their children. They also could not own property. There were cases in which a widow had her home or her farm sold out from under her by her son because she was not legally entitled to own it. Later, widows received some protection, but married women were still unable to own property in their own names.

Women lived entirely under the power of men. A woman with a drunken husband could not, for example, take in laundry, save her money, and buy a home for her children and herself. The house would belong to her husband, who could sell it out from under her at any time. A woman could be admitted to a mental institution by her parents or, after she was married, by her husband or adult son without a legal or medical hearing. And husbands were free to beat their wives to secure obedience or conjugal privileges so long, in most places, as they did not use "a stick greater in diameter than a man's thumb."

Of course, all the restrictions that applied to white women applied to black women as well. During the 1600s and early 1700s, free black men could often vote, own property, and even participate in some local government. Free black men voted in South Carolina until 1701, in North Carolina until 1715, and in Georgia until 1754. They also held public office. At the beginning of the seventeenth century, there was a black surety in York County, Virginia, and a black beadle in Lancaster County, Virginia. Later, white men robbed black men of these rights. *But at no time did black women share in them.*

The social and economic position of women paralleled their legal position. A white woman who did not come under the protection of a man, either husband or father, was in an unenviable position. Virtually her only hope for employment was to become a servant or farm worker, no matter what her family background or education might be. When married, she worked in the home and, usually, in the field. More than half of the total white immigration during the colonial period was made up of indentured servants who, even after they were released from servitude, scratched a living out of the soil. The gap between the handful of "aristocratic" women— who enjoyed a certain amount of leisure—and all other women was enormous.

Still, most white women could hope to be married and have families, while for black women this was not at all certain. Enslaved women in northern colonies were often isolated from other African Americans, living on farms that were at some distance from each other. Usually a woman would be the only slave—or one of two or three—living within the household. There might be no marriageable black man within a day's ride, much less an assortment to choose from. Especially after interracial marriage was made illegal, many black women were left without possible mates.

Some women married men from distant farms whom they saw only a few times a year, and some women ended up having short-term relationships that resulted in children. The mother and children in both cases became a family, but there were severe limitations on their freedom to live as such. Because the children were enslaved as well, there was always an authority higher than the parent's, for one thing. Because the children had to work from a fairly early age, their time was structured and their lives were shaped by someone outside the family. Most terrible of all, a child could be sold away at any time.

When enslaved women and men did marry—or have children without marriage—both parents suffered from the limitations on their families and their parental authority. Black men felt the pain of being unable to live as husbands and fathers and to care for their wives and children. And yet, defining oneself primarily as a worker rather than a parent was far more familiar to men. And the failure to be husband and father did not carry with it quite the social stigma and emotional devastation that the failure to be wife and mother did for black women.

White colonial America denied many African American women in these early years the ability to perform the roles upon which most women depended for self-fulfillment and self-respect. In addition, because they did not perform those roles, they lost the protection that white women who were wives and mothers received. However, even then, many black women participated in families of a more loosely defined sort. These were not necessarily made up of people related by marriage or blood, and often their members did not share the same race or culture. But they functioned as family units. Black women connected to the people around them. They nurtured, supported, leaned on, and laughed with others. And within a few generations, biological extended families began to evolve. The African American family began to take shape.

Limbs of Each Other

It took a tremendous commitment to make black families work in those early years, just as it has for the nearly three centuries since, but the difficulties were different. The first problem was the scarcity of potential mates. That was eventually overcome because, as there came to be two and three generations of African Americans in the colonies, the black population began to grow. For a number of reasons, the children of enslaved Africans were more likely than their parents to have children of their own who survived to adulthood. For one thing, the second and third generations of African American women began bearing children earlier than newly arrived African women had. When they reached the colonies, African women were many different ages—some past their peak childbearing years—and it often took years for women to recover from the physical debility caused by the Middle Passage. Also, African women were accustomed to nursing their children for a longer time and abstaining from sexual relations while they did. This significantly limited the number of children they bore. But, as they adapted to American culture, many black women began to wean their children earlier. They began to fall into the "every two years" pattern of white women.

Slowly, the black population grew, and the outlines of the black family emerged. It was not always the small nuclear family that has been perceived as the American ideal, but it was an emotionally potent and enormously cohesive entity, especially given the circumstances. Often family members were sold away, but at this time they were usually sold to nearby farms, making it possible to maintain some contact. Frequently, a family was broken up by an owner who had more than one farm. Again, enslaved Americans worked hard to keep up connections. Herbert G. Gutman, in *The Black Family in Slavery and Freedom,* recounts the story of the Addison family slaves.

> When Thomas Addison died in 1727, he was one of the county's [Prince George County] largest slaveowners, owning seventy-one slaves, many adult Africans among them. At his grandson's death in 1775, one hundred nine Addison slaves lived on three separate plan-

tations. Two were adjacent to each other, and the third three miles away. The forty-year-old Ned and his forty-six-year-old wife Joan lived on the main plantation with their four youngest children. Joan's older son Sam lived a few miles away. The sixty-four-year-old Jack Bruce and his fifty-six-year-old wife Sarah lived adjacent to the Addison's Oxon Hill place. Three sons, ranging in age from fifteen to twenty-six, lived at Oxon Hill as did another son, a twelve-year-old, who lived with his older sister and her child.

Early African Americans ensured the survival of the family by keeping roles flexible. Adults of whatever relationship took over the parenting responsibilities for children when necessary. Brothers and sisters provided care and support for each other. Even cousins could be as close as immediate family, especially if a person had been separated from closer kin. As late as 1799, George Washington's Union Farm in Virginia showed this sort of variety in family structure. According to historian Brenda Stevenson, "Of the 36 slaves who resided at Union Farm in 1799, none lived together as a married couple or within a nuclear-structured family: there were three married mothers residing with their children but with abroad husbands; only one married man, and his wife lived elsewhere; four single mothers; four single men; three single women; and one orphan child named Jesse." From what we know of kinship customs among early black Americans, Jesse was probably "adopted" by at least one of the adults. The entire group may have constituted a kind of extended family, with real and fictive cousins, aunts, and grandmothers.

There is clear evidence that black families did everything they could to keep in touch with each other. In a study of 589 advertisements for runaway slaves in eighteenth-century Virginia, for example, about one out of every three fugitives had left to visit a family member living at a distance. Charleston, South Carolina, merchant Robert Pringle explained in 1740 that his only reason for sending the slave Esther on a ship bound for Lisbon was that "she has a practice of goeing frequently to her Father and Mother, who live at a Plantation I am concern'd in, about Twenty Miles from Town."

In the cities a black woman's desire for marriage and family was more easily satisfied. By the late 1600s in Philadelphia, for example, there were eight thousand people, and half of the households had at least one slave. An enslaved woman who worked as a seamstress in one household could marry a man who worked as a carpenter in another. The father sometimes lived apart from his family, but he usually was an integral part of family life.

Free black women occupied a different position from their enslaved sisters, in part because most free black Americans in the colonies lived in the cities. Here, they were much more likely to find work and were somewhat less vulnerable to being kidnapped and reenslaved. (This was a constant fear for free blacks during the decades before emancipation.) In addition, the slaves who were most likely to be able to buy their own freedom or that of another were those who worked in skilled occupations, most of which were located in the city.

Free black women were often married. Indeed, many became free when their future husbands paid the slaveholder's price for them. Some of the proud families who would become prominent abolitionists and founding members of the black elite began building their dynasties in these early years. The Remonds, the Fortens, the Bustills, and the Douglasses—no relation to Frederick—all set down roots in colonial America at a time when opportunities for free African Americans were not as restricted as they would soon become.

A Sort of Freedom

If the conditions of slavery in the colonies are unfamiliar to most people, the very fact of free African Americans can be difficult to comprehend. And yet, by the middle of the seventeenth century, a free black population had begun to be a presence, and in the eighteenth century its members participated significantly in the life of the community as a whole. Before the hardening of laws and attitudes regarding slavery and black Americans, there was meaningful movement out of slavery and into the free state.

Enslaved women gained freedom in a number of ways. Some bought their freedom with money they earned outside their appointed workday. Some were purchased and freed by free black men so that they could marry. Some women were freed when a master or mistress died. There were even cases in which a white woman left her home to an enslaved woman who had lived and worked closely with her. The black women, when freed, often used these homes for boarding houses, inns, restaurants, laundries, and dressmaking establishments.

Over the years, a small but solid black working class emerged. By the eighteenth century, there were black business owners and town leaders as well. In 1736, for example, Mary Bernoon and her husband opened an oyster and ale house in Providence, Rhode Island, using the capital she had made by selling illegal whiskey. At about the same time, a black woman called "Duchess" Quamino set up a catering business in Newport. She was soon the most successful caterer in town. According to author Stephen Birmingham, "Free blacks virtually invented the catering business in America." And it was black women, who had developed their cooking skills in white kitchens, who led the way.

Lucy Terry Prince was a striking example of the possibilities for a black woman in colonial America. Her life is particularly significant because we know so many details, but it was because of her prominence in the town of Deerfield, Vermont, that we know so much more about her than about most women who lived in the colonial era. Lucy Terry Prince and her husband were active and respected members of their community. They expected and usually got treatment as equals with their white neighbors. And while the Princes were unusual, they were not unique among free African Americans.

There are other black women of the time, about whom we know somewhat less than we do about Prince, who entered significantly into the mainstream community. Nancy Lenox Remond, whose family later became important abolitionists, set up a cake-baking business in Salem, Massachusetts, in the late eighteenth century. Eventually, she came to dominate the catering trade in that city, running an exclusive restaurant as well. Her daughters Cecilia Remond Babcock, Maritcha Remond, and Caroline Remond Putnam operated the Ladies Hair Work Salon in the same city. They developed the largest wig factory in the state and manufactured a popular hair-loss tonic—Mrs. Putnam's Medicated Hair Tonic—which they sold wholesale and retail, both locally and through mail-order distribution.

Elleanor Eldridge's story comes down to us by way of a memoir. She was born free to Robin Eldridge and Hannah Prophet. Her father was captured in Africa and brought with the rest of his family to America on a slave ship. He received his freedom after serving in the American Revolution, although promises of material reward were not kept. Prophet, Elleanor's mother, was the daughter of a Native American woman who had bought a slave husband. The two had seven daughters, of whom Elleanor was the youngest. Eldridge's mother worked for the Joseph Baker family and, after she died, the family asked ten-year-old Elleanor to come live with them and work for them. The child's mother had apparently been close to the Baker family, since Elleanor was named after Mrs. Baker.

During her six years with the Bakers, Eldridge learned many of the skills she would use in her future business endeavors. According to her friend Frances Whipple McDougall, she was remarkably adept. "She learned all the varieties of house-work and every kind of spinning; and plain, double and ornamental weaving," McDougall told memoirist Frances Greene. "This double-weaving i.e. carpets, old fashioned coverlets, damask, and bed-ticking, is said to be a very difficult and complicated process; and I presume there are few girls of fourteen capable of mastering such an intricate business. Yet she was pronounced a competent and fully accomplished weaver. At her next job, she added cheese-making to the list of tasks at which she had the reputation of excellence. The cheese she made was labeled 'premium quality.' " Clearly, the still-teenaged Eldridge was a bright, accomplished person.

After the death of her second employer, Eldridge and her sister Lettise went into business together. In addition to weaving, they made soap and did some nursing. Soon, Eldridge bought a lot and built a house, which she rented out. A few years later, she went to live with another sister, in Providence, Rhode Island, and opened a painting and wallpapering business. She bought more real estate. And then more. An error, compounded by duplicity on the part of a white neighbor, led to the auctioning off of Eldridge's Providence real estate to pay a small debt. The illegal maneuverings were apparently covered up by the local sheriff.

Eldridge's success as a businesswoman is evident in her ability to pay $2,700 to recover the property. The obstacles a black woman had to face are evident in the fact that she was forced to pay this money for property she already owned because of someone else's mistake. A writer of the time stated, "No MAN would ever have been treated so; and if a WHITE WOMAN had been the subject of such wrongs, the whole town—nay, the whole country, would have been indignant: and the actors would have been held up to the contempt they deserve!"

The life of another free black woman of the time gives early evidence of the dedication of black women to education and to community service. Catherine Williams Ferguson was born on a schooner in about 1774. Her mother, a slave from Virginia, was being sent to a new owner in New York when she gave birth to the little girl who would soon be known as Katy. When Katy was very young, her mother taught her what she knew about Christian scripture, which made a deep impression on her. Even after the two were separated, when Katy was eight, the child went to church services and became a member of the Murray Street Church in New York City. She was not, however, taught to read and write.

By the time she was eighteen, with the help of two abolitionist women, Williams was free. Almost immediately, she got married to a man named Ferguson and began to have children, but both of the babies she gave birth to died when they were infants. Her husband died not long after the children. In the meantime, Katy had begun to make a living as a caterer and as a launderer of lace and other fine fabrics. But she was not satisfied with her modest financial success. She had other concerns. Katy Ferguson lived in a poor neighborhood near an almshouse, and all around her were children whose lives must have wrenched her heart. In 1793, when she was little more than a child herself, she started a Sunday school for them. Once a week, she took black and white children into her home to give them lessons in scripture and in the practical skills of life.

Soon, the pastor of her church, Dr. John M. Mason, heard about Ferguson's work and offered her space in his basement. He also found assistants who could provide the basic education that she, still unable to read and write, could not. Under Ferguson's supervision, the Murray Street Sabbath School continued for forty years. It was New York's first Sunday School. But Ferguson did not stop there. She helped the children find homes, and over the course of forty years, she took forty-eight of these children into her own home and cared for them until she could find them other places to live. Katy Ferguson died of cholera in New York in 1854. Her death was reported in the *New York Tribune,* which said that "thousands in this community have heard of or know Katy Ferguson." In 1920, the city of New York opened a home for unwed mothers and named it the Katy Ferguson Home.

We know about Elleanor Eldridge because the injustice committed against her led Francis Greene to write about her. We know about Katy Ferguson because her remarkable work with children led to recognition during her lifetime. But names and stories from this time of specific women—of any ethnicity—are extremely rare. For years the only names most people knew were Betsy Ross and Priscilla Alden, women who were known, respectively, for sewing and for saying, "Speak for yourself, John." It is of some significance, then, that these stories exist at all. Even more striking is the story of Phillis Wheatley, an enslaved woman whose accomplishments transcended her condition in life.

When Susannah and John Wheatley went to the docks in Boston in July 1761, they expected to come home with a personal servant for Susannah. They got more than they bargained for. They chose a pleasant little girl of seven or eight with the fine features of the Fulani, a people who lived at that time near the Gambia River in Africa. She was named Phillis, after the slave ship that brought her to America. Shortly after Phillis moved into the Wheatley home, the daughter of the house, Mary, saw her trying to make letters on a wall with chalk or charcoal. Mary decided to teach the young slave to read. Within sixteen months, Phillis could read and write English fluently and was learning Latin.

Phillis Wheatley's first published poem appeared on December 21, 1767, in the *Newport* (Rhode Island) *Mercury*. She was fourteen years old. Soon, she was a celebrity. Her poetry was being read and talked about all over Boston and throughout the colonies. Benjamin Franklin became a fan. Dr. Benjamin Rush wrote of her that her "singular genius and accomplishments are such as not only do honor to her sex, but to human nature."

Wheatley's poetic model was Alexander Pope, and she was highly skilled in his elegant style but was usually more passionate than that ironic English gentleman. Indeed, unlike her owners, she was a fierce apostle of freedom and a fiery American patriot. Susannah and John Wheatley were loyalists, attending the Old South Church with many other Tories. Phillis attended the Old North Church, a gathering place for patriots. Both her mastery of the heroic couplet and her ardent love of liberty are apparent in this excerpt from the poem "To the Earl of Dartmouth."

> *Should you, my lord, while you peruse my song,*
> *Wonder from whence my love of* **Freedom** *sprung,*
> *Whence flow these wishes for the common good,*
> *By feeling hearts alone best understood,*
> *I, young in life, by seeming cruel fate*
> *Was snatch'd from* Afric's *fancy'd happy seat:*
> *What pangs excruciating must molest*
> *What sorrows labour in my parents' breast?*
> *Steel'd was that soul and by no misery mov'd*
> *That from a father seiz'd his babe beloved:*
> *Such, such my case. And can I then but pray*
> *Others may never feel tyrannic sway?*

In 1772, Wheatley put together a volume of her work that included many patriotic verses. When her Boston supporters failed to come up with the money to publish it, she found a patron across the ocean. Selena Hastings, countess of Huntingdon, had read one of Wheatley's poems and offered to publish her work in London. The resulting book—with patriotic verse removed—was a success. The Wheatleys sent Phillis to London for its publication, and she met many of England's literary and social luminaries. She would have been presented at the Court of St. James, but Susannah Wheatley fell ill in Boston and asked her to return. The Wheatleys freed Phillis shortly after her return to Boston, in part because of pressure from her English admirers. She remained living with the Wheatleys for another four years and received financial support from them until John Wheatley's death in 1778, even though, when Susannah died in 1776, Phillis married John Peters.

An event that excites speculation occurred at the beginning of the Revolutionary War. When George Washington took command of the American army, Phillis Wheatley wrote him a letter in which she enclosed a poem in his honor. Washington invited her to visit him at his headquarters at any time and, later in the year, she did. Not long after, Washington reversed his long-held stand against black men serving in the Continental army.

The years after Wheatley's marriage were filled with financial hardship. Although Peters was a respectable black citizen who started out as a grocer and later became a lawyer, he was not a success in the world, and his pride apparently alienated Wheatley's white friends. She continued to write, but her spirit and her health were affected by the deaths of her first two children. Phillis Wheatley died in 1784, at the age of thirty-one, of complications arising from the birth of her third child, who died with her.

Sparse as they are, written records make it possible to report on these women who participated in the mainstream culture of the time. But it is important to remember that other African Americans, women as well as men, were simultaneously creating a separate culture. Its development was not usually recorded, and few names have come down to us. But that culture would influence American art, music, and dance forever.

Woven into the Fabric

In Albany, New York, on a sunny afternoon in the mid-1600s, a visitor could have climbed a low hill some distance from the center of town and looked down on a meadow filled with revelers. Hundreds of enslaved Americans gathered there, and at other spots around the colonies, to enjoy themselves at "slave festivals." At festivals in Albany and Manhattan that took place from the middle 1600s into the 1700s, huge crowds danced and sang almost without stopping, while an equal number of white spectators watched and applauded. Both women and men joined in the primarily African singing, dancing, and music-making.

In New Orleans during the 1700s, enormous crowds of slaves, both women and men, gathered every Sunday and on church holy days at a place called Congo Square, where the dancing and singing apparently began about three o'clock in the afternoon and went on until nine that night. There were many groups, or "tribes," that took part, each claiming a specific part of the square for its own. Each group had its own band, which played banjoes, drums, and rattles. Women participated in every aspect of these festivals, as instrumentalists and chant leaders as well as dancers.

The public festivals, and smaller gatherings on farms and plantations, were the cradles of what would become America's most significant musical form—jazz. Gradually, the European elements of church music mixed with African rhythms, repetitions, and call-and-response patterns to form, first, spirituals and, eventually, jazz itself. As Linda Dahl says in her book *Stormy Weather,* "The root of jazz is Africa uprooted; jazz had its beginnings in slavery, when European melodies, harmonies and instruments were combined with, and refashioned for, African-born rhythms. And the purpose of the music was African-born. . . . The music of black slaves married the pain and pleasure of physical life with a permeating spirituality; one of the great, enduring strengths was that it did not sever the life of the body from that of the spirit."

Black artisans, too, were contributing to the cultural richness of the new land. Slaves who worked with iron, clay, baskets, and textiles all used the techniques and images of their African heritage. Black women were particularly influential in weaving and quilt-making. Although slaves were usually constrained to produce European patterns when they were working for their masters, they often drew on their own cultural memories for objects made for their own use. Too, the artistic sensibility of the woman who dyes, spins, and weaves reveals itself in her work if she is given any latitude at all, and slave artisans often were. African colors, patterns, and symbols became part of the folk art tradition in America.

The artistic expressions of black women should also be recognized as part of a pattern of resistance. They affirmed an identity separate from that of "laborer," the only one recognized by most of white society, and that in itself was a significant form of resistance to their enslavement. At the same time, they often preserved African traditions and values, which reinforced their identity as a people of worth and heritage. They forged a community that would, at times, bond together to push back the tide of oppression.

And there *was* oppression, even if it was not rooted in the virulent racism that would later develop. Remember that, race aside, class divisions in the colonies were, as in England, extremely strong. The landowning classes believed themselves to be inherently superior, not just to slaves, but to anyone who had to hire out his or her labor. Workers and the families of workers were expendable as people and exploitable in the fields and kitchens. This was a time when physical force was considered an acceptable form of discipline for a stubborn or uncooperative servant. Children were put to work almost as soon as they could walk and talk. If you were a worker, life ranged from difficult to brutal. All of this was true of white and Native American servants, and it was true of African American slaves. Families were broken up by sale and inheritance. Restrictions on personal freedom ranged from onerous to intolerable.

Generally, the position of African Americans was worse in the South than in the North. The average number of slaves held by a single owner in tobacco country was not one or two, as in New England, but between nine and thirteen. In rice country, it could be anywhere from thirty-five to seventy-five. The work was hard and the workday long. Sunday was the only day workers did not spend, from dawn to dusk, in the fields. Women worked alongside men in virtually every aspect of the plowing, planting, and harvesting. The personal relationships that often arose between a single slave and the family she worked for and with in the North were extremely rare in the South.

Black Americans did not simply accept slavery itself or the conditions of slavery. There were many, in both the North and the South, who resisted slavery and resisted violently, including women. In 1663, African slaves and white indentured servants planned a revolt against their masters in Gloucester County, Virginia. Their plans were revealed, and they were beheaded. In 1681, an unnamed black woman was executed for burning down a barn in Roxbury, Massachusetts, presumably in an act of rebellion. In 1708, at least one black woman was involved in a slave revolt in Newton, Long Island, in which seven whites were killed. And black women were among those of the West African Coromantee and Pappa nations who participated in a slave revolt in 1712 in New York City. These were only a few of the dozens of slave rebellions in the 1600s and early 1700s.

There were other, less violent acts of resistance as well. An English traveler named John Josselyn tells of an African woman whose name is not recorded for us. "Mr. Mavericks Negro woman came to my chamber window," he recounts, "loud and shrill." Josselyn went out to the woman and saw that she was greatly grieving. He discovered from others on the farm that she had been a queen in Africa. He went to ask his host what the matter was with her and whether he could help her. He was told that "Mr. Maverick was desirous to have a breed of Negroes, and therefore seeing she would not yield by persuasions to company with a Negro young man he had in his house, he commanded him, wil'd she nill'd she, to go to bed with her, which was no sooner done, but she kicked him out again."

Black women resisted by refusing to work, by engaging in sabotage, even by running away, although that was rare. (The dangers of the American wilderness were daunting). Some committed suicide, which was not necessarily an act of despair and defeat. According to contemporary reports, most enslaved Africans believed that death would return them to their families and country. That was, for a great many, a consummation devoutly to be wished.

Accomplishment. Cultural expression. Resistance to oppression. These three characteristics distinguish the history of black women in America. At times they are in conflict with each other and at times they coalesce to create moments of glory, but they are always there. Within their scope, crucial values arise and develop, guiding the women of African America through a maze of cruelty and injustice.

Moving Apart

Gradually, the situation for slaves in the North and in the South began to differ more and more profoundly. While the northern colonies moved towards freeing slaves, southern colonies increasingly deepened the humiliation of slavery and denied freedom even to African Americans who were not enslaved. A 1668 law in Virginia had stated, "Whereas some doubts have arisen whether negro women set free were still to be exempt [from taxation] according to a former act, it is declared by this grand assembly that negro women, though permitted to enjoy their freedom yet *ought not in all respects be admitted to a full fruition of the exemptions and impunities of the English,* and are still liable to the payment of taxes [Italics added]." By 1670, free black men had been deprived of the vote. In 1692, the Virginia House of Burgesses enacted the Runaway Slave Law, making it legal to kill a runaway slave in the course of apprehending her. In 1705, Virginia declared slaves to be "real estate." Massachusetts, on the other hand, banned the importation of slaves in 1712 and started on the path that would eventually lead to emancipation. The journey would take more than sixty years, but it had begun.

By the time the colonies began their struggle for independence from the British, the North was turning its face against slavery, and the South had embraced it with a terrible fervor. It was quite a dilemma for men who professed to believe in human equality, but who knew that the new country would need the participation of every last colony in order to defend itself against its enemies and establish economic independence from England. Aside from their noble ideals, the northern colonists were secure in the knowledge that they did not need slaves. Economically, they did not depend on huge numbers of cheap workers. The southern colonies, with their growing plantation economies, very definitely did. The North could not—or believed it could not—make it without the South. And the South would not enter any endeavor without its slaves. The new country would come into being with slavery firmly in place and women firmly in their place. A century and a half had passed since black women first came to this country. Like Native Americans, they had symbolically stood on the shores of the New World to watch the arrival of the *Mayflower*. But they were still strangers in a strange land.

A great state is a well-blended mash of something

of all the people and all of none of the people.

ZORA NEALE HURSTON,

MOSES, MAN OF THE MOUNTAINS

A TALE OF
THREE CITIES

C H A P T E R   T W O

AMERICAN CULTURE HAS been compared to a potpourri, a tapestry, and a patchwork quilt. It's a salad or a gumbo or a stew, depending on the culinary tastes of the writer. It's almost anything, these days, except a melting pot. That vision of a nation where all diversity disappears into one undifferentiated mass has long since lost its credibility and its appeal. However, the idea that each ethnic group—or each ethnic and gender group—represents *one* element in whatever-concoction-you-prefer-as-your-metaphor has remained strong. We still talk about "black women" as though that were not only a meaningful category, which it is, but a homogeneous one, which it is not. The circumstances of African women diverged even before they were captured and brought to the New World. And though the experience of servitude gave most of them a commonality of interest, there were and are other elements to consider—time, region, even class or social status.

Differences among the American colonies in general were profound. Each had a character of its own, shaped largely by ethnicity and religion. As the colonies moved toward nationhood, those differences found expression in specific responses to the ideals of democracy and the break from England. Moreover, as each colony followed its own economic destiny, the institution of slavery grew to have a distinctive role in its development. As a result, the differences between a free black woman in Massachusetts and one in Georgia, or an enslaved black woman in New York and one in North Carolina, became enormous. To show this more concretely, we have chosen three cities to describe—Philadelphia, Pennsylvania; Charleston, South Carolina; and New Orleans, Louisiana. In each case, we will discuss the background of the city, its experience of the Revolutionary period, and its reaction to the incipient move towards freedom for black America.

In these three cities it is possible to distinguish some of the directions the history of black women would take, especially within the areas of accomplishment, cultural expression, and resistance to oppression. It is also possible to see very similar values developing in radically different environments. Emphasis on family, community, and the strategies of survival was strong in all three cities, different as they were.

Philadelphia, for example, was the free black capital of the colonies. Here, black women were part of an urban community that was striving for freedom, culture, and respectability. Churches, mutual benefit societies, and literary clubs formed a foundation on which, by the late nineteenth century, black women would build an extensive social service network. Here, too, black women discovered the dangers of living in, but not of, America's cultural mainstream, as they experienced social isolation, economic discrimination, and the danger of losing contact with their African heritage. Resistance took the form of political organization as the abolition movement was born and grew in importance.

In Charleston, African Americans were the majority and almost all of them were enslaved. However, because of their sheer numbers, they influenced every aspect of life in the southern city, participating in the economy in a unique way. Charleston's black daughters were traders, craftspeople, and fierce survivors. Because of the harshness of their oppression, they created a culture apart, preserving elements of their African heritage that are still visible today.

New Orleans was a city of Creoles, in every sense of that word—mixed blood, mixed language, mixed culture. During this period, it was not an American city, and that fact made an enormous difference to the black women who lived here. They enjoyed a very different kind of freedom from any experienced by women in the other two cities and participated in the creation of a vital spiritual and artistic milieu.

Each of these cities was created by a combination of historical accidents involving ethnicity, religion, economics, and at least a dozen other significant factors that shaped the lives of black women. At the same time, black women in each city also acted *upon* their society. They were among the factors that history must examine in order to understand all the rest. In the details of the lives of these cities there is a kind of history, and a kind of truth, that the most careful generalizations cannot reveal.

PHILADELPHIA

Sarah is an African American woman of thirty-four, let us say, a slave in the household of an English family in Philadelphia in 1776.

Sarah is walking to church one Sunday morning with her friend from two blocks over, Mary. Sarah is a weaver, and her work is in demand because of its quality and because of her remarkable feeling for colors. Mary, who is free, is a dressmaker with a good clientele. Their skills give them a certain status in the community. Too, they are respectable women, faithful churchgoers.

Sarah was married when she was younger, but her husband Tom was sold away from her, to a planter in Virginia. They write letters to each other, but Tom's owner has demanded that he take another wife, and Tom will not be able to resist much longer. Sarah's one daughter, Aggie, is fifteen and serving as a parlor maid. Sarah and Tom are praying that a miracle will happen and that Aggie will be free before she bears children.

Sarah hears a lot about equality and freedom, especially since the Declaration of Independence was signed. She can hardly believe that white people dare to talk about these things in front of her. She can hardly believe they don't understand what she feels. She would join the British in a minute if it would mean that she and Tom and Aggie would be free.

The first Quaker settlers arrived in Pennsylvania in 1681. Three years later, in 1684, the *Isabella,* out of Bristol, England, docked at Philadelphia with 150 enslaved Africans. They were all sold immediately. Since there were at the time about 1,000 English settlers, African Americans became, within a few days, 15 percent of the population of the city. In the decades to come, hundreds more enslaved Africans were brought into Philadelphia, usually from the West Indies or South Carolina. By 1750, almost half of Philadelphians who owned anything at all owned at least one slave. Most families owned only one or two slaves, hardly ever more than four. There was no gang labor. All during the colonial era, about 40 percent of Philadelphia slaves worked for mariners, artisans, and the owners of small factories. About one in every five male laborers on the wharves and in the shops of artisans such as bakers, printers, carpenters, and blacksmiths was black.

Black women were greatly in demand as well. They cooked and cleaned and tended children, of course. They became parlor maids and lady's maids. They also spun yarn and wove cloth. They were dressmakers and hairdressers and milliners. The kind of work a black woman did depended on the circumstances of the family for whom she worked. One woman might work alongside a blacksmith's wife hoeing and weeding the garden, while another reigned over a gourmet kitchen into which the wife of a wealthy merchant ventured only to consult about the menu.

In spite of Quaker scruples about unfree labor, within a few years there were about 1,400 slaves in a city with a population of 18,000. All of them lived in an area that covered no more than about twenty blocks, and they came into contact with each other regularly. A community formed in which black people knew each other, spent time together, fell in love with each other, married, and had children who played together. They continued to labor for the profit of others and were strictly limited by laws and custom, but they created networks of friendship and kinship that made up the greater part of their lives. This community even included a small but growing population of free black people that, by the mid-1700s, numbered around one hundred.

Because they lived in white households and worked alongside their owners, enslaved African Americans assimilated many European cultures and values. While the majority of settlers were English, any given household could be Germans, Swedes, or Sephardic Jews. Sometimes an African American's second language would be not English but Dutch or Norwegian. (The great Sojourner Truth spoke English with a thick Dutch accent.) In some advertisements, slaves offered for sale were described as multilingual, speaking three, four, or even six languages. There was a cultural cross-pollination that involved dozens of ethnic groups, including a great many from Africa. The English dominated, but they too were greatly affected by the others.

Philadelphia relied on slavery, but it was never comfortable with the institution. There was significant conflict among the Society of Friends about slavery almost from the beginning. One segment of the Quaker population always believed that holding other human beings in bondage went against Quaker beliefs. Gradually, this segment began to become more influential. Finally, the yearly meeting informed the local meetings that they must "testify their disunion" with any Friends who continued to have anything to do with slavery, and this reaction against slavery spread to other denominations. By 1783, there were only four hundred slaves in Philadelphia. Two thousand of the city's black population were free.

The Revolution

As Revolutionary feeling and rhetoric grew, so did black hopes for freedom, and those hopes were encouraged by sympathetic white Philadelphians. When the war finally swung into high gear, the primary concern of most black women and men was not freedom from England but freedom from bondage. On that front there were difficult decisions to be made, particularly when the British invaded and occupied the city in 1777. They remained for nine months, during which time slaves could escape slavery simply by leaving their masters' houses and reporting to the British army. This was fairly easy to do, since the British army had an outpost on virtually every block.

To avoid losing their investment, some fleeing owners took their slaves with them, and others sent their slaves into the country. Still, many enslaved Americans joined the British, including many women. Eventually, they would be relocated to Canada. The names of two young mulatto women, Phyllis and Poll, have come down to us. They were twenty-two and fourteen years old and set off into a world where they had no relatives, friends, or contacts, only the hope that they would be free. Others were faced with choosing between their network of families and friends in a place where they had grown up and freedom under a foreign power. Virtually all slaves had to decide whether to side with the British, who had promised freedom after the war, or remain on the side of America, in the hope that the movement toward abolition would escalate towards full-blown emancipation. A number of free black men, and a few slaves, chose to fight with the American troops, believing that Revolutionary principles of freedom and equality would extend to them after the war.

Black women, too, continually had to take sides. One story of a black woman's decision was preserved by the descendants of William Logan, a white landowner. Dinah, who had been a slave of the Logan family for many years, asked for and received her freedom from the family in 1776. During the occupation, British troops took over the Logan home, making it their headquarters. On October 4, 1777, the American army attacked, and two British soldiers were going to burn the house. While they were in the barn getting straw to set the fire, a British officer rode up on his horse and asked Dinah, who still worked for the Logans, if she had seen any deserters. She informed him that there were two of them hiding in the barn at that very moment. He arrested the soldiers, over their protests, and the home was saved. It is tempting to speculate whether Dinah would have done the same if the family had refused her request for freedom.

Many more black men would have enlisted in the Continental army or navy if they had been promised freedom in return for their service, but they were not. The British, on the other hand, offered not only freedom but the same rewards they offered any other male colonists—land and provisions. When the British left Philadelphia at the end of the occupation, the black Americans who had joined them left as well. Most of these—about a third of whom were women—were relocated by the British to Nova Scotia as free people. However, British attitudes during the occupation had led many to believe that their offer of freedom to those who fought for them was a bribe—and one that they apparently intended to honor—but that it did not reflect a commitment to equality or democracy. It looked as though the only hope for freedom for all black Americans—slim as it was—lay with an American victory. Many black Philadelphians continued to act on that hope.

Growing Freedom

After the British occupation and while the war was still raging, in 1779, the Pennsylvania legislature met in Philadelphia to discuss and eventually pass a gradual abolition bill. It was the first such bill passed in America. It was also the harshest of those passed in northern states between 1780 and 1804. Some slaves were freed immediately by the bill. However, those under twenty-eight years old remained enslaved until they reached that age. The children of the slave women among these would be free but would be indentured servants until they were twenty-eight. This was a way of continuing to reap, despite "abolition," the benefits of bonded labor.

Again, black womanhood was a legal curse. If a girl child was born to a slave one day before the passage of the bill in 1779, she would remain a slave until she was twenty-eight, and all the children she bore during that time would be locked into indentured servitude, remaining unfree workers for the first twenty-eight years of their lives. Fifty-six years after "abolition" there could be, and were, black people working out legally mandated indentures. The children of black men in the same situation were free—unless the other parent was an enslaved woman. Of course, many, if not most, of the children of enslaved black men were also the children of enslaved black women. Still, it was the status of the mother that determined the status of the child.

In some ways, freedom did not change the lives of African Americans nearly so much as they had hoped. Most free black men continued to be employed as mariners, day laborers, and artisans. Black women continued to work in white homes. But there were significant differences of detail. For one thing, according to the 1790 census, half of the two thousand African Americans in Philadelphia lived in independent black households. (About 14 percent of those households were headed by black women.) The other half were still working as live-in servants in white households. In 1795, a directory of well-established Philadelphia families contained the names of 105 African American heads of households, including 22 women. More and more, free African Americans in Philadelphia were of the respectable working class. Some were even better off. Indeed, there was a small, but growing, black upper class.

There were the Fortens, for example, headed by James Forten, Sr., who was born to free parents in 1766 and, after serving bravely on a privateer that fought on the American side in the Revolution, returned to Philadelphia to develop a sail-making fortune. His son, James, Jr., married a free woman named Charlotte Vandine in 1805. Charlotte and her daughters—

Margaretta, Harriet, and Sarah—were charter members of the Philadelphia Female Anti-Slavery Society, the first biracial women's abolitionist group in the country. Margaretta was a teacher. Harriet married the son of another prominent black Philadelphia family, the Purvises. When an English abolitionist, Sallie Holley, visited the family, she wrote that Harriet was "very lady-like in manners and conversation; something of the ease and blandness of a southern lady. The style of living here is quite uncommonly rich and elegant." The third daughter, Sarah, was a poet and essayist who also married a Purvis son.

To honor these accomplished and dedicated women, the New England poet John Greenleaf Whittier wrote a poem entitled "To the Daughters of James Forten." It praises their "excellence of mind / The chaste demeanor and the state refined" and ends with the declaration, "Still are ye all my sisters, meet to share / A Brother's blessing and a Brother's prayer."

The Bustills were another prominent family. Cyrus Bustill earned his freedom from slavery, served on George Washington's staff during the Revolution, and became a prosperous bakery owner. His daughter Grace Bustill Douglass owned a Quaker millinery store and was a member of the Philadelphia Female Anti-Slavery Society along with her daughter, Sarah Mapps Douglass. Sarah was tutored at home, as were many upper-class black children. She became a teacher and, in the early 1830s, opened a high school for black girls in Philadelphia, the only such school in the nation at that time. But Douglass did not stop there. She insisted on teaching science to her students, a course of study that was virtually unheard of for women.

Sarah Douglass was also the creator of the first European-style painting by an African American woman that we have yet been able to find. She came from a family of artists. Her brother, Robert, was a portrait painter who also painted signs. He sold his sister's hand-painted silk scarves in his shop. But the painting that we recognize as a historical marker in the history of African American women in art was in a school notebook. The traditional school notebooks were kept by students, who asked important people in their lives to contribute poems, thoughts, or pictures. In about 1836, Sarah Douglass contributed what art historian Tritobia Benjamin describes as "a stunning, signed painting of a rose-dominated bouquet and a prose dedication to an album belonging to Elizabeth Smith. Under her painting Sarah Douglass wrote, 'Lady, while you are young and beautiful / Forget not the slave, so shall Heart's Ease ever attend you.' "

One of the absolute priorities of the free black community in Philadelphia at this time was religion. Indeed, the institutional foundation of the black church in America was laid in the city. In 1786, Richard Allen, a black

Methodist, came to preach, and within a year he joined with Cyrus Bustill and another prominent black man, Absalom Jones, to form the Free African Society. This group was described by Methodist leader Charles Wesley as "the first evidence which history affords of an organization for economic and social cooperation among Negroes of the western world." Out of it came the African Methodist Episcopal (AME) Church, the first Christian denomination founded by and for African Americans. And while the official founders of the Free African Society were all men, we can be sure that such women as Cyrus Bustill's daughter Grace and Richard Allen's wife Sarah—later founder of the Daughters of Conference—were an important part of the unofficial group that gave rise to the Society. We know that, in 1793, just seven years after the founding, the welfare functions of the Free African Society were absorbed by the Female Benevolent Society of St. Thomas.

This group was one of hundreds of societies organized by free black women of the time to promote the welfare of the black community. By 1838 there were 119 mutual aid societies in Philadelphia alone, and more than half of them were founded and run by women. Women made up nearly two-thirds of the membership of all benefit societies, even those formed by men. Benefit societies generally collected dues, which remained as savings until they were needed by the members of the society. The funds were then used to help the sick and to bury the dead. However, these were far more than just burial societies. They were committed to the moral and social betterment of the community as well. Among the first benefit societies in Philadelphia were the Benevolent Daughters (1796), the Daughters of Africa (1812), the American Female Bond Benevolent Society of Bethel (1817), the Female Benezet (1818), and the Daughters of Aaron (1819).

Under the terrible burden of slavery, many of the boundaries of women's roles had broken down. They had to. Where there was a need, it was filled by anyone who had the skills, or the courage, to fill it. Those who could lead led. Those who could heal healed. And those who could preach had to do some maneuvering. The preachers at Mother Bethel African Methodist Episcopal Church were all men—officially—but women of spirit were very much a part of the life of the church. The participation of black women in the AME and in later Protestant denominations was modeled on that of women in white Protestant churches. That is, they were pivotal to the church, but their roles were strictly limited. The African American community, and especially women, adapted and modified this structure in its own way.

According to sociologist Cheryl Townsend Gilkes, there are four pillars of the Afro-Christian tradition—preaching, prayer, music, and testimony.

Women have been largely responsible for three of these—music, testimony, and prayer. They have served in the music ministry as choir members, choir directors, and organists. As early as 1828, a black church in Philadelphia, the St. Thomas Episcopal Church, hired a young woman, Ann Appo, as church organist. They have played the major role in testimony, which includes church visiting. In the area of prayer, black women were often better—and more in demand—than the preacher. Sophie Murray and Elizabeth Cole were both reported to be evangelists of the congregation at Mother Bethel, who "held many glorious prayer meetings [where] many souls were brought to saving knowledge." No one disputes the prevalence, indeed the dominance, of black women in these three areas.

Preaching, officially, was left to men. This division appeased the white Christians who, even in the free community, wielded power over black worship. It also satisfied the black men who believed their dignity as free men depended on maintaining traditional gender roles, even if the tradition those roles were derived from was white and European. But there were some black women who were unable to accept it. Three women of Philadelphia spoke loudly in their own time of a God they knew profoundly. Their names were Jarena Lee, Zilpha Elaw, and Rebecca Cox Jackson, and they were given the right to preach not by the white world or the male world, but by a power that was, to them, much greater.

In 1809, Jarena Lee petitioned Richard Allen for the right to preach in the Mother Bethel Church. He refused her request but eventually gave her permission to hold prayer meetings in her home. The meetings became very popular and, for a time, they satisfied Lee. And then, moved by the belief that she was called by God and that His word was higher than that of her religious brethren, she went out on her own. She became a traveling preacher, carrying her message and that of her Lord. Her example had a tremendous impact on other evangelical women.

Zilpha Elaw was attending a week-long revival meeting in 1817 when she fell into a trance. Awaking, she felt herself to be sanctified and was encouraged by other women at the revival to speak. Soon she was speaking regularly. After her husband's death, Zilpha Elaw, too, became a traveling preacher. Indeed, for a time she shared a platform with Jarena Lee. Elaw's sermons included fierce attacks against slavery, even when she was speaking in the South. Her audiences in both the North and the South included blacks and whites together. In 1840, she traveled to England, where she gave, according to her memoirs, some thousands of sermons.

The third, and in many ways the most interesting, of these charismatic preaching women was Rebecca Cox Jackson. Born in 1795 in a town near Philadelphia, Rebecca Cox was the daughter of a free black family. As an adult, she supported herself as a seamstress, marrying when she was thirty-five years old. The same year, a thunderstorm literally shook Rebecca Cox's life to its roots. As lightning crashed around her, she experienced a profound religious awakening. From that moment on, she followed only the voice within her. She began leading prayer meetings, at which her deep spirituality and her eloquence appealed powerfully to her congregations. Then she went on to preaching in public, a move that elicited a great deal of criticism.

Responding to complaints that Jackson was behaving improperly by "leading the men," AME Bishop Morris Brown attended one of her services. He later said, "if ever the Holy Ghost was in any place it was in that meeting." Jackson became even more controversial when she declared that holiness could not be achieved without celibacy. She became an open critic of the leaders of the AME Church and quarreled, for obvious reasons, with her husband. Finally, she left her family and the church to become an itinerant preacher.

In her travels, Jackson encountered and became associated with the Shakers. She found their beliefs very similar to hers and was drawn to their concept of a deity who embodied both genders. However, she took the Shakers to task for not carrying their message to African Americans. She left once and then returned to the fold. In 1857, Jackson and a disciple of hers, Rebecca Perot, founded a Shaker community made up almost entirely of black women. The community continued for more than twenty-five years after Jackson's death in 1871. Jackson's spiritual writings fell into obscurity until 1981. When they were published, writer Alice Walker coined the term "womanist" to describe Jackson's specifically black orientation toward women and their concerns.

All in all, the black community in Philadelphia became stronger and more substantial at the end of the eighteenth century and the beginning of the nineteenth. African Americans were certainly not accepted as equals by their white neighbors, but they were increasingly accepted as a contributing part of the larger community. That status seemed likely to rise when, in 1793, the city was struck by yellow fever, and black citizens, many of whom had some resistance to the disease because of their upbringing in tropical areas, turned out en masse to nurse the sick and bury the dead. However, they were not hailed as heroes. Even as black women and men bathed the feverish bodies of white neighbors, the tide of sentiment was turning against them. After the fever epidemic abated, African Americans were accused of charging for their services and profiting from the illness and fear of the white community.

By this time, the number of free blacks coming into the city from the South and other, more repressive states was beginning to frighten Philadelphia's white population. When the Haitian Revolution that had begun in 1791 turned out to be not only bloody but successful, white fears throughout the United States accelerated enormously. These fears had been a part of everyday life in Charleston, South Carolina, from its inception.

CHARLESTON

A young African woman in, let us say, 1760, is serving as a slave in the Charleston home of a planter whose ancestors came from Barbados.

Before the sun has risen in the sky, Benah is carrying heavy buckets of water into the kitchen for the cooking and cleaning she will be doing all day. Even at dawn, the air is thick and filled with the odors of fish and sewage. Work will be twice as hard today because of the fever. It has struck the mistress and Phoebe, and so there will be nursing to do along with everything else.

Benah turns the corner into the garden and an arm reaches out. "No, sir," she whispers. "Not now. Not today." The words are from her heart, but her mind knows that there is no point to them. She feels her skirt pushed up and she lets the buckets down to the ground so that they won't spill.

Again yesterday she had begged her mistress to hire her out in the marketplace. Just last week, her friend Abby had bought her freedom with money she'd made in the market. Once, Benah had dreamed of that, too. Now, she only wants to get away from the house, away from . . . away before she has a half-white child to raise in the small room behind the kitchen where she lives with three other slaves.

Alone again, Benah reaches down to pick up her buckets. Crushed under one is a plant she recognizes from her home in Africa. She recognizes it and knows what it can do. In an instant, she scoops a handful of leaves and tucks them into her apron pocket, hoping she will have the courage to use them. Tonight perhaps. In his tea.

South Carolina's history is very different from that of the northern colonies. After several failed attempts at colonization, the area was developed by planters from the island of Barbados, in the West Indies. Because slavery was well established in Barbados, slaves were a part of the plan for South Carolina from its founding in 1670. The first settlement was named Charles Town, after King Charles II of England. It was a port town and, as it grew, it behaved like one.

Here there was no Quaker insistence on virtuous behavior. There was instead a Barbadian love of comfort, elegance, and excess. Walter J. Fraser, Jr., described the settlers from Barbados in *Charleston! Charleston!:* "Ostentatious in their dress, dwellings, and furnishings, they liked hunting, guns and dogs, military titles like 'Captain' and 'Colonel,' a big midday meal, and a light supper. They enjoyed long hours at their favorite taverns over bowls of cold rum punch or brandy. In sum, the Barbadian well-to-do worked and played hard, drank and ate too much, spent recklessly, and often died young." This style of life required a great deal of labor, and the workers Barbadians were used to were slaves. They brought slaves with them, imported slaves, and within a few years had begun to enslave more Native Americans than any other English colony.

It took some time for the colonists to find a cash crop, something they could trade on the world market. The crop, it turned out, was rice. The legend is that the South Carolina rice economy began with a single bushel of rice. There is significant evidence that this bushel came into the colony on an African ship, and a Swiss writer stated in 1726 that "it was by a woman that Rice was transplanted into Carolina." But whether or not a black woman brought rice to the colony, it is certain that black women were among the primary reasons that the crop prospered. In parts of West Africa, rice was an important commodity, and women were primarily responsible for agriculture. These West African women, therefore, were far more knowledgeable in the cultivation of rice than the white colonists they worked for and even more skilled than African men. Basically, black women taught the white people of South Carolina how to grow the crop that would become the mainstay of their economy. As historian Peter H. Wood writes,

> When New World slaves planted rice in the spring by pressing a hole with the heel and covering the seeds with the foot, the motion used was demonstrably similar to that employed in West Africa. In summer, when Carolina blacks moved through the rice fields in a row, hoeing in unison to work songs, the pattern of cultivation was not one imposed by European owners but rather one retained from West

African forebears. And in October when the threshed grain was "fanned" in the wind, the wide, flat winnowing baskets were made by black hands after an African design.

The black hands that made those baskets were women's hands. It was women who brought the patterns with them in their memories and women who used the sweetgrass of the American South to fashion instruments for the cultivation, harvest, and refining of rice. It has recently been realized, as well, that black women were the makers of a great deal of the pottery used in the domestic lives of colonial slaves in South Carolina and neighboring states. Once thought to have been created by white men and then by Native Americans, the pottery called Colono Ware is now believed to have been made largely by African American women.

Black women were highly valued both as craftspeople and as rice hands. They worked side by side with men in the fields. As a result, the price paid for an enslaved woman from the Gambia River Valley was usually as high as that paid for a man. An 1852 slave inventory, for example, lists twenty-seven-year-old Callie May, a "Prime Woman, Rice." She was priced at $1,000. The same price was given for Deacon, a twenty-six-year-old "Prime Rice Hand."

The African workers' skills were not the only reason they were so valuable in the rice fields. Another factor was that the black population was more resistant to tropical diseases, especially malaria, than white workers were. While white slaveholders have over the years often justified abuse of black workers by falsely claiming that they were tougher and less vulnerable to pain and illness, in this case it was true. In the past few decades scientists have discovered that the genetic trait known popularly as "sickle-cell," which can cause a dangerous form of anemia, also protects those who inherit it from malaria. And West Africans had the trait in far greater numbers than anyone else living in the colony. Clearly, when choosing between European workers, who knew nothing of rice cultivation and were susceptible to a common disease, and African workers, who were skilled and often immune, the advantage of enslaved Africans was obvious.

Because black laborers were so important in the cultivation of rice, and because slaveowners became as eager to import women as men, the black population grew very quickly. In the first twenty years of rice production, from 1695 on, it outgrew the white population, and blacks remained a majority in the colony for more than a hundred years. By 1737, the disproportion was so great that a Swiss writer commented that "Carolina looks more like a negro country than like a country settled by white people."

The slave majority was one reason that measures used against black people in South Carolina were so much more vicious than in the northern colonies. The white planters lived in fear that their slaves would turn against and overpower them. They saw force as the only way to prevent rebellion. Another reason for the extreme harshness was Barbadian tradition. In that colony, laws and customs had long since been developed to control the slave population, and these "slave codes" were based on force and violence—in short, white terrorism.

The first rebellions against slavery in Charles Town began almost as soon as the colony did. Or at any rate, the colonists were convinced they did. It is difficult at this distance in time to distinguish between the real activities of slaves and the paranoid fantasies of slave owners, since the white population of Charles Town was so terrified of the black majority that it saw slave conspiracies behind every bush. White Charles Town formed slave patrols which, in 1721, were merged with the militia. Curfews were instituted, and laws were passed against groups of African Americans gathering in public places. Slaves who ran away repeatedly were branded with the initials of their owners or had portions of their bodies amputated.

In 1739, one of the most important slave revolts in colonial America took place at the Stono River Bridge, about twenty miles south of Charles Town. By sheer happenstance, planters from the surrounding area came to hear of it, and the revolt was defeated. However, the fears of the white populace increased. In 1740, the assembly passed a new Negro Act. The 1740 act, which remained in place until after the Civil War, was designed to ensure that slaves "be kept in due subjection and obedience." The means white Charlestonians were willing to use to accomplish that purpose were harsh. There was, however, a recognition in the act that slave owners could go too far, that brutal treatment might in itself endanger the "due subjection and obedience" of slaves. And so, it was forbidden to "willfully cut out the tongue, put out the eye, castrate, or cruelly scald" a slave. The penalty for thus mutilating slaves was a fine.

In 1749, an addition was passed to the Negro Act. It appears that enslaved African Americans, usually women, had become highly proficient at one particular form of resistance—poisoning. With the 1749 amendment, administering poison or even knowing about a poisoning became a capital crime—when it was committed by an African American.

At the same time, ironically, South Carolina slaves often had more independence from their masters than northern slaves. There were many plantations with absentee owners. Sometimes, a white overseer was hired and lived on the plantation. Often, however, black workers were left on their own, under the direction of a black manager, or driver. This was against the law, which ordained that there must be at least one white person for every ten African Americans, but the law was passed because of the custom, and the custom prevailed. In the city, too, slaves had a remarkable degree of autonomy, so long as they remained within certain traditional limits. By the 1760s, large numbers of slaves carried "tickets" from their owners, indicating that they were available for hire. When hired, the slaves fed and clothed themselves out of their earnings and turned over most of the rest to their owners.

That was how it was supposed to work. But the fact is that some slaves kept more of their earnings than they were "entitled to." And slaves without tickets were hired almost as readily as those with tickets. Even runaways could usually find work in the city. Workers who were particularly skilled at their jobs could often charge considerably more than the going rate, returning only the customary wage to their owners. And some groups of workers even combined to fix the cost of their services. In this way, enslaved African Americans sometimes accumulated very respectable fortunes, enough to buy their freedom and more.

This situation could exist only in a place where the concepts of "master's time" and "slave's time" had developed, as it had in South Carolina, in part because of the task system. Under this system, slaves were responsible for completing certain tasks, regardless of the time it took to do so. When they finished—if they finished—their time was their own. It was an efficient system in an area where whites were so far outnumbered because it required considerably less supervision. And, while it may not have demanded less work from slaves, it did give them more autonomy. It also gave the slave something—her time—to bargain with.

African Americans were brought to Charles Town to make money for their owners. They soon learned that the profit motive was so strong among white people that it could even lead them to break their own laws and protections against slaves. In the end, relations between blacks and whites were often a matter of negotiation. And it was this negotiation, combined with the skills and initiative of enslaved Africans, that led to one of the most remarkable phenomena in the history of African American women.

Freedom Within Bondage

The Charles Town Market was a place of tremendous activity. Farmers brought their produce in from the countryside. Fishermen hawked their catch. Peddlers sold bread and cakes. And at the heart of it all were the expert traders, who always got the best goods, knew how to corner the market on a highly desirable commodity, and could set the prices that the public would have to pay for virtually everything in the market. These traders were black women and they were slaves.

A great many of the women of West Africa were traders, and they knew the ins and outs of the marketplace. Their skills turned out to be as valuable in the New World as their ability to grow rice. From the late 1600s on, a slave in the Charles Town area would often be sent to the market to sell her master's goods and buy what was needed for the home. Sometimes, she would arrange with her master to take the money from selling the goods, buy other goods and resell them, making a larger profit. Out of the profit, she would pay her master a "wage," which remained the same no matter how much or how little she made. She would then keep the rest. Slave owners liked this practice because they got a steady income from their slaves, regardless of what they had to sell or whether they had any work for the women to do.

However, a lot of other people didn't like it. The women were very good traders, and soon they had almost complete control of the city's food supply. In 1686, a law was passed forbidding the purchase of goods from slaves. It had little effect. When an official marketplace was set up in 1739, part of its purpose was to prevent this kind of "black market" trading. That didn't work either. In fact, none of the many attempts to take control of the marketplace out of the hands of enslaved black women worked. A petition presented to the Charles Town assembly in 1747 describes the situation.

> [Their masters] give them all imaginable liberty, not only to buy and sell those commodities, but also . . . to forestall the markets of Charles Town by buying up the Provisions, &c. which come to town for sale, at dear and exorbitant prices, and take what other indirect methods they please, provided they pay their masters their wages, which they seldom or never enquire how they came by the same . . . [further] those Negroes and other slaves, being possessed of large sums of money, purchase quantities of flour, butter, apples, &c., all which they retail out to the inhabitants of Charles Town, by which

means leading lazy lives, and *free from the government of their masters.*
(Italics ours)

These women, using the skills of their foremothers in Africa, ruled the Charles Town market. Some of them amassed considerable wealth. And in the way they challenged white authority, they provided an example to other African Americans who lived as slaves.

The Revolution and Beyond

The dissatisfaction with British rule that swept through Philadelphia in the 1760s had its counterpart in Charles Town, and here the rage for freedom had another dimension. Because the slave population took the place of a solid working class, there was an enormous gap between wealthy whites and poor whites. The struggle for independence from Britain was accompanied and often overshadowed by a class struggle within the white population. When the colony entered the War for Independence, the population was severely divided. The Barbadians and their descendants were fiercely loyal to the British Crown. The laboring class supported, for the most part, the Patriots.

In 1780, the British army seized Charles Town. Their victory has been called the greatest of the war for the British, as they took America's last open seaport. Within the city, the Loyalists cheered, and others fell into line out of necessity. Huge numbers of runaway slaves poured into the city, some for safety and some to join the British army. British officers helped themselves to the comforts and indulgences of the city, throwing luxurious balls, to which enslaved women were "invited." The British remained in Charles Town for two and a half years. When they left, they agreed to take with them no slaves except those who had specifically sought them out to join them. They left the city with five thousand formerly enslaved women and men, most of whom ended up in Canada or British Caribbean territories.

Here in the Deep South, the ideals of the Revolution did not lead to emancipation as they did in Philadelphia. It was fear of slave revolts, not liberal sentiments, that led the South Carolina legislature in 1787 to pass a law forbidding the importation of slaves for a period of three years. The law was renewed each time its term had run, and the slave trade was officially over. Then, in 1794, the legislators went one step further in their attempt to control the black population when they banned the entry of any African American, free or enslaved. Still, the black majority remained. In 1800, there were 10,104 African Americans in Charleston and 8,820 whites.

Black Charlestonians continued to exercise a degree of independence, at least for a time. At the end of the 1700s and the beginning of the 1800s, the church became an important arena for black leadership, as it had in Philadelphia. It was the custom in Charleston for slaves to attend the churches of their owners. In effect, however, the black portion of the congregation remained separate from the white, organized into "classes" with their own leadership. These black church organizations raised funds to promote the welfare of their membership. This included buying burial ground, helping the sick and indigent, and—in secret, of course—buying and freeing their members. This last practice led eventually to a ruling in the Methodist Church that black members could meet only in the presence of a white member. As a result, in 1818, 4,367 African Americans in Charleston withdrew from the Methodist Church and formed the African Church, affiliating themselves with the AME Church in Philadelphia.

Keep in mind that most of these church members were still slaves. The free black population was not growing in Charleston as it had in Philadelphia. When nineteenth-century visitor John Lambert described black women who were "distinguished from the rest, by their coloured handkerchiefs tastily tied about their heads, the smartness of their dress, and long flowing shawls or muslin handkerchiefs thrown carelessly over their shoulders, a la Francoise [sic]," he was talking about enslaved women. When another visitor spoke of "the sleek, dandified negroes who lounge on the streets" making fun of the poor and tattered "cracker," he was talking about slaves. Powers quotes Sir Charles Lyell, who commented that "the negroes here have certainly not the manners of an oppressed race."

There was a curfew, but it was regularly flouted. It was illegal to sell liquor to slaves, but they were regular customers at the "grog shops" anyway. They drank, played cards or dominoes, and hung out with their friends. There were slave parties and balls. There were times when slaves outnumbered whites at the horse races. The irony of slave life in Charleston was that this freedom existed within a system that also allowed terrible cruelty to slaves. It did not reflect the liberality of slave owners, but the power slaves were able to take for themselves.

There were some African Americans in Charleston who were legally free. Almost two-thirds of them were women, and three-quarters of them were mulattoes. The most common way for a slave to become free in Charleston involved wills. Faithful servants were sometimes rewarded, at the deaths of their owners, with freedom. More often, those freed were black women who had served as mistresses, concubines, or unofficial wives. The second group accounted for the large proportion of free African Americans of mixed race since, when white men freed their mistresses, they also freed the children they had with their mistresses.

The sexual exploitation of enslaved women by white men was so common that South Carolinian Mary Boykin Chesnut would write in the middle 1800s, "Like the patriarchs of old, our men live all in one house with their wives and their concubines; and the mulattoes one sees in every family partly resemble the white children. Any lady is ready to tell you who the father is of all the mulatto children in everybody's household but her own." Many of these mulatto children were freed by their fathers and often given enough money or property to make their way in the world. They formed the basis of Charleston's free African American community.

Some of Charleston's free blacks became quite wealthy, including a number of women. Eliza Lee, for example, owned and operated the Mansion House, a hotel on Broad Street. Her guests were the white elite of Charleston. Others worked in the garment trade, owning and using slaves in their businesses. Maria Creighton, a free black woman of considerable wealth, left her estate to the Baptist Church for the benefit of indigent African Americans and her house to a black mutual benefit society connected with the church.

The accomplishments of the free and slave communities of Charleston were accompanied by growing tension between the races. Charleston's slave trading reopened in 1803 and its impact was horribly destructive. By 1820, almost 60 percent of the population was black. With the abolitionist movement growing in both the North and the South, Charleston's white community began to panic. They felt embattled and beleaguered. Their practical need to keep the slave population under control was increasingly bolstered by racist theories about the natural inferiority of black people. Their oppressive actions were justified now, not only by their stated suspicions that they were being plotted against, but also by specious arguments about the nature of the black race.

These views would have seemed incomprehensible to the people of our third city—New Orleans.

New Orleans

A young black woman named Marie is serving as a slave to a French household in, let us say, 1778.

Marie cleans, cooks, and does some sewing. She also dresses her mistress's hair. On Sunday when she is, by law, not working for her owner, she goes to the homes of three other women—one French, one free Black Creole, and one Spanish—to dress their hair. They talk and joke together in the Creole dialect. Marie goes home feeling tired, having worked on her one day off, but she has a feeling of accomplishment . . . and a few coins.

The small sums Marie makes go under her bed in a salt box she saved from being thrown out in the kitchen trash. Very early on Monday morning, before her work for the house begins, she gets up and makes a batch of cala, or rice cakes, which her sister, a free woman, takes to the market to sell along with her own. Another tiny contribution goes into the salt box. That Friday, the family has guests for dinner. One of them compliments her on her crab cakes and slips her a small coin. The salt box again.

It takes many years, but finally Marie has saved what she believes will be her purchase price. She goes to her owner and asks to buy her freedom. But Marie is a good worker and her owner does not want to part with her. So she is forced to go before the tribunal set up by the Spanish government. The tribunal decides that the sum Marie has saved is a fair price, and there is one more free black woman in New Orleans.

New Orleans was founded in 1718, about nineteen years after Louisiana became a French colony. Within a year, the first enslaved Africans were brought into the colony.

The timing of these two events was not coincidental. Louisiana had been limping along for its first two decades with little direction and less success, its only attraction being its strategic position at the mouth of the Mississippi River. No one particularly wanted to settle there. The few who did were usually rebels and rogues and others who did not fit into the fiercely repressive French society of the day. There weren't even very many of these renegades and misfits. In 1708, almost a decade after France claimed the land, the total population of Louisiana was 278. That included 80 enslaved Native Americans, 103 military personnel, 3 Canadians, 3 priests, 6 cabin boys, 6 "workers," 1 valet, and 77 settlers. None of the settlers had been allotted land.

Nine years later, Scottish exile John Law persuaded the King of France, without much difficulty, to give his Company of the West a charter to operate the colony. By this time, there was a grand total of four hundred French settlers in the colony, and they weren't doing very well. Under Law and his appointed governor, Jean Baptiste LeMoyne, Sieur de Bienville, the misfits were joined by scoundrels. For the next couple of years, French prisons were emptied into Louisiana. Vagrants, beggars, and military deserters were the majority, but there were also murderers and drunks to spice the gumbo. Louisiana now had a population, no matter how unsatisfactory and how sparse.

Bienville created a town for this motley crew, about a hundred miles from the mouth of the Mississippi River, where a Native American trading post already existed. He named it after a supporter of John Law's, the Duke of Orleans. It took a number of years to build a city in the swamp. It also took a great many workers, many of whom were Africans.

In 1719, the first two slave ships arrived from Africa. Within the next eight years, about 5,500 enslaved Africans were brought into Louisiana. The importation of enslaved Africans by the Company of the West basically ended in 1731. (Somewhat fewer than 600 more were brought in before France gave the colony to Spain in 1762.) It had lasted only twelve years, and it was ended, in essence, by the slaves themselves. They rebelled so often and so effectively in Africa, onboard the ships, and in Louisiana that the company had to give up.

In Africa, *captifs,* as they were called, were kept in camps to await the slave ships. Conditions in these camps were appalling, and the *captifs* were constantly rebelling. On the Company of the West ships, conditions were actually much better than on most that made the Middle Passage. In spite of the fact that the trip to New Orleans was significantly longer than to Charleston or the Caribbean—the major slave disembarkation points—the mortality rate was much lower, only about 3.6 percent, although this worsened in later years. Still, the *captifs* knew that they were being taken to a life of bondage and they rebelled. Historian Gwendolyn Midlo Hall quotes a description of an incident on board *l'Annibal* on July 13, 1729. It is from the ship's journal. On this journey, 7 people out of 249 had died. They included a mother and her nursing baby, two other nursing babies, two men, and a little girl. While the boat sat in port at St. Domingue (Santa Domingo),

> a flock of our *negresses* burst into the main bedroom and punched
> M. Bart, sublieutenant of the ship. Being suddenly awakened, he be-
> lieved that it was the *negres* [that is men, not women] who had come
> to murder him. He jumped out of his window into the sea [and then
> climbed back on deck]. This tumult had caused great alarm. We ran
> to arms and fired several rifle shots. Seeing that they were trying to
> come on deck with a crowd, and believing that it was the *negres,* the

gunfire had alarmed the entire port. Several boatloads of armed men came on board, one from the fort with a detachment of soldiers.

This attack by the enslaved women was only the last of a series of rebellions on board *l'Annibal,* and port officials suggested that the captain sell his cargo there, in St. Domingue, instead of trying to take the mutinous Africans on to Louisiana. He agreed, probably with considerable relief.

By 1746, there were about 3,200 white settlers in Louisiana and about 4,730 black. As in South Carolina, there was a clear black majority, and it was still in place when the Spanish took over the colony. But there were three circumstances that made these Africans and the world they helped to create very different from their counterparts in Charleston and Philadelphia:

The white settlers were poor and desperate.

The Africans were almost all from Senegambia.

The French believed in families.

These three facts would mean everything to the development of the Creole culture of the city. They would shape the lives of black women in a way that is still apparent in the city on the Delta.

The first point is important because, when the first slave ships arrived in New Orleans with their cargoes of enslaved people, they were not greeted by wealthy planters who needed workers to herd their cattle or raise their rice. Unlike the first slaves in Philadelphia, who were sold almost by the end of the day, the first slaves in New Orleans were not sold for *two and a half months*. No one had the cash.

The effect of this poverty on the lives of the enslaved Africans can be imagined. For one thing, they were poorly fed, clothed, and sheltered. Even their owners were barely able to escape starvation. But they were otherwise treated more humanely than slaves in South Carolina and most other southern colonies. This relatively humane treatment derived directly from the desperate condition of the slaveholders. Losing the labor of a slave for even a few days because of physical injury was disastrous. Losing the slave herself because she ran away from cruelty was a tragedy, at least to the slaveholder. Killing a slave, either deliberately or through abuse, was foolhardy to the point of idiocy.

Still, there were those in the colony who terribly mistreated slaves and denied their humanity. One man, Jacques Charpentier, was known to feed his slaves only one meal a day, and that of rotten beans. He worked them from several hours before dawn until late in the night, even in the driving rain. Charpentier raped enslaved women repeatedly and then beat them to make them miscarry his own children. He was known to have beaten many slaves to death. He was finally prosecuted for some of his crimes, but only because the slaves he had abused did not belong to him. Charpentier and his ilk were not ostracized by their white neighbors. Indeed, they were found useful. Other slaveholders threatened recalcitrant slaves with sale to such men. It was not a kinder and gentler world, just a poorer one.

The origin of the enslaved Africans powerfully affected life in the colony. Because the Company of the Indies had a concession in Senegal as well as in Louisiana, the vast majority of the slaves they brought to the colony were from the area around the Senegal and Gambian Rivers. In this area lived the Mande, the Fulbe, the Wolof, the Mandinga, and the Bambara. They spoke Sereer, Wolof, and Pulaar, which are closely related languages, and Malinke, which is intelligible to the speakers of the other languages. These peoples had lived, traded, and intermarried with each other for centuries. Their cultures had fed each other and fused. As a result, their experience of captivity did not include the terrifying loneliness that confronted most enslaved Africans. They were able to communicate with each other and, in many cases, they knew each other.

Culturally, there was strength in numbers. The assimilation that took place so thoroughly in Philadelphia, and to a considerable degree in Charleston, was much less profound in New Orleans. In fact, what happened between the races and the nationalities in that French city can much more accurately be described as a blending. Four cultures, including that of the Native American peoples in the area and later the Spanish, acted upon each other to produce the city of Creoles, one of the most colorful, fascinating, and appealing cities in the world and the most African city in the United States.

The Bambara were probably the most prominent among the Senegambian peoples who came to Louisiana. Later, the name would be used generically to refer to slaves, but the people who came to Louisiana during French rule were almost certainly actually of the Bambara people of Africa. According to Hall, they constituted a language community. Four hundred Bambara slaves speaking the same language were involved in the conspiracy of 1731, a situation that could not possibly have occurred in colonial Massachusetts, for example. There was even a Bambara court interpreter in Louisiana, and slaves, when they were testifying in court, identified their African nations.

These weren't isolated individuals striving to create a new life and set of values out of rags and tatters. Coming from the same area, with a shared language, they were able to re-create much of the life to which they were

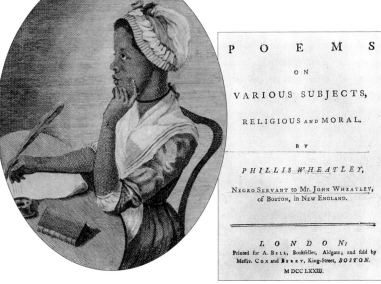

1. The second woman to publish a book in North America was poet Phillis Wheatley, an enslaved woman in Boston. *(Special Collections and Archives, W. E. B. Du Bois Library, University of Massachusetts, Amherst)*

2. Katy Ferguson opened the first Sunday school in New York, in 1793, when she was only nineteen years old. *(Engraving from* Homespun Heroines, *by Hallie Q. Brown, 1926)*

3. Alice, an enslaved woman, was profiled in the book *Eccentric Biography: or Memoirs of Remarkable Female Characters, Ancient and Modern*, printed by Isaiah Thomas, Jr., in 1804. She was apparently born in 1686 and died in 1802 at the age of 116. *(Beinecke Rare Book and Manuscript Library, Yale University)*

The Cruelest Years

SLAVE-BRANDING.

I

1. Antislavery literature publicized the brutality of chattel slavery in the antebellum South. (*Prints and Photographs Division, Library of Congress*)

2

2. Kidnapping and enslavement—or reenslavement—was a constant fear for free black Americans, especially during the antebellum period. (*Prints and Photographs Division, Library of Congress*)

3. Dissemblance of their true thoughts and feelings was a crucial survival skill for enslaved women. (*Rare Books and Special Collections Division, Library of Congress*)

3

4. Marie Laveau, the famous voodoo practitioner, was the most powerful woman in New Orleans in the nineteenth century. This painting by a German artist is said to depict her. (*Woman in Tignon, Adolph D. Rinck, 1844, oil on canvas, from the Permanent Collection of the University Art Museum, University of Southwestern Louisiana, Lafayette*)

5. The enslaved women who dominated the Charleston, South Carolina, market probably resembled this woman in a post–Civil War photograph. (*Prints and Photographs Division, Library of Congress*)

4

PUBLISHED BY
J.N.CHAMBERLAIN,

A Distorted
View

1. This cartoon from *Life in Philadelphia*, 1829, takes on a different meaning in the modern day. *(Prints and Photographs Division, Library of Congress)*

2. Richard Mentor Johnson, elected vice president of the United States, was the father of two biracial daughters, Adaline and Imogene, and openly acknowledged them. Not everyone approved, as this 1836 political cartoon shows. *(The Library Company of Philadelphia)*

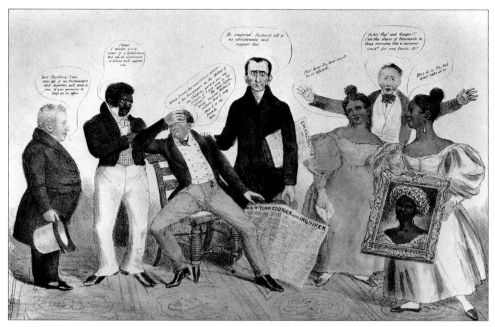

Free Choices

3. Mrs. Urias R. McGill had moved to Liberia from the United States and was living there with her husband when this photograph was taken by Augustus Washington in 1854. *(Prints and Photographs Division, Library of Congress)*

3

4

4. This 1844 lithograph was labeled "Mrs. Juliann Jane Tillman, Preacher of the A.M.E. Church," although women were not officially allowed to preach until more than a century later. *(Prints and Photographs Division, Library of Congress)*

Black Prosperity

1

1. Elizabeth Taylor Greenfield, often known as "The Black Swan," was the first black woman to receive recognition as a concert singer. She gave a command performance before Queen Victoria in 1853. *(Photographs and Prints Division, Schomburg Center for Research in Black Culture, The New York Public Library, Astor, Lenox, and Tilden Foundations)*

2

2. These three children—Eliza, Nellie, and Margaret Coplan—were the daughters of an affluent black businessman in Boston. They were painted in 1854 by W. M. Prior. *(Bequest of Martha C. Karolik for the M. and M. Karolik Collection of American Paintings, 1815–1865. Courtesy, Museum of Fine Arts, Boston)*

3

3. Clara Keaton, born in 1798, was the first depositor at the National Savings and Trust Bank in Baltimore. It is thought that this photograph was taken to commemorate the occasion of the deposit. *(Prints and Photographs Division, Moorland-Spingarn Research Center, Howard University)*

4

4. Many free black women worked on the Underground Railroad to help escaping slaves. One such woman, Chicagoan Emma Jane Atkinson, is portrayed here in a charcoal drawing based on a photograph. *(Franklyn Atkinson Henderson Collection [ICHi-22392], Chicago Historical Society)*

5. As the Civil War drew near, it became crucial to the North to keep England out of any conflict. Sarah Parker Remond traveled to the British Isles in 1859 and aroused indignation against slavery and sympathy for the Union cause. *(Courtesy, Peabody Essex Museum, Salem, Massachusetts)*

5

6. In 1855, escaping slave Ann Wood led her companions in armed resistance against a group of slave hunters who were after a bounty. *(from* Breaking the Chains, *by William Loren Katz, William Loren Katz Collection)*

6

The Civil War

1. Susie Baker King Taylor
was a nurse with a black
regiment during the war
and a teacher after.
*(Photographs and Prints Division,
Schomburg Center for Research in Black
Culture, The New York Public Library,
Astor, Lenox, and Tilden Foundations)*

2. Elizabeth Keckley, dress
designer for Mary Todd
Lincoln, raised money for
Contraband Relief during
the war. *(Prints and Photographs
Division, Moorland–Spingarn Research
Center, Howard University)*

3. During the war, recently
freed slaves were taught to
read and write by a veritable
army of teachers that included both black and white
women. Here, a white teacher
named Kate Foote works with
students in South Carolina
in 1862. *(Harriet Beecher Stowe
Center, Hartford, Connecticut)*

accustomed. They were virtually a community in exile, with traditions and customs already in place.

To pretend to sum up the Bambara in a few paragraphs would be to do them the greatest disservice. However, sketching in a few important elements of their culture should give us some insight into the black—and white—community in New Orleans. In Bambaran society, the family is the central spiritual grouping. Souls are recycled, so to speak, within the family. When a family member dies, the next to be born inherits his or her soul. And out of this belief comes an interpretation of power that is very different from the "manifest destiny" that guided American imperialism. "The Bambaran came to Louisiana," according to Hall, "equipped with a concept of sovereignty that was based upon control of people rather than of territory; with experience in creating new spiritual and legal communities; and with extensive experience in self-governing organizations." In other words, the enslaved Africans in Louisiana cared little or nothing about who owned the land or who controlled the territory. Their kingdom traveled with them. Control of their own spirits established it, and control of the spirits of others—including those of animals and of the earth—enriched and confirmed it.

Enslaved Bambara did not accept captivity docilely. They joined with Native Americans, both slave and free, to resist the French. They rebelled in groups and as individuals. The uprising in 1731 would have included all the Bambara in the area, but the conspiracy began to unravel when an enslaved woman owned by the Company of the Indies in New Orleans returned to company headquarters for lunch. She was tired from her work in a brick foundry, and when a French soldier demanded that she fetch him some wood for his fire, she refused. He hit her cruelly across the face. In a moment of rage, she cried out that French soldiers would soon have to stop slapping blacks.

That was all she said. She was immediately seized, taken to the governor of the colony, and questioned repeatedly. She denied that her words had any particular meaning. She insisted that she was just angry. But the governor sent a soldier and a Bambaran interpreter to the slave quarters to spy, and in the darkness outside one of the huts, they heard enough. The conspirators were tortured, but they never confessed or implicated anyone else. The woman was hanged. The men were broken on the wheel.

Running away was another common form of resistance. Africans were not deterred by a climate that often killed European settlers, and in spite of efforts on the part of the French to incite hostility between slaves and Native Americans, runaways found friends among the Choctaws. Indeed, the tribe ran what amounted to an underground railroad for runaway slaves who were willing to ally themselves with the British against the French. But violent resistance was not a regular part of the lives of Africans in New Orleans. They worked hard, played when they could, and raised families. This last was much easier to do in Louisiana than in a British colony. There may never have been, in all history, two more family-oriented cultures than the French and the Bambara. The blending of these two in New Orleans and the surrounding area was what produced the Creoles, whose feelings for family and family ties are legend.

In accordance with the French *Code Noir,* or Black Code, enslaved families were kept together. Husbands and wives were not sold separately, and children could not be separated from their parents until they were fourteen years old. It was also the law that everyone, slave or free, was required to be a member of the Roman Catholic Church. Further, slaves could not be required to work on Sundays or holy days. And they were to be adequately fed, clothed, and housed, even if they were too old or too ill to work. These laws were, of course, sometimes broken. Still, there is significance in their existence, and they were usually obeyed.

The result of all this was that, for many years, the usual slave family was made up of two parents, both African, and a number of children who grew up with a strong mixture of Senegambia and France in their culture. (Slaves from the West Indies and from other areas of Africa were few and came far too late to influence significantly the language and lore of the area.) The children in these African American families were called Creoles, as were their children and their children's children.

The word "Creole" has been defined in dozens of ways, changing over history. There have been those who insisted that there were no black Creoles and those who have claimed that *only* African Americans were Creoles. The Portuguese word *crioulo,* from which "Creole" comes, means "a slave of African descent born in the New World." The term was expanded to include those of European descent. Later, it was used to distinguish the mix of cultures that made up Louisiana in the early years from the Anglo-American people and influences that came in when the United States took it over.

French, African, and Spanish people all participated in forming the Creole culture. However, the Spanish were latecomers, and French and African influences predominate. The Creole language, for example, takes most of its vocabulary from the French, but it takes its grammar largely from Africa. The few African words that were incorporated often named things with which the Bambara and others were familiar from Africa, such as okra, or *gombo*. There is evidence that Creole derived from a Portuguese-based pidgin that was used in Senegal.

Creole, as a language, evolved so that enslaved Africans could speak to French settlers and to any Africans who did not share in the Mande language community. However, it eventually became popular among whites, even when they were speaking among themselves, and no wonder. Creole is colorful, rhythmic, and witty. It is also rich in the proverbs that the Bambaran immigrants were so fond of. Creole is the language in which a great deal of Louisiana folklore is written, including the Brer Rabbit tales which Joel Chandler Harris anglicized. The originals of the tales were Senegambian.

In addition to the Africanization of the city, slaves contributed, as they had in South Carolina, the technology needed to make its environs a profitable rice-growing area. Even more clearly than in South Carolina, the cultivation of this life-sustaining crop was dependent on the know-how of enslaved Africans. Swamps had to be transformed with dams, dikes, and valves that required the considerable skills of women and men from a rice-growing culture such as the Bambara.

However, in the middle 1700s New Orleans still had little to recommend it as a colony. Life was uniformly poor, sometimes desperately so. Blacks and whites starved, fell ill, and were exploited and abused by French officials and soldiers. Groups of runaways were made up of people of all ages, races, and conditions. And no one, anywhere, cared much about what was happening in this unfortunate municipality.

The "Revolution"

As the British colonies moved toward what would be the American Revolution, the Creoles of New Orleans confronted a huge change of their own. France finally got tired of dealing with its big, poor, and troublesome colony and gave it away.

When the Seven Years' War ended in 1763, France made a formal gift of Louisiana to its king's cousin, Charles III of Spain. Spain turned it down. France insisted. Spain begged off. France persisted. Spain gave in. In 1765, the colonists were informed that Louisiana was Spanish. The colonists had a fit. The French and an Irishman named "Bloody" O'Reilly helped the Spanish calm them down. In 1769, Spanish rule was established.

Under Spanish rule, the situation changed for the better for black women. There was considerably more intermarriage among racial and ethnic groups than under French rule. It was also the custom for a Frenchman or Spaniard who fathered a child with a black woman to free that child. Slaves who married free blacks were freed by law. There was even a law giving freedom to any enslaved woman whose master hired her out as a prostitute. In addition, any slave who could find the price could buy herself free, whether her owner wanted to sell or not. The matter was settled by a special tribunal set up by the Spanish government. In its recognition of the humanity of slaves, this was more like the slavery of Africa than that of the British—soon to be American—colonies.

According to figures compiled by historian Kimberly S. Hanger, there were 988 slaves freed in New Orleans between 1771 and 1803, the year of the Louisiana Purchase. Of these, 63 percent were women and 37 percent were men. This was at a time when the proportion of men to women in the slave population of New Orleans was approximately equal. Clearly, women gained their freedom more often than men. Was that because owners were more likely to free women? This was true, but only to a degree. Of the women freed, 54 percent were freed by their owners and 46 percent were bought out of slavery either by themselves or by someone else. Of the men, 48 percent were freed by their owners and 52 percent were bought out. Men were almost as likely to be freed by their owners as women were, and women were almost as likely to gain their freedom through purchase as men were. So where did the difference come in?

Were free and slave men buying black women out of slavery so that their children would be free? We have been told that was the case in Philadelphia and Charleston. What about here in New Orleans, where we have detailed records to back up generalizations of that kind? The answer seems to be no. Of the women who were bought out of slavery during this period, 54 percent bought themselves and 46 percent were bought by others. Of the men, only *40 percent* bought themselves. A full 60 percent were bought out of slavery by a third party. In New Orleans, then, women were more likely to purchase themselves. It was men who were more likely—by a large margin—to be bought out of slavery by someone else.

Black women clearly had a strong determination to be free and were able, even more often than men, to make freedom a reality. They apparently worked and saved to buy themselves out of bondage and, with the help of Spanish laws, were increasingly able to do so. The population of free black women in the colony grew. There was one segment of this population, however, who lived in a peculiar shadow society. They were by no means a majority among New Orleans' free black women but, like the women of culture in Philadelphia and the market women in Charleston, their story tells us something crucial about the society in which they lived.

Not Quite Free, Not Quite Wives

French men have historically had mistresses. The tradition is one that had great currency in New Orleans, and the mistress of choice was black. It is almost impossible to write about relationships between white men and black women without some ambivalence. Were these women traitors to black men, turning their backs on their heritage for the sake of nice houses and fine clothes? Were they heroines, sacrificing their love and self-determination in order to provide for their families and give their children a start in life? It is so easy to make culture-bound judgments about the past, so easy to look with twentieth-century eyes and distribute blame or praise accordingly. In this situation it is particularly dangerous to do so.

To begin with, most of these "women" weren't women. They were girls. The average *placage,* or unofficial marriage, began when the female partner was between twelve and fifteen years old. This is clearly before the age when a person can make a free, informed choice. The choice was made, instead, by the girl's family. The families, for the most part, believed that they were giving their daughters their best chance for a good life, since these alliances often lasted a lifetime and were characterized by mutual affection. It was a very different situation from the rape of black women by slave masters in other parts of the South. Still, girls of twelve and thirteen are children. These were arranged unions. The white men were oppressors and—there is the twentieth century falling over our eyes again.

Judgments aside, the situation gave a large group of free black women in New Orleans—and their children—a considerable degree of independence, wealth, and power. Property records of the second half of the eighteenth century list dozens of free black women who owned prime real estate in New Orleans in their own names, had houses built on the properties, and passed them on to their children.

Toward the end of the 1700s, more white women began to come to New Orleans. Apparently in an attempt to placate them, the Spanish governor declared that the free black women should support themselves, rather than live as "wives" to white men. He also declared that black women should not wear hats, clearly in an attempt to prevent them from looking as fashionable and fine as white women. Since all women in this Roman Catholic city were required to keep their heads covered in public, black women would be reduced to wearing kerchiefs, hardly a strong fashion statement. However, black women overcame this limitation easily and beautifully. They wound spectacular scarves in high, elegant turbans or draped them in the graceful *tignon* style and went about looking more lovely than ever.

Two women who represented different styles of life and attitudes towards the black community were Eufrosina Hinard and Marie Couvent. Hinard was born free in New Orleans in 1777, the daughter of a black mother and a white father. At the age of fourteen, she became the *placéed* companion of a Spanish counselor to the governor, Don Nicolás Vidal. They had two daughters, Carolina and Merced, and Vidal never entered an official marriage. Hinard and their children were his family. When he died in 1806, he left his estate to them. The estate included a number of slaves.

Hinard, although she was black herself, did not free the slaves she had inherited. Instead, she hired them out and bought more. They, as was the custom, gave a portion of their wages to her and kept the little that was left over after feeding and clothing themselves. Hinard encouraged them to save the money to buy their freedom. She charged them what they had cost her— or her husband—plus interest. Even after the United States government made it increasingly difficult to free slaves, Hinard continued her practice. She bought slaves, hired them out, and then allowed them to buy their freedom. She made a tidy profit in the process, enlarging the estate she would leave to her daughters. Hinard's attitude towards slavery was acquired from the Spanish culture in which she grew up, but it was remarkably similar to the African attitude. Slavery was a business practice, not a human condition. Everyone had a right to earn his or her way out of slavery, but she would have seen it as foolish to give away a good source of income.

Marie Bernard Couvent was born in about 1757, also in New Orleans. By the time she married Gabriel Bernard Couvent, they were both free. They accumulated real estate, among other things, and when Gabriel died in 1829, Marie inherited the lot. Three years later, she made a will leaving a valuable piece of land to be used for a free school for black orphans. However, L'Institution Catholique des Orphelins Indigens became more than a school for orphans and the impoverished. Founded some years before there was a public school system in New Orleans, and many years before black students would be admitted to public schools, it drew its students from all classes of the black community. The school still exists today and is the oldest continuing black Catholic school in the country.

Hinard and Couvent are striking examples of the wealth and power free black women could achieve in New Orleans. Many other free black women supported themselves as cooks, maids, hairdressers, or dressmakers. Some of the last were quite successful. Dressmaking was a significant area of business enterprise for black women here as in many areas in the South.

The most successful businesswoman in New Orleans, however, did not make her money with a needle, or at any rate, not a sewing needle.

Marie Laveau was born free in New Orleans sometime in the 1790s. She was a quadroon, one-quarter black. In 1819, she married a free black carpenter named Jacques Paris, whom she left a short time later. Although Paris was not dead, she began calling herself "the widow Paris" and moved in with another free black man, named Christophe Glapion. Laveau worked as a cook and hairdresser, and for some time she carried out these trades in the city jail. There she learned many dark secrets about New Orleans' citizens, black and white, rich and poor, free and slave.

Away from work, she developed a reputation as a practitioner of voodoo, a fetish religion that derived from a number of sources, including Roman Catholicism and African tribal beliefs. Consulted by white politicians and women of society as well as slaves and free black workers, Laveau was said to be able to cure illnesses, see the future, chart the course of true love, and see to it that the right candidate won the election. She was consulted for charms before marriages and, it is said, before many slaves made attempts to escape from their owners. She became so powerful, in fact, that little happened in New Orleans without the participation of the great Marie Laveau. Over the years, she also accumulated considerable wealth to go along with her power.

Laveau's daughter, also named Marie, was born in 1827. She joined her mother and, eventually, succeeded her. It is this Marie Laveau who is remembered in song and story in the city of New Orleans. However, the feats of both women are part of legend. This makes their accomplishments more difficult to assess and has prevented them from being taken with the seriousness they deserve. They were, however, highly influential in one of the largest cities in the South. The first Marie Laveau died in 1881, when she was in her nineties. Some have called her the most powerful black woman of the nineteenth century in America. Others still whisper her name in the dark. She is an intriguing part of the story of black women in America.

Marie Laveau and her daughter were not the only voodoo queens in New Orleans. As a group, practitioners of voodoo—most of whom were women—have fascinated generations, black and white. They have appeared in songs, mystery novels, and movies. Their image is one that has become familiar to us. And the familiarity derives from more than just a group of women in New Orleans. Enormously, even *absurdly* powerful women are part of a black mythology. This is not the stereotyping demanded by white culture, but an expression of resistance and rebellion. In her book *Stormy Weather,* Linda Dahl points out, for example, that the "defiance, pride, posturing and boastfulness, and the vivid symbolism of these voodoo-queen songs [are] qualities that mark the later compositions of the blueswomen." She cites this song, taken from a New Orleans newspaper in 1924 and recorded many times.

> They think they frighten me
> Those people must be crazy
> They don't see their misfortune
> Or else they must be drunk.
> I—the Voodoo Queen
> With my lovely handkerchief
> Am not afraid of tomcat shrieks
> I drink serpent venom!
> I walk on pins
> I walk on needles
> I walk on gilded splinters
> I want to see what they can do!
> They think they have pride
> With their big malice
> But when they see a coffin
> They're as frightened as prairie birds.
> I'm going to put gris-gris
> All over their front steps
> And make them shake
> Until they stutter!

In 1803, the United States took over Louisiana. According to the figures from the 1805 census, free African Americans made up 30 percent of the free population of New Orleans. They also accounted for one-third of the nonwhite population. In other words, when New Orleans became an American city, almost one of three free citizens was black and one of three black citizens was free. For all African Americans, free or slave, the entry of Louisiana into the Union changed life tremendously, and not for the better.

THE SHADOW FALLS

In the first decades of the nineteenth century, while slavery was disappearing in Philadelphia, as it was in much of the North, it was becoming more economically compelling and far more deeply entrenched in the South. It was also becoming more cruel. Free African Americans heard daily about the atrocities being committed on plantations to their black sisters and brothers. They also saw their own progress towards freedom and prosperity grinding to a halt as economic and class discrimination were bolstered by the deep racism that would corrode American democracy for the next two centuries.

Ironically, slavery might actually have died out in this country were it not for the coming together of several crucial factors at the same time. In the North, by the end of the eighteenth century, it was virtually gone. In the Chesapeake states—Virginia, Maryland, and Delaware—tobacco planting had begun to wear out the land. Farmers were turning to grains, which did not require vast numbers of slaves. Inspired by the Revolutionary attitudes, many farmers began to free their slaves.

Then, Eli Whitney invented the cotton gin. It was able to clean the seeds out of hardy, easy-to-grow short-staple cotton in about one-fiftieth of the time that it took to do it by hand. Suddenly, there was a crop that would grow all over the Deep South and that, like the more temperamental rice crop, required a huge labor force. Slave labor was again the easiest way for a plantation owner to make a fortune.

But there were no slaves coming in from Africa. In 1807, the importation of slaves had been outlawed. Suddenly, the demand far outstripped the supply. The result was horrendous. Slaveholders in the Chesapeake states stopped freeing their unwanted slaves and began selling them down the river. Some of them even began operating "slave farms," where the sole crop was slaves to be sold. Southern slaveholders began to view their slaves as stock that would have to reproduce themselves rather than as people who could be replaced if they were freed or ran away. The world of black America—the world of slavery—changed.

What set chattel slavery in the antebellum South apart from other forms of unfree labor was the suspension of virtually all regulation of behavior towards slaves. Slave codes in Africa, Louisiana, and all over the world had usually recognized the essential humanity of the person enslaved and treated slavery as a temporary, economically dictated condition. The American South changed all that. Being a slave became part of the definition of a black person. And being a slave meant having absolutely no rights. In 1809 in South Carolina, a judge declared that "young slaves . . . stand on the same footing as other animals." In 1829, a woman named Lydia tried to defend herself against her master and was shot. The judge trying the case stated, "The power of the master must be absolute to render the submission of the slave perfect. The slave, to remain a slave, must be made sensible that there is no appeal from his master."

The irony is that the "peculiar institution" might not have developed if this country had taken freedom less seriously. We as a nation had declared that "all men" were equal and entitled to certain inalienable rights, which included liberty, not to mention the pursuit of happiness. We were very proud of taking that position and, indeed, our national identity was based on it. We were the "land of liberty."

How then could millions of people be kept in bondage? The answer was clear. They must not be "men." This avoided the paradox of slavery in the land of liberty. A simple denial, however, was not good enough. Slaveholders set out to dehumanize black Americans in the eyes of white Americans. The approach was remarkably successful. Racism spread throughout the country, affecting free African Americans as well as slaves.

To accomplish the dehumanization that the institution of slavery demanded in a freedom-loving country, the South created an entire mythology. The mythology incorporated character traits for black Americans that justified everything from beatings to rape to stealing childhood from hundreds of thousands of children. The public relations campaign to spread this mythology was intense. Most important of all, the people of the South came to believe it themselves. The use of force and violence to control human property became, increasingly, a matter of course. A curtain of cruelty had lowered over the United States, North as well as South.

I had much rather starve in England, a free

woman, than be slave for the best man that ever

breathed upon the American continent.

ELLEN CRAFT,

RUNNING A THOUSAND MILES

FOR FREEDOM

SURVIVAL AND OTHER FORMS OF RESISTANCE

CHAPTER THREE

I can sit on the gallery, where the sunlight shine bright, and sew a powerful fine seam when my grandchildren wants a special pretty dress for the school doings, but I ain't worth much for nothing else, I reckon.

These same old eyes seen powerful lots of tribulations in my time, and when I shuts them now I can see lots of little children, just like my grandchildren, toting hoes bigger than they is, and they poor little black hands and legs bleeding where they was scratched by the brambledy weeds, and where they got whippings 'cause they didn't get done all the work the overseer set out for them.

I was one of them little slave girls my own self, and I never seen nothing but work and tribulation till I was a grown woman, just about. . . . It was the fourth day of June in 1865 I begins to live . . .

KATIE ROWE, SPEAKING TO AN INTERVIEWER FROM
THE FEDERAL WRITERS PROJECT IN THE 1930S

The eyes of slave women look to us across the centuries, still filled with strength and sorrow, bewildered, but seldom dulled by pain. These women of the southern plantations have stood so long as a symbol of endurance that it is difficult to look into the faces in old photographs and see the complexities that we must see if we are to understand them and their history. They lived through the most terrible time in American history *as individuals.* Each one got up in the morning with feelings in her heart's core that might have been despair or something that resembled hope. When she was herded into the field before dawn, she cried out, if only in her silent self, against this life that held her like the iron teeth of an animal trap. When she made love, she shivered with desire. When she gave birth, she ached— with yearning to feel her child's soft body next to her and with desolation at the thought of its future.

The plantation South in the decades before the Civil War was not the world of Lucy Terry Prince and Phillis Wheatley. It was not a place where Elleanor Eldridge could build up a business and buy real estate, no matter what the obstacles. It was a place of gang labor, slave quarters, and bearing children that the master thought of as stock. In the perverse universe of the slaveholder, whipping another human being until she bled was just another management technique and keeping her from a sick or dying child nothing but an economic necessity. In the life of an enslaved woman, violence was expected, and cruelty was commonplace.

But cruelty is only the background for the real story. Even here, where life was most difficult and choices most limited, black women had victories.

They reared children who loved and respected them. They passed on from generation to generation values that made life possible and worth living. They turned survival into an art and a form of resistance to oppression. This is where we really begin to learn from the women of black America.

CHATTEL SLAVERY IN
THE ANTEBELLUM SOUTH

Take a look around you. Look at your neighbors, the merchants and other people you do business with, the minister at the church on the corner, the people who teach your children. Now, go a little further afield. Look at the people you see on the evening news: the executives of corporations who put profits before public health concerns, the drug dealers, the sex offenders and child abusers. Imagine that *all* of these people were allowed to own other people. Think about it. Let it really sink in. Any one of them could own a person who, if she ran away, would be tracked down by the police and returned to her owner. They could own people who would not be allowed to testify against them in court, no matter what they did. And they would automatically own the children of the women who were their property.

They could do anything they wanted, understand, with any of the people who were their property. No one would punish them or put them in jail. Most people probably wouldn't even refuse to invite them to parties. They could overwork their human belongings, starve them, beat them, sexually abuse them. Or, on the other hand, they could clothe their property well, provide decent meals, and assign reasonable tasks to perform. It would be entirely up to them, with virtually no interference from outside.

How would each of those individuals treat the people they owned— the men, women, and children who were entirely in their power, over whom they had complete control? What do you think life would be like for them? In most countries of the world, it would be almost impossible to achieve this act of the imagination. In the United States we don't have to. We know what would happen because we know what did happen. We can look at our own history for the answers.

Human nature was very much the same in the antebellum South as it has always been and still is today, and there are tremendously wide variations in the way people behave in any given situation. If we forget that, we will find it difficult to believe some part of the truth about slaveholders and slaves. A story of some terrible atrocity will seem too evil, too extreme to be genuine. Or, on the other hand, the remembrance of an ex-slave that the "master and missus" were always kind and "took good care of their people" will seem some kind of obscene sugar-coating of the bitter truth. And yet both are real aspects of the history of black women. There are some very good people in the world along with some exceptionally bad ones, but if there is one thing that history has taught us, it is that there is no one good enough to own another person. There is no one good enough to own a slave.

Indeed, owning a slave could make a good person, or at any rate an ordinary person, bad. In the first studies of rape, which appeared in the 1970s, a strange phenomenon came to light. It might be expected that the greatest brutality would occur when a woman is raped by one man and the necessity for overpowering her is great. In fact, however, by far the greatest brutality occurs in gang rapes, when overpowering the woman is hardly an issue. The brutality, it appears, is part of the process of dehumanizing the woman. It is essential that no one of the men should stop, see the woman suddenly as someone's sister or daughter or wife, look at the other members of the group and cry out, "What are you doing to this person? What kind of monsters are you?" Brutality towards slaves, too, was a method of dehumanization, one more way of making them seem less than human so that no one would cry out the word "monster."

But enslaved Americans themselves cried out. Up to this point, we have heard few voices of black women who lived the history we have described. A handful left behind journals or letters, but these women were almost entirely absent from public discourse, so their thoughts and feelings about their lives generally have been lost. However, a remarkable project initiated by Franklin Roosevelt's administration during the Great Depression passed down to us the actual words of women and men who lived in slavery in the antebellum South.

The Federal Writers Project, during the 1930s, sent fieldworkers into former slave states and interviewed more than two thousand people who had been enslaved. To keep the words in perspective, remember that these people were talking about things that had happened seventy and eighty years before. They were talking to white interviewers at a time when there was little reason for black people to trust whites. And they were comparing memories of childhood with their lives as old people during the worst depression the country has ever seen. Still, the histories have been enormously valuable to historians. Combining them with records kept by plantation owners, diaries, journals, and other sources, we have a fairly clear picture of what life was like during this terrible time. And we can hear the voices of black women as they grew from babies left behind when their mothers went to the fields to teenagers flirting with young men on Sundays to mothers themselves trying desperately to protect their own children from slavery's pains and sorrows.

SOMEBODY'S CHILD

I been eight year old when they took me. Took me from me mother and father here on the Pipe Creek place down to Black Swamp. . . . I never see my mother or my father anymore. Not till after Freedom. SILVIA CHISOLM

All of us children, too little to work, used to have to stay at the "Street" [slave quarters]. They'd have some old folks to look after us—some old man or some old woman. They'd clean off a place on the ground near the washpot where they cooked the peas, clean it off real clean, then pile the peas out there on the ground for us to eat. We'd pick 'em up in our hands and begin to eat. REBECCA JANE GRANT

When I was little, I used to play in that big cave they calls Mammoth Cave, and I was so used to that cave it didn't seem like nothing to me. But I was real little then, for soon as they could they put me to spinning cloth. LULU WILSON

Childhood, for most slave children, lasted only a few years. During those years, they played as other children do. They jumped rope and climbed trees and played games. And then, in a heartbreakingly short time, they went to work. Some enslaved children began to do small chores when they were four or five. By seven, many slave children were working regular hours. Most ten-year-olds were considered "hands." Girls usually began working at an earlier age than their brothers, and they shifted from the jobs accorded children to their adult jobs earlier as well.

Slave children did a number of jobs. Both boys and girls were enlisted for child care. Mothers, of course, worked all day. On a small plantation, the slaveholder's wife might care for the babies and toddlers, with help from slightly older children. Other places, a slave who was too old for fieldwork might be assigned the child-care duties, again with the help of children of seven or eight years. On some plantations, children of that age took care of their younger brothers and sisters alone.

Children, of course, are not the best caretakers of other children.

Sometimes, when Marster hear the babies cry, he come down and say, "Why the children cry like that, Ellen?" And I say, "Marse, I get so hungry and tired I done drink the milk up, instead of giving it to the baby." . . . I was so little I don't know no better.   ELLEN BETTS

Slaveholders also used small children to gather firewood, weed garden patches, run errands, and keep birds out of the garden. Children swept the yard, fed chickens, and helped with household chores. Some children were taken, at a very early age, into the owner's house to be trained as house servants. It was conventional wisdom in the South that the best way to get a good house servant was to raise one. Often, children were taken from their parents to sleep in the Big House as well as to eat, work, and play there. Their families were replaced by the families of their owners, with their position in those families clearly defined.

I was kept at the Big House to wait on Miss Polly, to tote her basket of keys and such as that. Whenever she seed a child down in the quarters that she wanted to raise by hand, she took them up to the Big House and trained them. I was to be a housemaid. The day she took me, my mammy cried, 'cause she knew I would never be allowed to live at the cabin with her no more.   SARAH DEBRO

In many ways, children who were taken into the house were fortunate. Certainly they ate better and had better clothing and more comfortable working conditions than children in the field. Some became "pets" of the slaveholding family and developed relationships that could, without much of a stretch, be called friendships. At the same time, both children and adults who served in the house were on call twenty-four hours a day. They had not a moment that was completely their own. And they were in no less danger of violence than a field hand. In the house, as in the field, "discipline" was swift and often cruel. Too, southern plantations had their share of outright sadists. Without the constraints of law or social disapproval, these people, both women and men, were free to commit extremes of physical violence on even the youngest slaves, especially when they were separated from their families.

Children who were house servants also missed out on the support and camaraderie of the slave quarters, with its powerful sense of community. That was no small loss. To enslaved Americans, community meant survival—emotional, psychological, and often physical survival. They were under constant assault from the white world, which did everything it could to make them "good slaves." A good slave, obviously, is *not* a healthy, secure, "self-possessed" person. Self-respect was a treasure to be cherished in the quarters. It was a quality that parents worked hard to instill in their children and that the slave community encouraged in all its members. Separated from that atmosphere, a child was vulnerable to all sorts of attacks on her sense of self-worth.

I was just a little girl, about eight years old, staying in Beaufort at the missus' house, polishing her brass andirons and scrubbing her floors, when one morning she say to me, "Janie, take this note down to Mr. Wilcox Wholesale Store on Bay Street and fetch me back the package the clerk give you."

I took the note. The man read it, and he say "Uh-huh." Then he turn away and he come back with a little package, which I took back to the missus.

She open it when I bring it in and say, "Go upstairs, Miss!"

It was a raw cowhide strap about two feet long, and she started to pouring it on me all the way upstairs. I didn't know what she was whipping me about, but she pour it on, and she pour it on.

Directly, she say, "You can't say 'Marster Henry,' Miss? You can't say 'Marster Henry?'"

"Yes'm. Yes'm. I can say 'Marster Henry!'"

Marster Henry was just a little boy about three or four years old. Come about halfway up to me. Wanted me to say "Marster" to him—a baby!

REBECCA JANE GRANT

In this atmosphere, without the help of the community, a child's spirit was easily broken. In the quarters, a black mother or father taught the child, instead, the lessons of survival.

LEARNING HER LESSONS

Survival in slavery meant obedience to the slaveholder. The laws saw to that. The whip guaranteed it. But, even more important, there was loyalty to the family and to fellow slaves. A black mother taught her daughter to do her own work and to help other slaves when they were unable to complete their tasks. She taught her daughter never to tell a white person anything that could possibly harm another slave. From a very early age, black children learned that the family and the community came first. In an America where rugged individualism has always been prized so highly, such impassioned loyalty to a community was not a commonly accepted value, especially as it was practiced in slave quarters.

Historians and sociologists all over the Western world have noted that, under conditions of great hardship, the men of a community will bond, often at the expense of their families. They develop strong loyalties toward each other so that they can trust each other in battle against the enemy, whether that is a hostile tribe or an exploitative employer. Women, on the other hand, have usually bonded with their children, defending them against the callousness and brutality of both the outside world and their embattled husbands and fathers. However, enslaved people, both women and men, seemed to have stressed loyalty to the entire community of slaves. And black women, while they did bond strongly with their children, also bonded with each other. They formed a subculture as a base from which they could protect themselves—against all white people, on the one hand, and against all men, on the other.

Indeed, as Deborah Gray White points out in *Ar'n't I a Woman?*, "Slave women have often been characterized as self-reliant and self-sufficient because, lacking black male protection, they had to develop their own means of resistance and survival. Yet, not every black woman was a Sojourner Truth or a Harriet Tubman. . . . The self-reliance and self-sufficiency of slave women, therefore, must not only be viewed in the context of what the individual slave woman did for herself, but what slave women as a group were able to do for one another."

This sense of community was fostered when women worked together. Often, work such as spinning, weaving, and sewing was a communal activity. On some plantations there were "spinning and weaving" cabins. Certainly quilting was done by a group. These were times when women bonded, as were the more profound experiences of childbirth. The strength of black women, again and again, has been drawn from other black women.

The development of a community is one of the most powerful of all survival skills, and it is a skill that black women have mastered.

Another skill mastered by enslaved women was protection of the inner person. A black mother taught her daughter to develop two faces. She was to seem accommodating and tractable to the slaveholder, smiling and ready to please. At the same time, she was to have a secret place inside her full of self-respect. Janie might learn at the end of a whip to call a white baby "Marster Henry," but there was a part of her that could laugh at the silliness of it or be contemptuous or angry or whatever would keep her own sense of self intact.

As daughters got older, of course, there were other lessons to be taught. Even very young girls were subject to sexual abuse from white men. This was a reality black parents faced from the moment a girl baby was born. There was no real defense against it, but black mothers counseled their daughters in modesty and dignity, in the hope that those qualities might provide some protection. They also taught them lessons of guile and trickery. There was nothing dishonorable in deceiving the slaveholder. Indeed, the ability to overcome force by the use of wits was a highly valued one in the slave community. Certainly, if a girl could protect her sexual integrity, anything was justified.

Black mothers taught their daughters many such lessons. None of them, however, involved textbooks and slates.

The white folks did not allow us to have nothing to do with books. You better not be found trying to learn to read. Our marster was harder down on that than anything else. You better not be catched with a book.
HANNAH CRASSON

The white folks didn't never help none of we black people to read and write no time. . . . [I]f they catch we black children with a book, they nearly about kill us.
SYLVIA CANNON

White people in the South held paradoxical views about the intelligence of African Americans. On one hand, they insisted that Africans were an inferior race and not possessed of the intelligence to function equally with whites. On the other, they declared that it was "dangerous" to teach blacks how to read and write. It unfitted them for the role of slave. This second position was, to some extent, true. Being able to read opens up the world. People who know something other than slavery are unlikely to remain convinced that it is their only option. Slaveholders knew this and most did everything they could to keep enslaved people illiterate.

In fact, in many states this was one area in which slaveholders did not have complete control over their slaves. It was illegal for anyone to teach a slave to read. Historian William Loren Katz cites a case in which "Margaret Douglass, a white woman of Norfolk, Virginia, was tried and found guilty, according to the court, 'of one of the vilest crimes that ever disgraced society.' She had taught Kate, 'a slave girl, to read the Bible. No enlightened society can exist where such offenses go unpunished,' ruled the court."

Enslaved Americans, however, often managed to learn in spite of all obstacles. There were secret schools in the quarters where, behind closed doors and with lookouts posted, a slave with some skills in reading and writing would teach others. Sometimes black children learned to read from their white playmates. This usually meant hiding from the white child's father, although some mothers seemed to have known and not interfered. Sometimes children who worked as house slaves would listen in to the white children's lessons and pick up the basics that way.

Depriving black people of the opportunity to learn was an absolute priority in the South. In the words of one Virginia legislator, "We have, as far as possible, closed every avenue by which light might enter their minds. If you could extinguish the capacity to see the light, our work would be completed; they would then be on a level with the beasts of the field, and we should be safe!"

Milla Granson, a slave born in about 1800 in Kentucky, persuaded her master's children to teach her to read. She believed that, somehow, education would lead her to freedom. It led her first to teaching. With the little learning she had gained from the other children, she began to teach other slaves. At this first farm, which was not in the Deep South, she had the permission of her owner for her teaching. However, when her master died, she was sold to a plantation owner in Mississippi. There, in the middle of the night, she taught class after class of slave students to read. People who had worked hard all day in the field sat awake from 11:00 P.M. to 2:00 A.M. to pick up the rudiments of knowledge that Milla Granson could pass on. When she had taught them all she could, they would graduate, and she would take on another class. Hundreds of slaves learned to read and write from Milla Granson. For many of them, as Milla Granson had hoped, their literacy led to freedom.

WORK

*In course of time, I was took off nursing and put to the field. I dropped
cotton seed, hoed some, and picked cotton. I never learned to read or
write.*

*At certain times we worked long and hard, and you had to be particular.
The only whipping I got was for chopping down a good cornstalk near a
stump in a new ground.*   ADELINE JACKSON

When it was time to move from childhood chores to adult jobs, the differences between girls and boys became more marked. All field slaves, it is
true, did hard manual labor, and men and women did many of the same
jobs, but outside the fields there were differences. Field hands worked long
hours at backbreaking jobs. The planting of cotton began in March. From
April on, slaves hoed, thinned, and weeded it. August brought picking,
which continued until sometime in January. Then slaves ginned the cotton,
getting out the seeds, and pressed it into bales. Finally, they loaded it into
wagons. At the same time, there were the other chores to be done. There
was food to be grown and livestock to be raised to feed both the owner's
family and the slaves. There were the usual farm chores, such as clearing
land and building fences.

Women participated with men in virtually all of these jobs. When
there were at least sixteen slaves, they were usually divided into hoe gangs
and plow gangs, and there were not as many women on the plow gangs as
men. Slave women, with boys and older men, made up the hoe gangs. But
there were exceptions. A Mississippi traveler wrote, "Seeing a wench
ploughing, I asked him [the overseer] if they usually held the plough. He
replied that they often did; and that this girl did not like to hoe, and, she
being a faithful hand, they let her take her choice."

The plowing "wench" had good reason to dislike hoeing. The hoes
were not the small, streamlined garden hoes of today. They were made of
pig iron hammered into a width as broad as a shovel. One former slave
commented that "they make them heavy so they fall hard, but the biggest
trouble was lifting them up." Lifting and swinging these hoes hour after
hour, day after day, was exhausting and painful, even if it was "women's
work." And there was no respite. The British actress Fanny Kemble, who was
briefly married to a southern slaveholder, described black women in the
fields as "human hoeing machines."

On small holdings, both men and women plowed and hoed. And on every cotton plantation, large or small, everyone picked. Women, men, and children all went into the fields on the coldest days of the year and pulled the prickly bolls off cotton plants until their hands bled. Slave women and girls often picked even faster than the men. Other plantation crops—rice, sugar, tobacco—demanded labor that was just as intense.

There were some jobs on plantations for artisans and craftspeople. Estimates of how many slaves held those jobs vary. Some say that as many as one-quarter of the male slaves worked as blacksmiths, carpenters, wagon and coach drivers, and so on. Others make that number closer to 10 percent. But all agree that women were not employed in these "skilled" jobs. Historian Wilma King suggests that the reason for this was that childbearing "interrupted work which could not be completed as easily by a substitute as picking cotton or pulling corn." Jacqueline Jones, on the other hand, argued that slave owners considered the work women did in the winter, such as spinning and weaving, to be too important to interrupt to hire a woman out as a mechanic or driver. These are important points, made by two percipient historians. Still, it seems likely that the most fundamental reason that black women were not allowed to learn traditionally male crafts is that those crafts were *traditionally male.* White women were not allowed to learn them. Why would a white man make an exception for a black woman that he would not make for the daughter of a white sharecropper? Certainly he used black women in the fields, but poor or working-class white women worked alongside their men in the fields, too. Using a hoe did not require "male know-how" in the sense that using a hammer did.

Slaveholders were practical enough to violate the basic principles of sexism when it was to their advantage and when it did not require them to acknowledge in a woman a level of equality that was of any importance. Allowing any woman, black or white, to learn and exercise male craft skills would have been far too threatening to the principle of male supremacy. (One does suspect, however, that on some small plantation in the back country, there was a large, strong African American woman who worked a forge because there didn't happen to be a man around who was fit for the job.)

The other point that comes unavoidably to mind here is that almost all historians make a distinction between "skilled" work and the sort of work that women did—nursing, midwifing, cooking, spinning, weaving, seamstressing. The fact is that these are clearly forms of skilled labor. We may lose sight of this fact because so many women acquired these skills, but it is a very important one. In cities, these were the very skills that enabled free black women to open businesses and become self-supporting. In 1860, 15 percent of free black women were dressmakers and hairdressers.

Of course, the point that King and the others were making was a crucial one. Black women on plantations did not have the privileges that traditionally male skilled labor brought with it. Dressmakers did not have the mobility, for example, that came with being hired out to do carpentry on another plantation. Within riding distance of a plantation, there were unlikely to be more than a few women with money to pay a dressmaker, and most of them owned slaves to do the work for them. Women were also not used as supervisors and therefore did not gain the privileges granted to men in those positions.

There are instances, however, of enslaved women whose skills helped ease the burden of slavery for themselves and their families. Nancy Williams, of Loudon County, Virginia, made quilts from fabric scraps and sold them for ten dollars apiece to white neighbors, for example. Other women made and sold baskets. And there were two jobs that gave some enslaved women status and certain privileges. These were cook/housekeeper and midwife.

The cook in the Big House of a sizable plantation was usually as skilled as the chef in a reputable restaurant. Plantation owners often enjoyed a level of luxury in their homes that was comparable to the wealthiest families anywhere, so a truly proficient cook was valued and respected. She often had a degree of privacy enjoyed by neither field-workers nor other domestic slaves. She ate the same food that she cooked. And when she doubled as housekeeper, she was a kind of "foreman" over the other domestics. She was, however, "on call" her entire life. And, of course, she enjoyed no more mobility than any other slave.

The midwife, on the other hand, often traveled all over the area in which she lived. Indeed, enslaved midwives in rural areas delivered virtually all babies, black and white, unless there was a medical complication. A doctor in Virginia estimated that, during the antebellum years, black midwives delivered half the white babies in the state.

I was always good when it come to the sick, so that was mostly my job. I was also what you call a midwife, too. Whenever any of the white folks around Hanover was going to have babies they always got word to Mr. Tinsley that they want to hire me for that time. Sure he let me go—'twas money for him, you know.   MILDRED GRAVES

A slaveholder who had among his slaves a midwife had a valuable property. She could be hired out at least as easily as a carpenter or blacksmith, and her fees considerably enriched her owner. Mildred Graves's owner gave her a few cents of her fee to keep herself, and she was able to use that money to make her life somewhat more comfortable. The midwife also enjoyed a position of respect in both the black and white communities. She usually passed her skills on to her daughters or, sometimes, to other women apprentices.

Still, whatever her position, an enslaved woman worked long, hard days. And even when working the same job and hours as a man in the field, she was usually given less food. The clothing provided by the slaveholder—skirts and dresses—was far less appropriate for the work than a man's. And then, when her job was finally done, she continued to work.

> *Master had four overseers on the place, and they drove us from sunup till sunset. Some of the women plowed barefooted most all the time, and had to carry that row and keep up with the men, and then do their cooking at night.*   HENRY JAMES TRENTHAM

As we've seen, American mainstream gender roles had a lot of power in the plantation South. When it was convenient for the slaveholder to shatter the stereotypes—putting women into the fields, for example—he did. But most of the time a woman was expected to fulfill a woman's role, and that included doing "women's work." On some plantations, food was doled out from a central kitchen. On others, however, women came in from the fields to cook for their families, mend clothes, and then, late into the night, spin and weave. Often, enslaved men were issued a seasonal allotment of clothes, including perhaps a shirt, a pair of pants, and a jacket. Women, on the other hand, were allotted cloth, buttons, thread, and a needle.

This aspect of the enslaved woman's life has caused a degree of controversy among historians. Some have said that this additional work could not be considered a burden of slavery because black women did it out of love, to care for their families. Since historians began to debunk the myth of the "absent black family," this view has gained even more currency. However, even if every enslaved woman loved desperately the man she lived with, that fact would not justify added burdens that could have been, but usually were not, shared. "To say that women did housework for 'love,' " writes historian Claire Robertson, "is not to mitigate its severity but to paper it over with romantic ideology." The fact is that, while there was considerably more equality between enslaved women and men than between middle-class white couples, gender still dictated roles. And while everyone suffers from the limitations of sexism, women suffer more.

In slavery, that sexism was complicated and reinforced by racism, as it so often has been in the history of black women. Marriage, for the black woman, was a two-edged sword that often cut deep into her identity and her heart.

Courtship and Marriage

Who married the slaves? Man, folks didn't get married then. If a man saw a girl he liked he would ask his master's permission to ask the master of the girl for her. If his master consented and her master consented then they came together. She lived on her plantation and he on his. The woman had no choice in the matter. KATIE BLACKWELL JOHNSON

Sexual love is the most intimate of human relationships. For this love to be subject to the whims and economic considerations of a third party, as it was in slavery, was humiliating. It was also destructive, painful, and unwholesome. Enslaved men and, especially, women fought against the control of the slaveholder in this most personal area of their lives with any and every means. Often they lost the battle. But often, miraculously, they won. On some plantations, young women were even permitted to choose their husbands.

As a young woman reached late adolescence, the question of love and marriage inevitably arose. If she lived on a large plantation, there were many young men for her to talk to and flirt with. On Sundays, she would take the scarf from around her head and fix her hair. She might put on her best dress, if she had one, or perhaps just add a necklace made of seeds and dried berries.

If a young man asked her to marry, and she accepted him, he would then go to her owner and seek permission. But there were often others involved in the process—the women of the community. Sometimes one woman, by virtue of her age and wisdom, held the power to approve or disapprove any marriage in the quarters. This was the case with the woman known as "Ant Sue," according to former slave Caroline Johnson Harris. When Harris and her beau approached Ant Sue for permission to marry,

"She tell us to think about it hard for two days, 'cause marrying was sacred in the eyes of Jesus." After two days' thought, the couple returned to the older woman, who called together the other members of the community and asked them to pray for Caroline and her future husband.

The slaveholder usually determined the nature of the wedding ceremony. Since slave marriages were not legal, there were no licenses, and there was no necessity for an ordained minister or judge. Sometimes the slaveholder performed the ceremony himself, and sometimes a black preacher or an elder in the community, such as Ant Sue, administered the vows. Many of the slave narratives mention "jumping the broomstick," a ritual in which the bride and groom do exactly that—jump over a broomstick together or one after the other—as a way of formalizing a marriage. This is sometimes thought of as an African holdover. In fact, writes Brenda Stevenson, it was a pre-Christian ritual from Europe, "probably passed down to later generations as an amusing, perhaps quaint, relic of their 'pagan' past. By imposing this cultural albatross on slaves, southern whites suggested the lack of respect and honor that they held for their blacks' attempts to create meaningful marital relationships. The slaves' acceptance of this practice, on the other hand, demonstrated the ability of slave culture to absorb, reconfigure, and legitimize new ritual forms, even those masters imposed out of jest or ridicule."

It is certainly true that the broomstick ritual came to hold an honored place in the wedding customs of enslaved people. And the marriages it initiated were taken with great seriousness, regardless of their lack of legal force. However, it is important to remember how slavery affected these marriages. First, most enslaved women had no choice about whether or not they were to become wives and mothers. It was not only expected of them, it was demanded. The joys of courtship could not disguise the fact that, if a woman did not choose a husband, she would be assigned one. It was part of her job. It was also part of a woman's job to bear children.

> When a girl became a woman, she was required to go to a man and become a mother. There was generally a form of marriage. The master read a paper to them telling them they were man and wife. . . . Master would sometimes go and get a large, hale, hearty Negro man from some other plantation to go to his Negro woman. He would ask the other master to let this man come over to his place to go to his slave girls. A slave girl was expected to have children as soon as she became a woman. Some of them had children at the age of twelve and thirteen years old. Negro men six feet tall went to some of these children. HILLIARD YELLERDAY

In Loudon County, Virginia, which Stevenson studied, enslaved women usually had their first children at the age of nineteen. However, slave narratives from Deep South plantations often mention "marriages" of girls in their early to middle teens.

One young woman, Rose Williams, was enormously grateful to her owner, a man named Hawkins, for having bought her together with her mother so that they wouldn't be separated. Her gratitude was put to the test when she was sixteen years old. Hawkins informed Rose that she must go to live with a man named Rufus. Young and ignorant of sexual matters, Rose thought this meant that she should take care of the cabin for him. That night, when Rufus tried to get into bed with her, she protected herself with a poker. The next day, Rose went to Mrs. Hawkins to protest Rufus's behavior and was told that she was to do as Rufus wanted. Again, Rose refused. That night, she kept Rufus at a distance with the poker again. But the morning brought Hawkins to her. He informed her that she must bear children with Rufus or be whipped at the stake. "I thinks about Massa buying me off the block and saving me from being separated from my folks, and about being whipped at the stake. There it am. What am I to do? I decides to do as the master wish and so I yields."

Later, after freedom, Rose remained single. She said one experience was enough for her and that the Lord would have to find someone else to replenish the earth. Childlessness was a luxury for Rose Williams, a luxury enslaved women could seldom enjoy.

If a woman didn't bear children, she would first be assigned a different husband. If there were still no children, she would usually be sold. Even the most amiable slaveholder was unwilling to support the expense of a woman who did not supply him with little slaves. If the slaveholder was reluctant to lie about her barrenness to a buyer—or unable to pull off the deception—her price would be small, and her new owner would assign her the hardest, dirtiest jobs to make up for her uselessness as a source of children.

Enslaved men, on the other hand, could and did sometimes refuse to marry.

> *I determined long ago never to marry until I was free. Slavery shall never*
> *own a wife or child of mine.*   J. W. LOGUEN

Some women attempted to take this attitude and a handful got by with it, for one reason or another, but not many. Enslaved women were almost universally condemned to marrying men they might be parted from and bearing children they must watch go through the pains of slavery. And most enslaved women had few of the satisfactions of "doing for" their families that even the poorest free woman might have. Almost everything was controlled by the slaveholder, including the food she had to prepare and the clothing her family wore. And of course, everything she did for her family was done when she was already spent from a day's hard labor.

Also, not every enslaved woman loved her husband. Indeed, it is remarkable that so many did, given the conditions under which they all lived. Still, black women on the plantations were not saints, and neither were black men. They were ordinary human beings managing to survive in an appalling situation. And ordinary human beings, no matter who they are or how they live, do not always love their mates. Some of the men were surly, unlovable, and even abusive. Some of the women were jaded and dead to "the finer feelings." And some were simply very practical.

Deborah Gray White cites the case of Fannie, slave of Ned Eppes of Florida. When Eppes proposed to sell Fannie to her husband Essex's owner so that the two would not be separated when Essex's owner moved to Florida, Fannie refused to go, "preferring to stay with her mistress, the woman who had previously purchased her from a cruel owner. Fannie's experience with a mean master had taught her a lesson she took to heart: 'I knows . . . dat it's might easy ter git a good husband, an' might hard ter git a good mistis.' " Fannie soon remarried, explaining that she needed someone to chop wood.

Having said all that, we get to the remarkable part. At the end of the Civil War, with the opportunity before them to escape from marriages that were sanctioned only by slaveholders, the great majority of freed couples chose to remain together. There were, for example, twenty thousand slaves in seventeen counties of North Carolina who paid a fee to register their marriages, making them legally binding. There were 2,817 slave marriages officially confirmed in six counties of Virginia.

Slave marriages were, for the most part, strong and caring unions. And sometimes they were love stories that rival those of Antony and Cleopatra or Romeo and Juliet. Another young woman named Fannie, for example, wrote to her husband after his master had taken him along into the Confederate army, a letter filled with passion and sweetness, from which this excerpt is taken.

> I haven't forgotten you nor will I ever forget you as long as the world stands, even if you forget me. My love is as great as it was the first night I married you, and hope it will be so with you. My heart and

love is pinned on your breast, and I hope yours is to mine. . . . There is no time night or day but what I am studying about you. . . .

Your Loving Wife,
Fannie

Motherhood

A Georgia slave trader appeared at the door of a small cabin. He was there to take delivery of a boy who lived within. The boy's mother, however, hid him and went to guard the door. "You are here to get my son," Harriet Ross said, "but the first man that comes into my house, I will split his head open." The master's son, not wanting to lose the money from the sale, tried to physically subdue Mrs. Ross, but she took up a pole and beat him instead. Nearby, Mrs. Ross's daughter, Araminta, stood watching and learning. When she grew up, she married a man named Tubman and changed her name to Harriet, to honor her mother.

Not all stories about black mothers are this dramatic, but they are nonetheless powerful and inspiring. Slave narratives are filled with accounts of the devotion of enslaved women to their families. These are not merely nostalgic memories of childhood. They are specific descriptions of the ways black women nurtured and cared for their kin with the smallest material resources and the tiniest bits of time. Black women, with black men beside them when possible and, when not, alone, made a loving, caring place for young people to grow up in. It was their most difficult task and their greatest joy.

> *I remember well my mother often hid us all in the woods, to prevent master selling us. When we wanted water, she sought for it in any hole or puddle . . . full of tadpoles and insects: she strained it, and gave it round to each of us in the hollow of her hand. For food, she gathered berries in the wood, got potatoes, raw corn, etc. After a time the master would send word to her to come in, promising he would not sell us.*
>
> MOSES GRANDY, WHO ESCAPED TO ENGLAND
> AND DICTATED HIS AUTOBIOGRAPHY THERE

Pregnancy and childbirth are never easy things. For enslaved women, they were fraught with danger and filled with pain. There was little or no actual prenatal care for enslaved women, although midwives in the community may have given advice and some medication. The kindest slaveholders would allow a woman to take a month or two away from field labor to bear and care for an infant. A great many made virtually no allowance, working a pregnant woman up to the moment she went into labor and expecting her to be back in the field the next day. And pregnancy did not protect a woman from the whippings that were the usual form of discipline on a plantation. In fact, some slaveholders developed a method for dealing with the situation. They dug a hole into which a pregnant woman's swollen stomach would fit while she lay on the ground to receive a beating.

Because of this treatment and because slaves, including pregnant women, were poorly nourished, a great many babies were born dead or died soon after birth. Those who survived belonged to what Wilma King ironically refers to as an "actuarially perilous category." They died of malnutrition, of illnesses that did not receive proper treatment, or of ones, like sickle-cell anemia, that had no cures; sometimes they died by violence. They died at two years or five years or seven years. They died and were entered into the books of the plantations as this child was (by South Carolina slave owner David Gavin): "Celia's child died about four months old[,] died saturday the 12. This is two Negroes and three horses I have lost this year."

In spite of the difficulties, mothers did everything they could to help their children to survive. Mothers sometimes carried infants on their backs while they worked so that they could care for and nurse them. Others laid their babies under trees where they might be tended to when the mother reached the end of a row. Domestic workers tried to keep their infants with them in the kitchen or wherever they were doing their chores. On some plantations, women workers were forced to leave their infants while they worked. They would run back to the quarters from the fields on lunch breaks to nurse their babies. Seldom, when a child was ill, was the mother able to be with her. Again and again, women toiled in the fields while their sick children were cared for, or ignored, by someone else. Sometimes, a message would be sent to a working mother to tell her of her child's death.

During slavery it seemed like your children belong to everybody but you.
CAROLINE HUNTER

The slave narratives tell of women who stole from, lied to, and cheated their owners in order to provide for their children. They took tremendous chances, defying owners and overseers when they had to. And they were not alone. One of the most striking aspects of life among enslaved Americans was the degree to which the extended family and the community took responsibility for all children. As a corollary to this, the structure of the family itself seems to have been almost infinitely variable.

The question of the structure of the African American family is an important one historically. Black sociologist E. Franklin Frazier wrote a book entitled *The Negro Family in the United States*, which indicted white society for the destruction of the black family during slavery. The indictment served, ironically, as a basis for discriminatory descriptions of African American family structure, rife with negative comments about "absent fathers" and ever-present "matriarchs." In 1968, white political thinker Daniel Patrick Moynihan declared the black American family to be "pathological," basing much of his argument on the number of female-headed households.

Then, in 1976, Herbert Gutman published a landmark book, *The Black Family in Slavery and Freedom,* which presented evidence that the average black family in the South was a nuclear family with two parents and a fundamentally patriarchal structure. This was his way of opposing the prevailing view of slave families as unstable. Instead of challenging the mainstream definition of a workable family, he accepted that definition and tried to show that enslaved families fit it. Many of the statistics he used to support this view reflected the situation in the Deep South on large plantations.

Twenty years later, Brenda E. Stevenson, in *Life in Black and White,* put forth a very different view.

> There . . . is very little evidence which suggests that a nuclear family was the slave's sociocultural ideal. Virginia slave families, while demonstrating much diversity in form, essentially were not nuclear and did not derive from long-term monogamous marriages. The most discernible ideal for their principal kinship organization was a malleable extended family that, when possible, provided its members with nurture, education, socialization, material support, and recreation in the face of the potential social chaos that the slaveholder imposed.

Stevenson based her conclusions on evidence that was, largely, not from the Deep South, but from Virginia, where there was a considerably higher proportion of small slaveholdings. In this context, fewer adults could find marriage partners on their own plantations. There were many "abroad" marriages, in which a man lived apart from his family and visited, sometimes once a week and sometimes far less often. Families were separated when owners who had more than one plantation "redistributed" their slave workers. And, in the antebellum years, many owners became involved in the thriving domestic slave trade. They sold their slaves for profit. All these conditions made tremendous demands on family cohesion. Enslaved Americans rose to meet the challenge of those demands.

In other words, an African American family might, as Gutman suggested, be made up of two parents and their children, if the situation allowed it. But, as Stevenson pointed out, it might equally be composed of a mother and her children, a grandmother and her grandchildren, three or four male cousins, a brother and sister and his child. Family structure depended on geography, economics, and of course, the time in which the family lived. In the end, the important thing is not whether families fit the American patriarchal ideal, but whether they worked. They did. The black response to an institution that tore families apart in the name of economics was to improvise other families. African Americans were tremendously flexible, in part because their African heritage gave them a variety of models.

Enslaved Americans were also deeply committed to the idea of family, at any cost. At the core of this response was the need to care for children. At the same time, however, enslaved women and men used families of all shapes and sizes to fill the need for companionship, support, intimacy, and a sense of belonging. When combined with their powerful sense of community, this commitment to family provided black women with a source of strength that would continue to serve them throughout the period of slavery and far beyond.

THE MAKING OF A CULTURE

"Around the quiet campfires or in the privacy of their huts," writes William L. Katz, "the slave community gathered to swap tales of turtles that outdistanced hares, of little Davids who slew huge Goliaths, and of tiny animals that tricked lions and bears who wanted to eat them. People nourished morale with jokes about refusing to be buried near their masters because the devil might take the wrong body."

Those campfire gatherings must have been remarkable. Out of them came songs, stories, dances, and humor that would prove the most powerful influence in the formation of a genuinely American culture. African American "entertainment" was filtered through the minstrel show—a truly extraordinary cultural phenomenon—all through the nineteenth century. It would eventually become one of the two most important sources of the American musical comedy. African American music also yielded blues, jazz, gospel, and rhythm and blues. But for enslaved people on the plantations, it was simply another powerful way of surviving.

Music was an important aspect of the lives of enslaved Americans, and black women were integrally involved in both of the two major forms of music that evolved during the antebellum years. One was an exuberant, largely African music that was given new form by contact with European instruments and musical idioms. That strain produced jazz, ragtime, and other forms of popular music. The other was a melding of European sacred music with African rhythms and spirituality that produced what came to be called "spirituals." Of course, the two also influenced each other.

First there was the music used by enslaved Americans to accompany their dancing. Instead of using instruments—or sometimes in addition—women and men "patted juba (or juber)." This involved making music by tapping their feet to keep the strong rhythm and embroidering that rhythm by clapping hands and slapping thighs. One person, the "juber rhymer," would improvise lyrics, which were spoken, not sung.

On one plantation in Maryland, the main juber rhymer was a young woman named Clotilda. A book entitled *The Old Plantation, and What I Gathered There in an Autumn Month,* by James Hungerford, published in 1859, records some of Clotilda's juba song lyrics. As in square dancing, the words tell the dancers what steps to do. At the same time, they tease people in the community. Hungerford's notes indicate that the people answered back, chiding Clotilda for her cheekiness.

Not all dancing was accompanied by clapping. There was also instrumental music, called "fiddle-sings," "jig-tunes," and "devil songs." Most of these are lost. Perhaps their lyrics, which were usually nonsense, didn't seem worth preserving.

> *There was a girl named Cora from over to the Herndon place. Slaves sure would hoop and holler when Cora got to stepping. Gal was graceful as a lily—bend her arms and elbows to the music just as pretty as a picture. Long, tall, slim gal she was and when she "cut the corner," tossing her head and rolling her eyes, everybody knowed she was the best.*
>
> MARTHA HASKINS

These songs and dances made their way to the streets of southern cities and, in New Orleans, were seen by a white performer named Thomas Rice, who adopted them for his own. He did the black dances while wearing blackface and using exaggeratedly "black" speech and movement. In no time at all, he was one of the most popular entertainers on the stage. Soon, groups of white entertainers adopted the form and the minstrel show was born. Black music had made it to the stage. Black performers, on the other hand, had not. It was not until after the Civil War that minstrel shows with black dancers and musicians became popular.

Religious music, the other strain of African American music that would become so much a part of American life, began to develop when enslaved Africans were converted to Christianity. In early colonial times, church music in America largely consisted of psalms set to music. Enslaved Americans learned this music in white churches that they attended with their owners. Then, in the 1730s, a religious revival called The Great Awakening infused religious services with a more emotional tone. This new tone was particularly welcome to people from West Africa, where music and dancing were so often a central part of religious practices. Black Americans took this new emotional freedom and ran with it.

In 1816, Richard Allen, founder of the AME Church, published *A Collection of Spiritual Songs and Hymns Selected from Various Authors*. This hymnal reflected the music that African Americans liked and created. It was the first to use what musicologists call the "wandering refrain." Allen not only added refrains to standard hymns, he added, as music historian Eileen Southern puts it, *"any* refrain to *any* hymn." This kind of improvisation would become a mark of African American music.

As Southern and others have reconstructed it, black congregations would sing a phrase from a favorite hymn. Then they would begin to add choruses, shouts, repeated lines, and outbursts of praise or joy until a new song was born. They did this at camp meetings—outdoor revival-type services—that lasted for hours. After all the whites went home, black worshipers stayed and sang for hours, sometimes all night.

On southern plantations, enslaved Americans were sometimes allowed to attend white church services. From the late eighteenth century until the repression that began in the 1820s and 1830s, they even had their own churches. Then, however, African Americans were usually forbidden to gather together without whites present, even to pray. It was at this point that much religious activity went underground.

We never heard of no church, but us have praying in the cabins. We'd set on the floor and pray with our heads down low and sing low, but if Solomon [the driver] heared, he'd come and beat on the wall with the

stock of his whip. He'd say, "I'll come in there and tear the hide off you
back." . . . Once my maw and paw taken me and Katherine after night to
slip to another place to a prayin-and-singin'. . . . We prays for the end of
tribulations and the end of beatings and for shoes that fit our feet.

MARY REYNOLDS

Even in these secret services, often held in the woods, the slaves sang. And
the songs they sang would take on a new meaning as the antislavery movement grew. *"Steal away,"* they would sing. *"Steal away/Steal away to Jesus/*
Steal away, steal away home/We ain't got long to stay here." And all the others
who heard the words knew that there were two meanings. Singing became
an important method of communication.

Meetings, of course, were not allowed. At work in the fields, enslaved people could not talk. The overseer or the driver was always there.
Written correspondence was impossible when so few could read or write.
But singing was allowed. Singing, the masters knew, made the work go
faster.

Sometimes the message of a song was general, encouragement to believe that there was hope for escape. *Good news, chariot's acomin'/Good news,*
chariot's acomin'/Good news, chariot's acomin'/and I don't want it to leave me
behind.

At other times, it was quite specific. *Follow the drinkin' gourd! Follow the*
drinkin' gourd/For the old man is awaitin' for to carry you to freedom/if you fol-
low the drinkin' gourd. The message was delivered. A conductor from the Underground Railroad was nearby, waiting to guide fugitives to freedom if they
went in the direction of the Big Dipper—the drinkin' gourd. Harriet Tubman, most famous of the Underground Railroad conductors, had her own
signature song. *Dark and thorny is the pathway where the pilgrim makes his*
ways/but beyond this vale of sorrow lie the fields of endless days. Those who
heard it knew that the legendary "Moses" was in the area, ready to help
them.

Today when we hear these songs it is difficult to believe that owners
and overseers failed to understand their messages. But when we hear the
words, we fill in between the lines with our knowledge of the antislavery
movement and the Underground Railroad. We also hear them, or read
them, out of context, a context in which singing was an ever-present part
of life. Work songs set the tempo for scythes and threshers. Field hollers
were cries for help. Enslaved people sang about family sold down the river,
about children dead, about all the sorrows of the cruel life they were forced
to live.

Poor Rosy, poor gal/Poor Rosy, poor gal/Rosy break my poor heart/Heav'n shall-a be my home.

Enslaved people were also forced to sing. Owners believed that singing "livened them up." So those who were about to be auctioned were made to sing. And after the auctions, on forced marches to the plantation, drivers demanded songs of weary and footsore slaves. But it was the slaves who chose what they would sing. Time and again, they lifted their voices in songs that comforted, consoled, and finally, spoke of freedom.

GROWING RESISTANCE

My maw was cooking in the house and she was a "clink"—that am the best of its kind. She could cuss and she wasn't afraid. Wash Hodges [the slaveowner] tried to whop her with a cowhide, and she'd knock him down and bloody him up. Then he'd go down to some his neighbor kin and try to get them to come help him whop her. But they'd say, "I don't want to go up there and let Chloe Ann beat me up." I heard Wash tell his wife they said that.
LULU WILSON

Resistance was part of life. Sometimes it produced the kind of story that Lulu Wilson recounted with such pride. Sometimes it was hidden and never told to anyone. But it was constant. It was a part of every theft of food to feed a child and every lie told to get out of fieldwork for a day. Survival itself was a form of resistance. And resistance was crucial to the survival of the spirit.

There were, in essence, two kinds of resistance. Black women and men resisted the conditions of their slavery. They also resisted slavery itself.

I Just Can't Do More

Our folks will work and be as reasonable as any other group about it. As slaves, Negroes did some real work, but even the Negro had his limit. My mother used to tell me about such an instance. One day she had worked and worked and worked until she just couldn't go any faster. The overseer told her to work faster or he'd beat her. She said she simply stopped and told them, "Go ahead, kill me if you want. I'm working as fast as I can

and I just can't do more." They saw she was at the place where she didn't
care whether she died or not, so they left her alone. VIRGINIA HAYES SHEPHERD

"If resistance in the United States was seldom politically oriented, consciously collective, or violently revolutionary," writes Deborah Gray White, "it was generally individualistic and aimed at maintaining what the slaves, master, and overseer had, in the course of their relationship, perceived as an acceptable level of work, shelter, food, punishment, and free time. . . . Slave resistance was aimed at maintaining what seemed to all concerned to be the status quo."

In this spirit, a woman who was worked too hard while she was pregnant might run away. Or she might refuse to work and be supported by other women in the community in her protest. Often, direct resistance was met with terrible punishment, but it happened nonetheless. Frederick Douglass wrote in his autobiography of that pivotal moment in his life when he refused to be whipped by Covey, the slave breaker. "My dear reader, this battle with Mr. Covey . . . was the turning point in my life as a slave. . . . I was nothing before; I was a man now."

Douglass spoke of his experience in terms of becoming a man. And yet there were many enslaved women who met that moment and proved themselves as thoroughly as Douglass ever did. Indeed, as historian James Oliver Horton points out, "When Douglass was resisting Covey, a slave woman named Caroline was ordered to help restrain him. Had she done so, Douglass believed her intervention would have been decisive, because 'she was a powerful woman and could have mastered me easily. . . .' "

In Southampton County there was another woman something like my
mother in spirit. This woman would work, but if you drove her too hard,
she'd get stubborn like a mule and quit. Her name was Miss Julian Wright.
Julian worked in the field. She was a smart, strong, and stubborn woman.
When they got rough on her, she got rough on them and ran away in the
woods. They found her by means of bloodhounds. . . . The evidence of her
punishment was so horrible that the sight of it fifty years afterwards
sickened my daughters. VIRGINIA HAYES SHEPHERD

Given the dangers of open resistance, the more usual course was to find a covert way of restoring the "status quo." Sometimes this involved lying or stealing. Deception of all kinds was considered an honorable tool in the enslaved woman's arsenal. Often, nobody knew but the woman herself that the score had been settled.

How many times I spit in the biscuits and peed in the coffee just to get back
at them mean white folks. DELIA

Resistance of this kind sometimes took on the character of negotiation, especially with enslaved women who had some influence in the household. "After her mistress died, Alcey, the cook on the Burleigh plantation in Virginia," writes White, "decided she no longer wanted to work in the kitchen. When her request to be transferred to the field was ignored, she found another way to make her desire known. 'She systematically disobeyed orders and stole or destroyed the greater part of the provisions given to her for the table.' When that failed 'she resolved to show more plainly that she was tired of the kitchen.': 'Instead of getting dinner from the coop, as usual, she unearthed from some corner an old hen that had been sitting for six weeks and served her up as a fricassee!' Alcey achieved her objective and was sent to the field the following day without even so much as a reprimand."

This kind of "negotiation" took place far more often than most people would suppose. In law, the power of the slaveholder was absolute. In practice, many factors entered into the relationship between owner and slave. Personalities were significant, as well as strength of character. The desire on the part of a slaveholding family to live a peaceful, pleasant life was often of great consequence in the negotiation. Women who lived and worked in the Big House were able to take advantage of these factors to chip away at the power of the owners.

This may be one of the reasons that there were different styles of resistance for women and for men. Women were more likely to engage in verbal and even physical confrontations, while men far more often ran away altogether. Women did, however, run away on occasion. They simply didn't often stay away. They ran away to visit family or to avoid punishment, and then they returned to the plantation, often to be reunited with other family. Sometimes they just ran away for a night.

You know they used to wear petticoats starched with hominy water. They
were starched so stiff that every time you stopped they would pop real loud.
Well, [my mother] would go out at night to a party some of the colored
folks was having and she would tell us kids to stay in the house and open
the door in a hurry when we heard her acomin'. And when we heared them
petticoats apoppin' as she run down the path, we'd open the door wide and
she would get away from the patteroll [patrol]. ANNIE WALLACE

Truancy was a way of life for many enslaved women. It reconciled their need to remain on the plantation, usually because of children, with their equally strong need for freedom, if only for a day, a week, or a month. "Such a woman was Celeste," according to White, "another Louisiana slave who, determined not to be beaten by the overseer, built her own rude hut from dead branches and camouflaged it with leaves of palmettos on the edge of a swamp not far from the master's residence. Every evening she returned to the plantation for food and lived like this for the better part of a summer."

To Be One's Own

Black women and men also rebelled against slavery itself, regardless of conditions. They fought, not only for their own freedom, but for freedom as a principle and for each other. This kind of resistance was much rarer among the slave population than resistance to daily oppression. Much of the battle against slavery, against the very idea of owning other people, was carried out by free African Americans and their white allies on behalf of their enslaved sisters and brothers. However, there was one aspect of "ownership" that enslaved women regularly challenged. Thousands, even tens of thousands of women, declared that this one part of their humanness was not for sale to or by anyone. And every day, across the antebellum South, they suffered and died to protect that essential part of themselves.

The slave experience itself, remember, was different for women than for men. In their work life, this difference was often a result of preconceptions about gender, a cultural question rather than a biological one. However, in another area—the sexual—the difference was directly connected to biology. Women were exploited sexually as well as economically. Men were forced to work for the master. Women were forced to work and, in addition, they were forced to have sexual intercourse, bear children, and often, nurse the children of others with their own bodies.

Enslaved women, in other words, were subjected to "forcible sexual intercourse," the legal and moral definition of rape. The amount and kind of force used varied. So, too, did the person a woman was forced to give her body to. Sometimes the white master or overseer would force her to the ground in the fields. Sometimes she was locked in a cabin with another slave whose job was to impregnate her. For another woman, the force involved might be less obvious. She was forced to have sex in the same sense that an enslaved man was forced to plow a field, as a job. Still, it was rape, and black women experienced it every day.

Not surprisingly, enslaved women resisted this sexual exploitation, sometimes fiercely. But their resistance has seldom been recognized for what it was—resistance to the concept of ownership itself. Most historians seem to have seen resistance to rape as essentially a refusal to accept one of the *conditions* of servitude, as though it could be classed with complaints about inadequate food or clothing or with a refusal to work beyond certain limits. Some women, it could be said, simply refused to do a certain kind of work—sexual work.

The refusal by large numbers of slaves to do one specific kind of work would have been enough to make us pay special attention. There is no other instance of this kind of refusal on record. However, from the emotional weight given to the act in all available records and narratives, it is clear that rape was not seen as part of the job, even a particularly abhorrent part. It was seen as a violation of the self, in exactly the same way women see it today. When women resisted, they were saying, "You do not own this—not *this* part of me."

> You know, there was an overseer who used to tie mother up in the barn with a rope around her arms up over her head, while she stood on a block. Soon as they got her tied, this block was moved and her feet dangled, you know, couldn't touch the floor. This old man, now, would start beating her naked until the blood ran down her back to her heels. . . . I asked mother what she done for them to beat and do her so. She said, "Nothing other than refuse to be wife to this man." ANNIE WALLACE

It is impossible to know how many times enslaved women endured beatings because they resisted the sexual demands of owners and overseers. There are many cases in the FWP interviews, often related by sons and daughters, sometimes by the women themselves. Indeed, there are so many reports that it almost seems as if resistance to rape was more common than submission.

> I was one slave that the poor white man had his match. . . . These here old white men said, "What I can't do by fair means I'll do by foul." One tried to throw me, but he couldn't. We tusseled and knocked over chairs and when I got a grip I scratched his face all to pieces, and there was no more bothering Fannie from him. But, oh, honey, some slaves would be

beat up so, when they resisted, and sometimes if you rebelled, the overseer
would kill you.   FANNIE BERRY

One of the most important published slave narratives has at its center this form of resistance. In *Incidents in the Life of a Slave Girl,* Harriet Jacobs described her prolonged efforts to avoid sexual relations with her master, Dr. Flint. For years she kept him at bay, but only with great difficulty. She recalls that she was able to use the presence of her grandmother on the plantation to avoid her master's advances because "though she had been a slave, Flint was afraid of her. He dreaded her scorching rebukes. Moreover, she was known and patronized by many people; and he did not wish to have his villainy made public."

Jacobs finally turned to another white man, one of her own choosing, as protection against Flint. It was only a partial victory, a compromise with honor. However, she saved her children from slavery by choosing a man she knew would buy and free them. She also cheated Flint of his pleasure and the ownership of her children. She successfully resisted the demands of the slaveholder and, therefore, of slavery.

Elizabeth Keckley, who toward the end of her life became a designer/dressmaker for Mrs. Abraham Lincoln, also discussed this form of resistance in her narrative, *Behind the Scenes: Thirty Years a Slave and Four Years in the White House.* Born a slave of the Burwell family, she was sold while she was in her teens to a North Carolina slaveowner. She recalls that she was "regarded as fair-looking for one of my race," and that as a result of her appearance her new master pursued her for four years. "I do not care to dwell upon this subject," she wrote, "for it is fraught with pain. Suffice it to say, that he persecuted me for four years, and I—I—became a mother. The child of which he was the father was the only child I ever brought into the world. If my poor boy ever suffered any humiliating pangs on account of birth, he could not blame his mother, for God knows that she did not wish to give him life; he must blame the edicts of that society which deemed it no crime to undermine the virtue of girls in my then position."

Keckley's effort at resistance may seem to have failed. She did, after all, submit at last. However, her story could have been very different if she had not resisted so successfully for so long. Shortly after the birth of her child, she was repurchased by one of the Burwell daughters, who took her and her son to St. Louis. There, Keckley worked as a dressmaker. Her owners were paid for her work, of course, but several of her customers lent her the money to pay for her freedom and that of her son. Within a short time, she had paid off her loan, learned to read and write, and moved to Washington, D.C. She was so successful that she ended up designing all of Mary Todd Lincoln's clothes. She employed twenty seamstresses in her shop, and her most famous design, Mary Todd Lincoln's inaugural ball gown, is in the Smithsonian Institution. A re-creation is exhibited at the Black Fashion Museum.

How much of that would have happened if she had succumbed easily to her owner and borne him three or four children?

Ellen Craft and her future husband, William, escaped from slavery together. Young Ellen was so reluctant to have children while she remained in slavery that she and William agreed to delay their marriage until they reached the North. In their narrative, *Running a Thousand Miles for Freedom,* William Craft perceptively explains his wife's motivations. "My wife was torn from her mother's embrace in childhood, and taken to a distant part of the country. She had seen so many other children separated from their parents in this cruel manner that the mere thought of her ever becoming a mother under the wretched system of American slavery appeared to fill her very soul with horror. . . ." Ellen Craft's future husband understood her horror, and the two of them made their escape before they had children.

The FWP interviews give many accounts of resistance to forced sex. Some of them are certainly accurate reports of what happened. Some may have acquired the quality of legend as they were told over and over, a source of inspiration for other women.

One day Sukie was in the kitchen making soap. Had three great big pots of lye just coming to a boil in the fireplace when old Marsa come in for to get after her about something.

He lay into her, but she ain't answer him a word. Then he tell Sukie to take off her dress. She told him no. Then he grabbed her and pulled it down off her shoulders. When he done that, he forgot about whipping her, I guess, 'cause he grab hold of her and try to pull her down on the floor. Then that black gal got mad. She took and punch old Marsa and make him break loose and then she gave him a shove and push his hindparts down in the hot pot of soap. Soap was near to boiling, and it burnt him near to death. He got up holding his hindparts and ran from the kitchen, not daring to yell, 'cause he didn't want Miss Sarah Ann to know about it.

. . . Marsa never did bother slave gals no more.   FANNIE BERRY

All of these women resisted sexual exploitation. They also resisted becoming "breeders" for the men who owned them. Every time an enslaved woman managed to refrain from bearing slaves, she struck a blow against her owner in particular and the slaveholding system in general. Thwarting the desires of the slaveowner challenged his total control and it also damaged him financially. It was an enormously difficult thing to do. Both Keckley and Jacobs were helped in their struggles by moral pressure brought to bear on their male owners by other women, and this was not an uncommon situation. Moral pressure was seldom enough, of course. Still, some enslaved women were strong, determined, and lucky enough to accomplish this highly meaningful protest, and many achieved it to some degree or another.

There was one group of enslaved women, however, who were almost powerless in this regard. They were the women who were chosen specifically as "sexual workers."

> *If God has bestowed beauty upon [the enslaved woman], it will prove her greatest curse. That which commands admiration in the white woman only hastens the degradation of the female slave.*
> HARRIET JACOBS, *INCIDENTS IN THE LIFE OF A SLAVE GIRL*

There was a part of the slave trade particularly designed to profit from the sale of attractive black women, or, as they were known at the time, "fancy girls." Slave traders prided themselves on the numbers of such women they had for sale and on the high prices commanded by their physical appearance. Often these women were sold for prices that far exceeded those that planters were willing to pay for a field laborer. In 1857, for example, the *Memphis Eagle and Enquirer* ran an editorial in which it was observed that "a slave woman is advertised to be sold in St. Louis who is so surpassingly beautiful that $5,000 has already been offered for her, at private sale, and refused."

In a novel of the antebellum South, the life of that "surpassingly beautiful" woman would have been filled with luxury enough to offset her duties as a sexual servant. She was, after all, worth more than $5,000. But that money was paid to her owner, not to her. And prostitution is a wearing job, even when it is not forced, as it was under slavery. Slave prostitution robbed a woman of all self-determination, all control of her life and her body, and it seldom had a pretty ending.

For other enslaved women, there was not even the hint of glamor.

Mr. Mordicia had his yeller gals in one quarter to themselves, and these gals belong to the Mordicia men, their friends, and the overseers. When a baby was born in that quarter, they'd send it over to the black quarter at birth. They do say that some of these gal babies got grown, and after going back to the yeller quarter, had more children for her own daddy or brother. MATTIE CURTIS

Old Marster was the daddy of some mulatto children. The relations with the mothers of those children is what give so much grief to Missus. The neighbors would talk about it, and he would sell all them children away from they mothers to a trader. My missus would cry about that. They sell one of Mother's children once, and when she take on and cry about it, Marster say, "Stop that sniffing there if you don't want to get a whipping." She grieve and cry at night about it. SAVILLA BURRELL

Strikingly, when this issue has been dealt with in the past, historians have usually stressed how difficult the sexual exploitation of "their women" was for black men and how destructive their inability to prevent it was to their "masculinity." Certainly it must have been horribly difficult for a man to watch the woman he loved beaten for resisting rape. And it must have been even more painful when she could not resist. It is beyond imagining what a father felt when he saw his daughter sold to the "fancy trade." But to conclude that black men were thereby emasculated is to make a huge and erroneous leap of emotional logic. As historian James O. Horton points out, "Women knew what was and what was not possible and respected their men within the context of the realities of black life. In fact, that respect itself became an act of resistance." And beyond the question of respect from mates, pain at the suffering of a loved one knows no gender. Women suffered as they watched their husbands whipped. Both parents suffered when children were punished. All black people suffered for each other; men had no monopoly on that.

Sexual exploitation of women, then, was hurtful primarily to women. And their refusal to be exploited was a powerful, effective form of resistance. Indeed, it was possibly the most effective form of slave resistance on record and, in some cases, certainly the most terrible.

Two other intimately related forms of resistance peculiar to women emerge from the narratives—abortion and infanticide. The conscious decision on the part of a slave woman to terminate her pregnancy was one act that was totally beyond the control of the master of the plantation. Herbert Gutman offers evidence of several southern physicians who commented upon abortion and the use of contraceptive methods among the slave population. He recounts a situation in which a planter had kept between four and six slave women "of the proper age to breed" for twenty-five years and that "only two children had been born on the place at full term." It was later discovered that the slaves had concocted a medicine with which they were able to terminate their unwanted pregnancies. He also found evidence of a master who claimed that an older female slave had discovered a remedy for pregnancies and had been "instrumental in all . . . the abortions on his place."

This last instance suggests that even those women who did not resist slavery through actually having an abortion themselves resisted covertly by aiding those who desired them. It is therefore possible that a sort of female conspiracy existed on the southern plantation. In an interesting twist to the apparently chronic problem of unwanted and forced pregnancies, there is evidence that female slaves, recognizing the importance of their role in the maintenance of the slave systems, sometimes feigned pregnancy as a method of receiving lighter work loads. The success, however limited, of this kind of ploy would also require the aid of other female slaves on the plantation—a midwife, for example, who might testify to the master that one of his slaves was indeed pregnant.

Possibly the most psychologically devastating means that the slave mother had of undermining the slave system was infanticide. The frequency with which this occurred is not at all clear. Several historians have contended that infanticide was quite rare, and Eugene D. Genovese writes that "slave abortions, much less infanticide, did not become a major problem for the slave holders or an ordinary form of 'resistance' for the slaves. Infanticide occurred, so far as the detected cases reveal anything, only in some special circumstances." The subject of infanticide under slavery is clearly in need of further study. However, it is important to note that the relatively small number of documented cases is not as significant as the fact that it occurred at all.

There are a number of instances in which a slave woman simply decided to end her child's life rather than allow the child to grow up enslaved. Genovese writes that "for the most part, however, the slaves recognized infanticide as murder. They loved their children too much to do away with them: courageously, they resolved to raise them as best they could, and entrusted their fate to God." It is certainly true that the enslaved parents who reared their children with courage and resourcefulness loved those children. However, Genovese's statement fails to acknowledge the motivations for infanticide offered repeatedly by the slave parents themselves. Slave parents who took their children's lives appear to have done so out of love as well, a different form of love. They had a clear understanding of the living death that awaited their children under slavery and said to others that they killed the children because they loved them. Since this explanation is the one offered most frequently in the narratives, and since there does not seem to be any evidence at this time that contradicts the slaves' statements, it should be accepted as reflective of their true motivations.

The daily resistance of enslaved women was, as White stated, "seldom politically oriented, consciously collective, or violently revolutionary," but it was effective. It often changed their own lives and those of their children. At the same time, it affected slaveholders in a practical, often economically related way. And out of the spirit of resistance came a stronger and stronger impulse toward the kind of action that would change the country itself.

WHAT DOES NOT KILL ME . . .

Not every enslaved woman was a heroine.

At night the overseer would walk out to see could he catch any of us walking without a note, and to this day, I don't want to go nowhere without a paper.   SYLVIA CANNON

Oppression destroyed some souls as it destroyed so many bodies. Pain doubtless diminished as many characters as it ennobled.

All my white folks was good to me, and I reckon that I ain't got no cause for complaint. I ain't had much clothes, and I ain't had so much to eat, and a–many a whupping, but nobody ain't ever been real bad to me.
                                                                        JOSEPHINE SMITH

But certain values emerge when we study the lives of these women, and those values seem so clear and so extraordinarily potent that it is difficult not to romanticize the women who forged them. An enslaved woman learned to compose an inner reality that her oppressors could not touch. This self was to remain intact no matter what she had to do to meet the demands made upon her by slaveholders, white society, or black men. Dissemblance was required to protect this self, and so dissemblance became a valued skill. Honesty, to various degrees, might be a characteristic of her dealings with friends or kin. Complete truthfulness was reserved for those with whom she was most intimate . . . and for herself.

She also learned to build a community to sustain her and those she loved. She knew the value of loyalty and discretion and of courage in the face of challenges to the well-being of the whole. Survival was not possible alone. She learned that there were limits to what could be accepted, even at the point of a gun or the lash of a whip. But she also learned that death is not always the only alternative to dishonor.

Finally, she learned that slavery must end.

Many will suffer for pleading the cause of oppressed Africa,

and I shall glory in being one of her martyrs; for I am firmly

persuaded, that the God in whom I trust is able to protect me

from the rage and malice of mine enemies, and from them that

will rise up against me; and if there is no other way for me to escape,

he is able to take me to himself . . .

MARIA W. STEWART, *RELIGION AND THE*

PURE PRINCIPLES OF MORALITY

RESISTANCE BECOMES REBELLION

CHAPTER FOUR

I N T H E F I R S T half of the nineteenth century, there was a hotel in Cincinnati, Ohio, called the Dumas. It was a black hotel and it was usually full of black travelers, many from the South. When slaveholders came through town and stayed at prestigious white hotels, their personal servants often put up at the Dumas. Black boatmen also stayed at the hotel as they passed through the Ohio town.

Over the years, free black citizens of Cincinnati became accustomed to stopping by the Dumas and talking with the travelers. They especially asked for news of the South and the people they had left behind there. They also asked the travelers to deliver messages for them to relatives and friends. One woman sent letters year after year to her children, still in slavery in North Carolina. Another sent messages to her mother for more than three decades, starting in about 1810. James O. Horton writes, "During these years she consulted her mother about her choice of a husband and informed her of the birth of children. Thus in 1843 the news of her grandchild's enrollment at Oberlin Collegiate Institute found the proud grandmother in a Mississippi slave hut, bound in body, she reported, but free in spirit."

Slavery oppressed every black person in America. In the antebellum years, tens of thousands of African Americans were free, but every one of those thousands felt the sting of slavery in one way or another. They had family still in chains—brothers, sisters, parents, and even children. They remembered slavery themselves. Or their closest friends grieved for loved ones lost to bondage. In some places they had to fear capture and reenslavement. Even those least affected, those who had been free for generations, knew that the color of their skin would always stigmatize them so long as any of their color was enslaved. Free black women were separated from slaves by distance and by condition, but their lives were linked, and so were their destinies.

Twice in the history of the United States, questions of race and gender have impelled great movements for social change. The second and more familiar of those took place in the 1950s, 1960s, and 1970s. The first preceded it by more than a century, gathering force in the 1830s. In both these movements, black women occupied a unique position. Because they were doubly oppressed, they had more at stake than anyone else in the success of the movement for change in both areas. And because they were doubly oppressed, they found it most difficult to occupy positions of leadership. Still, they worked for freedom with their whole hearts.

The resistance of enslaved women to slavery, as we have seen, was very personal, often an individual act. When it was collective, it was not usually planned and organized. It grew out of deep needs within individual women and found expression in the same way, shaped only by the enslaved woman's character and situation. Free black women resisted in very personal ways as well. They saved money to buy their enslaved relatives out of bondage. They helped their enslaved loved ones escape. And always they hoped and prayed for an end to slavery. But they also channeled their resistance into the organized abolition movement, joining the struggle for freedom, lifting strong and articulate voices or working quietly in support of the more public activities of black men. Like Harriet Tubman, they served as part of the Underground Railroad or, like Sojourner Truth, they traveled and spoke for justice.

During the antebellum years—about 1830 to the Civil War—this resistance became intense. The abolition movement gained force as northern attitudes against slavery hardened, and black women were among the earliest organizers of this new push to end slavery. But in the abolition movement, they often found further discrimination, as women. Indeed, the movement became the cradle of the crusade for women's rights. It served also to foster the true beginnings of black women's literature and the entrance of black artists into mainstream culture.

Origins of the Movement

The abolition movement did not begin in the nineteenth century. It began, in a sense, with the first resistance by an African to enslavement and grew with the formation of such groups as the Society of Free Negroes in Boston. It "officially" began with white sympathizers, mostly Quakers, in Philadelphia in the middle of the eighteenth century, but their idea of abolition was, to say the least, paradoxical. These were white men who believed that slavery was a sin but did not necessarily believe that black people were their equals or that the races could live together in harmony. In fact, most of them fervently did *not* believe these things and strongly supported efforts to establish a colony in Africa and ship all African Americans to it.

While these men did a lot of good, rescuing hundreds of black people from illegal slavery and building schools for free black children, most of them were not, in any real sense of the word, abolitionist. They believed that slavery would die out naturally and that their duty was simply to encourage this natural process, mitigating some of the horrors of slavery in the meantime. Ironically, because they used the word *abolitionist,* they forced later and more radical groups, such as those founded or co-founded by African Americans, to use the weaker *antislavery*.

The movement began to change in the late 1820s. One of the catalysts for that change was *David Walker's Appeal*. The *Appeal* was a pamphlet of seventy-six pages published in 1829 in Boston, and it pulled no punches. Far from advocating a gradual and "natural" end to slavery, it called for action, immediate and militant. "Remember Americans," David Walker wrote, "that we must and shall be free and enlightened as you are, will you wait until we shall, under God, obtain our liberty by the crushing arm of power? Will it not be dreadful for you? I speak Americans for your own good." This was a new and inspiring note. For the South, of course, it was a terrifying one. The governors of three states called special sessions of their legislatures to confer about the message of the *Appeal*. Mayors of several southern towns sent messages to the mayor of Boston, asking him to throw Walker in jail and burn his book.

David Walker's Appeal may have inspired Nat Turner's Rebellion of 1831, the largest and most threatening slave insurrection to that date. After "Nat's Fray," as many black southerners called it, panic filled the South. By 1833, most southern abolition societies, of which there were many, had disappeared. Abolitionist activity, which continued, went underground. In the North, new organizations were founded and new voices were heard. William Lloyd Garrison, a young white abolitionist, came into prominence in 1831 when he started his newspaper, the *Liberator*. As militant as any African American of the time, his credo was "I will not equivocate—I will not excuse—I will not retreat a single inch—AND I WILL BE HEARD." Garrison and his paper received tremendous support from the black community. However, important as Garrison was to the cause, the time had clearly come for African Americans to become leaders in their own struggle. Among the first of these leaders were black women such as Maria W. Stewart, Mary Ann Shadd Cary, and of course, Sojourner Truth.

SOJOURNER'S SISTERS

Maria W. Stewart has come down in history as the first American woman to lecture publicly to an audience of both men and women. This is a significant identification, but, as is often the case with "firsts," it oversimplifies and therefore diminishes Stewart's importance. In 1831, Stewart published a small pamphlet entitled *Religion and the Pure Principles of Morality, the Sure Foundation on Which We Must Build.* Its impact on the abolition movement was not as great as that of *David Walker's Appeal,* but it was greeted with great interest because it addressed not only abolition but also related issues such as black autonomy. She is often cited as one of the first black nationalists. In 1832, she gave her first lecture, in Boston, before an audience of black and white women and men. Her message, in this and later speeches, was one of self-determination and economic independence for African Americans. She spoke strongly for racial pride and had nothing but scorn for black people who expected—or even allowed—white people to solve their problems for them. She could be quite critical of black men for failing to educate themselves and prepare themselves for leadership. She also demanded that black women take an active part in business, politics, and education and that they uphold the highest moral standards, in order to refute the myths of the white South that said black women were ignorant, lazy, and degenerate. "O, ye daughters of Africa, awake!" she wrote. "Awake! Arise! No longer sleep nor slumber, but distinguish yourselves. Show forth to the world that ye are endowed with noble and exalted faculties. O, ye daughters of Africa! What have ye done to immortalize your names beyond the grave? What examples have ye set before the rising generation? What foundation have ye laid for generations yet unborn?"

Because her views went against a great many cherished beliefs, and she had no time for the platitudes that might have softened them, Stewart alienated a lot of people. However, seen from the vantage of today's political realities, many of her ideas about the need for African Americans to throw off dependence on white society seem remarkably modern and to the point.

Mary Ann Shadd Cary was another ardent proponent of black self-determination, a forerunner, like Stewart, of the black nationalist movement. Her first published work, a political pamphlet, came out in 1849, when she was twenty-six years old. *Hints to the Colored People of North America* was a powerful call for self-reliance. *Notes on Canada West,* published three years later, went even further. Having moved to Canada herself after the passage of the Fugitive Slave Law, young Mary Ann Shadd roundly declared that African Americans should simply give up on their own country and immigrate to a more civilized place. More striking than her call to Canadian immigration, however, was her denunciation of black antislavery agents, especially from the Refugee Home Society, who traveled the country begging for funds. Their methods and their sometimes corrupt practices grossly offended her racial pride, and she did not hesitate to say so. Carolyn Calloway-Thomas writes, "By nineteenth-century norms, Shadd Cary's caustic, jolting language seemed ill-suited to a woman. She used phrases such as 'gall and wormwood,' 'moral pest,' 'petty despot,' 'superannuated ministers,' 'nest of unclean birds,' 'moral monsters,' and 'priest-ridden people' in order to keep her ideas before the public.' "

Of a different ilk altogether was Sojourner Truth. Born into slavery in 1799, she was the second youngest of the ten or twelve children of James and Elizabeth Bomefree. Their owners were Dutch, from an area north of the city of New York, and since the family's first language was Dutch, as noted previously, Truth's English was always heavily accented. Her parents named her Isabella.

Young Isabella Bomefree had several owners, but she went to the John Dumonts when she was eleven years old and remained with them until she was freed by state law in 1827. She was then twenty-eight years old. When she was fourteen, the Dumonts had married her to another of their slaves, and she had five children. She was also a recently converted, and very ardent, Methodist. After her emancipation, she moved to New York City with her teenaged son, leaving her daughters in the care of their father. She supported herself doing household work and began to preach at camp meetings. For a time she lived in a commune headed by a charismatic preacher who called himself Matthias. After the commune broke up, she went back to work in New York for another eight years. Then, in 1843, as a sign of her spiritual and political awakening, she renamed herself Sojourner Truth and began her true career as a traveling "exhorter."

On her travels, she met up with both abolitionists and feminists. Although she remained primarily a religious speaker, she was soon moving audiences with her messages against slavery and for the rights of women. According to historian Nell Irvin Painter, "The symbol of Sojourner Truth that is most popular today turns on two speeches of the 1850s: one in Akron, Ohio, in 1851, the other in Silver Lake, a small town in northern Indiana, in 1858." In the first instance, she responded to a man who put forth the "pure womanhood" notion that women were frail and needed the helping arm of a strong man to help them into carriages and over mud puddles. Nobody had ever helped her in this way, Truth is reported to have said.

And a'n't I a woman? Look at me! Look at my arm! (and she bared her right arm to the shoulder, showing her tremendous muscular power). I have ploughed, and planted, and gathered into barns, and no man could head me! And a'n't I a woman? I could work as much and eat as much as a man—when I could get it—and bear de lash as well! And a'n't I a woman? I have borne thirteen chilern, and seen

'em mos' all sold off to slavery, and when I cried out with my
mother's grief, none but Jesus heard me! And a'n't I a woman?

The thirteen children, of course, were closer to her mother's experience
than her own, but the point was powerful and powerfully made.

At the Silver Lake meeting Truth made a gesture that has become legend. "Faced with a hostile audience that questioned a black woman's right
to speak in public and that intended to shame her out of presenting her
case," writes Painter, "Truth confronted men who claimed she was too
forceful a speaker to be a woman. After they demanded that she prove her
sexual identity through a performance intended to humiliate, Truth bared
her breast in public, turned the imputed shame back upon her tormenters,
and, transcending their small-minded test, turned their spite back upon
them."

Since Truth could neither read nor write, reports of both of these
meetings come from others, and the accuracy of those reports has been
questioned. But there is no question whatever that Sojourner Truth powerfully affected those she came into contact with. She was a woman of deep
faith and raw eloquence. When she stood on stages around the country to
awaken audiences to the urgent need for justice, she sang and led the audiences in singing antislavery songs she had written herself. Eugene D. Genovese, in his book *Roll, Jordan, Roll,* quotes abolitionist Harriet Beecher
Stowe. "She seemed to impersonate the fervor of Ethiopia, wild, savage,
hunted of all nations, but burning after God in her tropic heart and stretch-
ing her scarred hands towards the glory to be revealed."

Another antislavery activist, Sarah Parker Remond, was born into the
prominent Remond family of Massachusetts. Remond was the daughter of
successful businesswoman Nancy Lenox Remond and sister of Cecilia, Maritcha, and Caroline, who owned and operated a large beauty salon, a wig
factory, and a company that manufactured and distributed a medicated hair
tonic. Their brother Charles was a lecturer for the Massachusetts Anti-Slavery Society. Sarah herself, who attended private schools and was characterized in later years as impressively well read in English literature, began
making public appearances with her brother in 1842, when she was sixteen
years old. She continued her antislavery activity through the 1840s and
1850s. In 1853, she and two friends attended a Mozart opera at the Howard
Athenaeum in Boston and refused to be shunted into the seating area set
aside for African Americans. As they were being ejected by the police, Remond fell and tumbled down the stairs. She sued. She was awarded five
hundred dollars in damages, and the Athenaeum was desegregated.

In 1856, Remond became a lecturer for the American Anti-Slavery Society, touring New England along with her brother Charles, Wendell Phillips, and Susan B. Anthony, among others. She wrote to a friend, "We have attended some interesting meetings in this state, and my only regret is that I did not sooner begin to do what I might, in this particular field of labor." Shortly thereafter, in January of 1859, she left for England. For two years Remond traveled all around the British Isles, giving more than forty-five lectures in England, Scotland, and Ireland. Unlike such emotionally powerful speakers as Sojourner Truth, she spoke in a quiet, carefully reasoned style that appealed to her English audiences. Often, she dealt specifically with the terrible situation of enslaved women. When she spoke to a primarily female audience in Warrington, near Liverpool, she was given a watch with the inscription "Presented to S. P. Remond by Englishwomen, her sisters, in Warrington, February 2d. 1859." Her lectures earned her and, more important, her subject enormous attention in the press.

There were many others who wrote and spoke out against slavery as well. Among them were Ellen Craft, who had escaped with her husband to Canada, and the legendary Harriet Tubman. In most instances, these women went about their work without the practical and emotional support that male abolitionist leaders expected and usually got from their wives. When married, they continued to carry out their domestic responsibilities. When mothers, they relied on other women, relatives and friends, to care for their children.

The free black community basically adopted the gender roles of their white, middle-class neighbors. It was a reaction to slavery, of course. If gender roles were broken down by slaveholders, then they would be, *must be,* upheld by free people. The "masculinity" of the black man became a symbol of freedom. Upholding that masculinity became a part of the black woman's duty to the race, and the way she did that was to embrace, as best she could, white standards of femininity. In other words, in order to prove that they deserved to be free, black men and women had to become unequal with each other.

Women—black or white—were not allowed active participation in any male-dominated antislavery societies until about 1840. In that year, the American Anti-Slavery Society split when the Garrison contingent managed to elect a woman to the executive committee. Garrison's opponent, Lewis Tappan, declared his position in no uncertain terms. "When the Constitution of the A. AntiS. Soc. was formed in 1833, and the word 'person' introduced, *all concerned* considered that it was to be understood as it is usually understood in our benevolent Societies. All have a right to be *members*, but the *business* to be conducted by *men*. . . . Women have equal rights with men, and therefore they have a right to form societies of women only. Men have the same right. *Men* formed the Amer. AntiS. Society." (Italics in original) On this petulant note, Tappan and his supporters left the organization.

Until the 1840 split, women formed their own societies. In 1832, the Female Anti-Slavery Society of Salem, Massachusetts, was founded. It was a landmark event in the history of the struggle against slavery because it was the first women's antislavery society in the country, and because all of its founders were free black women. Two years later, it reorganized as the Salem Female Anti-Slavery Society, with both black and white members.

The Philadelphia Female Anti-Slavery Society (PFAS), founded in 1833, was the first group formed by both black and white women. The nine black women who were charter members were members of the free black middle class. This would become the pattern in the decades to follow. It required significant resources and support for a woman to involve herself in the struggle. A domestic servant would, for one thing, be too vulnerable to losing her job or some other form of reprisal. The Boston Female Anti-Slavery Society was also founded by both black and white women. Among the black women were Susan Paul, Louisa Nell, and Nancy Gardner Prince. Anna Murray Douglass, wife of Frederick Douglass, was active in the group, although her name is not found on membership lists.

These separate female societies did not, as a general rule, present the voice of the black community to white society. That remained the role of black men. They did not formulate policy or strategies of resistance. These, too, were considered male prerogatives. Perhaps their major activity was raising money for the struggle. In a letter to feminist friend Elizabeth Smith Miller, Sarah Forten described a PFAS Christmas fund-raiser.

> I have delayed replying to your kind letter until now because I wished to give you an account of our Anti Slavery *Fair*—and I knew you would be gratified by a description of it—and of the good success we had. Our Society had been making Preparations for the last four months to get up this Sale—and many very beautiful fancy productions did they manufacture for the occasion. We hired the Fire Mens Hall in North St—below Arch—and decorated it with evergreens—and flowers—and had it brilliantly lighted. There was six tables—including a refreshment Table—on which most of the eatables were presented—three large Pound Cakes—Oranges—and Grapes were given to us—so our expenses were not great—and the proceeds amounted to more than three hundred Dollars.

They also got the word out. PFAS members built an antislavery hall for meetings and lectures. They distributed antislavery material and were in the forefront of a petition campaign to outlaw slavery in the nation's capital. The Colored Females' Free Produce Society, founded in 1831, took a different approach. Also based in Philadelphia, it was dedicated to supplying its members with goods that had not been produced by slave labor. Its members also encouraged the black community to boycott goods that had involved the labor of slaves. Grace Douglass, one of the founding members of the PFAS, was also active in the Free Produce Society.

Not all women's antislavery groups were biracial by any means. An entry from the diary of a white abolitionist in Fall River, Massachusetts, reveals what happened when three black women—who had been attending meetings of the Female Anti-Slavery Society of Fall River—applied for membership. The diary writer, Elizabeth Buffum Chace, along with her sister Lucy Buffum Lovell, had visited the women and invited them to join. "This raised such a storm among some of the leading members," wrote Chace, "that for a time, it threatened the dissolution of the Society." These leading members, it seems, objected to the implication of equality that membership would entail. Justice prevailed, and the women were admitted.

This was by no means always the case. And even when there was a mixed membership, racism could cause terrible embarrassment and pain for black women. Still, although denied membership in male antislavery societies and faced with ostracism or indignities in women's antislavery societies, black women continued to work for freedom. Indeed, the origins of the movement for women's rights in this country can be traced to the efforts of women in the abolitionist movement to receive recognition from men in the movement.

In 1837, black and white women came together at the Anti-Slavery Convention of American Women to insist on their right to speak in public against slavery. Prominent at that meeting were the members of the Philadelphia Female Anti-Slavery Society. At the second meeting of the convention, on May 15 of the following year, the group gathered at the newly constructed Philadelphia Hall. They were interrupted, however, by an angry mob of white Philadelphians protesting the mixing of the races. When the women refused to give in to demands that they segregate their seating and cease walking together, black and white, to the meetings, anger grew. On May 17, the building was burned to the ground. Accompanying this racialist anger, though much less violently, was male prejudice within the abolitionist movement. In that same year, for example, black women were involved in the rescue of a fugitive slave in New York. The *Colored American* condemned the women. "Everlasting shame and remorse seize upon those females that so degraded themselves yesterday," its editor wrote. "We beg their husbands to keep them at home and find some better occupation for them."

The issue of women's rights was not a new one. Abigail Adams had brought it up while the Declaration of Independence was being drafted. Maria Stewart spoke to black women of their rights as early as 1832. "Do you ask the disposition I would have you possess?" she demanded. "Possess the spirit of independence. The [white] Americans do, and why should not you? Possess the spirit of men, bold and enterprising, fearless and undaunted. Sue for your rights and privileges. Know the reason that you cannot attain them. Weary them with your importunities." But the abolitionist movement, as it gathered steam, brought the idea to the fore politically. Both black and white women were regularly denied the right to speak and heard men who talked eloquently about equality deny that women were equal.

In 1840, Lucretia Mott represented the PFAS at the World's Anti-Slavery Convention in London. She and the other women delegates, however, were refused recognition by the convention. The exclusion led directly to the organization of the Seneca Falls Convention on women's rights in 1848. For more than a century and a half, the beginning of the American struggle for women's rights has been placed at that convention, where Lucretia Mott and Elizabeth Cady Stanton, with the support of Frederick Douglass, gathered a small group of supporters to send out a call for equality for women. Symbolically, this has been a problem, since there is no record of the attendance of black women at the event, in spite of Mott's close association with some of the most prominent black women activists.

Historian Ann D. Gordon has made the eminently sensible suggestion that this event was in fact *not* the pivotal one. She has put forward instead the 1837 meeting of the Anti-Slavery Convention of American Women, when American women first publicly insisted on their right to be heard. In a resolution of that convention, black and white women declared that "as moral and responsible beings, the women of America are solemnly called upon by the spirit of the age and the signs of the times, fully to discuss the subject of slavery, that they may be prepared to meet the approaching exigency, and be qualified to act as women, and as Christians, on this all-important subject." This resolution has no less force simply because it specifies the particular subject upon which women were demanding to be heard. Indeed, it is highly appropriate that the American woman's first public insistence on her right to speak should be on behalf, not only of herself, but also of what the resolution goes on to call "the oppressed in our land."

The Seneca Falls convention was the result of a logical progression from the Anti-Slavery Convention of American Women of 1837 to Mott's experience at the London convention of 1840 to any number of other experiences of black and white women in the abolition movement. If it is true that no black women were present at Seneca Falls, that omission, while baffling, is trivial. It should be remembered that even Susan B. Anthony was not present at that meeting. And black women were evident in the women's rights movement both before and after Seneca Falls. Sojourner Truth's first recorded women's rights lecture took place within the next year, in 1849. Sojourner Truth and Susan B. Anthony lectured together often. The combination of the sternly righteous New England schoolmarm and the magnificently eloquent former slave was a powerful one. Other black women who were notably active in the movement were Sarah Jane Woodson Early, Harriet Forten Purvis, Margaretta Forten, and Sarah Remond. Nancy Gardner Prince was an active participant in the 1854 National Woman's Rights Convention.

The failure of history to recognize the dedication of black women to the cause of equal rights for women might seem inexplicable, but it is the result of certain easily recognizable factors. The first and most potent is the tendency to oversimplify. Spotting that tendency is easy. It shows itself in statements like "The Pilgrims came to this country for religious freedom," "Abraham Lincoln freed the slaves," and "The New Deal ended the Great Depression." Complexity is difficult for history to acknowledge, and the position of black women with regard to black men, white men, and white women has always been complex. In the nineteenth century, they wanted two things—freedom for women and freedom for African Americans. When asked to choose between these two things, most of them refused, and history therefore has failed to recognize their dedication to both causes.

OUTSIDE THE MOVEMENT

There were, of course, less organized oppositions to slavery than the antislavery societies, and free black women were thoroughly involved in these. Mary Ellen Pleasant, a black businesswoman, helped to finance John Brown's raid on Harper's Ferry. Another businesswoman, Elizabeth Gloucester, helped Brown with money she made buying and selling real estate in Brooklyn. In Boston, when two fugitive slave women stood before a judge, about to be taken back to the men who claimed to own them, a group of free black women rushed the courtroom and carried them to freedom. In 1857, black abolitionist Nancy Gardner Prince was involved in the ejection of a slave catcher from a woman's home, according to Thomas B. Hilton.

> One day between eleven and twelve o'clock, A.M., there was a ripple of excitement in the rear of Smith's Court. Some children had reported that a slaveholder was in Mrs. Dorsey's. It being working hours scarcely a colored man was seen in the vicinity, but there were those around that showed themselves equal to the occasion. Among these was Mrs. Nancy Prince, a colored woman of prominence in Boston who, with several others, hurried to the scene. Mrs. Prince had seen the kidnapper before. Only for an instant did [her] fiery eyes rest upon the form of the villain, as if to be fully assured that it was he, for the next moment she had grappled with him, and before he could fully realize his position she, with the assistance of the colored women that had accompanied her, had dragged him to the door and thrust him out of the house. By this time quite a number, mostly women and children had gathered near by, whom Mrs. Prince commanded to come to the rescue, tell them to 'pelt him with stones and any thing you can get a hold of,' which order they proceeded to obey with alacrity. The slaveholder started to retreat, and with his assailants close upon him ran out of the court. Only once did the man turn in his head-long flight when, seeing them streaming after him terribly in earnest, their numbers constantly increasing and hearing in his ears their exultant cries and shouts of derision he redoubled his speed and, turning the corner was lost to view.

Women were also among the group of armed African Americans who, in 1851, went to the defense of four escaped slaves in Christiana, Pennsylvania, in defiance of the Fugitive Slave Law. Thirty-six of the group were arrested but were acquitted in court. Even these acts of tremendous courage, however, were open to criticism, as we have seen.

Black women also bought slaves in order to free them. An elderly New York woman named Hester Lane purchased and liberated eleven slaves, including two teenagers, a single man, a family of three, and a family of five. In all, she spent almost $2,000 to free these enslaved people, and then she paid for the educations of all the children and set them up in business. Jane Minor, a nurse/midwife in Petersburg, Virginia, gained her freedom in 1825 after nursing some prominent white citizens during an epidemic. She continued to work and save, using her earnings to emancipate others. In 1840, she bought and freed Phebe Jackson, who followed in her footsteps as a healer. Before she was through, Minor freed sixteen women and children.

And then there were the women of the Underground Railroad. Pivotal to this extraordinary effort, they helped thousands escape from the brutality of life in the slave South.

THE UNDERGROUND RAILROAD

Few political actions in history have so captured the imagination as the Underground Railroad. It was courageous, daring, bold, and startlingly effective. The entire purpose of the "railroad" was to help enslaved people escape from the South. There were several routes, going from the South to the North to Canada. Its "conductors" guided fugitives. Its "stops" were places where the fugitives could rest, be fed, and hide from their pursuers. Its "station masters" were people—white and black, men and women—who risked their lives to offer refuge, usually in their own homes, to those who were running desperately towards freedom. The most famous conductor on the railroad was a black woman.

Harriet Ross Tubman has achieved fame of mythic proportions as the best-known conductor on the Underground Railroad. Her heroic exploits included many trips—most sources say fifteen—into the South to rescue more than two hundred slaves and deliver them to freedom. Since Underground Railroad operators did not keep records of their activities, the exact number of trips Tubman made is unknown. Tubman herself remembered the number as eleven.

Tubman began her legendary career after making her own escape from slavery in 1849. In Philadelphia, she worked as a domestic, saving her meager earnings until she had the resources and contacts to rescue her sister, Mary Ann Bowley, and her two children, in 1850. This was the first of many rescue missions Tubman would undertake as an agent of the Underground Railroad.

In her numerous trips South, Tubman followed various routes and used different disguises. She might appear as a hooded, apparently mentally impaired, wretchedly dressed man loitering about or talking in tongues. She might be an old woman chasing hens down the street. She usually chose a Saturday night for the rescue since a day would intervene before a runaway advertisement could appear. She carried doses of paregoric to silence crying babies and a pistol to discourage any fugitive slave from thoughts of disembarking the freedom train. Within two years of her own escape she had returned to Maryland's eastern shore to lead more than a dozen slaves to freedom in northern states. Maryland planters saw her as such a threat that they offered $40,000—an astronomical sum at that time—for her capture.

Tubman eventually developed close, mutually supportive relationships with black abolitionist William Still of Philadelphia and white abolitionist Thomas Garrett of Wilmington, Delaware. William Still, the leading black figure in the Underground Railroad, described Tubman as "a woman of no pretensions; indeed a more ordinary specimen of humanity could hardly be found among the most unfortunate-looking farm hands of the South. Yet in point of courage, shrewdness, and disinterested exertions to rescue her fellowman, she was without equal."

As part of the Compromise of 1850, the Fugitive Slave Law placed fugitive cases under federal supervision and empowered special U.S. commissioners to receive $10 for each arrest that returned a slave to his or her owner. With the passage of this legislation, the entire federal government machinery and power could be called upon to assist in the capture and return of escaped slaves in any section of the country. This law cast an ominous shadow on northern communities. Tubman, having been forced to relocate many fugitives to Canada, herself moved to Saint Catharines, Ontario, just beyond Niagara Falls.

In December 1851, Harriet went South and returned with eleven slaves, including her brother and his wife. The following year she made another trip into Maryland and retrieved nine more slaves. On June 4, 1857, Tubman achieved a long-desired goal when she rescued her parents. She made her last rescue in late 1860 when she returned to Dorchester County to free Steven Ennets, his wife Maria, and their three children. Tubman took great pride in having never lost a passenger. These long journeys of courage and faith inspired her friends and the runaways to call her "Moses."

Although illiterate, Tubman gave speeches and personal testimony. She conspired with John Brown in his doomed effort to provoke a massive armed slave rebellion by raiding the federal arsenal at Harpers Ferry, although illness prevented her direct participation in the raid. Frederick Douglass wrote to Harriet Tubman on August 28, 1868, and eloquently summed up her life.

The difference between us is very marked. Most that I have done and suffered in the service of our cause has been in public, and I have received much encouragement at every step of the way. You, on the other hand, have labored in a private way. I have wrought in the day—you the night. I have had the applause of the crowd and the satisfaction that comes of being approved by the multitude, while the most that you have done has been witnessed by a few trembling, scared, and foot-sore bondmen and women, whom you have led out of the house of bondage, and whose heartfelt "God bless you" has been your only reward. The midnight sky and the silent stars have been the witness of your devotion to freedom.

Tubman was not the only black woman to serve her people through the Underground Railroad. One of the first and most important agents of the Underground Railroad, Anna Murray Douglass would have been remembered by history for her contributions to the struggle for freedom if it had not been for one thing: she was married to Frederick Douglass. While her extraordinary husband overshadowed her, however, she was a memorable woman in her own right.

Anna Murray Douglass was the eighth child of Bambara and Mary Murray and the first to be born free. Her parents gained their own freedom just one month before she was born. At seventeen, she left the family home and traveled to Baltimore, where she found work with a French family. She quickly became involved in the black community, joining the East Baltimore Improvement Society, a somewhat exclusive group, whose membership was small and limited to free blacks. There was before long, however, one exception to the latter restriction, a young, intelligent, articulate slave named Frederick Augustus Washington Bailey. The two young people fell in love.

Bailey was determined not to marry until he was free, so he and Anna Murray began to plan his escape. They used her savings of nine years to finance the plan, and she sewed him a disguise—the uniform of a sailor. He borrowed from a friend the papers that would allow him to travel as a free man. In September of 1838, he arrived in New York. She followed a few days later, and they were married. They began a new life in New Bedford, Massachusetts, where they adopted the new name of Douglass. While her husband worked in the shipyards, the young Anna Murray Douglass worked as a domestic. She also resumed her involvement in community activities. After her husband became prominent in the abolitionist movement and began to travel a great deal, Douglass reared their five children and virtually supported the family by taking work binding shoes. In 1847, the family moved to Rochester, New York, where the Douglass home became a stop on the Underground Railroad. Since Frederick was not often home, it fell to Anna to carry out the duties of agent. In the meantime, the Douglass sons worked as conductors, leading fugitive slaves from one stop to another on the path to freedom.

Tubman and Douglass were only two of the many free black women who risked everything to rescue their sisters and brothers from enslavement. Free themselves, they were determined that others should be free. And these abolitionist women had another powerful impact on the black community, one that went beyond the specifics of emancipation. This movement for freedom became the cradle of black women's literature. Aside from Lucy Terry Prince and Phillis Wheatley, virtually all of the early black woman writers and poets came out of the struggle for emancipation.

ANOTHER WORLD, ANOTHER CULTURE

The abolition movement had significance for black women far beyond the elimination of the legal institution of slavery. Culturally, it brought many free black women into the mainstream in a number of different areas, including literature, the arts, and education.

A tradition that has continued through Maya Angelou's autobiographical series and even the fiction of such writers as Alice Walker and Toni Morrison was begun in the early nineteenth century as part of the battle against slavery. Among the weapons abolitionists used were the true stories of slaves themselves, or rather, former slaves. Abolition groups often paid for the publication of these narratives and helped to distribute them, hoping to raise public consciousness and elicit sympathy for those held in bondage. Most of the slave narratives were written by men, but there were women writers as well. The information in them has been of critical importance to historians, and they were also crucial to the formation of the literature of black women.

The earliest of these autobiographical narratives, published in 1831, was written by a West Indian, Mary Prince. It told of the appalling conditions of slavery in the Caribbean. The most significant of the narratives, literarily, is probably Harriet Ann Jacobs's *Incidents in the Life of a Slave Girl: Written By Herself*, published in 1861. Originally thought to be a novel written by a white woman, it was not revealed until 1987 as the work of a black woman and essentially autobiographical. *Incidents* is particularly important because it deals with the sexual aggression of a slaveholder and tells how one enslaved woman averted abuse. In the process, she lived for seven years in an attic crawl space too small to allow her to sit up. After escaping at last, Jacobs fled to New York, where she lived, with her children, for a number of years. One of the women for whom she did domestic work was moved by her story and, without her knowledge, "purchased" her and her children in order to free them. Jacobs then decided to write her story. She published it herself, with help from African American abolitionist William C. Nell and white abolitionist Lydia Maria Child.

Many other slave narratives were published after the Civil War, including those of itinerant preachers Jarena Lee and Zilpha Elaw. Elizabeth Keckley's *Behind the Scenes at the White House* was also published following the war, causing a huge furor because of its inside look at the Lincolns' marriage. It contained forty letters written by Mary Todd Lincoln to Keckley, who had become her confidant. But slave narratives, loudly as they echo in the work of many writers today, were not at the time considered as important literarily as the poetry and essays of free black women who began to express themselves in writing because of the abolition movement. As the movement grew, antislavery periodicals such as the *Afro-American Magazine* and the *National Anti-Slavery Standard* gave black women, for the first time, an outlet for their writing.

The Forten women again were among the leaders in this wave of black women's literature. Sarah Forten Purvis, for example, wrote against slavery with great eloquence in articles with such titles as "The Abuse of Liberty" and "The Slave Girl's Address to Her Mother." Charlotte Forten Grimké is of even greater significance. Educated at home by tutors, she began writing poetry at an early age. Her work was published primarily in abolitionist journals, but slavery was not her only subject. She wrote about love and the loneliness that is so much a part of the human condition. Her style was the style of the times, much as Phillis Wheatley's had been. John Greenleaf Whittier was a supporter of Forten Grimké's, praising her work and encouraging her career. During the Civil War, she wrote about her experiences as a teacher of recently freed African Americans on South Carolina's Sea Islands. These essays were published in the *Atlantic Monthly* in 1864, but this was the only time she was published in the mainstream white press. Unfortunately, Charlotte Forten Grimké was never able to find a niche outside the abolitionist movement.

The first black woman to publish a book of essays in the United States was born and died in obscurity, but her need to express her thoughts and feelings pushed through the limitations of her position and guaranteed her a place in history. Ann Plato was born in Hartford, Connecticut, probably in about 1820. As a very young woman, she became a teacher. Her book, *Essays: Including Biographies and Miscellaneous Pieces in Prose and Poetry,* was published in 1841. In it are sixteen essays and twenty poems dealing with death and the changing of the seasons, as well as with religion, benevolence, employment, and education. They are not particularly original or elegantly written, but the book is of importance historically because it was only the second ever published by an African American woman. The first, a book of poems by Phillis Wheatley, had been published almost seventy years before.

One woman would go on through most of the nineteenth century as the preeminent black woman writer. Frances E. W. Harper, an active member of the abolition movement and worker in the Underground Railroad, toured as a lecturer, speaking against slavery and for women's rights. Her first volume of poetry, *Poems on Miscellaneous Subjects,* was eagerly snatched up by those who already knew and admired the work she had first published in the *Liberator* and the *Christian Recorder* and then read at her lectures. The book sold more than ten thousand copies in the first three years after its publication, a phenomenal number at that time. Twenty editions were issued during the next twenty years.

Harper was the first African American woman to publish a short story. "Two Offers" appeared in 1859, six years after Frederick Douglass's "The Heroic Slave," the first short story published by an African American. In spite of the time that had passed, Harper's was only the second short story published by an African American of either gender. She went on to have a fifty-year career as a novelist, poet, and essayist.

Harper was not, however, the first African American woman novelist. The first black person of either gender to publish a novel in America was Harriet E. Wilson. She was also one of the first two black women to publish a novel in any language, anywhere in the world. Startlingly, her accomplishment was not acknowledged for more than a century. Wilson registered the copyright of her novel on the eighteenth day of August 1859. The publication date of *Our Nig: or, Sketches from the Life of a Free Black, in a Two-Story White House, North. Showing That Slavery's Shadows Fall Even There* was September 5. Wilson asked her "colored brethren," in the preface, to buy the book so that she might support herself and her child. Five months later, her son was dead. The novel, *Our Nig,* was largely autobiographical, as are many first novels. It was well plotted and well written. But it was never reviewed, not even in the abolitionist journals, according to Henry Gates, Jr.

> [T]his remarkable accomplishment was virtually ignored for a century after its publication. A systematic search of all extant copies of black and reform newspapers and magazines that were in circulation contemporaneously with the publication of *Our Nig* yielded not one notice or review, nor did searches through the Boston dailies and the Amherst *Farmer's Cabinet.* Other black fiction of the time, though not popularly reviewed, was reviewed on occasion. That such a significant novel, the very first written by a black woman, would remain unnoticed in Boston in 1859, a veritable center of abolitionist reform and passion, and by a growing black press eager to celebrate all black achievements in the arts and sciences, remains one of the troubling enigmas of African American literary history. The list of people and publications who do *not* mention Wilson and her book is too long to insert here, but it includes Du Bois's three important bibliographies, Murray's *Preliminary List of Books and Pamphlets by Negro Authors* (prepared for the American Negro Exhibit at the Paris Exhibition of 1900), and all of the late-nineteenth- and early-twentieth-century black biographical dictionaries.

Until 1983, when Gates championed the novel and prepared for publication a new edition of it, *Our Nig* was lost in obscurity. Gates suggests two reasons for this. First, the book is not about slavery but rather about the trials of a free black woman living and working as a domestic servant. "The villains of *Our Nig* are not slaveholders and overseers. They are the women of a northern white household. Their crimes will not be destroyed by the abolition of slavery but only by a complete reexamination and amendment of the economic and social position of black women in American society." That may account for the lack of welcome on the part of northern white abolitionists. And second, the book treats sympathetically the marriage of the main character's parents—a white woman and a black man. That probably antagonized a great many more readers. It was not an easy book for anyone in the early nineteenth century to read, and so history misplaced it.

Strangely, *Our Nig,* like *Incidents in the Life of a Slave Girl,* was thought to have been written by a white author. Until the 1980s, two of the most important literary works by black women were not attributed to them at all, but to white authors. This is just one measure of the disrespect in which black women have been held. Still, they managed to write about their lives and feelings, and finally their writing is being given the credit it deserves.

It was not only in literature that abolitionist sentiments brought opportunities to a select few black women. Elizabeth Taylor Greenfield, one of the first great black women concert singers, was born in about 1819 in Natchez, Mississippi. Her parents, named Taylor, were slaves on the estate of Mrs. Holliday Greenfield. When Elizabeth was a year old, Mrs. Greenfield freed the child's parents and sent them to Liberia, but she took Elizabeth with her to Philadelphia. When the young woman's remarkable voice was noticed by a neighbor, Mrs. Greenfield encouraged her talent, and Elizabeth Greenfield began performing as a soloist at private parties. After Mrs. Greenfield's death, the young singer was taken up by other members of affluent white society. She toured the country, singing in all the free states.

In New York, in 1853, Elizabeth Taylor Greenfield debuted at Metropolitan Hall, which held an audience of four thousand, white patrons only. Because of a threat that the building would be burned if she appeared, police were stationed in the hall during the concert. After the concert, Greenfield apologized to her own people for their exclusion from the performance and gave a concert to benefit the Home of Aged Colored Persons and the Colored Orphan Asylum. In England, she appeared in a command performance before Queen Victoria. Critics praised her emotional power and the weight and sweetness of her voice. Audiences responded also to her intelligence and personality.

Literature and the arts were important to free black women, but education was the "salvation of the race," and it was not a great deal easier to come by for free black women than it was for those enslaved. In 1833, for example, a white Quaker woman named Prudence Crandall tried to admit a young black girl, seventeen-year-old Sarah Harris, to her school. All of the other students in Crandall's school were white, most of them from the community of Canterbury, Connecticut. The other students' parents first howled in protest, then withdrew their children from the school, claiming that Crandall was encouraging social equality between the races that would lead to intermarriage. Crandall closed the school. But then she reopened it, and this time she admitted only black girls. This should have met the community's objections, but it didn't. The townspeople were furious. They ostracized Crandall. They put manure in her well. Finally, they set her house on fire. As if this weren't enough, they forbade her family to visit her, threatening them with fines of $100 for the first offense and $200 for the second offense. Town officials arrested Crandall herself and tried her twice.

Finally, she gave up, defeated by frenzied opposition to the education of black women.

In spite of such experiences, free African Americans continued to believe in the possibility of, as well as the necessity for, education. Teaching became the vocation most often chosen by young middle-class black women, as it was for the same class of white women. But there was a difference. For black women, teaching was not simply employment. It was an almost holy calling, an opportunity for service to the race.

For some of the earliest teachers, education was literally a holy calling. The Oblate Sisters of Providence were black nuns who ran a school for French-speaking black immigrants in Baltimore. The school's founder, Elizabeth Lange, was born in a French colony in the Caribbean and came to the United States in 1817. In 1827, she settled in Baltimore and opened the school. When Pope Gregory XVI recognized the value of her work and her dedication to the church, he granted her the right to found a religious order dedicated to education. In 1843, the priest who had supported the founding of the order, Father Jacques Hector Nicholas Joubert, died. With him died virtually all of the order's assistance from the Catholic church. In order to keep their school open, the nuns took in laundry. Some years later, they found another priest to sponsor them and again received some support from the church.

When Ann Marie Becroft was only fifteen years old, she founded a day school for black girls in the Georgetown section of Washington, D.C. Eight years later, in 1828, a Catholic priest asked her to open a school sponsored by the church. Moving to larger facilities, she ran a boarding and day school until 1831, when she left to join the Oblate Order.

Although some women found help for their educational efforts in various churches, others went it alone. In 1819, for example, a black woman from Santo Domingo named Julian Froumountaine opened a free school for African Americans in Savannah, Georgia. When restrictive laws were passed in the 1830s, Froumountaine went underground. Mary Smith Kelsey, a member of the black elite in Hampton, Virginia, began teaching both enslaved and free black Americans secretly in the 1850s. She was one of a number of black women whose teaching was, a few years later, officially sanctioned by the Union army as the United States entered the Civil War. Many black women taught in their living rooms, secretly. Catharine Deveaux managed to run a school in Savannah for twenty-seven years, from 1834 until the Civil War, hiding its existence from the white community the entire time.

No one knew, when the abolition movement began, that it would nurture black women and men in so many different fields. What's more, no one knew how it would end. Some must have envisioned legislation that would destroy the legal basis for slavery. Others may have believed that educating slaveholders to the immorality of their ways would bring about a gradual and voluntary abolition. At least a few thought the United States, like Haiti, was headed towards revolution. In the end, however, abolition was achieved only through one of the worst wars in history.

Before the Dawn

The Civil War was the turning point in African American history. Before and after it, there were poverty and discrimination, evils and exploitation. In its practical aspects, life for many black people was much the same after the guns ceased firing as it had been before they began. And yet, everything was different. After the Civil War, there was freedom.

The war itself took an enormously heavy toll on black Americans. They starved on plantations from which supplies had been cut off. They died in battle. And they suffered from the anger and fear of slave owners who were seeing their fortunes and their way of life being destroyed. But they were not merely victims of the conflict. They were active and fiercely committed participants who worked and fought and prayed. Black women were at the very center of the struggle as America entered the bloody half decade of the Civil War.

So the beginning of this was a woman and she had

come back from burying the dead.

ZORA NEALE HURSTON,

THEIR EYES WERE WATCHING GOD

THE WAR
FOR FREEDOM

CHAPTER FIVE

Outside of the Fort were many skulls lying about; I have often moved them one side out of the path. The comrades and I would have wondered a bit as to which side of the war the men fought on, some said they were the skulls of our boys; some said they were the enemy's; but as there was no definite way to know, it was never decided which could lay claim to them. They were a gruesome sight, those fleshless heads and grinning jaws, but by this time I had become used to worse things and did not feel as I would have earlier in my camp life. SUSIE BAKER KING TAYLOR, NURSE, UNION ARMY

When the first guns were fired at Fort Sumter on April 12, 1861, those in power on both sides insisted that they were not fighting about slavery. Confederates claimed they were fighting for the right of each state to make its own policies. The United States government, on the other hand, was fighting to preserve the Union. So long as politicians and statesmen could believe that—or pretend to believe it—there was hope for compromise and reconciliation. African Americans, however, recognized that slavery was at the core of the conflict and that their future was at stake. In the first days of the war, when Abraham Lincoln announced the need for 75,000 volunteers to fight, black men rushed to join the army and were refused. A year later, this policy would change and black men *and* women would serve with honor and distinction, but in that initial refusal, the complex and contradictory forces at work in the North were clearly revealed. Still, there was no question where African American loyalties must, and did, lie. In the words of Frederick Douglass, "The American people and the Government at Washington may refuse to recognize it for a time but the 'inexorable logic of events' will force it upon them in the end; that the war now being waged in this land is a war for and against slavery."

Whether free or slave, black women knew that their fate was being decided on the battlefields at Manassas and Gettysburg. Thousands of them had that knowledge forced on them every day, because they were there, in army camps. Others continued to work on the plantations of the South, seeing the fear in the slaveholders' eyes at the thought of losing their slaves, their workforce, their livelihood. These women took an active, aggressive role in the Civil War even when it meant tremendous sacrifice, and the historical significance of this has never been explored. Indeed, the extraordinary participation of black women in the war effort is seldom mentioned, even in African American histories. Of course, women had been involved in war before, but their participation had usually been limited to rolling bandages, knitting socks, and keeping things going on the home front. Black women were actually at the battle sites, nursing the wounds of black soldiers. They served as cooks and laundresses and spies, carrying out reconnaissance missions for Union officers. The legendary Harriet Tubman even led a raid into enemy territory. Many of these women had followed the army as it swept through the South, walking away from their plantations and their lives in slavery. They worked for the army in part because they had nowhere else to go and in part because they wanted to be involved in the struggle for freedom. Others sought out the opportunity to serve.

Black women also served in the propaganda effort. In the lecture halls of the North and even as far afield as Liverpool and Dublin, they elicited support for the Union by evoking antislavery sentiments. And when tens of thousands of slaves fled the South during the war, black women undertook the tremendous task of finding food, clothing, and sometimes, housing for the fugitives. Harriet Keckley, Mary Todd Lincoln's dressmaker, used her contacts with the wealthy and influential to raise funds. Refined and sheltered Charlotte Forten traveled to the Sea Islands to teach basic literacy. The women's antislavery societies mobilized in an unprecedented way to provide the services so desperately needed by the newly freed.

Black women knew that this was their war, the step toward freedom they had prayed and struggled for in the decades just past. It divided the country and killed almost an entire generation of young men. There was in it no sense and little righteousness. But it was a bloody opening in the insurmountable wall of oppression, and enslaved Americans walked through the horror to freedom.

OUR FREEDOM, OUR STRUGGLE

All too often, history books give the impression that enslaved people waited on the plantations of the South to be freed while white men of both armies fought and died on the battlefields of the Civil War. In fact, from the time that war was declared, hundreds of thousands of enslaved people ran to Union lines to escape from slavery, and tens of thousands of them helped to wage the war.

This mass exodus from bondage presented an enormous and immediate problem in the beginning. It apparently never occurred to anyone that it would happen, and there was simply no federal program in place to deal with the fugitives. There was not even a policy for commanding officers to follow in the field. After all, the slaves had not yet officially been freed. So far as both Union and Confederate laws were concerned, these people still belonged to the slaveholders. And so, for the first month of the war—and in some cases longer—Northern troops actually *returned fugitives* to their "owners."

Then, in May, General Benjamin Butler, who was stationed in Virginia at the time, declared that the enslaved people who escaped to his troops were contraband. They were, in other words, property taken in war. With this inspired technicality, Butler changed the Union's position. Other Union generals followed suit. On August 6, Congress passed the first Confiscation Act, which provided that any property used by the owner's consent and with his knowledge to aid and abet insurrection against the United States was forfeit and could be confiscated by Union forces. Property in this case might mean a wagon or a load of grain. It might also mean a slave. A slave who was thus used, according to the act, would be forever free.

President Lincoln, however, refused to order that the law be strictly enforced. He felt strongly the need to be cautious about slavery. Indeed, he stated very clearly that, if he could preserve the Union without freeing a single slave, he would do so. That would not prove possible. In March of 1862, he proposed a plan to Congress that called for gradual emancipation, with financial compensation for slaveholders, but it was opposed by both abolitionist delegates and those from the slave states that had remained loyal to the Union—Delaware, Kentucky, Maryland, Missouri, and West Virginia. In April, slaves in the District of Columbia were freed. However, when General David Hunter issued orders freeing all slaves in the area under his command—Georgia, Florida, and South Carolina—using the "contraband of war" argument, President Lincoln overturned the orders. Over the next few months, the federal government's approach to the situation evolved. In June, Lincoln signed a bill that abolished slavery in federal territories. In July, Congress passed the second Confiscation Act, which freed slaves whose masters cooperated with the Confederacy. And in September, Abraham Lincoln issued the Emancipation Proclamation, declaring that all enslaved people in the Confederacy would be free as of January 1, 1863.

Now, as Union troops marched through the South, black families walked off the plantations where they had been enslaved, leaving behind the whipping post and the auction block and days of labor that lasted from daybreak to last light. They also left behind the closest thing to a home that most of them had ever known. Gathering their few belongings, these newly free people simply fell in line behind their liberators and began to walk. Historian Noralee Frankel reports that "when William Tecumseh Sherman advanced through the state of Mississippi in 1863–64, behind his army were

'10 miles of negroes . . . a string of ox wagons, negro women and children behind each brigade that equaled in length the brigade itself.' "

When Union troops reached the cities where they were stationed, the hundreds or even thousands of former slaves stopped walking. Legally, they were free. However, there remained for the Union officers the practical problem of what to do with these thousands of people who arrived on the Union's doorstep with nothing more than the clothes on their backs and an occasional cooking pot. To begin with, the army put the men to work digging trenches and doing other noncombat labor. Women and children were more problematic. Many of them remained in camps nearby in tents or shacks put together out of whatever they or the army could find. The camps were crowded and dirty, and food was hard to come by. If Union troops left the encampment, the African Americans left behind were undefended and often killed or recaptured by white Southerners.

In July of 1862, the federal government had begun allowing black men to serve in the army. Before the war was over, 178,975 African Americans would serve in the Union army as combat troops, according to the Adjutant General's Office. Of those men, almost 70,000—more than one in three—lost their lives. There were another 200,000 black men in service units. The soldiers in black regiments saw combat in more than two hundred battles. About 29,000 others fought in the Union navy. Indeed, African American men were admitted into the navy as early as September 1861— almost a year before the army began accepting black volunteers—and they made up almost one-quarter of that arm of the services. The black troops fought with distinction. As one white general wrote after a battle at Big Black River in Mississippi, "Of this fight I can only say that men could not have behaved more bravely. I have seen white troops fight in twenty-seven battles and I never saw any fight better."

Equality of risk and sacrifice did not, however, mean equality of conditions. Black soldiers were paid less than their white counterparts. (White soldiers were paid $13 per month plus $3.50 for clothing, and black soldiers were paid $10, including clothing allowance.) They served in segregated regiments. They were at first not allowed to become officers. Often, black soldiers were put to work doing manual labor instead of fighting. When they did fight, they were given inferior weapons and equipment.

Most contraband wives lived near the army barracks where their soldier husbands and fathers were stationed. Gradually, they moved out of army tents and into boarding houses or shanties. Many of the women living near army camps worked for the army as cooks, laundresses, or servants.

When the troops went into battle, the women followed behind, serving the Union cause and remaining close to their soldier husbands. Susie Baker King Taylor was one of these.

CIVIL WAR NURSE

Susie Baker King Taylor was born in 1848 into an old American family. In her book, *A Black Woman's Civil War Memoirs: Reminiscences of My Life in Camp with the 33rd U.S. Colored Troops, Late 1st S.C. Volunteers,* she traces her family back through the maternal line to her great-great-grandmother, one of the first African slaves in the colony of Georgia. "My great-great-grandmother was 120 years old when she died. She had seven children, and five of her boys were in the Revolutionary War. She was from Virginia, and was half Indian. She was so old she had to be held in the sun to help restore or prolong her vitality." One of this woman's daughters, Taylor's great-grandmother Susanna, had twenty-three daughters of her own and one son. One of these daughters, Taylor's grandmother, Dolly Reed, was in part responsible for Taylor's upbringing.

When Susie Baker was seven, she was allowed to leave the plantation where she and her mother were enslaved to go to live in relative freedom with her grandmother, who had been hired out to work in Savannah. There she learned to read with the help of two white children who were her friends and a black teacher who held a secret school in her living room.

> My brother and I being the two eldest, we were sent to a friend of my grandmother, Mrs. Woodhouse, a widow, to learn to read and write. She was a free woman and lived on Bay Lane, between Habersham and Price streets, about half a mile from my house. We went every day about nine o'clock, with our books wrapped in paper to prevent the police or white persons from seeing them. We went in, one at a time, through the gate, into the yard to the L kitchen, which was the schoolroom. She had twenty-five or thirty children whom she taught, assisted by her daughter, Mary Jane. The neighbors would see us going in sometimes, but they supposed we were there learning trades, as it was the custom to give children a trade of some kind. After school we left the same way we entered, one by one, when we would go to a square, about a block from the school, and wait for each other.

Dolly Reed found another teacher, a Mrs. Beasley, for her granddaughter, but soon that teacher, too, had taught the little girl all she could. Fortunately, Susie had a white playmate, Katie O'Connor, who went to a convent school. Katie offered to give her lessons so long as they could hide them from Katie's father. With her mother's consent, Katie taught Susie every evening for four months before entering the convent permanently. Young Susie then got lessons from the landlord's son, a white student at the nearby high school. She lost that tutor when he went to serve in the Confederate army. (During the first battle of Manassas, he deserted to the Union side.)

The young girl and her grandmother were also active members of the black community and, in 1862, they were discovered attending a secret political meeting in a black church. Dolly Reed was placed under strict control by the guardian her owner had appointed for her, and young Susie was sent back to the plantation. Shortly thereafter, she and her family escaped to the Union encampment on St. Catherine, in the Sea Islands. From there they were taken to St. Simon's Island. While on the journey, Susie and her skills were discovered by the commander of the boat. Three days after she arrived on St. Simon's, she was put to work teaching. It was soon clear, however, that the island was not safe from Confederate attack. The fourteen-year-old teacher was evacuated, with others, to Camp Saxton in Beauford, South Carolina. There she went to work as a laundress for Company E.

Company E, or the first South Carolina Volunteers, was an unusual unit. When it was formed, Lincoln was still opposing the participation of African Americans in combat. However, two white generals helped a group of free black men and fugitive slaves to form a regiment, led by General Rufus Saxton. Later, the troops would receive official authorization. Susie Baker remained with Company E throughout the war. Among its members were many men from her own family and an old friend named Edward King, who became her first husband. She also became the unit's nurse.

Clara Barton, Elizabeth Blackwell, and Dorothea Dix were among the white women who worked to train and organize field nurses during the Civil War, but their efforts did not affect most of those who served. Only about 20 percent of army nurses were women, and in the South this percentage was even lower. Most Civil War nurses were men who had little or no training. The majority learned their jobs by doing and by observing. They had compassion and common sense to help them and not much else. It was the same for Susie Baker King. The scenes she describes would have daunted a M.A.S.H. unit. "About four o'clock, July 2, the charge was made," she wrote in her memoirs. "The firing could be plainly heard in camp. I hastened down to the landing and remained there until eight o'clock that morning. When the wounded arrived, or rather began to arrive, the first one brought in was Samuel Anderson of our company. He was badly wounded. Then others of our boys, some with their legs off, arm gone, foot off, and wounds of all kinds imaginable."

It was not only contraband women who were involved in the war effort. Most free black women were ardent in the war for freedom. Harriet Tubman, for instance, earned distinction as the only woman in American military history to plan and execute an armed expedition against enemy forces. She was a spy, scout, and nurse for the Union army stationed in the Carolinas and Florida.

Tubman had a bounty on her head most of her life. After the war began, Southern states continued to offer rewards for her capture as she passed back and forth between Confederate and Union lines, gathering intelligence for the Union. She carried with her a pass issued by General David Hunter which read, "Pass the bearer, Harriet Tubman . . . wherever she wishes to go; and give her free passage, at all times, on all government transports." She might as well have been invisible to the prejudiced eyes of Southern soldiers. The short woman with her dark skin and head wrapped in a bandanna was a familiar and innocuous sight, just another "Mammy." In this guise she "made many a raid inside the enemy's line, displaying remarkable courage, zeal and fidelity," according to General Rufus Saxton. Her most famous adventure during the war came when she was acting as assistant to Colonel James Montgomery on a raid from Port Royal, South Carolina, inland up to the Combahee River in June 1863. Her first task was to make contact with enslaved men and women on the plantations that were about to be raided by Montgomery's soldiers. She was able to calm their fears of the dreaded Yankees and help them escape to safety. She also helped to plan the raids, during which many plantations that had been providing food for Confederate troops were destroyed. The Boston *Commonwealth* reported one of these battles on July 10, 1863.

HARRIET TUBMAN

Col. Montgomery and his gallant band of 300 black soldiers, under the guidance of a black woman, dashed into the enemy's country, struck a bold and effective blow, destroying millions of dollars worth of commissary stores, cotton and lordly dwellings, and striking terror into the heart of rebeldom, brought off near 800 slaves and thousands of dollars worth of property, without losing a man or receiving a scratch. It was a glorious consummation.

The account went on to describe speeches given after the battle by Montgomery and Tubman, as well as some of her intelligence activities. "Many and many times she has penetrated the enemy's lines and discovered their situation and condition, and escaped without injury, but not without extreme hazard." Tubman was also present at the Fort Wagner battle and was purported to have served the last meal to Colonel Robert Gould Shaw, white commander of the Black Massachusetts Fifty-Fourth Regiment, celebrated in the 1990 film *Glory*. She recorded a powerful description of the battle that ended in the deaths of approximately 1,500 black troops: "Then we saw the lightning, and that was the guns; and then we heard the thunder, and that was the big guns; and then we heard the rain falling, and that was the drops of blood falling; and when we came to get in the crops, it was dead men that we reaped."

Following the Civil War, Tubman recounted her life story to her friend, Sarah Elizabeth Bradford, and received a small stipend from the sale of the resulting biography, *Scenes in the Life of Harriet Tubman*. For thirty years, Tubman fought to receive a pension from the U.S. government for her military services and eventually won a $20 per month stipend, not for her own services but for those of her second husband.

Among Tubman's fellow spies for the Union was Mary Elizabeth Bowser, whose dazzling espionage activities passed on vital information from Jefferson Davis, president of the Confederacy, to General Ulysses S. Grant. Bowser was born on a plantation outside Richmond, Virginia, a slave of the Van Lew family. When John Van Lew died in 1851, however, the abolitionist women of his family freed all of his slaves. They are reported even to have bought and then freed the members of their servants' families who lived in other households. Bowser remained at the Van Lew home as a servant for a time, and then the Van Lew family sent her to Philadelphia to receive an education. She was there at the beginning of the Civil War.

Elizabeth Van Lew, the daughter of the family, was a strong Union sympathizer. For the first few months of the war, she nursed Union soldiers in nearby Libby Prison. Later, her activities became more daring. She became a spy. Feigning weakness of the mind, she allowed herself to be called "Crazy Bet" in order to avert suspicion from herself. Then she began to aid prisoners escaping from Libby Prison by hiding them in a secret room in her house. While they were there, the prisoners would tell her everything they had been able to learn by listening to their guards while in the Confederate prison. Van Lew wrote down the information in code and sent it through the lines to Grant, General Benjamin J. Butler, and other Union officers.

Van Lew's ardor did not stop there. She decided that she should have an intelligence agent in Jefferson Davis's own home. She sent for Bowser to come back to Richmond. Bowser did, and she soon became a servant in the Confederate White House. Like Van Lew, Bowser pretended to have a mental deficiency. She was therefore disregarded while her sharp wits garnered information from the Davises' conversations with their guests. She also read dispatches as she dusted, and carried all this information home with her in her head. Back at the Van Lew home each night, she recited from memory everything she had learned, and Van Lew put it into code.

The coded messages were carried to the Union officers in a variety of ways. A black servant of Van Lew's—an old man—went from Richmond to the Van Lew farm for provisions every day. He carried a pass that allowed him to make the journey. The story goes that one egg in each batch of provisions was a dummy and that messages were carried in that egg. Another servant, a black seamstress who worked for a family named Carrington, carried the materials of her trade between the homes of Union sympathizers. Cipher messages were worked into her dress patterns.

Spying for the Union was a task many black women undertook, using their "invisibility" to advantage. Lucy Carter spied for the Sixteenth New York Cavalry stationed at Vienna, Virginia, carrying a pass from its commanding officer that allowed her to cross the lines of the Sixteenth "at pleasure." Sojourner Truth spied for the Union in the Northern states. She also lectured and raised funds for the contraband camps.

In 1863, after the terrible battles at Gettysburg and Vicksburg, President Lincoln sent out a call for more soldiers. African American activist Mary Ann Shadd Cary was one of those who responded by volunteering to become a Union army recruiting officer, alongside such prominent men as Frederick Douglass and Charles Remond. In August of that year she received her official appointment, the only one given to a woman. (Other women worked unofficially to recruit black soldiers, including Harriet Jacobs and Josephine Ruffin.) In a sketch in the book *The Rising Sun*, edited by William Wells Brown, William Still wrote of Cary's work, "Mrs. Carey [sic] raised recruits in the West, and brought them on to Boston with as much skill, tact and order as any recruiting officers under the government. Her men were always considered the best lot brought to head-quarters. Indeed, the examining surgeon never failed to speak of Mrs. Carey's recruits as faultless. This proves the truth of the old adage, that 'It takes a woman to pick out a good man.' "

Still other black women, such as Elizabeth Keckley and Harriet Jacobs, became extremely effective at raising funds to aid fugitive slaves. In 1862, Keckley, whose son George was killed in action while fighting for the

Union, helped to found the Contraband Relief Association, an organization of African American women formed to provide assistance to former slaves who had come to the District of Columbia. She solicited and received contributions from her employer, Mrs. Abraham Lincoln, as well as from white abolitionists and members of the black community. "I suggested the object of my mission to Robert Thompson," she wrote, "Steward of the [Metropolitan] Hotel, who immediately raised quite a sum of money among the dining-room waiters. Mr. Frederick Douglass contributed $200, besides lecturing for us. Other prominent colored men sent in liberal contributions. From England a large quantity of stores was received. In 1863 I was re-elected President of the Association, which office I continue."

Harriet Jacobs, author of *Incidents in the Life of a Slave Girl,* also raised money and supplies for the people in contraband camps. She went personally to Washington, D.C., and Alexandria, Virginia, with her daughter Louisa to work with the people of the camps there. When they arrived in early 1862, they found four hundred people living in crowded barracks. By 1863, there were ten thousand refugees in Washington and three thousand more in Alexandria. The Jacobses did what they could to provide much needed medical care and the basics of subsistence, such as clothing and bed linens. Harriet Jacobs also used her considerable talents as a writer to report conditions in the camps to Northern sympathizers. William Lloyd Garrison published her letters in the *Liberator.*

> I went to Duff Green's Row, Government headquarters for the contrabands here. I found men, women and children all huddled together without any distinction or regard to age or sex. Some of them were in most pitiable condition. Many were sick with measles, diptheria, scarlet and typhoid fever. Some had a few filthy rags to lie on, others had nothing but the bare floor for a couch. . . .
>
> Some of them have been so degraded by slavery that they do not know the usages of civilized life; they know little else than the handle of the hoe, the plough, the cotton-pod and the overseer's lash. Have patience with them. You have helped to make them what they are; teach them civilization. You owe it to them and you will find them as apt to learn as any other people that come to you stupid from oppression.

When white teachers tried to take over a school built by freedmen, Jacobs stepped in. She went to a meeting of the trustees of the school and asked that her daughter Louisa and another black teacher, Miss Lawton, be put in charge. "After this discussion," she wrote to a friend, "the poor people were tormented. First one then another [white person] would offer to take the school telling them they could not claim the Building unless a white man controlled the school. I went with the trustees to the proper authorities, and their lease for the ground on which the building was erected secured to them for five years." She went on to explain that she did not "object to white teachers but I think it has a good effect upon these people to convince them their own race can do something for their elevation. It inspires them with confidence to help each other."

One of the primary worries of the North was that England would weigh in on the side of the Confederacy in order to protect their interests in Southern cotton. It was clear that the strongest argument against their intervention was the moral one that slavery was an abhorrent institution. As a result, a determined effort was made to influence public opinion in Britain. Sarah Parker Remond was one of the most effective of those who waged this public relations war. When war was declared in the states, Remond realized that her antislavery lectures in Britain were more important than ever. She remained in that country throughout the war. Her primary goals were to sway public opinion to support the Union blockade of the Confederate states and to raise funds to aid newly freed African Americans, an effort she continued after the war.

Other black women spent the war teaching, preparing former slaves for their new life as free people. Young women who had entered teaching because they believed it was the "salvation of the race" were inspired to test their belief under the most difficult circumstances. They came into Southern areas in the wake of the Union troops, armed for their own battle with primers and Bibles. Mary Smith Kelsey Peake was born in Norfolk, Virginia, in 1823, the daughter of a white father and a free black mother. Her parents were unable, under Virginia law, to marry. Mary was educated in Alexandria, Virginia, where she lived with an aunt until she was sixteen. Eight years later, she moved with her mother and a new stepfather to Hampton. She worked as a seamstress and founded a mutual benefit society called the Daughters of Benevolence. She married Thomas Peake and took her place in the elite black society of the city. In secret, she taught slaves and free African Americans to read.

In the first months of the Civil War, Confederate soldiers set fire to homes in Hampton in retaliation for the Union sympathies of black citizens. Thomas and Mary Peake lost their house and fled to Fort Monroe. There, in September 1861, as soon as Confederate forces left Hampton, Mary Peake's teaching went public. She opened a school that was officially sanctioned by

Union officers at Fort Monroe. Soon she was teaching more than fifty students during the day and twenty adults in the evening. One of the first teachers to be supported by the American Missionary Association, she died of tuberculosis less than a year later, still teaching from her bed.

Many other black women taught before and during the Civil War, moving from secret schools in back rooms to school buildings bought and paid for by former slaves. Some, like Mary Peake, received help from the AMA or the federal government. Others were paid in corn and eggs by the parents of their students. A number of black teachers were involved in one of the most interesting episodes in the war.

THE PORT ROYAL EXPERIMENT

The Civil War engendered a number of experiments in which myths and stereotypes about African Americans were tested. One myth was that black people would not work on their own, that they needed force and coercion or, at best, the guiding hand of a white supervisor. The Port Royal experiment offered a graphic illustration of black self-determination and longing for economic autonomy. It also occasioned a historically important action on the part of black women as laborers.

When Northern troops expelled the Confederate army from the South Carolina Sea Islands in the spring of 1862, the Southern planters who lived there abandoned their homes and plantations, leaving behind a highly valuable cotton crop and several thousand formerly enslaved workers. Secretary of the Treasury Salmon Chase conceived the notion that these workers could prepare for their future life and, at the same time, save the crop. The federal government sent agricultural supervisors to the islands to work with the former slaves and teachers to provide them with needed education. The government was following in the footsteps of a young abolitionist named Edward S. Philbrick, who had conceived a simple idea—growing cotton with free laborers rather than slaves. Conventional wisdom had always had it that such a radical approach would be unprofitable at best and financially disastrous at worst. But no one had ever really tried.

Philbrick gathered a group of Northern investors and bought one of many plantations in the South Carolina Sea Islands that had been abandoned by their owners. Then he hired former slaves who had been left behind by the planters to raise cotton, paying them by the bale. Each family of workers was also allotted a garden space to use however it liked. Most used their spaces to grow produce to eat and sell. In his first year, 1862, Philbrick made a profit of $5,000, only a third of what he expected to make. In the second year, however, there was a net profit of $80,000. The experiment had obviously been a financial success.

In the opinion of some of the workers, though, it had been too much of a success for Philbrick and not enough for themselves. Harriet Ware, who witnessed the confrontation, wrote, "The women came up in a body to complain to Mr. Philbrick about their pay—a thing which has never happened before and shows the influence of very injudicious outside talk, which has poisoned their minds against their truest friends. The best people were among them, and even old Grace chief spokeswoman." Some time later, Philbrick was again confronted by "old Grace" and her delegation of women.

I'se been working for owner three years, and made with my children two bales cotton last year, two more this year. I'se a flat-footed person and don't know much, but I knows those two bales cotton fetch enough money, and I don't see what I'se got for them. When I take my little bit of money and go to the store, buy cloth, find it so dear, dear Jesus!—the money all gone and leave children naked. Some people go out yonder and plant cotton for theyself. Now they get big piles of money for they cotton, and leave we people way back. That's what I'se looking on. . . .

This may have been the first time in the history of the American South that free African Americans attempted to negotiate wages and working conditions with a white employer. They were unsuccessful, but they had served notice that times had changed and that the people intended to change with them.

Another aspect of the government's "social experiment" at Port Royal was education, and a number of white teachers were brought from the North to teach. The first black teacher sent to the Sea Islands was Charlotte Forten, granddaughter of Charlotte and James Forten, two of Philadelphia's most prominent black citizens. Her grandmother, three aunts, and mother had all been founding members of the Philadelphia Female Anti-Slavery Society. Charlotte, educated by tutors in her home and then at the integrated public schools of Salem, Massachusetts, became a deeply sensitive young woman, often melancholy and intensely aware of the limitations her race would put on her acceptance as a serious literary person. She turned to the struggle for freedom as an outlet for her feelings and her talents.

After graduating from Salem Normal School, Forten took a job teaching in Salem. She was the first black teacher of white students in that city. Although health problems interfered, she continued to teach for the next several years, but she was not satisfied. She wanted a more active role in the struggle for freedom. It was at the suggestion of poet John Greenleaf Whittier that she took on the work in the Sea Islands. Charlotte Forten was hired for the project and worked alongside Laura M. Towne and Ellen Murray, two Philadelphia teachers. In a school in the Central Baptist Church on St. Helena Island, the three women worked literally day and night. During the day, almost one hundred children attended classes where they learned reading, writing, spelling, history, and mathematics. Then, in the evenings, adults who had worked all day came in for tutoring in reading and spelling.

In her diary Forten recorded her feelings. "Thursday, Nov. 13 . . . Talked to the children a little while to-day about the noble Toussaint [L'Ouverture]. They listened very attentively. It is well that they sh'ld know what one of their own color c'ld do for his race. I long to inspire them with courage and ambition (of a noble sort), and high purpose. . . . This eve, Harry, one of the men on the place, came in for a lesson. He is most eager to learn, and is really a scholar to be proud of. He learns rapidly. I gave him his first lesson in writing to-night, and his progress is wonderful."

Forten wrote an account of her work, "Life on the Sea Islands," that was published in two parts in the *Atlantic Monthly* in May and June of 1864. It told of a newly liberated people who were ready for education and work and all that freedom could bring them. For most African Americans in the South at this time, the picture was very different.

LEFT BEHIND

Every soldier's family, black or white, lived in sorrow and fear. They prayed, they hoped, and they waited for the news they feared—that the men they loved would not come home. The terrible casualty rate of the Civil War meant that that news would come for hundreds of thousands. For the families of formerly enslaved soldiers, however, there was another concern, and it was a critical one. Families left behind were usually in desperate straits. On the reduced wages of a black soldier, wives could not support their families. In the South, still enslaved wives of men who escaped and joined the Union army were subject to vengeful actions on the part of slaveholders. Some of the homes where they waited were slave quarters on

Southern plantations, in the very heart of enemy territory. And some had no homes at all in which to wait.

There were also thousands of marriages among former slaves who served in the army. For many, legal marriage was only a confirmation of the vows they had made to each other while enslaved. Army chaplains performed marriages for a multitude of African Americans who had lived as committed couples for years. Indeed, the army demanded that marriages be legalized before it would recognize them, regardless of how long a man and woman had thought of themselves as husband and wife and fulfilled the obligations of that state. Only if a couple were legally married would the woman and any children be allowed to live near the camp. And then, as the war progressed, even that sanction was withdrawn.

One of the most terrible and fiercely resented aspects of slave life was the separation of families. To have white people—in the shape of army officers—separating them again was a dreadful thing for former slaves. It called into question the very idea that they were free. And yet, when U.S. officials began instituting programs for women, children, and men unfit to serve in late 1862, women were often forced to leave the cities where their husbands, legal or not, were stationed. The reason given was that they interfered with military procedure. In one city—Natchez, Mississippi—the excuse was the public health.

"It is to be apprehended," said the announcement of Major A. W. Kelly, the titular health officer of the troops stationed in Natchez, "that serious danger to the health of this City will result from the congregation within its limits of the large number of *idle* negroes which now throng the streets, lanes and alleys, and over-crowd every hovel. . . . To prevent these evil effects it is *hereby ordered* that after the first day of April, 1864, no contraband shall be allowed to remain in the city of Natchez, who is not employed by some *responsible white person. . . .*" The term "contraband" was defined in the order as "all persons formerly slaves who are not now in the employ of their former owners." Hundreds of people were expelled from the city, including many who had lived there for decades and were self-supporting. A group of black residents protested.

NATCHEZ, Miss., April 1, 1864

General Tuttle:

SIR: The undersigned citizens of Natchez would respectfully ask you to modify the recent order of the Health Officer of this city. . . . It certainly cannot be the interest or policy of the Government of the United States at this time to alienate the colored people from it and make them its enemies. The colored soldier in the field hearing that his mother or his wife has been driven from her quiet and comfortable home, simply because she supported herself and was not dependent upon some white person, may feel less inclined to hazard his life in the cause of his country. . . .

In the execution of the order referred to, the most flagrant wrongs have been inflicted upon the better class of the freed people. An old woman who has lived fifty years in this city, and was not disturbed before, was driven at the point of the bayonet to the camp. Mothers . . . having young infants and attending to lawful business were arrested, and were not allowed to see their babes. . . . Many others who had paid their taxes and rents in advance, and who had official and personal security of protection and safety, were suddenly turned out of their neat and comfortable houses, without any time allowed them to arrange their affairs, and driven away to the camp, without shelter or clothing for the night.

The litany of abuses went on. Women and children who were not herded into contraband camps were sometimes taken to abandoned plantations and set to work raising cotton. They received minimal wages—out of which they were expected to buy food—or no wages at all. In some cases, they were required to carry passes if they left their plantations. And, again, they were vulnerable to raids by Confederates intent on reenslaving them.

Separation from families. Picking cotton. Little or no wage. Restricted movement. The situation of the "contraband" women was hauntingly similar to the slavery they had left behind. For the wives of other black soldiers—those who still lived in Southern states—slavery was exactly what they continued to face every day. Life was enormously difficult and it only grew worse. Those who remained behind included a disproportionate number of women and children, especially later in the war, when Union policies about black troops had changed. The women and children were forced to do work that was often beyond their capacity. There was seldom enough to eat. In addition, soldiers from both armies raided plantations for food, leaving more hunger behind them.

When Union soldiers came looking for grain and livestock, enslaved people were caught on the horns of a dilemma. If they did not cooperate, the soldiers were quite capable of treating them harshly. If they did help the Union army, their owners were likely to punish them after the soldiers were gone. When Union soldiers took food and destroyed food stores, knowing the hardship it would cause, enslaved Americans became confused in their loyalties. When the soldiers did worse—and they did far worse—slaves saw little difference between Yankees and the Southern whites they had always known. They had been told that the war was being fought to free them and that Union soldiers were their saviors. This was not the way saviors should behave.

"[O]ne day I was in the field working, the Yankee soldiers was marching, about six of them stopped and took a razor blade and cut off my hair," Mildred Graves recalled. "I had long black hair that hung way down my back. I kicked and fit as much as I could, but I couldn't stop them." Another time, Graves went on, "it was a Sunday afternoon and five of us colored girls was walking out, some Yankees stopped us and took razors and cut us on our arms, legs and on our backs." Other enslaved women told of Union soldiers who stole livestock not only from white planters but from poor black families or who sexually abused black women.

Not all experiences with Yankee soldiers were negative, of course. Many fought out of antislavery conviction. More were seeing a way of life they had never witnessed before and were sympathetic to its victims. During an FWP interview, Eliza Sparks remembered Yankee kindness. After she had given directions to a lost soldier, he gave her some money and asked her child's name. She told him it was Charlie Sparks. "Well, you sure have a pretty baby," the soldier said. "Buy him something with this; and thank you for the directions. Goodbye Mrs. Sparks." No one had ever called her "Mrs." before, and Sparks remembered it the rest of her life.

If African Americans were sometimes puzzled by the Yankees, they were seldom confused about slavery itself. They fervently believed that freedom was near, and their belief was translated into action. Slavery had always existed only so far as it could be enforced. As soon as enslaved women and men saw that the power of slave owners had been diminished by the war, they began to exercise the freedom that they knew was inherently theirs. On some plantations slaves refused to work or caused as much trouble as they could. According to historian Catherine Clinton, "Most slaves stayed behind—recalcitrant, rebellious, and, in the end, an effective fifth column. Historians suggest that the failure of nerve and the failure of rule in the plantation South undermined Confederate independence. And they document women's roles in disrupting plantation work patterns and, in some cases, initiating work stoppages or strikes in the fields. These and other activities by black women behind the lines disheartened plantation mistresses, at the least. At the most, they prevented the plantation owners from maintaining discipline and productivity at a time when continued productivity was crucial to Confederate success."

In the North, things were not much better for those left behind. And on some occasions, they were worse. As the war changed focus, becoming more clearly a war against slavery, hostility increased among whites in the North. The ground was fertile for bitterness. Tens of thousands of men were dying on the battlefields, more than anyone could possibly have imagined. It sometimes seemed as though no able-bodied man would be left alive at the end of the war. If the war ever ended. And what were all these men dying for? The answer to that question was the crux of the problem.

Black Americans, while they could vote in some states and serve on juries, were getting poorer and poorer. Their position in Northern society was becoming more and more marginal. Afraid of competition for "white jobs," the Illinois legislature passed a law in 1862 barring black immigration into the state. Other Northern legislatures considered such legislation. Even most Northerners who opposed slavery did not see African Americans as equal and valued members of the community, as people worth fighting and dying for. Starting as far back as 1829 there were race riots in a number of Northern cities. In Detroit, for example, rioting broke out on March 6, 1863. The alleged cause of the riots was the attack on two young girls—one white and one black—by a black man named Thomas Faulkner. In fact, Faulkner happened to be white. But his crime and his supposed race were the justification for a vicious attack on the black citizens of Detroit.

However, racial animosity did not reach its peak until the antislavery focus of the war intensified. At the same time, the federal government instituted a draft law with one very disturbing provision. Any man who could afford it could pay $300 for a substitute draftee. Men of the working class were unable to pay, of course, and so they were unfairly and disproportionately subject to the draft. Their anger was quickly turned against the people they saw as the cause of the war—African Americans. On Saturday, July 11, 1863, the first draft lottery was held. In New York the next day, the newspapers printed the 1,236 names of local men chosen in the lottery. Resentment began to build. As it was Sunday, people around the city had all day to get drunk and get angry. Before dawn on Monday, five hundred of them marched toward the draft office.

Police were outnumbered and the state militia was off fighting the war. The protesters made their way virtually unchecked into midtown Manhattan. They broke into the draft board office, destroyed files, and burned the building. And then the riot began. It was the worst in New York history, an infamous title that still stands. A witness later wrote that First Avenue was filled with "thousands of infuriated creatures, yelling, screaming and swearing in the most frantic manner. . . . Up came fresh hordes faster and more furious; bare-headed men, with red, swollen faces, brandishing sticks and clubs or carrying heavy poles and beams; and boys, women and children hurrying on and joining with them in this mad chase up the avenue like a company of raging fiends."

The riot tore through the black community like a tornado of hatred. African Americans were killed and beaten, their homes destroyed. The sixty thousand rioters even attacked the Colored Orphan Asylum on Fifth Avenue. Fortunately, the orphanage's administrator was able to get the 237 children out, because the mob set the building on fire. When the fire department arrived to put out the fire, the mob slashed their hoses.

Listen to fifteen-year-old Maritcha Lyons's description of the riot. Her family lived in Brooklyn.

> On the afternoon of July [13th] a rabble attacked our house, breaking windowpanes, smashing shutters and partially demolishing the front door. Before dusk arrangements had been effected to secure the safety of the children. As the evening drew on, a resolute man and a courageous woman quietly seated themselves in the hall, determined to sell their lives as dearly as may be. Just after midnight a second mob was gathering. As one of the rioters attempted to ascend the front steps, father advanced into the doorway and fired point blank into the crowd. The mob retreated and no further demonstration was made that night. The next day a third and successful attempt at entrance was effected. This sent father over the back fence while mother took refuge on the premises of a neighbor.
>
> In one short hour, the police cleared the premises. What a home! Its interior was dismantled, furniture was missing or broken. From basement to attic evidences of vandalism prevailed. A fire, kindled in one of the upper rooms, was discovered in time to prevent a conflagration. Under cover of darkness the police conveyed our parents to the Williamsburg ferry. Mother with her children undertook the hazardous journey to New England. We reached Salem tired, travel-stained, with only the garments we had on.

Everything the family owned, including Mr. Lyons's business, was destroyed. They were, compared with others in the city, relatively fortunate. Others were killed, beaten, or raped. Hundreds were homeless. There was an investigation, but no one was indicted.

What happened next was a kind of turning point. City officials rallied behind black citizens. They immediately began to raise money for the riot victims. They petitioned the War Department for authorization to raise a black regiment. According to Sterling, "Eight months after the riot, the Twentieth Regiment U.S. Colored Troops marched down Broadway to Union Square, and whites as well as blacks lined the streets to wave handkerchiefs and cheer. 'There has been no more striking manifestation of the marvelous times that are upon us than the scene at the departure of the first of our colored regiments,' said a *New York Times* editorial. 'It is only on such occasions that we can realize the prodigious revolution which the public mind everywhere is experiencing.' "

The *Times* was overly optimistic, although the phenomenon it noted was real, and the hostility of Northern whites was further mitigated by the courage and sacrifice of these African American soldiers. Still, the war continued to churn up a complex brew of emotions and attitudes concerning slavery and race. It was never entirely clear whether allies were friends and whether enemies were those most to be feared. While the war was raging, black Americans could focus on victory and freedom, but in their hearts they must have wondered what would happen, how much would really change, after the war.

GOING ON

After the war. Those were words to conjure with. The Emancipation Proclamation had declared that Southern slaves were free forever, but a victory by the Confederacy would have wiped out all thoughts of freedom for any black person within its borders. It was not until Robert E. Lee surrendered at Appomattox on April 9, 1865, that the dream became a reality.

The reality, however, was not what anyone had hoped. The most difficult transition in our nation's history, one that would have taxed the intellectual powers of political scientists, sociologists, philosophers, and Solomon himself, was instead shaped by accident and assassination. It was designed by ignorance, hatred, and bitter resentment on one side and self-interest on the other. The North vastly underestimated the magnitude of the task and overestimated their own capacity for patience and sacrifice.

Through this maze of calamity, black women made their way. Daily life changed far too little for most of them. Their new resources were seldom better than their old. Their freedom was severely limited. And yet, in the first decade after the war, there emerged the first black woman lawyer, doctor, and sculptor. Two black women pioneered what would become the black theater. Black churches sprang up like mushrooms. And a generation of black children—along with an astounding number of adults—gained the basic skills of literacy. In the words of Susie Baker King Taylor, "A new life was before us now, all the old life left behind."

I heard [my grandmother] say some people came early one morning and said they

[the slaves] were free. Some cried, but my big mom just called her whole family

together and walked away. My great aunt said that by noon my grandmother had

found work for herself and had a shed for everybody in the family to live in.

She'd say, "Freedom never scared a colored person—that's one lie told."

ELIZABETH CLARK-LEWIS,

LIVING IN, LIVING OUT

FREE WOMEN
IN SEARCH OF FREEDOM

CHAPTER SIX

RACE IS ONE of the central issues of American history. It is probably not too much to say that, in the nineteenth century, it was *the* central issue. The great congressional battles were fought over slavery. Political careers were made or destroyed over it. And then, in a final, terrible attempt to resolve the issue forever, the nation split and fought a bloody civil war, the only one in its history. And when it was over, race remained the central issue in American life.

For black Americans, freedom was glory. It was the long awaited, the fervently desired, the fulfillment of dreams. But it turned out that emancipation was only the first step on the road to freedom, not the last, and the obstacles along the way would be formidable. The liberal and sympathetic North was easily tired and not prepared to commit the tremendous resources that would be necessary to complete the job. The slaveholding South was not prepared, even in defeat, to give up its death grip on the black labor force. Reconstruction politics, under the leadership of Charles Sumner and Thaddeus Stevens, gave with one hand what the Ku Klux Klan would take away with another.

Through all of this, black Americans had three goals—to find their family members and reestablish their families; to make a living; and to live, as far as possible, lives that did not resemble slavery. They were fervent in their pursuit of all three. None of these goals turned out to be easy to attain, but this, in the minds of black women and men, was what it meant to be free.

Others were not so clear about what freedom meant for black Americans. When the Civil War ended, no one really knew what to do with several million former slaves, although many white southerners knew what they *wanted* to do with them. Abraham Lincoln considered deporting them. He even asked one of his generals to look into the logistics of the situation. The general reported back that it would be infeasible. No one will ever know what Lincoln would finally have decided. Symbolic of so many horribly charged issues, he became the first American president to be assassinated. Black America hugely mourned the emancipator's death and waited with trepidation to see what his successor would do.

President Andrew Johnson, himself a former slaveholder, seemed to be of the opinion that the fate of black people in the South was of little importance compared to that of white people. He would doubtless have been willing for former slaves to live free and happy lives, but he was completely unwilling for their former masters to suffer any inconvenience to make that possibility a reality. He was determined that all plantations would be returned to their former owners and all offices should be filled by white officeholders. Beyond that, he was willing to be cooperative.

White southerners, of course, believed that black people should remain slaves in all but name, working in the fields as always and in the kitchens as usual. They even enacted laws, called Black Codes, to try to enforce this condition. In 1865 and 1866, for example, the provisional government appointed by President Johnson passed laws in South Carolina that prohibited freedmen from working in any occupations except farming and menial service and gave "masters" the right to whip servants under the age of eighteen. In Mississippi, a law passed in November of 1865 compelled African Americans to have jobs by the second Monday in January of 1866. Black Americans, in various states, could be jailed or otherwise punished for "insulting gestures" or quitting their jobs. In Alabama, an African American who attended a meeting after work could be fined $50 and, if unable to pay, could be sentenced to work without pay for up to six months. In Florida a black person found with any kind of weapon could be whipped thirty-nine lashes on the bare back.

In the words of Union General Carl Schurz, "although the freedman is no longer considered the property of the individual master, he is considered the slave of society. . . . Wherever I go—the street, the shop, the house, the hotel, or the steamboat—I hear the people talk in such a way as to indicate that they are yet unable to conceive of the Negro as possessing any rights at all." This was not simple racism. Enslaved Americans were the South's workers. Their labor had built the southern agricultural economy and their labor was necessary to maintain it. Some former slaveholders simply refused to tell their slaves that they were free. Others took advantage of the poverty and fear of their laborers to keep them in virtual slavery.

Frederick Douglass had a radical approach to the problem of what to do with the black man. "If you see him plowing the open field, leveling the forest, at work with a spade, a rake, a hoe, a pick-axe, or a bill—let him alone; he has a right to work. If you see him on his way to school, with spelling book, geography and arithmetic in his hands—let him alone. . . . If he has a ballot in his hand, and is on his way to the ballot-box to deposit his vote for the man whom he thinks will most justly and wisely administer the Government which has the power of life and death over him, as well as others—let him *alone*."

While white America debated about what to do with them, black women and men went about trying to construct lives, to construct freedom.

Gathering the Fold

The first summer of freedom was a time of searching. Black women traveled from town to town, from farm to plantation, looking for their children. "They had a passion," said one officer of the newly formed Freedmen's Bureau, "not so much for wandering as for getting together. Every mother's son seemed to be in search of his mother; every mother in search of her children." If word came through the grapevine that a daughter—sold off at ten or twelve—was working on a farm sixty miles away, her mother would begin walking and would not stop until she stood at the gate of that farm with her daughter in her arms. Black men, too, searched for and found their wives and children.

Putting the family back together was not always an easy thing to do. Just finding children who had been sold away years before was a daunting task. Even when a child's location was known or discovered, there were obstacles to be faced. Getting back to a plantation she had left, for whatever reason, was often difficult, painful, and frightening for a mother. And securing the children was not always easy. In *Memories of Childhood's Slavery Days*, Annie Burton tells of the day her mother came to take her away from their former owner. Her mother had escaped from the plantation three years before. When the war ended, she came back to claim her children. Her husband had died a short time before.

> My mother came for us at the end of the year 1865, and demanded that her children be given up to her. This, mistress refused to do, and threatened to set the dogs on my mother if she did not at once leave the place. My mother went away, remained with some of the neighbors until supper time. Then she got a boy to tell [my sister] Caroline to come down to the fence. When she came, my mother told her to go back and get Henry and myself as quick as she could. Then my mother took Henry in her arms, and my sister carried me on her back. We climbed fences and crossed fields, and after several hours came to a little hut which my mother had secured on a plantation. We had no more than reached the place, and made a little fire, when master's two sons rode up and demanded that the children be returned. My mother refused to give us up. Upon her offering to go with them to the Yankee headquarters to find out if it were really true that all negroes had been made free, the young men left, and troubled us no more.

Other mothers were not so fortunate. Although enslaved Americans were now free by law, they were living among white people who did not accept that law and, indeed, were determined to keep things just as they had always been.

In anticipation of the war's outcome, many slaveholders had drawn up apprenticeship agreements binding their young slaves to them before the war ended. The courts usually upheld these agreements. In addition, children could be made apprentices against their will and that of their parents if a white farmer or plantation owner claimed that it was in the child's best interests. This was virtual slavery, and it was painfully frequent. In Kent County, Maryland, alone, 130 slave children were apprenticed by late November of 1865. The parents of 102 of the children protested the actions of the court, but their protests were usually futile.

Parents did not give up easily, though. Some worked and struggled for years to recover their children and consolidate their families. All too often the struggle had to be carried on by a woman alone. Many black women had lost their husbands in the war. Others had been separated from the fathers of their children a decade before the war ended and had no hopes of finding the men again. Still others knew that the husbands sold away from them had been forced to remarry or, in some cases, had chosen to do so. Sometimes the women themselves had remarried and now faced first husbands with the children of their successors. The challenge for former slaves was often not so much rebuilding families as creating them. The fact that African Americans were able to put their families together as well as they did is a tribute to the abiding respect for family in the culture. In every state, tens of thousands of couples legalized the marriages they had committed themselves to during slavery. These couples, along with the multitude of solitary women, gathered their children together as well as they could and began to build new lives.

Economically, that was no easy task. At no time during the ten years of Reconstruction or in the decades that followed did the federal government or anyone else "reconstruct" the economy of the South to accommodate the millions of recently freed people. Promises were made and broken. A "welfare" program called the Freedmen's Bureau was established to try to keep mouths fed and bodies together with souls. But no effort was made to provide what those former slaves needed more than anything—a decent, honest way to make a living.

The only jobs that were available in a South devastated by war were the jobs black Americans had held in slavery. There would be a difference, of course. Now, they would receive wages. They would provide their own food and clothing. They would not be subject to every whim or perverse urge of their master's. It would not be the same as slavery. It would, however, be damned close, and for most African Americans, it would be too close. Freedom was a desperately desired, long-awaited prize. Black people wanted not only to know that they were free, but to feel it. And so they tried, in every way they could, to forge lives that were different from slavery. That is one of the important reasons that sharecropping, with all its drawbacks, became the chosen way of life for southern African Americans.

SHARECROPPING

Recently freed Americans, along with most rural Americans of the time, dreamed of owning their own land and farming it with their families. But white southerners were almost universally unwilling to sell land to their former slaves. The American idyll was closed to most black people, and so they took the closest they could get. They farmed, as a family, land that belonged to someone else, in exchange for part of the crop.

Since the advantages of this way of life were not financial, many pragmatic northern sympathizers were frustrated by it. Neo-abolitionists, following the war, tried very hard to turn former slaves into exemplary workers on the northern model—people who held down reasonably well-paying jobs and worked to get ahead, and who turned over virtually all control of working conditions to their employers. However, since the South was an agricultural region, holding down a job meant working on a gang in the fields, under the supervision of an overseer. That was too strong an echo of slavery for African Americans. Virtually every black male wanted to "be his own man." Virtually every black wife wanted to work only after she had fulfilled her domestic responsibilities. The sharecropping system came much closer to filling those needs.

Black women were central to this decision. They and their husbands wanted certain things for them, certain *differences* from slavery. First, they wanted never again to be forced out of their homes before dawn, leaving behind children too small to take care of themselves and housework that would never get done. Second, they wanted never again to work under the supervision of white men who might physically or sexually abuse them. Third, they wanted to be seen as women, not workhorses. They were willing to pay a high price for these things, so crucial to the sense of freedom.

Part of the price was enormously long hours, for black women ended up working in the fields when they were needed—as they often were—in addition to their work at home. Another price was the disdain of most of white society. Both southern landowners and northern reformers considered the desire of black women to work at home rather than in the fields to be evidence of laziness, and they were outraged by it. Southerners saw it as "acting the lady," since no black woman could actually *be* a lady in their eyes. Black women should do one thing and one thing only—work for white people. Northern neo-abolitionists were almost equally appalled. They believed strongly that good, honest work was both an evidence and a guarantor of morality.

Even when a family was sharecropping, the landowner would often try to force women and children into the fields so that more work would be done and a larger crop raised. He would insist that women and children could not live in the house that was provided with the sharecrop if they did not work. Black families tried to hold out against this coercion, but it was not always possible. It was far too easy to throw a family off a sharecrop. Nonetheless, black families did everything they could to keep women and girls out of the fields as much as was humanly possible. According to the 1870 census, only 40 percent of black wives in the Cotton Belt reported "field laborer" as their occupation. (Among white women, 98.4 percent said that they were "keeping house.") Given the situation, it was remarkable that more than half of all black married women did *not* work in the fields.

Of course, the assumption that census workers were told the truth is probably an unwarranted one. When one woman interviewed by historian Elizabeth Clark-Lewis was told that the census records had her own mother "keeping house," she replied, "Who'd tell them Cooks Mill people what anybody really did? Not us who'd know. Or maybe my daddy did, and he'd say that knowing different, I guess." Another woman, when told the same about her mother, said, "Is that what those papers says? Oh, I guess that record said right. Keeping house . . . 'tis true. But they didn't ask *whose* house she was keeping. I guess they need to ask 'where do you keep house?' Then they'd heard 'for Miss Neill, Miss Campbell, the Ricks or the Dickersons.'" Many black women did domestic work to help supplement the painfully little made by farming. Over the years, this became more and more common, until virtually every black girl-child, except for the most affluent, knew that at some time or another she would be cleaning house for white folks.

There were few white Americans who concerned themselves with this gradual slide back into slavery. Two men who did were Charles Sumner and

Thaddeus Stevens, the prime movers of the Reconstruction. If their ideas had been fully implemented, instead of being adopted piecemeal and with enormous reluctance, the history of the South and of the United States would have been very different.

RECONSTRUCTION

Representative Thaddeus Stevens was a lawyer from Philadelphia who had often defended runaway slaves in the days before emancipation. He proposed to Congress that large plantations, which had been legally forfeited by the owners under the Confiscations Acts during the war, should be divided into forty-acre lots and distributed to the recently freed, but Congress refused. Indeed, federal officials went to South Carolina, where former slaves had actually been given temporary title to land during the war, and *took it back*. It was restored to its slaveholding, Union-opposing, treasonous former owners. Senator Charles Sumner supported Stevens's efforts to provide the recently freed with land. When that failed, the two men continued their efforts on behalf of African Americans in the South. Eventually, they began to make progress among those in Congress who mistrusted former Confederates or who wanted to keep the Republican party in power.

Sumner and Stevens and their congressional allies were perversely helped in their efforts by the white South itself. In the two years since the end of the war, southern efforts to keep former slaves in their place had involved armed violence, mass murder, beatings, and rape. Police and government officials staged phony riots in which hundreds of the recently freed were killed. When northern politicians and voters heard about these police-directed riots in which black Union veterans were slaughtered, black women were raped, and black churches were burned, they began to lose faith in the ability of the white South to assimilate their former slaves into society peacefully.

In 1867, Stevens managed to gain control of Reconstruction efforts. The South was placed under military control, and new elections were held. The word "harsh" is often used to refer to Reconstruction laws, but it takes only a few examples of what black Americans were up against to see that "harshness" was called for. When elections were held to choose delegates to the Alabama constitutional convention, for example, former slave James Alston was elected along with four other black men. Not long after, his house was surrounded in the night by armed men. In minutes, 265 shots were fired into the house. Two of them hit Alston, and the night riders left him for dead. He wasn't. Alston then received a warning to leave town. When he didn't, his house was again attacked. Alston escaped and managed to make his way to the Alabama constitutional convention. He was the only black man there. The other four were dead.

Officially, Reconstruction lasted ten years, from 1867 to 1877. During that time, there were both positive and sinister developments. The Ku Klux Klan held its first meeting and, along with hundreds of other secret organizations, began their campaign of terrorism. All during Reconstruction, night riders haunted the countryside. There was not a month, week, or day when black Americans were not intimidated, harassed, and killed to prevent them from exercising their rights. But also during this time, the Thirteenth, Fourteenth, and Fifteenth Amendments were passed, and black Americans enjoyed a degree of political power and self-determination they had not known before and have not known since. Black men were able to vote for the first time. There were black representatives in all southern legislatures. There were black lieutenant governors, treasurers, and secretaries of states.

There was even a political salon, under the gracious auspices of the Rollin sisters of South Carolina. A reporter for the *New York Herald* described them in extravagant terms. "[In] periods of transition and choosing, as, for instance, during the French and our own Revolutions, and as in the case of the late Paris Commune, women of tact, pluck, education and experience have always governed masses of men. France had her Madame de Tencin, Madame du Deffon, Madame de Genlis, her Theresa Cabarrus and her Madame Roland. . . . And South Carolina is not to-day without her feminine celebrities, albeit they may not be of the orthodox and Caucasian shade of skin."

There is no doubt, from all reports and descriptions, that the Rollin sisters—Frances Anne, Charlotte (Lottie), Kate, Louisa, and Florence—were beautiful and well educated. Their father owned a successful lumberyard, enabling them to go to Charleston's Catholic schools and then, for finishing, to schools in Boston and Philadelphia. The Rollin family moved to Columbia, South Carolina, after the war, and the young women became forces in Reconstruction politics. Their home was the place for political figures, black and white, to be seen and to make contacts. Frances married state senator and future judge William J. Whipper. Kate was engaged to marry a white state senator but died when she was only twenty-five. However, their involvement in political activities was not merely social. They wielded considerable power, largely because of their intelligence and knowledge. They were not just pretty faces.

Frances was the author of a biography of Martin R. Delany, famed abolitionist and emigrationist. She also taught on the Sea Islands during the war. She was her husband's law clerk before they were married. After marriage, she taught at Avery Institute. Louisa was a strong feminist and, in 1869, addressed the South Carolina House of Representatives on behalf of universal suffrage. Lottie Rollin was elected secretary of the South Carolina Woman's Rights Association, an affiliate of the American Woman Suffrage Association (AWSA). In 1871, she chaired a meeting at the state capital to promote women's suffrage. In 1872, she was elected to represent South Carolina as an ex-officio member of the executive committee for the AWSA.

These members of the black elite were not the only black women who held political opinions or affected the political lives of their communities. In March of 1867, schoolteacher and former slave Isabella Gibbins expressed herself about the hypocrisy of the South and its politicians. She left no doubt whatsoever about her incredulity and scorn. She also left no doubt that slavery had not crushed her spirit or diminished her intelligence.

> We have lived to see the fortieth Congress and to behold a change of affairs. The rebels begin to see the error of their way at last, and do all they can to better our race. They say, "the colored people are not only free but have a right to vote. Now let us be kind to them; they have been our slaves, and we must do something for them. It will not do to leave them to the care of those hated yankees. . . . They are a good people, and so fond of their old masters, they will do what we want they should. Most of them love us, and have forgotten what happened while they were slaves. They know we are their friends."
>
> This is a grand story for them to tell, but let us answer them. Can we forget the crack of the whip, cowhide, whipping post, the auction-block, the hand-cuffs, the spaniels, the iron collar, the negro-trader tearing the young child from its mother's breast as a whelp from the lioness? Have we forgotten that by those horrible cruelties, hundreds of our race have been killed? No, we have not, nor ever will.
>
> If the Northern people who have given their life's blood for our liberty are not our friends, where can we find them? O, God help us to love these people.

Virtually all of the political power that black women possessed during Reconstruction was behind the scenes, as it was for all women in the United States, of whatever color. But like the Rollin sisters, many black women fought hard to change that situation. Their desire to stand on a level of equality with men required them, in the years following the Civil War, to make some very difficult decisions and take some unpopular stands.

THE VOTE

Most abolitionists, black and white, agreed on one thing. Freedom, as poet Amiri Baraka would say a century later, "is like life. It cannot be had in installments." There could be no gradual emancipation, no small steps on the road to political equality. If a man was free, he was free. But what about a woman?

The Thirteenth Amendment to the U.S. Constitution prohibited slavery in 1865. Then the Fourteenth Amendment was passed in 1868, saying that no citizen could be denied the rights guaranteed by the constitution. Suddenly woman suffragists saw the opportunity to grasp justice. They declared that, as they were citizens of the United States, they could not be denied constitutional rights, including the right to vote. In an attempt to take their claim to the U.S. Supreme Court to be tested, several feminists attempted to vote in local elections. Susan B. Anthony went to the polls in New York State, Sojourner Truth in Michigan, and Mary Ann Shadd Cary in the District of Columbia.

When these attempts failed, many black and white feminists turned their attention to the proposed Fifteenth Amendment to the Constitution. The amendment guaranteed the right to vote to black men. These women insisted that it should also grant that right to black and white women. This demand created an uproar in the abolitionist movement. Many were outraged that women—of any race—should "stand in the way" of obtaining the vote for black men. Women should step back and wait their turn, lest they jeopardize the fate of men who so desperately needed political power. Frances Ellen Watkins Harper was an advocate for this point of view.

Sojourner Truth articulated the other point of view in a speech delivered in 1870. "There is a great stir about colored men getting their rights," she declared, "but not a word about the colored women; and if colored men get their rights, and not colored women get theirs, there will be a bad time about it. So I am for keeping the thing going while things are stirring; because if we wait til it is still, it will take a great while to get it going again."

This matter of priorities has come up again and again for black women, and it is not an easy one. It split the women's suffrage movement right down the middle in the nineteenth century. Those who fought to make the Fifteenth Amendment cover women as well as black men allied themselves with the National Woman Suffrage Association, which numbered among its members Sojourner Truth, Mary Ann Shadd Cary, Susan B. Anthony, and Harriet Forten Purvis. Those who discontinued their work for woman's suffrage until black male suffrage was won joined the American Woman Suffrage Association, which included Frances Harper, Caroline Remond Putnam, and Lottie Rollin, under the presidency of white abolitionist Henry Ward Beecher.

When the battle was over and the Fifteenth Amendment was passed in 1870, it declared that the right to vote could not be denied to any citizen on the basis of race, color, or previous condition of servitude. It did not mention gender. Black women had not been granted the vote along with their husbands and fathers. But they did manage to make their presence known.

One Man, One Vote

Political power was not viewed in the black community in exactly the same way that it was in white society. The difference involved the concept of family. A white family was in possession of one vote, that of the man, the husband and father. He decided, subject to whatever coaxing and cajoling his wife could get away with, how that vote would be cast. After the passage of the Fifteenth Amendment, a black family also had one vote. How *that* vote was cast, however, was decided by the entire family, communally. This view, put forward by historian Elsa Barkley Brown, explains many things that have baffled white historians, sociologists, and feminists for more than a century. To see how this difference operated in practice, it is only necessary to look at the postwar state constitutional conventions.

The Reconstruction Act of 1867 required that each formerly Confederate state hold a constitutional convention, at which black men had the right to vote for delegates and on ratification ballots. Each political party, in preparation for this convention, held its own. The Republican convention in Virginia opened in Richmond on August 1, 1867. On that day black men, women, and children abandoned all other pursuits and gathered at the convention site. According to Brown, tobacco factories were forced to shut down because most of their workers, male and female, were at the convention. This mass exodus from tobacco factories, fields, and white people's kitchens happened every time a particularly important issue was raised at the convention during the course of the summer. When the time came to vote for delegates to the larger convention, the *New York Times* reported that "the entire colored population of Richmond" was there to make its will known.

When the state convention was held, black Virginians again gathered *en masse*. Outside convention hours, the black community held mass meetings, attended by all ages and both genders, at which the issues of that day's deliberations would be discussed. There were even suggestions that the will of these meetings should be binding on black delegates. Although that did not happen, the meetings were enormously influential, as were the crowds of black women and men who gathered in the galleries during the day and participated vocally in debates.

After the constitutional conventions, when black men exercised their right to vote in state and federal elections, the participation of black women continued. They formed women's political organizations that campaigned for particular candidates, raised funds, and got out the vote. They wore campaign buttons that put them in danger of reprisals from the white community. They accompanied black men to the polls and to political meetings. One crucial role they played at these meetings was to guard the guns that were necessary to defend the delegates in case of white attack. They played a similar role on election day, accompanying men to the polls, according to a contemporary report, "in arms, carrying axes or hatchets in their hands hanging down at their sides, their aprons or dresses half-concealing the weapons."

This evidence of gender equality in the black community is something of which both black men and black women can be proud. And it may help to explain why so many black women activists were willing to put aside women's suffrage until the vote was secured for black men. They saw that vote as shared.

Many black women also acquired considerable influence in local politics because of their work in another area of life—education. As a result of southern laws and customs against teaching slaves to read and write, the vast majority of the newly freed were illiterate, unable to read contracts, deeds, and street signs, or even to sign their names. A number of organizations were formed to meet this need, the largest of which was the American

Missionary Association. The AMA sent more than five thousand teachers to the South between 1861 and 1876. The combined efforts of the other groups supported thousands more teachers, a great many of whom were black women. By 1868, fifteen black colleges had been chartered to train these teachers.

The undertaking would require women who were highly dedicated, strong in both mind and body and, most important of all, good at their jobs. There was not enough money in the world to recruit this kind of force. Fortunately for black Americans, money was not the highest priority among black women.

To Educate a Race

In an 1879 commencement address at the Institute for Colored Youth, educator Fanny Jackson Coppin told her graduating students, "You can do much to alleviate the condition of our people. Do not be discouraged. The very places where you are needed most are those where you will get least pay. Do not resign a position in the South which pays you $12 a month as a teacher for one in Pennsylvania which pays $50." She was speaking to young, educated women who had been brought up to believe that service to their people was the highest good. Most left behind comfortable homes, good prospects, and even love and marriage to fulfill what they believed was their duty and their destiny.

The task was daunting, and so were the conditions of their life as they undertook it. These northern women were often shocked by the poverty of the rural South. In a letter from James City, Virginia, a teacher wrote, "I am in the most convenient and comfortable dwelling there is in the neighborhood but that is not saying much, for the wind has free access to my room in spite of all my efforts to the contrary. I have 4 panes of glass in my sash which affords me sufficient light to write by in the daytime. I had to be very persevering or I should have had none. My room was the most forlorn looking place I ever saw for respectable people to live in, minus everything but dirt and something they nicknamed a bed."

The people of these communities, however, had a way of making up for the poverty of the surroundings. They were desperately hungry for learning, and they gave these black teachers respect that bordered on veneration. They also faced, with the teachers, the dangers that came with combining the words "black" and "education" in the South. A black schoolteacher from New York, Edmonia Highgate, gave a revealing description of life in rural Louisiana in a letter to a friend, dated December 17, 1866. "There has been much opposition to the School," she wrote. "Twice I have been shot at in my room. My night scholars have been shot but none killed. The rebels here threatened to burn down the school and house in which I board before the first month was passed yet they have not materially harmed us. The nearest military protection is two hundred miles distant at New Orleans. Even the F. M. B^{au} agt [Freedmen's Bureau agent] has been absent for near a month. But I trust fearlessly in God and am safe."

If living conditions were often wretched and dangerous, the work was always exhausting. Emma Brown was the first teacher at the first free, tax-supported school for African Americans in Washington, D.C. With her white assistant, Frances W. Perkins, she started with forty students in one room. Soon, the enrollment had tripled, but the room remained the same size. While Perkins had her primary students chanting out loud in one corner of the room, Brown taught all the other grades in another. In a letter to a close friend, she expressed her frustration. "This is hard work—it has been too hard for me and Dr. Breed closed the school a week earlier than he intended because I was too sick to teach longer. I gave completely out," she wrote in despair. She went on, "Would you believe that I hate teaching now? I grow sick at the very thought of going back to teaching. I can scarcely realize that I who loved teaching so dearly should feel so. Dr. B. is kind and considerate, Miss P. I am devoted to, she is a faithful friend and an excellent teacher, the children have been good, yet the mere thought of going back to that school makes me sick."

Brown did go back. She continued to teach. But life was difficult, and not just in the classroom. Not all white teachers and administrators were like "Miss P." In another letter she described a teachers' meeting.

> Rev. Kimball rose and said, "Teachers, how many of you think these children can learn as well as white children?" The teachers voted on that. Then he said How many think that these children are as honest as white children of the same class? One damsel said she thought they were not as honest as their favored brethren and sisters. One other teacher who looked to be of the "poor white trash" species, said in a very injured tone that she had "never associated with or come into contact with the low class of whites." I looked at her and perceived that her bump of benevolence had not begun to sprout. The colored teachers as though they had known of this ridiculous performance beforehand and had together resolved on their course,

declined taking any part in the debate. None of us voted. All looked just what they thought. At the close I wished I had remained in school teaching my children to be as honest as white folks.

These black women had great influence in the communities in which they taught. Their responsibilities went far beyond the classroom. Often, in addition to teaching children during the day and adults in the evening, they organized special classes in sewing and cooking. They wrote letters, read and explained contracts, organized discussions of issues that concerned the community. They became, in most communities, leaders whose opinions on political matters, as well as other issues, were consulted and respected.

Other black women were breaking down educational barriers in another sense—as students—and invading the white male preserves of law and medicine. Just about one decade before the beginning of the Civil War, in 1849, a white woman named Elizabeth Blackwell had managed to overcome all obstacles to enter and to graduate from a small, rural medical school in New York State. She became the first woman doctor in the United States or Britain. Just fifteen years later, at a time when race mythologists were still insisting that black women were incapable of moral or intellectual effort, Rebecca Lee Crumpler graduated as a doctor of medicine from the New England Female Medical College in Boston. She was the first black woman doctor. Three years later, Rebecca J. Cole graduated from the Woman's Medical College of Pennsylvania. And in 1870, Susan Smith McKinney Steward earned a degree from the New York Medical College for Women.

Crumpler was born in Richmond, Virginia, in 1833 and reared in Pennsylvania by an aunt. This aunt provided young Rebecca's early exposure to medicine, acting as a kind of doctor to her community. In her late teens and twenties, Crumpler worked as a nurse in Massachusetts. Her employers, however, recommended that she try to enter the New England Female Medical College. After graduating, she set up a private practice in Boston. When the Civil War ended, Crumpler moved back to Richmond to work with the newly freed. Her practice was a success in these Reconstruction days, and in 1883 she published *A Book of Medical Discourses in Two Parts*. It was addressed to women, advising them on how to take care of themselves and their children.

Rebecca Cole was a student at the Institute for Colored Youth in Philadelphia until 1863. She then attended the Woman's Medical College before moving to New York. There she became resident physician at the New York Infirmary for Women and Children. This hospital was owned and operated by women physicians, who otherwise found great difficulty in finding hospitals in which to treat their patients. Cole broke new ground when she was given the work of visiting slums and ghettos to instruct women in hygiene, prenatal care, and the care of infants. In 1873, after having returned to Philadelphia, Cole and fellow physician Charlotte Abbey started the Women's Directory Center. Its function was to provide medical services to destitute women and children. Cole had a fifty-year career in medicine and died in 1922.

Susan Smith McKinney Steward had a much more visible career. A member of the Brooklyn black elite, she was African, Native American, and European. Reared in affluence, she attended the New York Medical College for Women and was the first black woman to practice medicine in the state of New York. She developed a highly successful practice with a diverse group of patients. The *New York Sun* once stated in a description that she had "a handsome bank account and lives well." She read papers before the Homeopathic Medical Society of the State of New York and was active in community affairs. In 1871, she married William G. McKinney, with whom she had two children. Four years after his death she married Theophilus Gould Steward, a U.S. army chaplain. She moved with him to Montana and points west until her retirement in 1907. They both then became teachers at Wilberforce University in Ohio. Steward delivered a paper at the First Universal Race Congress in London in 1911. When she died seven years later, W.E.B. Du Bois delivered her eulogy.

These three women, remarkable as they were, did not signal an end to discrimination against black women in medicine. Indeed, the situation for both black and white women was discouraging. Between about 1855 and 1890, nineteen medical schools for women were founded. By 1895, eleven of them had closed and only a tiny number of men's medical schools admitted an occasional woman. For black women, the difficulties were almost overwhelming. During Reconstruction and in the decade or so after, there were 115 black women physicians in the United States. By the 1920s, there were only 65.

The circumstances for black women in the law were very similar. In 1872, at a time when women could not yet vote, Charlotte E. Ray became an officer of the court. She graduated from Howard University Law School and was admitted to the bar of the District of Columbia. She was particularly unusual in that she attended law school before applying for the bar— and she actually practiced law. There were a few white women who had been admitted to the bar in the various states, although Ray was the first woman in the District of Columbia, but virtually none of them had gone to law school. Most of them were wives of attorneys and had studied in their husbands' offices. Few of these white women were practicing attorneys. The most prominent among them was Myra Bradwell, who edited the *Chicago Legal News* instead of practicing law.

Ray opened a law office in Washington, D.C. Reports of her work make clear that she was capable, but as she was unable to defeat both sexism and racism, she could not make a living as an attorney. She did, however, become active in the suffrage movement, lending her knowledge and skills to the National Woman Suffrage Association.

In 1883, activist Mary Ann Shadd Cary earned her law degree, also graduating from Howard University Law School. She would have preceded Charlotte Ray, having attended Howard's law school in the late 1860s, but, in her own words, she was "refused graduation on account of my sex." Cary, too, was an active suffragist. In 1880, as white women suffragists became more discriminatory against their black allies, she organized the Colored Women's Progressive Franchise Association.

Ray and Cary were able, by law, to argue in the nation's courts and unable to vote in the nation's elections. They both died before women were granted suffrage.

Night Falls

Black men voted. Black women studied law. Black women and men enjoyed a certain amount of freedom for about a decade, and they used it to the fullest. But at no time was the threat of white reprisal absent. And when the North tired of trying to protect those whom they had so recently fought to free, there was no longer any bar to violence and discrimination in the South. In 1877, Rutherford B. Hayes withdrew the troops. The South rose again. An era began that was in some ways worse than slavery, and black women were forced to call on every ounce of their strength to endure.

To be a woman of the Negro race in America, and

to be able to grasp the deep significance of the

possibilities of the crisis, is to have a heritage,

it seems to me, unique in the ages.

ANNA JULIA COOPER

BLOSSOMING IN HARD SOIL

CHAPTER SEVEN

BLACK AMERICAN WOMEN have never had only one enemy to fight, one obstacle to overcome. Throughout history, there have been three—law, custom, and violence. Law made black women and their children slaves, robbed them of their human rights, and bound them to often cruel and exploitative owners. Custom constrained them within limitations of gender and race and rendered their attempts to protect their sexual integrity virtually useless. Violence permeated their lives. These three enemies have worked together, and black women have seldom been able to attack one without finding themselves painfully ensnared by the others. In the last decades of the nineteenth century, the three old enemies recombined to destroy the freedom for which so many had fought so hard before and during the Civil War.

With the withdrawal of federal troops from the South in 1877, the era of Jim Crow began. At first it must have seemed the end of hope. Reconstruction had promised much and, for a time, given African Americans a sense of citizenship. Now all political liberty was systematically destroyed, and white terrorism became the custom of the country. Black people worked in the fields and in the homes of whites as they had under slavery, and they were subject to much of the same violence and repression.

Black women and men, however, evinced a powerful will to freedom and dignity. Many black families left the South, making homes for themselves in other parts of the country, especially the West. Among those who remained, there were tens of thousands of women who organized into the black women's club movement, a truly remarkable phenomenon that became virtually the sole provider of social services to the black community. While caring for the impoverished and the aged and building hospitals and schools, the clubs also became training grounds for political action as their members learned to work together, organize, raise funds, and garner support from the rest of the community. Black women developed their organizing and leadership skills in the church as well. The hub of the black community, it served many purposes beyond worship and religious instruction, and black women were its motive power. Of no less significance were the artists and artisans. From quilters in sharecropping cabins to the first black playwrights, they affirmed African American identity and inspired a spirit of resistance that would grow in the decades to come.

JUMP JIM CROW

In the minstrel show tradition, Jim Crow was a funny little man who danced and sang. *Wheel about and turn about / An' do jist so— / An ebery time I wheel about / I jump Jim Crow. . . .* But there was nothing funny about what came to be called Jim Crow in the southern United States. It was a determined and largely successful effort on the part of white southerners to rob African Americans of all political power, economic opportunity, and social equality. The white South had been compelled by defeat in war to accept the end of slavery. Without the military force of the North actually in occupation, however, they were prepared to return to as near an approximation as they could get. They were ready for what the Democratic party of the time called "Redemption."

For the South to be "redeemed," it was first necessary to make sure that black men could not vote. All else could follow from that. In the years just following Reconstruction, hesitant to use the law and fearful that the federal government would step in and rule unconstitutional state and local attempts at disfranchisement, white southerners turned to violence and threats of violence. Terror spread through the black South. At the slightest sign of black political initiative—or at no sign at all—armed white men called "bulldozers" burned homes and even entire towns, raped women, and lynched both men and women. According to Ida B. Wells-Barnett, between 1878 and 1898, about ten thousand people were lynched in America, primarily in the South. A statement issued by white supremacist General M. W. Gary of South Carolina stated, "Every Democrat must feel honor bound to control the vote of at least one Negro, by intimidation, purchase, keeping him away or as each individual may determine how he may best accomplish it. Never threaten a man individually. If he deserves to be threatened, the necessities of the time require that he should die."

In testimony to a Senate committee in 1880, former slave William Murrell stated, "The white people in Louisiana are better armed and equipped now than during the war, and they have a better standing army now in the State of Louisiana than was ever known in the State, and I defy any white man in Louisiana, Democrat or Republican, to deny that assertion." The entire force of that "army" was enlisted to deprive black people of the least vestige of political power.

The 1878 elections were the occasion of a massive intimidation effort. It was to be made clear, once and for all, that the vote no longer belonged to the black man. In many counties of Louisiana and Mississippi, black men were told that, if they appeared in town on election day, they would be shot. Night riders roamed the countryside, murdering black men who had shown some intention of voting. The "bulldozers" were out in force, and their terrorism virtually repealed the Fifteenth Amendment.

In the years that followed, other methods were developed. Polling places were built in areas black voters could not travel to. Bridges between black communities and polling places were burned. Sometimes, polling places were moved and only white voters were notified. In one parish in Louisiana, the polling place was set up in the wilderness far outside of town, and white voters gathered at their church to be told how to reach the spot. Even in the safety of the church, the location was passed among them in whispers. In another parish, white voters appeared at the polls in the early morning hours to cast their votes by candlelight, and then the polls were closed for the day. Black voters arrived to find that, at dawn, they were too late to vote. Eventually, election procedures were changed by law to make it very nearly impossible for any black man to vote. Registrars could, for example, demand that potential voters pass impossibly difficult literacy tests. Since the tests were not mandatory and the demand was never made of white voters, black voters were effectively barred from exercising their legal rights. And since these restrictions were not based, theoretically, on race, the Supreme Court did not object.

Education was also a target. Segregated schools had been customary even during Reconstruction, but there was, as yet, no *legal* bar to black attendance at white schools. Southern legislators soon remedied that. By the end of the 1870s, all southern states had passed laws segregating their public schools. In addition, black southerners were virtually barred from owning land, so most were reduced to tenant farming or sharecropping. To complete the oppression of black southerners, little more was necessary at this point.

Socially, two separate and thoroughly unequal societies evolved during these years. Custom dictated that African Americans should not mix in white society, including that to be found in restaurants, parks, libraries, bathrooms, and railway cars. Black Americans turned to the law to combat custom only to find the two joining hands. While the Civil Rights Act of 1875, passed during Reconstruction, had stated that there could be no discrimination in public places or on any means of transportation within the United States, a Supreme Court ruling on the Civil Rights Cases of 1883 stated that the Fourteenth Amendment guaranteed only that *states* could not discriminate. Individuals and corporations could. This ruling made legal *all* forms of discrimination except those specifically enacted by state government agencies. Then, in 1896, the Supreme Court heard the case of

Plessy v. Ferguson and made an infamous ruling. It affirmed state laws allowing "separate but equal" facilities for black and white citizens. "The object of the [Fourteenth] Amendment," the judges wrote, "was undoubtedly to enforce the absolute equality of the two races before the law, but in the nature of things it could not have been intended to abolish distinctions based on color, or to enforce social, as distinguished from political equality, or a commingling of the two races upon terms unsatisfactory to either."

Justice John Marshall Harlan, in voting against the opinion, said, "in view of the Constitution, in the eye of the law, there is in this country no superior, dominant, ruling class of citizens. There is no caste here. Our Constitution is color-blind. . . ." If Harlan was right, the Constitution was the *only* thing in the country that was color-blind. Within the decade, there was legally enforced Jim Crow seating on streetcars in Georgia, North Carolina, Virginia, Louisiana, Arkansas, South Carolina, Tennessee, Mississippi, Maryland, and Florida. There were segregated prisons, hospitals, funeral homes and cemeteries, sports arenas, and orphanages. Black facilities were grossly inferior and, in some cases, barely existed. A black "hospital ward," for example, might be a room in the basement of a white hospital, formed by hanging blankets from water pipes. A black school could count itself lucky to get the used and outdated books from white schools nearby.

Over water fountains, bathrooms, and doorways, demeaning "whites only" and "colored only" signs were posted. They were even to be found on vending machines. African Americans were exiled from amusement parks and swimming pools, concert halls and zoos. In courtrooms, they were sworn in on a separate Bible. From *Plessy v. Ferguson* until the 1954 *Brown v. Board of Education* ruling, "separate but equal" was the law of the land, and "equality" was pretty much whatever the white sheriff, mayor, or school board decided. This was not simply a matter of priorities; humiliation was a strategy, not an accident. And behind every hardening custom of inequality there stood the threat of violence. Beatings. Lynching. Rape.

Lynching and the threat of lynching were powerful weapons in the southern battle to keep black people in a slavelike condition. So, too, was rape. Until recently, however, when historians talked about the rape of enslaved women and free women who lived under white dominance, they often concentrated on the damage that this act did to the black male's sense of esteem and self-respect. He was powerless to protect his woman from white rapists and was therefore robbed of a crucial part of his masculinity. Few scholars have assessed the effect that rape, the threat of rape, and domestic violence had on the psychic development of black women. In the late nineteenth and early twentieth centuries, lynching, not rape, came to represent the horrors of white domination. Author Hazel Carby put it baldly in *Reconstructing Womanhood*.

> The institutionalized rape of black women has never been as powerful a symbol of black oppression as the spectacle of lynching. Rape has always involved patriarchal notions of women being, at best, not entirely unwilling accomplices, if not outwardly inviting sexual attack. The links between black women and illicit sexuality consolidated during the antebellum years had powerful ideological consequences for the next hundred and fifty years.

The power of rape as a symbol *against* the black man and its lack of power as a symbol of the oppression of the black woman derives in part from the nature of the crime in law. Most people think of rape as a crime against women. Morally, of course, it is. But historically and legally, it is not. Rape originated in English law as a crime of property. The offended party is the person who "owns" the right to sexual access to a woman's body. Traditionally, that has almost never been the woman herself. The right to a woman's body has belonged to her father until she was married and, thereafter, to her husband. This right was a valuable property. It could be bartered, at marriage, for a camel or an oxen or half a kingdom. If it was stolen—by a man who had sex with the woman without her father's permission—a significant financial loss was incurred. As a result, statutory rape (in which the young woman consented) and forcible rape were crimes of approximately equal gravity. After marriage, of course, the offended party was the husband. As a result, adultery (on the part of a woman) and forcible rape were also of approximately equal gravity. They were, in fact, virtually the same crime.

It is not difficult to see how this traditional definition of the crime of rape would be interpreted during slavery. If *everything* about a woman belonged to the slaveholder, then obviously the right of sexual access would be included in that. A slaveholder could no more be held legally guilty of raping a slave than a husband could be held guilty of raping his wife. And if some other man should force a slave woman, the offended party was not the woman, but the slaveholder.

This legal situation made for an emotionally distorted world in the South. A slave woman stood in much the same legal relationship to a slaveowner as did his wife *and vice versa*. He had the legal right to the bodies of both. He was responsible for feeding and clothing both. He had authority over and responsibility for the children of both. When a man took sexual possession of either, he was acting on his legal rights. And many did. They established multiple "wives" and multiple families. (This was in addition to the more "casual" rape of enslaved women in fields or pantries.)

In this situation, obviously, it became very important for white women to distinguish themselves from their husbands' other legally sanctioned sexual partners. There *must* be a distinction of some kind, but legally it wasn't clear. And so, apparently, white society turned to the time-honored antithesis of good women and bad women, saints and whores, angels and temptresses. A wife was a good woman from a good family, and the only way to gain access to her body was to marry her. A slave was the *opposite*. White women had to pretend to be the former, and black women were doomed to be seen as the latter. The distinction gave white society some protection for the institution of marriage, and it was ardently upheld by men and women both. The iron maidenhood in which it encased white women led to mental and physical illness, loveless marriages, and broken hearts. For black women, the situation was much worse. Any claim they might have to being moral entities was sacrificed to the need to sanctify white marriage. They became, in the peculiar morality of the South, "unrapeable."

The distinction did not fade when slavery ended. All through the years of Reconstruction and Jim Crow, black women could be raped with impunity by white men. And since a huge majority of employed black women worked in white households under the authority of and in proximity to white men, they were continually exposed to sexual harassment. Rape was just one of the weapons of southern terrorism, a terrorism that would make many African Americans decide to leave the South.

The 1878 elections triggered the first of the large black migrations north that would continue throughout the Jim Crow years. The people who loaded themselves and their belongings onto wagons and set out for the unknown were looking for many things, including economic opportunities. But the immediate cause was often more basic. They were fleeing the violence. Men fled beatings and lynchings. Women fled sexual assault and rape. Families fled a world in which not one of their members was free from fear. For black women, the farms of the West and the factories of the North held out hope of a better world economically, and that motivation cannot be underestimated. But they also promised, and sometimes delivered, human dignity and decency.

WEST TO FREEDOM

When Moses led the people of Israel out of Egypt and into the promised land, they called it the "Exodus." Black Americans who fled the Deep South for Kansas between 1878 and 1881 called themselves the "Exodusters." Not for the first time, the black community found inspiration in a biblical parallel, and not for the first time, their faith was somewhat misplaced.

In the late nineteenth century in America, the West was the land of opportunity, and most movement was in that direction. Wide open spaces, it seemed, could be easily translated into endless fields of grain and grazing land. The idyllic vision of the small family farm led both black and white Americans to leave the crowded North and the impoverished South for "land, lots of land under starry skies above." African Americans did not, however, decide separately and spontaneously that the American West was the land of milk and honey. Two men, Benjamin Singleton and Henry Adams, worked very hard to present a westward move as the answer to the problems of Jim Crow. Each of the men traveled around the South, giving speeches and passing out handbills, spreading his message. There were many who listened, and among them were thousands of black women.

Most black women traveled West with their families, as wives or daughters, expecting to work on farms, with no landowner to answer to. Many realized that modest dream. Others found jobs or opened businesses. One black woman drove a stagecoach, and another struck it rich in a Yukon gold mine. There were, among the black women of the West, laundresses and real estate speculators and even a Buffalo soldier. They did not find complete freedom from racialism, but they did find a world that was much closer to the democratic ideal than the Jim Crow South they left behind.

The fifty thousand African Americans who migrated to Kansas between 1878 and 1881 met with considerable resistance. White southerners did not want to share political power, property, or even streetcars with black people, but they certainly didn't want them to leave. Former slaves and their families made up a pool of cheap labor that southern property owners had no intention of trying to do without. As a result, southern sheriffs arrested black travelers for vagrancy, southern legislators passed laws against encouraging migration, and southern employers hired hoodlums to beat up anyone involved in the migration in any way. Resistance came from another source as well. Some black leaders, including Frederick Douglass, felt that migration out of the South would doom that area. Still hoping to regain the vote and, therefore, political power, they saw the exodus as a stream of potential voters pouring out of the desperately needy South. And finally there was resistance from white Kansans. Some were afraid that a large black population would deter other white settlers. They also believed a great deal of the southern mythology about African Americans and feared that the black families trudging wearily into their towns beside their wagons were actually bands of thieves, cutthroats, and prostitutes. In spite of opposition, however, the Exodusters persisted, and by 1880 black women made up 4.6 percent of the Kansas population.

Most African Americans who found their way to Kansas hoped to become independent farmers, but few—perhaps a third—had the resources to do so. The rest got jobs as farmhands, domestic servants, or general laborers. Some were unable to find work and were reduced to begging. But the farmers were undeniably better off than most black Americans, and so were many of the hired workers. Former southerners founded several black towns in Kansas. The largest, Nicodemus, had more than seven hundred residents at its peak. On the streets of Nicodemus and other black towns, African Americans could walk with their heads up. Dignity would not be punished as "uppitiness." Laughter need not be hidden. Breathing the air of freedom was a heady sensation and one for which great sacrifices would be made.

The Nicodemus school was the first in Graham County, Kansas. Its teacher, Francis Fletcher, taught fifteen pupils from books donated by a former Kentucky slave. The students attended classes in the winter, when there was no work to do on the farms, and learned arithmetic, literature, moral values, and hygiene. Another Nicodemus teacher, Lulu Sadler Craig, came to the town with her family in 1879, when she was eleven. She later recalled that Native Americans in the area were friendly to the black settlers, sharing with them food that they had received from an Army fort. And the settlers needed all the help they could get. Most of the farmers did not have plows and so they dug in the earth with their hands.

The situation in Oklahoma was very different from that in Kansas. The first African Americans to reach Oklahoma had come with the Five Civilized Tribes on the Trail of Tears earlier in the century. Forced by the federal government to travel on foot from the southeastern United States to the much less fertile lands just north of the Red River, the tribes included the Cherokees, Choctaws, Chickasaws, Creeks, and Seminoles. According to records of the time, people of African descent accounted for 18 percent of the Cherokees, 14 percent of the Choctaws, 18 percent of the Chickasaws, and 10 percent of the Creeks. These statistics are available because most of the black tribal members were slaves. However, their status was not that of chattel. They lived in family groups and intermarried with other tribal members. In the fifth tribe, the Seminoles, African Americans were not enslaved. In the antebellum years, a large number of runaway slaves had fled from Georgia and the Carolinas to Florida and joined the Seminoles in fighting against U.S. soldiers. That fighting lasted for forty-two years, ending with the Civil War. Among the Seminoles, African Americans were first neighbors and allies and then friends and family.

By the time of the 1860 census, there were 7,362 slaves in Oklahoma belonging to Native Americans. There were also an uncounted number of nonslave tribal members who were of African descent. In 1866, the federal government decided that the Five Civilized Tribes should be punished for siding with the Confederacy during the Civil War, even though their loyalties had actually been split. The government took away a large part of the tribes' territory, presumably to be assigned to other Native American groups that would be resettled in the future. They also required that former slaves of the tribes should be given land allotments and membership in the tribes. Most received between 40 and 160 acres. It was the only instance of land redistribution to freed slaves after the Civil War.

When the Oklahoma Territory was opened for settlement in 1889, the numbers swelled. In 1890, promoter Edwin P. McCabe told the *New York Times,* "I expect to have a Negro population of over 100,000 within two years in Oklahoma . . . [and] we will have a Negro state governed by Negroes." Oklahoma did not become a black state, of course, but black people played an enormously important role in its history. Thirty black towns were founded between 1890 and 1906, and, when the Oklahoma Territory achieved statehood in 1907, about 137,000 of its half million citizens—more than one in four—were black.

Langston, Oklahoma, was built immediately after the 1889 Land Rush. By 1891, it had one hundred citizens who were busy building homes and businesses. The Langston *City Herald* soon had the largest circulation of any newspaper in the state—four thousand readers. By 1892, there were six hundred respectable working-class and middle-class African Americans in the city. The women of Langston, a remarkable and remarkably dedicated group, urged the town to build a public school that offered classes up to the eighth grade. Not long after, they started a high school. By 1900, according to historian William L. Katz, Langston "boasted a literacy rate among the highest of any frontier community in the United States: 72 percent of its citizens could read and 70 percent could write." The figures for Langston's women were nothing short of astounding. Ninety-five percent could both read and write. In 1897, Langston became the home of Langston University, an important historically black college.

The women of Boley, Oklahoma, could also make an astonishing boast about their success in promoting education. In the early years of the twentieth century, one-half of Boley's high school students went on to college, girls as well as boys. For any high school in the country, this was an impressive statistic. For a rural black high school, it was miraculous.

At least one woman was among the official founders of these western towns. Josephine Allensworth and her husband founded a town near Bakersfield, California, in 1908. After settling in Los Angeles at the end of the Civil War, they decided to establish what they called a "race colony" so that they and other black people could live "free from the restrictions of race." In the town of one hundred, Josephine Allensworth was president of the school board, established a library for the colony, and sponsored organizations for self-improvement.

Black towns apart, there were black women in all parts of the West. Most of them lived in towns and cities and were five times as likely as white women to have jobs. Although many worked as domestics, others broke through traditional racial and gender boundaries. Their lives provide a striking contrast to those of black women in the Jim Crow South.

There was Mary Lewis, who ran the Alhambra Cafeteria in Tucson, Arizona, in the 1890s. Elvira Conley opened a laundry in Sheridan, Kansas. Sarah Miner ran an express and furniture-hauling business in Virginia City, Nevada. Annie Neal opened the Mountain View Hotel in Oracle, Arizona, in 1895. There, her guests enjoyed nursing care, a private school, and monthly church services. But perhaps the most colorful of the black women of the West was Mary Fields. She stood six feet tall and weighed two hundred pounds, smoked cigars, and carried a .38 Smith and Wesson. And she drove a stagecoach. She was Gary Cooper's childhood idol.

Born a slave in Tennessee, Mary Fields went to work for Mother Amadeus of the Ursuline Convent after the Civil War. In 1884, Mother Amadeus went to Montana to found a school for girls, and Fields joined her three years later. For ten years, she drove a wagon for the school to and from town and then left after a shootout with a cowpuncher. The cowpuncher was unharmed, as was Mary Fields, but the bishop demanded that she be fired. In the nearby town of Cascade, Montana, she opened a restaurant. It was a popular place, but Fields went broke because of her habit of feeding people who could not pay. For the next eight years, she was a stagecoach driver for the U.S. mails.

In her later years, "Stagecoach Mary" took in laundry and tended her garden. The only black resident of Cascade, she was apparently well loved. When her laundry burned down, the town rebuilt it with donated materials and labor. At the saloons in town, no women were allowed except Stagecoach Mary Fields. When the owner of the Cascade Hotel leased it to another man, he made it a condition of the lease that Fields continue to receive her meals there free. The town even closed the schools and had a celebration on Fields's birthday. Since no one knew when that was, the town celebrated when Mary Fields felt like it. As she got older, Fields curbed her legendary temper. She worked for long hours in her garden and was the number one fan of the Cascade baseball team, presenting bouquets to home run hitters. She cared for the altar at Wedsworth Hall for the Catholic Society. It was during this time that Cooper, then a boy of nine, first met Mary Fields. She was, as Cooper put it, "one of the freest souls ever to draw a breath or a thirty-eight."

Another woman who proved to be as tough as the Wild West around her was Cathy Williams. The daughter of Martha Williams, an orphanage worker in Arizona and New Mexico, Williams disguised herself as a man and, under the name William Cathy, served from 1868 to 1870 in the Buffalo Soldiers. The Buffalo Soldiers were four black units of the army that served on the frontier through the late 1800s. Always aware that the army offered most of them better lives than they would have as civilians, the black troops became famous for their dedication and courage. A Montana newspaper of the time stated, "There are no better troops in the service." After honorably serving in the Buffalo Soldiers, Williams went back to the Southwest and ran a farm.

May B. Mason was another remarkable woman. A Seattle widow, she went to the Yukon to look for gold, returning in 1898 with a land claim and $5,000 worth of gold dust. Later that year, she was offered $6,000 for her claim and refused it. The Seattle *Post-Intelligencer* reported that, for her marriage to Attorney Con A. Rideout, she wore "a black silk gown, and her ears and fingers sparkled with diamonds." She used some of her precious dust to help finance her husband's political ambitions. She and other black socialites in Seattle enjoyed themselves at concerts of the most popular black performers and even presented their own evening of Shakespeare at the Opera House. They did excerpts from *Richard III* and *Macbeth.* A favorite amusement was lunch on yachts in Puget Sound.

When black women fleeing Jim Crow reached Colorado, they found the path had been paved for them by a woman named Clara Brown. A former slave from Kentucky, she had hitched a ride on a covered wagon to Denver with some prospectors in 1859, in exchange for cooking and washing. After a couple of years there, she bought a miner's cabin in Central City and opened a laundry. In addition to serving as the Methodist Church, her house became, according to a local paper, "a hospital, a hotel and a general refuge for those who were sick or in poverty." That included whites, blacks, and Native Americans. Soon, Brown took in a partner, expanded her business, and began buying real estate. By 1864, she owned seven houses in Central City and sixteen lots in Denver. She also owned property in Boulder and Georgetown. If she had held on to her business and property, she might have become one of Colorado's wealthiest women. Instead, when 1865 brought emancipation, she went back to Kentucky to find her children. She failed, but she returned to Denver with twenty-six former slaves, for whom she found homes and jobs. She also helped pay for their education. In 1883, the Colorado Pioneers Association changed its bylaws so that it could vote Clara Brown its first woman member.

Mary Fields, May Mason, and Clara Brown found a freer life in the West, where racial and gender discrimination, while they still existed, were considerably less harsh than in either the South or the industrial North. They were among thousands of black women who enjoyed lives that had more scope and, often, more material comforts than were possible in other areas. But there were *hundreds* of thousands who remained in the South, through necessity or choice, to battle against the deepening atmosphere of repression. And although they did not leave in search of freedom, they did not remain behind to be victims.

LIFTING AS WE CLIMB

The term "woman's club" usually conjures visions of sweet-faced ladies in flowered hats sipping tea, usually because they have nothing better to do with their time on a weekday afternoon. This image has never been particularly accurate, even of white women's clubs. With regard to black women's clubs it could hardly be further from the truth—except, probably, for the flowered hats. The thousands of organizations black women formed to promote the welfare of their community were a very different proposition. In the late nineteenth century, the black community was faced with poverty, illiteracy, and discrimination on a massive scale. When black women found that white governmental agencies and other organizations had no intention of providing services to the communities in which they lived and worked, they stepped into the void. It was a monumental task.

One city might have ten women's organizations, another twelve or thirteen. In Richmond, Virginia, there were twenty-five "female benevolent orders," the most historically significant being the Independent Order of St. Luke. In the last decade of the nineteenth century, these organizations went in two enormously important, and very different, directions. The Order of St. Luke and others like it became instruments for economic self-determination, while still others grew into the influential black women's club movement. Out of both of these came women of great power.

Boston, New York, and Washington, D.C., were the centers of what would eventually become the national black women's club movement. Along with Philadelphia and, to a lesser degree, some southern cities, these three were the homes of the black elite. Here, in conservatively affluent homes, lived the daughters and granddaughters of families that had been free for generations, building modest fortunes. Here were wives of respectable black working men—barbers, porters, postal workers. And here, too, were the dressmakers and hairdressers who made up such a significant proportion of the black entrepreneurial class.

In Washington, these women gathered at the Bethel Literary and Historical Society to hear the great women leaders and speakers of the day, including Mary Ann Shadd Cary, temperance lecturer Hallie Q. Brown, and educator Anna Julia Cooper. In 1892, members of the Bethel group joined with others in Washington to form the Colored Woman's League of Washington, D.C. That same year, a group of New York's black women leaders honored Ida B. Wells-Barnett at a testimonial dinner. Out of that meeting came two important clubs—the Woman's Loyal Union and the Woman's Era Club of Boston, founded by Josephine St. Pierre Ruffin. Within a few years after the founding of these clubs, two events, involving exclusion and slander, led to the formation of the national black women's club movement.

In the early 1890s, the United States proclaimed that it would host a world's fair, the biggest, most spectacular one ever. Almost immediately, white feminist Susan B. Anthony set to work. Determined that the fair would include representation for women, she brought a group of socially acceptable feminists together with a group of influential Washington ladies in a parlor of the Riggs House in Washington, D.C. (She herself stayed upstairs during the gathering, so as not to frighten anyone.) In December, Anthony submitted a petition to Congress that was signed by, among others, the wives of three chief justices of the Supreme Court. She proposed that women be represented at the fair. Congress voted on the proposal and she got her way. In a way.

The Columbian Commission was made up of the most influential men in Chicago, where the fair was to be held. When they got together to appoint a group of women to take responsibility for the women's representation, they did not appoint Anthony, or any other suffragists for that matter. They appointed their wives, the leaders of Chicago's high society, with Bertha Honore Palmer at the helm. When Palmer, wife of hotelier and real estate magnate Potter Palmer, was ready to make up a "board of lady managers," she got the ladies she wanted. This board, too, was virtually devoid of suffragists, and it was entirely, completely, and unalterably devoid of black women. It was a sign of the growing confidence and pride of black women that they spoke up. Indeed, a group of Chicago women presented a petition for participation. It was rejected.

Palmer's rationale for refusing the proposal was that it was not presented by a national organization. Indeed, she said, there was no national organization of black women and, therefore, there could be no black representatives on the Board of Lady Managers. Quickly, the Colored Woman's League of Washington, D.C., tried to organize a national convention of black women's clubs, but it did not succeed in putting the convention together in time to qualify for the board.

In the meantime, Fannie Barrier Williams, the wife of a prominent black Chicago attorney, made her own proposal to the board. She was far more acceptable to Palmer and her cronies. She was beautiful, well spoken, rich, and from Chicago. In addition, she did not ask to be put on the board itself. Her proposal was that she be appointed a clerk in charge of exhibit installations, and it was accepted. Then, through the power of her personality, she gained some influence with the board, at least to the degree that she was invited to speak at one of the Women's Congresses at the fair.

The incident, which infuriated black clubwomen, brought them together. The Colored Woman's League of Washington continued to push for a national organization. There was already a kind of national publication, called the *Woman's Era*, published by the Woman's Era Club of Boston and circulated around the country. Here, the Colored Woman's League placed an announcement asking for delegates from other clubs to come together to form a national black women's organization at the National Council of Women convention in 1895. A number of clubs responded and became the National Colored Woman's League.

And so it was that the exclusion of black women by white women at the fair prompted the first step toward union. The second was inspired by the slander of a lone white man who put into words one time too many the falsehood that had plagued black women for more than a century. Hearing that Englishwoman Florence Belgarnie greatly admired Ida B. Wells-Barnett for her courage in the antilynching struggle, journalist James W. Jacks decided that it was his duty to set her straight about black women. In an open letter, he explained that she should not encourage or support such a person, accusing black women of having "no sense of virtue and of being altogether without characters." He didn't stop there. He also declared that all black women were "prostitutes, thieves, and liars." The letter was circulated to black women's clubs around the country.

At length it reached Josephine Ruffin in Boston. This brilliant, respectable, and respected woman found that she had been pushed too far. Her response to the letter was a charge to black women, entitled "A Call: Let Us Confer Together." In it, she called black women together "to teach an ignorant and suspicious world that our aims and interests are identical with those of all good aspiring women." Ruffin went on to sound the two notes that would remain themes of the black women's club movement well into the twentieth century. She declared that black women must teach the world this lesson "not by noisy protestations of what we are not, but by a dignified showing of what we are and hope to become." And she insisted that the task had to be accomplished collectively. White society could and did dismiss the character and accomplishments of individual women as exceptions. "Because all refutation has been tried by individual work," she wrote, "the charge has never been crushed." The response to Ruffin's call was enthusiastic. A total of 104 women from twenty clubs came together at a conference in Boston and formed the National Federation of Afro-American Women. Eventually, the membership included thirty-six clubs from twelve states. The National Colored Woman's League, however, was not among them.

Two national organizations of black women's clubs now existed. They had the same goals and the same values. They even had the same date and place for their national conventions—Washington, D.C., in July of 1895. The absurdity of the situation became evident when members of one "national" organization ran into members of the other "national" organization as they all scurried to meetings. As a result, a committee was formed and, that same year, the two groups merged. The new organization was called the National Association of Colored Women (NACW). The NACW was the first truly national black organization that functioned with strength and unity. It would be another fifteen years before the National Association for the Advancement of Colored People (NAACP) was formed.

The motto of the NACW was "Lifting as We Climb," and its members took that motto very seriously. They believed that African Americans were judged by others as a group, not as individuals. If they were to receive the respect to which they were entitled, therefore, they would have to make sure that *all other black women* were equally worthy. This was, to say the least, an unrealistic goal. But it powered an enormously important enterprise, providing the black community with virtually all its social services.

When it came to serving their community, the women's clubs were quite extraordinary. Their first priority was caring for the aged and infirm. Since many former slaves had no families to take care of them and, of course, no pension or savings, this was a huge job. With the closing of the Freedmen's Bureau, black women's clubs took on the burden largely by themselves. Next in importance were medical care, child care, and other services for black families.

It is difficult to communicate the scope of the work done by these organizations, but a look at the work done in just one state gives some idea. The state association of black women's clubs in Colorado, for example, supported the Colored Orphanage and Old Folks' Home in Pueblo, Colorado. In the same state, a smaller group of clubs, the Negro Women's Club Home Association, was formed for the specific purpose of creating a home for single working girls and a nursery for working mothers. The home was opened in 1916, and in 1921 a health clinic was added. The Colored Women's Republican Club of Denver was so effective in its voter registration drive that it could report, in 1906, that a higher percentage of black women than white women had voted in the past election. (Colorado was one of those western states that extended the franchise to women ahead of the 1920 Constitutional amendment.) The black women of Colorado were, in the early years of the century, providing for orphans, the aged, single working women, and the children of working mothers, as well as getting out the vote. It is an impressive record.

There were dozens of Phyllis (or Phillis) Wheatley Clubs around the country, honoring the first African American woman poet. Most of them were homes for young working women, who were denied housing at the Young Women's Christian Association (YWCA) facilities around the country. They often included day nurseries for working mothers, classes in domestic skills, and other services. A Phyllis Wheatley Home was founded by black clubwomen in Detroit in 1897. The Nashville Phyllis Wheatley Club established a Phyllis Wheatley Room and later founded a home for aged women.

Often, women's clubs worked hand in hand with professional women such as teachers, librarians, and social workers. The Virginia Federation of Colored Women's Clubs bought the farm on which Janie Porter Barrett built her Virginia Industrial School for Colored Girls at Peake Turnout, Virginia.

Judith Ann Carter Horton persuaded the Excelsior Club in Guthrie, Oklahoma, to raise the money for a public library. The club also supported a school for black young people who had been in trouble with the law.

In some cases, professional women founded women's clubs to help them in their missions. Jane Edna Hunter, for example, was trained as a nurse. However, after moving to Cleveland, Ohio, she found that there were no positions available for her in area hospitals. She was also unable to find decent housing. Her response to this was to get any paying work she could find—private-duty nurse, cleaning lady, laundress—and to form the Working Girls' Home Association in 1911 to help other young black women in her situation. She and her friends each contributed five cents a week from their meager earnings and began looking for other members. By 1913, they had opened a twenty-three-room residence for single, black working women. By 1917, they had replaced it with a seventy-two-room building. By 1928, the residence—which was now called the Phillis Wheatley Association—had 135 bedrooms, 4 parlors, 6 clubrooms, a cafeteria, and a beauty salon. There was also an employment agency for black women.

There are hundreds of stories like Hunter's. Black professional women considered it part of their job to serve the community. Many times, they were able to get education and training only because a church or a community group paid their way, and service was their way of repaying the debt. But even when no such tangible help was received, they believed that it was their absolute duty to themselves and their families to "advance the race." The "Lifting as We Climb" philosophy, however, effective as it was in providing the black community with social services, had another, less fortunate effect—the tendency to adopt certain white, middle-class values.

Now, that is an accusation made all too freely in discourse about race in America. In this case, however, there are clear and specific issues involved, the most important of which is gender. In her book *What a Woman Ought to Be and to Do,* Stephanie J. Shaw tells this story. As a child in the late 1860s, Mary Church Terrell was traveling by train with her father when he left the first-class car to smoke. While he was away a white conductor tried to move Mary to the "colored" car, a second-class coach. Terrell recalled her effort to explain the incident to her mother.

> I assured her [that] I had been careful to do everything she told me to do. For instance, my hands were clean and so was my face. I hadn't mussed my hair. . . . I hadn't soiled my dress a single bit. I was sitting up "straight and proper." Neither was I looking out of the window, resting on my knees with my feet on the seat (as I dearly

loved to do). I wasn't talking loud. In short, . . . I was behaving "like a lady" as she told me to do.

This poignant story serves as a parable for race relations during the Jim Crow era. A large part of the black community believed that the way to defeat racism was to obey every rule of proper behavior to the letter, to offer no provocation for discrimination. In hindsight this conviction seems both moving and intensely frustrating. It is, however, completely understandable. We have learned in recent years that victims of abuse develop a need to feel that they have some control over what happens to them. If they can believe that the abuse has, at least in part, arisen from their own behavior, they can also believe that it may be preventable in the future. The victims need only change the behavior that caused the abuse. African Americans during the Jim Crow era, then, clutched at the idea that lynching, rape, economic oppression, disfranchisement, and social ostracism were to some degree grounded in the "improper" behavior of people who had been degraded by slavery. Change the behavior, they reasoned, and white people would stop the abuse.

One of the behaviors the club movement focused on was sexual. During the antebellum years, quite respected black women had made the choice to refrain from marriage to their life partners for a number of reasons, including the desire to protect their property and financial status. Now, this option was discarded, at least by the vast majority of the respectable black community. Because of the intense desire to contradict the image of immorality with which black women had been burdened, the clubwomen put their feet on the straight and narrow path and expected everyone else to do the same. It was all right not to marry, but you made that choice because, in the words of Anna Julia Cooper, you were not "compelled to look to sexual love as the one sensation capable of giving tone and relish, movement and vim" to your life. If you were not going to marry, sexual love was off limits entirely.

This attitude, while it did not permeate the entire community, had a very powerful effect on those parts of the community it touched. And it was upheld not only by the club movement, but by another powerful, woman-driven element in black America—the church.

THE SUBSTANCE OF THINGS HOPED FOR

The heart of the black community, all through the nineteenth century, was the church. It was often the only public building the community had access to, and in it took place not only religious services but classes, clubs, social events, and political meetings. The leaders of the church were usually the leaders of the community. At a time when no black person could aspire to being a member of the city council, being a deacon was highly prestigious. Decisions concerning the building fund or the use of the fellowship hall became as crucial as the apportionment of city taxes or floating a new bond issue. This may be one reason that black men carried their emulation of the male-dominated white church so far. Power was at least as much at issue as scriptural soundness.

At Sunday services, women were significantly in the majority, both in the pews and in the choir. The organist, or pianist, and choir director were usually women. Women were the chief fund-raisers for the church and for mission work. They were the church visitors, taking comfort to the sick and sick of heart, as well as food to the hungry. Men stood in the pulpit and sat on the church board; women did everything else.

There were women, however, who did not accept this situation without protest. As early as 1868, women in the AME pressured the church government to allow women some official position. The response was the position of stewardess. Chosen by the minister of each church, a stewardess was formally allowed to "render service to the church." But not all women were happy with this compromise. They felt the call to preach, and preaching remained strictly off-limits, officially. Still, women did preach. Like Zilpha Elaw and Jarena Lee, they became traveling evangelists. And the AME's position was not always upheld by the local churches. Some ministers welcomed the women and allowed them to carry on revivals in their churches because, it seems, the women were highly effective.

Almost twenty years after the stewardess compromise, in 1884, the AME finally agreed to license women preachers. These women were not ordained ministers, and they could not administer the sacraments—communion, marriage, and so forth. They were also not allowed to have their own churches. They could, however, preach. This compromise, too, left the women dissatisfied. At the 1888 General Conference, they presented church officials with a fait accompli. Bishop Henry McNeal Turner had already ordained a woman known to us only as Sarah A. H. of North Carolina. He was immediately reprimanded, and the conference refused again to sanction the ordination of women.

The AME did not give in until 1948, but the women didn't give in, either. Among their most powerful tools were the women's missionary societies, formed against male opposition. In 1874, they created the Women's Parent Mite Missionary Society and, in 1904, the predominantly southern Women's Home and Foreign Missionary Society. The general superintendent of the latter came to be one of the most influential women to that date in the black church.

In Baptist churches, the participation of women was even more restricted. They were sometimes seated separately from men in church services and were, for a time, forbidden to organize their own women's societies. And yet the women who attended Baptist churches, because they were relatively poorer than those in the AME, were even more likely to center activities in the church. For women whose lives were otherwise made up of cleaning other people's homes, sharecropping, or working in a tobacco factory, the church was often the only refuge. It was the source of social interaction and meaningful activity. Within its walls they became leaders and organizers, recognized for skills that had nothing to do with getting anything clean.

At the end of the nineteenth century, black Baptist churches began to organize into a separate convention. This move resulted in the formation of the National Baptist Convention (NBC) in 1895, and it gave the black churches a larger measure of self-determination. However, women were excluded from the convention, despite their considerable majority in church membership. And so, throughout this period and into the twentieth century, black Baptist women formed their own local and state organizations. These women's organizations focused on the needs of the community, and one of their highest priorities was education. Indeed, some of them were specifically formed to support educational activities.

The women's groups raised their own money, and, to the chagrin of Baptist men, they controlled their own money. The men tried to force male officers on them, but the women resisted and allowed men to be involved only as honorary members. Mary V. Cook, a professor at the State University of Louisville, wrote of ministers and male laymen locking women's societies out of church buildings. Virginia Broughton, a schoolteacher and missionary, wrote in her autobiography that there were physical threats made against the women and even confrontations that held the threat of injury or death.

In 1900, one young woman took it upon herself to chide the men for their obstructiveness. At a meeting of the National Baptist Convention, twenty-one-year-old Nannie Helen Burroughs stood to speak on the subject

"How the Women Are Hindered from Helping." The title was a reference to the scripture, "Ye entered not in yourselves, and them that were entering in ye hindered." Burroughs eloquently expressed the women's dissatisfaction, and with the help of two sympathetic men, the women won approval for the formation of a women's auxiliary to the NBC. The Women's Convention (WC) immediately elected officers, and Burroughs became corresponding secretary. During the WC's first year, Burroughs delivered more than two hundred speeches and wrote more than nine thousand letters. By 1903, the WC had almost one million members. A powerful force in the anti-lynching movement, the organization also worked against segregation of public facilities, discrimination in employment, and colonialism in Africa.

In the course of their struggle for empowerment, and in their work within individual churches, black women had found another training ground for political action. In the future, their hard-won skills would be enlisted in the push towards real freedom, the Civil Rights movement. Skills alone, however, do not engender action. The longing for freedom, the affirmation of culture, the pride in heritage must all find expression if they are to intensify to the point of ignition.

THE SEED OF THE FLOWER

"And so," wrote Alice Walker, "our mothers and grandmothers have, more often than not anonymously, handed on the creative spark, the seed of the flower they themselves never hoped to see: or like a sealed letter they could not plainly read." The lives of black women in the final decades of the nineteenth century were not all striving and achievement and struggle. In poverty and in prosperity, there was art. The artistic expressions of black women during this time ranged from quilts to paintings that were exhibited in Paris. They included grand opera and the first plays by and about black people. In all these expressions, there was resistance to oppression, a striving to affirm the culture and identity of black women.

In 1886, while a white artist from Athens, Georgia, was visiting the Athens Cotton Fair, she saw on display there a quilt of such originality and beauty that she tracked down its maker. She found the quilter, Harriet Powers, living on a farm with her husband. It was a fairly prosperous farm, and although Powers welcomed Jennie Smith, she refused Smith's offer of ten dollars for the quilt. Later, during a financial setback, Powers wrote to Smith offering the quilt for sale, but Smith did not have the funds to make the purchase. Another year passed before she was able to make another offer for the quilt. She explained later how the magnificent quilt came into her possession:

> Last year I sent her word that I would buy it if she still wanted to dispose of it. She arrived one afternoon in front of my door in an oxcart with the precious burden in her lap encased in a clean flour sack, which was still enveloped in a crocus sack.
>
> She offered it for ten dollars, but I told her I only had five to give. After going out consulting with her husband she returned and said, "Owin' to de hardness of de times, my ole man lows I' better teck hit." Not being a new woman she obeyed.
>
> After giving me a full description of each scene with great earnestness, she departed but has been back several times to visit the darling offspring of her brain.
>
> She was only in a measure consoled for its loss when I promised to save her all my scraps.

It was Smith's purpose to exhibit the quilt in Atlanta at the Cotton States and International Exposition of 1895. The black community had raised $10,000 for a special building at the exposition, and there were exhibits from eleven southern states. Powers's name is not on the list of exhibitors, but there is evidence that her quilt was there. In 1898, a group of faculty wives from Atlanta University commissioned Powers to create a second quilt as a gift for Reverend Charles Cuthbert Hall, president of Union Theological Seminary. The quilt owned by Smith passed, at her death, into the hands of a friend. He kept the quilt for some time and then gave it to the Smithsonian Institution. It is now on exhibit there. The quilt owned by Hall is on exhibit at the Museum of Fine Arts in Boston.

Much of the imagery on the Powers quilts derives from the Judeo-Christian Bible, but the quilts are done using an appliqué method that originated in Africa. It was used in tapestries made by the Fon people of Abomey, the ancient capital of Dahomey in West Africa. Interestingly, in Dahomey the appliqué was usually done by men, but in America the technique was perpetuated by black women.

Quilts are often the only physical evidence we have that reveals aspects of the inner lives and creative spirits of otherwise obscure black women. Historically, they illuminated women's reflections on the everyday activities, values, and beliefs of members of the black community we seldom hear from. The art of quilt-making also brought black women together in protected spaces where they could cement friendships, share ideas, acquire information, and find and give to one another essential support and encouragement. Quilting is a striking illustration of black women's culture.

Looking at the two quilts of Harriet Powers that have been preserved causes profoundly mixed feelings. It is wonderful to see the work of an artist preserved. It is important to value the medium available to her. But it is impossible not to feel great sadness that she was denied the opportunity to fulfill her potential. Her race and gender put her outside the world of "art" as we know it. Her class, too, militated against her, but it was by no means the most significant factor. Even upper-class white women could not break through the barriers built around the artistic establishment of the time.

In the middle of the nineteenth century, all American art schools were closed to both white women and all African Americans. In the 1850s, some white women were admitted to a few schools, but they were severely restricted in what they could study and how. They were not, for example, allowed to take life drawing classes, a serious handicap in an artistic tradition that highly values the ability to draw the human figure. By the 1880s, the first African Americans were being admitted to art schools. Women were still not allowed to see nude people; they were drawing from statues. And African American women found that whatever small concessions were made for black men or white women were still not being made for them.

Annie E. Anderson Walker was a case in point. Born in Flatbush, New York, she became a teacher, married an attorney, and moved to Washington, D.C. In 1890, having taken private art lessons, she applied to and was accepted at the school of the Corcoran Gallery of Art. However, when she showed up for classes, the admitting instructor said that "the trustees have directed me not to admit colored people. If we had known that you were colored, the committee would not have examined your work." In spite of intervention by Frederick Douglass, the committee refused to back down. Walker eventually went to New York City to study at Cooper Union for the Advancement of Science and Art and then to Europe, where she exhibited with some success. She was able to do this because of her husband's financial position, but being the wife of a successful man had its disadvantages as well. When she returned from Europe, the strain of trying to discharge her duties as her husband's hostess and at the same time fulfill her destiny as an artist proved too much. She broke down and became an invalid. Her money and connections had, to some degree, overcome the obstacles of racism, but they only reinforced the obstacles put in her way by the sexist attitudes of the time.

At the end of the nineteenth century, the only black woman artist who had participated in and been recognized to any degree by the American artistic mainstream was sculptor Edmonia Lewis, who emerged during the crisis-filled days of the Civil War. The next important black women artists would also be sculptors, but they would not emerge until the first decades of the twentieth century.

In theater, the situation was similar in some ways. Nineteenth-century popular entertainment was dominated by the minstrel show. Based on exaggerated and mocking images of black people and employing black music and dance, these shows were performed by white men in blackface until after the Civil War. Then, black men began to form minstrel troupes. They, too, performed the exaggerated characters and, much of the time, wore blackface. Strange as it may seem to us now, this was all America's favorite form of entertainment for almost ninety years. No women were involved in it. And needless to say, no black women were involved in the mainstream legitimate theater. And yet, the real beginning of black theater in America came in 1875 through the agency of two black women. Anna and Emma Hyers, two sisters, formed a traveling troupe called the Coloured Operatic and Dramatic Company to produce musical plays about the black experience. It was the first time in the history of black America that plays by black people and about black people were presented on the stage.

The Hyers sisters began their career as child prodigies. As concert singers, they made their professional debut at the Metropolitan Theater in Sacramento when Anna was eleven and Emma was nine. The sisters, guided by their father, did not perform again until 1871. Then, having spent five years in preparation, they embarked on a national tour. They were greeted with enthusiasm. Within a few years, the Hyers sisters were celebrities. In 1875, they and their father formed their musical drama troupe and began the part of their career that would become so important in the history of black drama.

Their first production was *Out of Bondage,* which traced the history of black people from slavery to freedom and what the Hyers sisters called "attainment of education and refinement." This production was revolutionary in that, unlike other musical productions of the time, it had a storyline, consistent characters, and serious music. It was very successful, and the troupe followed their new direction. According to music historian Eileen Southern, "By the late 1870s the Hyers had staged *In and Out of Bondage* (1877), a three-act musical drama adapted by Sam Hyers; *Urlina, or The African Princess* (1877; copyright notice filed in 1872 by E. J. Getchell); *Colored Aristocracy* (1877), a musical drama in three acts written by black novelist Pauline Hopkins . . . and *The Underground Railroad* (1879), a four-act musical drama also written by Hopkins." One of the stars of the Hyers's first production was Sam Lucas, a well-known black actor whose primary success came in minstrel shows. However, he returned to work with the Hyers sisters on at least two other occasions, leaving his highly paid appearances on the blackface stage to make theater art of distinction.

Another important step in the history of black theater was also taken by a woman. Sissieretta Jones, a great beauty with a magnificent voice, was often compared to the white singer Adelina Patti. In 1892, the "Black Patti" signed a contract to appear at the Metropolitan Opera. She was already famous, having enjoyed tremendous success in both the United States and the West Indies. She had appeared at the White House and been given orchids by Mrs. Benjamin Harrison. However, the Met proved to be not quite ready for her. She was not allowed to perform, and she went on to other ventures. She sang in Europe and at Carnegie Hall, gave a command performance for the Prince of Wales, and sang at the Royal Opera House in Covent Garden. She had triumph after triumph, but the one thing she most wanted eluded her. She wanted to perform dramatic roles on stage. When the world of opera remained closed to her, she finally formed "Black Patti's Troubadours." The Troubadours required many compromises on Jones's part because its basic format was the minstrel show. In the second act, however, the traditional cakewalk was replaced by a medley of operatic selections. These were not just arias, but excerpts from great operas performed by Jones and her company. Later, Black Patti's Troubadours, in the heyday of the black musical, became the Black Patti Musical Comedy Company.

In 1900, Pauline Hopkins wrote, "Art is of great value to any people as a preserver of manners and customs—religious, political, and social. It is a record of growth and development from generation to generation. No one will do this for us: we must ourselves develop the men and women who faithfully portray the inmost thoughts and feelings with all the fire and romance which lie dormant in our history." The quilters affirmed black identity, contradicting all the messages white America attempted to force on black people. The Hyers sisters used their talents and celebrity to preserve and celebrate the history of black people. And Sissieretta Jones took to the people evidence of the excellence of black people. All of these undertakings have been part of the mission of the black woman artist throughout the centuries, and they continue to be so today.

THE COMING STORM

"Men and women are not made on trains and on streetcars," said educator Nannie Helen Burroughs of Jim Crow discrimination. "If in our homes there is implanted in the hearts of our children, of our young men and of our young women the thought they are what they are, not by environment, but of themselves, this effort to teach a lesson of inferiority will be futile." Many black families were able to do this, to make "separate countries" within their homes, where to be African American was to be beautiful and proud, whether they left the South to found black towns in the West or remained behind to battle Jim Crow. But, while instilling dignity and self-respect in the young was one way to fight the brainwashing, it was not enough. Dignity cannot mend a perforated appendix or keep hunger from knotting a six-year-old's stomach. The tangible effects of oppression had to be addressed as well, and black women took this huge task to heart, working through their clubs and churches.

Black women were embattled at the end of the nineteenth century, but their triumphs were in some ways more consequential than their adversities. The club movement, the church, the individual achievements of artists—these all compel our attention and admiration in a way that almost overshadows the bigotry. In the first decades of the twentieth century, however, America fell to new depths of hate. It became increasingly difficult to believe that people of goodwill could move gradually and without animosity to a reconciliation. The eradication of this country's deep dishonor seemed impossibly difficult, and reliance on white humanity naive. In that discovery, however, lay the best hope for the future.

We are not the first to suffer, rebel, fight, love and

die. The grace with which we embrace life, in spite

of the pain, the sorrows, is always a measure of

what has gone before.

ALICE WALKER,

REVOLUTIONARY PETUNIAS

NO MOUNTAIN
TOO HIGH

CHAPTER EIGHT

WITH THE *PLESSY v. Ferguson* ruling in 1896, it became official. No white person or institution, no school or employer or restaurant or street car conductor was obligated to treat a black person as they would treat a white person. The separate-but-equal doctrine had made legal the efforts of the white South to establish a caste system, and black America faced a time bleaker than any before or since chattel slavery.

White southerners lynched more than one hundred black women and men every year. Countless thousands of black women were raped. Homes, schools, and churches were burned to the ground to avenge imagined rebellions or simply from hatred.

Poll taxes and other restrictive legislation robbed black men of the vote; black women, of course, had never had it. By 1902, poll taxes had been instituted in every formerly Confederate state. In Louisiana, 130,000 black men were registered to vote in 1898. By 1902, four years later, there were only 5,000. In Alabama, after an amendment to the state constitution, the numbers went from 181,000 to 3,000. To seal this disfranchisement, southern states universally declared that political parties were private clubs and therefore that the Democratic party could legally bar black men from their primaries. Since the Democratic party at that time won virtually all general elections in the South, black men were excluded from all meaningful political activity.

The situation in the North also deteriorated. In Massachusetts, black men had made considerable progress in the 1880s, but by 1902 the last black representatives were voted out of the state legislature. At the same time, much legislation that had been passed in the North to protect black rights in public places and on transportation fell into disuse. It simply was not enforced. The rising power of labor unions, which should have improved the lot of black workers, accomplished the opposite. During the 1880s, The Knights of Labor had made efforts to include black workers, recruiting some sixty thousand black members. In the 1890s, the Knights were supplanted by the American Federation of Labor, which rigidly excluded African Americans.

Even America's national pastime closed its ranks. In 1883, White Stockings coach Cap Anson refused to let his team play against Toledo when it fielded a black player. In 1887, when the New York Giants put black pitcher George Stovey on the mound, Anson, in the words of baseball historian Alex Chadwick, "exercising all his tremendous influence in baseball circles, was able to prevent it at a time when it was still possible that blacks might have become permanently established in white organized baseball's structure."

In addition, an unholy alliance was formed between southern racist politicians and northern academics. Scientists and social scientists began to support race mythology with spurious "research" and "scientific" theories. White supremacy, they declared, was the natural and desirable order of things. To interfere with it was to stand in the way of progress. But in its fervor to demonstrate its power, white America went too far. In the South, the will to flee Egypt was again awakened in black people. And resistance in the country at large began not only to strengthen, but to organize.

The black community responded in many ways to the increasing violence and exclusion, from Booker T. Washington's conservative concept of self-improvement to the fiery antilynching crusade of Ida B. Wells-Barnett. Everywhere, there was a growing political consciousness, a sense that the time had come to work together for change in ways that went beyond the prevailing social service focus. That consciousness extended into business, where bank president Maggie Lena Walker and millionaire entrepreneur C. J. Walker preached a gospel of financial independence from the white world. It even inspired the musical protests of blues singers "Ma" Rainey and Bessie Smith. The search for freedom continued in a newer, bolder way.

STANDING INSIDE THE FIRE

Ida B. Wells-Barnett began accepting large responsibilities at the age of sixteen when her mother and father died during a yellow fever epidemic and she became sole "parent" to her five younger brothers and sisters. She supported her siblings by taking a job as a teacher for $25 a year at a school six miles from their home and continued to teach for a number of years. Her first overt political activity occurred in May of 1884, when she was twenty-two. Having taken a seat in the ladies' coach on a Chesapeake and Ohio Railroad train, she refused to give it up and was forcibly removed. In response, she sued the railroad and was awarded $500. Although the ruling was overturned on appeal to the state supreme court, she was the first black person to initiate a legal challenge to the Supreme Court's nullification of the 1875 Civil Rights Bill.

Active in the black community in Memphis, Wells-Barnett developed a reputation for intelligence and eloquence and was offered the editorship of a weekly black newspaper, the *Evening Star*. Her work there led to her becoming editor of another black weekly, called *Living Way*, for which she wrote a column under the pen name "Iola." The column greatly increased her renown and, when she began to contribute articles to publications around the country, the young newspaperwoman's stature grew. Still in her twenties, Wells-Barnett became editor and part-owner of the *Memphis Free Speech and Headlight*. Her early journalistic emphasis was on children and education, but that changed suddenly and dramatically in 1892, when three friends were lynched.

Thomas Moss, Calvin McDowell, and Henry Steward owned and operated a successful grocery business in a primarily black area outside Memphis. Their competition was a white grocer whose store had previously been the only option for black customers. Angry and resentful that the black grocers had cut into his business, he threatened them. Other African Americans supported them, and foreseeing trouble, armed black men were waiting inside the store when a white gang attacked one Saturday night. In the melee that followed, three whites were shot. Police arrested the store owners and one hundred other African Americans, who were charged with conspiracy. Although the three white men recovered, Moss, McDowell, and Steward were taken from the jail and lynched.

Wells-Barnett was grieved and outraged. Moss was one of her best friends. Suddenly, she took another hard look at lynching in the South. The white rationalization that black men were lynched for raping or attempting to rape white women was thin, but it had been given surprisingly wide credence, even among the black community. This case, however, was startlingly different. Three successful, reputable black men had been lynched not for their acts, however minor or manufactured, against white women, but simply for their business success. Wells-Barnett began to review other lynching cases and to rip aside the thin veil of deception that had hung over them for years.

The editorials that Wells-Barnett wrote after the lynching of Moss, Mc-Dowell, and Steward were probably the most radical statements made by an African American leader of the time. In the most inflammatory of these editorials, she declared that the charge of rape against black men was an excuse, not a reason, for lynching. She called for Memphis's black citizens to "save our money and leave a town which will neither protect our lives and property, nor give us a fair trial in the courts, when accused by white persons." She then went further and made the statement that would send white southerners into a frenzy. She declared that no one really believed black men were raping white women and, "If Southern men are not careful, they will overreach themselves and public sentiment will have a reaction. A conclusion will be reached which will be very damaging to the moral reputation of their women."

White response to the editorial highlights its radical nature. Wells-Barnett was on her way to Philadelphia when it appeared, and in her absence the newspaper office was destroyed. She was also informed by white newspaper reports that if she dared to return to Memphis, she would be the next to be lynched. Clearly, she had made her point. Just as clearly, if she wanted to continue to do so, she would have to stay out of the South. The impassioned young editor took a job with the *New York Age* and continued to research lynching. In October of 1892, she published the results, a powerful exposé entitled "Southern Horrors: Lynch Law in All Its Phases." She then began touring the country—and eventually Europe as well—to speak against this form of terrorism.

In 1893, Wells-Barnett made her presence felt at the Columbian Exposition in Chicago, where she stood outside the gates and distributed twenty thousand copies of a pamphlet she had coauthored with her future husband, Ferdinand Barnett. *The Reason Why the Colored American Is Not in the Columbian Exposition* continued the Wells-Barnett attack on lynching. After the fair, she remained in Chicago, where she co-founded the Ida B. Wells Club and served as its president for five years. She also married Barnett, owner of the *Chicago Conservator.*

The influence of Wells-Barnett on the black community cannot be overestimated. The radical nature of her message and the aggressiveness of her style—and especially her refusal to accept white justifications of racial violence—were in striking contrast to those of the dominant black leader of the time, Booker T. Washington. The man who would later be called the Black Boss, the Wizard of Tuskegee, and the Savior of the Race came to the attention of the black community through the Tuskegee Institute, which he ran with his partner and wife, Olivia Davidson Washington. After she died, he was joined by another powerful black woman, Margaret Murray. The two of them made Tuskegee an important center of black education and Washington's power base. Murray later married Washington and was a forceful ally in propounding his particular philosophy for African Americans.

That philosophy was, from one point of view, a matter of common sense. Recognizing the implacable nature of racism in the South, where 90 percent of black Americans lived, he declared to the world that social and political equality were not priorities for black people. They wanted—and should be willing to work very hard to get—a measure of economic prosperity, out of which all else might follow. Someday. His school, therefore, trained students for jobs in agriculture and industry or, in the case of women, for serving as nurses, teachers, and wives and mothers to the race. Subjects such as literature, art, music, history, science—beyond that which was necessary to repair a thresher—were all luxuries black people could not afford.

Washington's conservatism went beyond educational theory into all aspects of black life, and it appealed mightily to white America. He was soon courted by politicians from both North and South. From the position of eminence he thus achieved, he sent his message out to all black America, and many responded to the safety that Washington seemed to offer. That large group of African Americans who believed they could earn the respect of white America if they worked hard enough and behaved well enough saw in Booker T. Washington their belief confirmed. Here was a man who began in slavery and now visited the White House. They cherished his example and clung to his beliefs. Unfortunately, Washington was willing to use his power to discourage and obstruct any black leaders who opposed him. If you were a rival, he could prevent white philanthropists from donating money to your organization with a word, induce the governor to deny your requests for permits or licenses, even get the sheriff to throw you in jail for asking too many awkward questions at one of his lectures.

When Ida B. Wells-Barnett launched her antilynching campaign, she did not expect Washington to applaud her and he didn't. He certainly did not approve of the young journalist's explosive style and very public persona. Indeed, apart from the educated wives who worked incredibly hard to help him run his school, he did not appear to approve of women who stepped outside the realm of the home. Although two of his three wives and his daughter had some college education, he states in his autobiography that educated women learned too many things that had nothing to do with housekeeping.

In 1898, Wells-Barnett helped to revive the Afro-American League, a national organization that was originally founded in 1890 to promote black unity. Although it had become defunct, activist T. Thomas Fortune persuaded Wells-Barnett that they could bring it back to life. The group was renamed the Afro-American Council, and Wells-Barnett was elected president. She led the organization in a much more radical direction than Fortune had intended, taking a strong stand against lynching and Jim Crow and Booker T. Washington.

Shortly after Wells-Barnett took over the council, Wilmington, North Carolina, erupted in a riot. A white mob that included some of the most prominent citizens of Wilmington destroyed a black newspaper office and killed eleven black people. Charles S. Morris, a local clergyman, movingly described the scene as he saw it. "Nine negroes massacred outright; a score wounded and hunted like partridges in the mountains; . . . thousands of women and children fleeing in terror from their humble homes in the darkness of the night. . . . All this happened, not in Turkey, nor in Russia, nor in Spain, not in the gardens of Nero, nor in the dungeons of Torquemada, but within three hundred miles of the White House, in the best State in the South, within a year of the twentieth century, while the nation was on its knees thanking God for having enabled it to break the Spanish yoke from the neck of Cuba." Wells-Barnett called an emergency meeting of the council, which censured President McKinley for failing to denounce the rioters. In the statement issued, she made one of her most famous declarations. "If this gathering means anything," she said, "it means that we have at last come to a point in our race history where we must do something for ourselves and do it now. *We must educate the white people out of their 250 years of slave history."*

That was the crux of the difference between Wells-Barnett and Washington. While his message suggested that black people were largely responsible for their own continued oppression, she placed the blame for racism directly on the shoulders of whites. Midway between these two stood another woman, Mary Church Terrell. The daughter of millionaire Robert Church, she was also devastated by the lynching of Thomas Moss, who had attended her wedding to Robert H. Terrell a year before. In the years that followed, she was at first uncertain what path her life would take. She could afford to become an expatriate, moving to Europe and living in an atmosphere that was free of America's deadly racism, and she did try that. But after two years, she returned to the United States and became active in the women's club movement. In 1896, she became president of the first truly national black women's organization, the National Association of Colored Women (NACW). Wells-Barnett and Terrell were two of the most influential black leaders of the time, and they worked together in spite of their differences in viewpoint and philosophy. The NACW, for example, became one of the strongest supporters of Wells-Barnett's anti-lynching campaign.

Other young black leaders, encouraged by Wells-Barnett's example, began to oppose Washington. Among these were William Monroe Trotter and the brilliant W. E. B. Du Bois. In 1905, these Civil Rights pioneers gathered near Niagara Falls to form an organization they called the Niagara Movement. Its goals were as radical as those of Wells-Barnett's Afro-American Council, and it was more active in trying to achieve those goals. The Niagara Movement was an important step forward, but the birth of the

The Search for Literacy

I

1. This 1890 photograph of a mother and daughter reading in Mt. Megis, Alabama, shows a scene that was common throughout the decades following the Civil War, as African Americans fervently sought the education that had been denied them so long. *(Photograph by Rudolf Eickemeyer, Photographic History Collections, National Museum of American History, Smithsonian Institution)*

2. Eliza Campbell Taylor, born in Chicago in 1850, was the first black schoolteacher in the city. She began teaching in the 1860s, while she was still a teenager. *(Franklyn Atkinson Henderson Collection [ICHi-22379], Chicago Historical Society)*

1. DeMandge Tolliver Duesse was the first black child on record to be born in the Wyoming territory. *(Photograph by Edgar D. Meyers, Wyoming State Archives, Wyoming Division of Cultural Resources)*

2. "Stagecoach Mary" Fields was Gary Cooper's childhood idol, living a free but rugged life in Montana. *(from* Black Women of the Old West, *by William Loren Katz, William Loren Katz Collection)*

3. Truth and Grace Hannah are photographed on the Hannah homestead in Nebraska. More than fifty thousand black Americans moved west to escape Jim Crow in the three years between 1878 and 1881. *(Solomon D. Butcher Collection, Nebraska State Historical Society)*

West to Freedom

4. Carlotta Stewart-Lai moved to Hawaii from Brooklyn, New York, in 1898 and became a high school principal. Her substantial salary and her family's affluence allowed her to dress exquisitely and to travel extensively around the islands. (*Stewart-Flippin Papers, Moorland-Spingarn Research Center, Howard University*)

5. The Black Women's club movement included both black-originated groups such as the New Era Club of Boston and black branches of white-originated organizations that were exclusionary. This group is the Frances Harper branch of the Women's Christian Temperance Union (WCTU) in Seattle, Washington, circa 1900. (*from Seattle's Black Victorians, by Esther Mumford, [Ananse, 1980], Esther Mumford Collection*)

4

We Specialize in the Wholly Impossible

1. Nannie Helen Burroughs, seen here (left) with an unidentified friend, was president of the National Training School for Women (NTSW), which was founded in 1901 and had as its motto "We Specialize in the Wholly Impossible."

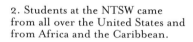

2. Students at the NTSW came from all over the United States and from Africa and the Caribbean.

3. The Women's Convention of the Black Baptist Church founded and supported the National Training School for Women. (All photos from Nannie Helen Burroughs Collection, Prints and Photographs Division, Library of Congress)

3

On Stage

4. Anna M. Hyers and her sister Emma were the first to stage theater written by and for black Americans, from 1875 until the early 1890s. (*Prints and Photographs Division, Moorland–Spingarn Research Center, Howard University*)

5. Florence Mills was the first black woman superstar. When she died young, 150,000 people crowded the streets of Harlem for her funeral. (*Courtesy of Richard Newman*)

6. The Spillers were a musical group that performed from 1906 until 1940 and toured internationally. At the time of this 1906 photograph, the prejudice against women instrumentalists was not yet strong in the black community. (*Isabele Talliaferro Spiller Papers, Moorland–Spingarn Research Center, Howard University*)

MAY YORKE   MAYDAH YORKE   ALICE CALLOWAY   NATHAN SPILLER

1. W. E. B. Du Bois compiled and prepared several albums for the Negro Exhibit of the American Section at the Paris Exposition of 1900 to show the economic and social progress of black Americans since the Emancipation. This photograph illustrated the beauty and diversity of the American black woman. (*Daniel Murray Collection, Prints and Photographs Division, Library of Congress*)

2. These women, whose experience of life shows in their faces, were attending a convention of former slaves in 1916 when this photograph was taken. (*Prints and Photographs Division, Library of Congress*)

More Than One Kind of Beauty

Freedom in Action

3. Long active in the battle to acquire the right to vote, black women faced further obstacles in most parts of the country when they tried to exercise that right. *(Photographs and Prints Division, Schomburg Center for Research in Black Culture, The New York Public Library, Astor, Lenox, and Tilden Foundations)*

4. During the 1920s, there was a rise in black athletic clubs and teams, in which women participated fully. *(Photograph by E. Elcha, Photographs and Prints Division, Schomburg Center for Research in Black Culture, The New York Public Library, Astor, Lenox, and Tilden Foundations)*

The Legacy of Madame C. J. Walker

1. A'Lelia Walker, daughter of beauty products entrepreneur Madame C. J. Walker, became a social leader in New York and a patron of the Harlem Renaissance. This photograph was taken in about 1925. *(Photograph by P. E. Mercer, Photographs and Prints Division, Schomburg Center for Research in Black Culture, The New York Public Library, Astor, Lenox, and Tilden Foundations)*

2. Two beautiful women advertise a hair cream in this photograph by famed black photographer James Van Der Zee, taken in 1925. *(New Orleans Museum of Art: Museum purchase, City of New Orleans Capital Funds and Mrs. P. Roussel Norman Fund)*

most important organizational warrior in the battle for Civil Rights was three years in the future.

Those three years were brutal ones for black America. In August of 1906, three entire companies of black soldiers were discharged without honor—and without a trial—after a fight with Brownsville, Texas, civilians. Having put up with racist taunts for as long as they could, the soldiers had responded and been summarily and harshly punished. Later that year, twelve African Americans were killed and seventy wounded in a riot in Atlanta, during which police disarmed black people who tried to defend themselves. In 1908, after a false accusation of rape by a white woman against a black man, white rioters in Springfield, Illinois, torched a black neighborhood. For six days, they beat and lynched black women, men, and children. They destroyed homes and businesses, looting and vandalizing everything in their path.

When word of the Springfield riot reached New York, a white social worker named Mary White Ovington reacted with outrage. She had been present as a journalist at the founding of the Niagara Movement, worked every day among members of the black community, and had a deep sympathy with the plight of black Americans. Her emotions were engaged by an article written about the riots by white journalist William English Walling in the *Independent.* She quickly got in touch with Walling and another white social worker, Henry Moscowitz, to organize a conference on racial discrimination. White journalist Oswald Garrison Villard of the *New York Evening Post* "issued a call" to supporters of black rights, both black and white. Sixty people signed the call. Twenty of those people were women. Two were black women—Ida B. Wells-Barnett and Mary Church Terrell.

The National Negro Conference took place on February 12, 1909. Wells-Barnett spoke of the pressing need to reclaim the right to vote, as did W. E. B. Du Bois. The delegates resolved to form a new organization, the National Association for the Advancement of Colored People (NAACP). One of its first officers was a black woman, Kathryn Johnson, who served as field secretary. Johnson, however, was an exception. The earliest officers of the NAACP were white. Later, most of the officers were black. However, early and late, they were men. Ironically, women were the ones who kept the organization going from day to day. They organized local chapters and raised funds. They recruited new members and worked to keep old ones. In short, they used, in support of the NAACP, all those skills they had developed over many years in the church, the schools, and the black women's club movement. In 1912, for example, Mary Cable organized the Indianapolis branch of the NAACP. Already president of the Colored Women's Civic Club, she became Indiana's first NAACP president. All of the other officers and members of the board of the Indianapolis branch were also clubwomen. After thirteen months, however, the women asked the men of the black community to take over because, as the women put it, the men "have more time."

This is an important point in understanding black America and the Civil Rights movement. For decades, in dealing with this most important crusade, books of history have recorded the names and pictures of men almost exclusively. However, a more recent—and closer—look has revealed a very different pattern. Black women organized and operated the structures of the movement, the groups that got things done, while men were spokespersons who interacted with white male leadership. This was only a pattern, of course, and not an invariable one. Women were sometimes spokespersons, especially on a local level and in situations where only women were involved. Certainly few people of whatever race or gender have been as powerful in representing a cause as Ida B. Wells-Barnett. Too, there were certainly men who circulated petitions and passed out handbills. But generally men were at the front and women worked behind them. It is important to keep that in mind when looking at the history of the Civil Rights movement in the United States. Appearances can be deceptive.

As the black community became more political, so, too, did the black women's club movement. Mary Talbert, when she became president of the NACW, recruited the support of women's groups all over the country for the antilynching movement. In 1922, she organized the Anti-Lynching Crusaders, a group that worked to bring white women into the antilynching movement. They had considerable success in this effort. Indeed, they were able to influence the National Council of Women to support the movement. Even more important, they inspired the formation of the Association of Southern Women for the Prevention of Lynching, a group of white women who repudiated the role they had been assigned as the justification for violence against black men.

These early signs of growing political consciousness were enormously important in the history of black Americans. And the part that such women as Ida B. Wells-Barnett and Mary Church Terrell played in the fledgling movement was critical. There were other women, however, who were developing a different approach. They believed that the black community should take power over its own destiny economically.

Bankers and Businesswomen

The story of Maggie Lena Walker is rooted deep in the black community and the special place that women have occupied in it. It is the story of a woman who believed fervently in the capacity of—and the absolute need for—black people to take their destiny into their own hands. That belief grew out of the history of black America, as did the organization she took over and transformed at the end of the nineteenth century.

The Independent Order of St. Luke was founded originally in Baltimore in 1867, by a woman named Mary Ann Prout. An offshoot of the order was founded in Richmond a few years later. For some time its primary function was to help its members when they were sick and bury them after they were dead. The various "councils" of the organization also served as a way for businesspeople and others to make useful contacts. However, as the end of the century approached, the order began to show signs of age.

Maggie Walker, the woman who would revitalize and entirely reconstruct the Order of St. Luke's, was born a few years before the order was founded. Her mother, Elizabeth Draper, worked for Elizabeth Van Lew, the prominent member of Richmond's white society who organized a small, private spy ring for the Union army. Maggie Walker's father, Eccles Cuthbert, was an Irish-born newspaperman, a correspondent for the *New York Herald* for many years. He was not married to Walker's mother. She married a black man named William Mitchell a few years after Maggie was born. A waiter at the luxurious St. Charles Hotel, he was murdered when Maggie was an early adolescent.

Maggie Walker's life seems to have touched, at every turn, important elements of black American history. Her mother, for example, did laundry for a living. That may seem a prosaic enough occupation but, historically, it was far from it. For one thing, laundresses didn't "live in" as did most other domestic workers. This gave them an autonomy that others didn't have. For another, they worked in groups, doing their tasks at one home one day and at another the next. While they rubbed clothes against their washboards, the women traded stories and information. They also discussed the concerns of the black community, argued with each other, and came to conclusions about important issues. What the laundresses thought became a real force in black community politics. In the 1880s, they were among the first black workers to organize, going on strike in large cities all over the South.

The young Maggie went to a school with an all-black faculty. It was from her teachers as well as her mother and the laundresses that she began to learn the philosophy of black self-reliance. Maggie joined the Order of St. Luke when she was fourteen and continued to participate after she graduated from high school and became a teacher. When marriage forced her to give up her teaching position in 1886, she became more active in the Order of St. Luke, working in the office and becoming a collector of dues. She also attended several St. Luke conventions. At an 1895 convention, she made a proposal for the formation of a juvenile department and what she called a "Council of Matrons." Soon after, she was elected Grand Matron, a position she held for the rest of her life.

At the 1899 convention, Maggie Walker was elected to head the Order of St. Luke. She immediately began building a new kind of organization. Calling the order a women's organization that gave equal opportunities to men, Walker and her followers helped to found a school for delinquent girls, raised money for scholarships, supported women's suffrage, denounced the theft of the vote from black men, and spoke out against lynching. They led the 1904 boycott of Richmond's segregated streetcars. They also created the St. Luke Penny Savings Bank, a weekly newspaper called the *St. Luke Herald,* and a department store, the St. Luke Emporium. By 1920, the order had more than one hundred thousand members in twenty-eight states.

When the St. Luke Penny Savings Bank came into existence, Maggie Lena Walker became, most historians agree, the first woman bank president in America. Later, because of new regulatory laws, the bank was separated from the order. At that point, St. Luke's became primarily an insurance company. The St. Luke Bank and Trust Company, as it was now called, merged with other black banks to become the Consolidated Bank and Trust Company, with Maggie Walker as chairman of the board. The bank still thrives today.

While running her various enterprises, Maggie Walker traveled to preach and promote economic autonomy for the black community through business. She was convinced economics was the key to freedom for the African American people and was scornful of any support of white financial interests by the black community. She was also a passionate feminist and advocate of black women. "And the great all absorbing interest," she said in 1909, "this thing which has driven sleep from my eyes and fatigue from my body, is the love I bear women, our Negro women, hemmed, circumscribed with every imaginable obstacle in our way, blocked and held down by the fears and prejudices of the whites, ridiculed and sneered at by the intelligent blacks."

At the same time, there were other women working fiercely towards the goal of economic self-sufficiency in a field in which black women had long been active. It was a complex, paradoxical, and politically controversial issue—hair.

Black Beauty

The New York mansion of Madame C. J. Walker was just a few blocks from that of John D. Rockefeller. It was an appropriate location for the home of the first American woman to become a millionaire through her own efforts, without an inheritance from either father or husband. Indeed, Walker was born in a sharecropper's shack, and her husband benefitted far more from his association with her than the other way around. Walker's accomplishments are so striking that it is hard to imagine why she is not yet renowned for her leadership of the black community during the period from 1890 to 1920. She overcame almost overwhelming obstacles of race, gender, and class to leave a legacy that even today affects millions of African Americans daily. Tens of thousands of black women were able to escape from the limitations of domestic work through her company, and hundreds of thousands of others found a new way of defining and presenting themselves through her products and her philosophy.

"I am a woman who came from the cotton fields of the South," Walker said to the National Negro Business League convention in 1912. "I was promoted from there to the washtub. Then I was promoted to the cook kitchen, and from there I promoted myself into the business of manufacturing hair goods and preparations. . . . I have built my own factory in my own ground." The rest of her speech—which she gave from the floor because she had been refused the podium—was so impressive that Booker T. Washington overcame his reluctance to allow a woman to address the convention and, the following year, Walker was the keynote speaker.

In the late nineteenth and early twentieth centuries, black women advanced in business in the areas they had already staked out—beauty and fashion. As more African Americans moved to the cities and got jobs in industry, a demand grew for products that would help them improve their appearance. (Improvement, of course, was in the eyes of the beholder.) Many white-owned firms exploited the market in the 1890s, appealing to prejudices about color and the desire of many black people to be accepted in white society. The most popular products were those promising to straighten hair and lighten skin. The white firms, however, were not alone in their development of the black market. The leading black beauty entrepreneurs of the time were Anthony Overton, Annie Turnbo Malone, Madam C. J. Walker, and Sarah Spencer Washington, all of whom sold hair tonics, pressing oils, face creams, and other products.

The most significant figures in the fields were women. Annie Turnbo Pope Malone's Poro Company was one of the first in the field of black beauty products. Walker, nee Sarah Breedlove, probably first became interested in beauty products while working for Malone, in 1904. In 1906, Sarah Breedlove married Charles Joseph Walker and adopted the name by which she would be known for the rest of her life. In the meantime, she had developed her own line of beauty products and now, with her husband's help, began marketing them from door to door. She also adapted a French invention to black hair needs, coming up with the "hot comb."

Soon Walker began to hire other black women to sell her products and opened a training school for them. The company grew so quickly that it was necessary to move the headquarters from Denver to Indianapolis in 1910 to take advantage of that city's transportation opportunities. Walker put together a staff that would remain with her for years and divorced her husband. In 1913, she bought a townhouse in New York to house her training school, a beauty salon, and living quarters for herself and her daughter. However, she spent little time there. Instead, according to her great-great-granddaughter, A'Lelia Perry Bundles, she "crisscrossed the country and gave slide lectures promoting her business, as well as other Black institutions, at conventions held by Black religious, fraternal, and civic organizations. To expand her market internationally, she traveled to Jamaica, Cuba, Haiti, Costa Rica, and the Panama Canal."

When Madame Walker gave her keynote address at the National Negro Business League, she stressed the role of black women. "The girls and women of our race," she said, "must not be afraid to take hold of business endeavor and . . . wring success out of a number of business opportunities that lie at their very doors. . . . I want to say to every Negro woman present, don't sit down and wait for the opportunities to come. . . . Get up and make them!" In the meantime, Walker was making a lot of those opportunities herself, for other black women. By 1916, the Walker Company had twenty thousand agents. Most of them were black women, and they made three or four times as much as they could make as maids. They also achieved a level of autonomy and respectability that they could not have aspired to as domestic workers.

In the turbulent year of 1917, Walker joined with W. E. B. Du Bois and James Weldon Johnson to call for black support of the war effort. In the same year, when a terrible race riot broke out in East St. Louis, Walker was on the planning committee of the Negro Silent Protest Parade. About ten thousand black New Yorkers marched in silence down Fifth Avenue to protest the rioting. Increasingly, Madame Walker was the one woman present when prominent African Americans gathered to exert their influence for the benefit of the race. In 1918, she was the keynote speaker for the NAACP at antilynching fund-raisers around the country. It was during that year that she opened her estate near the Rockefellers. The wealthiest black woman in America and the first self-made American woman millionaire, she had become a symbol of black economic independence.

When Walker died, she left tens of thousands of dollars to Mary McLeod Bethune's Daytona Normal and Industrial School and the Tuskegee Institute, as well as to other black schools. Her support of education was, of course, typical of black women, in part because the education of black Americans has, from the beginning, been largely in their own hands. At the beginning of the twentieth century, it was largely in the hands of black women.

Strengthened By Her Presence

In his book *Black Education in the South, 1860–1935,* James D. Anderson notes that the white South all but abandoned black education after 1900. From 1900 to 1920, tax appropriations for school building increased sharply in every single southern state, but virtually none of the money was used for black schools. In her book *Proud Shoes: The Story of an American Family,* Pauli Murray described the kind of school black students were forced to attend.

> West End looked more like a warehouse than a school. It was a dilapidated, rickety, two-story wooden building which creaked and swayed in the wind as if it might collapse. . . . Outside it was scarred with peeling paint from many winters of rain and snow. At recess we [were] herded into a yard of cracked clay, barren of tree or bush, and played what games we could improvise like hopscotch or springboard, which we contrived by pulling rotted palings off the wooden fence and placing them on brickbats.
>
> . . . the floors were bare and splintery, the plumbing was leaky, the drinking fountains broken and the toilets in the basement

smelly and constantly out of order. We'd have to wade through pools of foul water to get to them. . . .

In Atlanta in 1913, at least one thousand black children were denied schooling because of overcrowding. Another five thousand attended only 3½ hours a day because their schools were in double session. Nonetheless, when a $3 million bond issue was proposed—half of it earmarked for schools—only $37,000 was allocated to black education. The entire sum was allotted to repairs of existing buildings.

In 1914, the average public expenditure for education for a white child in school in the South was $10.82. For a black child, it was $4.01. In 1930, the gap was even wider. $42.39 was being spent for each white child and $15.86 for a black child. In the late 1920s, the annual state expenditure for education in South Carolina was $52.60 for each white student and $5.20 for each black student. Schools in the North were not a great deal better.

In these schools, and with enormously limited resources, black women faced the challenge of educating the race. In 1890 the numbers of male and female black teachers were roughly equal, according to the U.S. Census—7,864 women and 7,236 men. Ten years later, the number of men had remained very much the same, and the number of black women had risen to 13,524. By 1910, two-thirds of all black American educators were women. What they faced when they went out to teach is difficult to comprehend. Often, there was not even a school. The teacher would find that part of her job was to raise funds to build the school building or even to build it herself. Stephanie Shaw cites Genevieve Nell Ladson, a graduate of the American Missionary Association's Avery Institute. "When I say I built a school . . . I mean I built it, from helping them cut down the trees with my saw, to hammering boards in place."

There was a fund endowed by Julius Rosenwald (president of Sears, Roebuck and Company) that provided money for black schools on the condition that members of the black community match the donation. Often the teacher found herself canvassing for dimes and dollars or organizing bake sales and quilt raffles to raise the matching funds. In 1915, a black teacher helped citizens in Wake County, North Carolina, mortgage their property and borrow $3,500 from a local bank. Parents pledged to repay, at harvest time, the people whose homes were put up for security. Once there was a building, teachers often begged or borrowed textbooks, blackboards, maps, and any other equipment they could find. Then they set out to teach far more students (64 percent of black schools in the South were one-teacher schools and 19 percent were two-teacher schools), with a wider range of aptitudes, with less help than white teachers. They were also paid considerably less.

There was one other major obstacle in the way of these remarkable women. School boards and others who provided funds for black schooling usually believed that black children did not need and could not use anything beyond agricultural and industrial training. They had been encouraged in this belief by Booker T. Washington, and at first glance, the idea that black children should be trained to do the only kind of work that would be available to them makes sense. This kind of training was certainly needed, but to limit black Americans to vocational education would have been grossly unfair and dangerous. It was up to teachers to find a way to go beyond mere "training" to offer black children the kind of enlightenment that a liberal education can offer.

First, many of them used the practical training they were required to offer as a way of improving the community. Second, they often used this part of the curriculum as a way to raise money for other kinds of education. Historian Valinda Littlefield writes, "They deliberately concealed their activism for educational improvements under the cloak of industrial education. Such invisibility created a dual perception. On the one hand, these educators were viewed as doing exactly what they were told, as evidenced by the writings of such historians as Horace Mann Bond and Carter G. Woodson. And, on the other hand, they were quite visible in the black community raising funds for educational needs and working tirelessly to improve the living conditions of the race."

One particular group of teachers stands out during this period. The Jeanes supervisors went far beyond their appointed tasks to become leaders of their communities. Anna T. Jeanes was a white Quaker woman who donated $1 million to set up a fund to support the "rudimentary education of Colored people residing in rural districts" in the southern states. The Jeanes teachers were asked to model their work after that of Virginia Randolph, an African American teacher in Honrico County, Virginia, who had developed a method of combining academic subjects with practical education and of working closely with the community. Beginning in 1908, they went out to rural communities at a salary of about $45 a month for seven months of the year. Many stretched their salaries to cover the other five months so that they could stay in their communities year-round.

Jeanes teachers organized "improvement leagues" and "betterment associations." They raised money, created gardens and gardening clubs, participated in reading circles and study groups, started libraries and summer schools. They formed "moonlight schools" to teach adults. And they managed to place enough emphasis on academic subjects—in between raising beans and feeding livestock—to please parents who did not want their children relegated to manual labor all their lives. One Jeanes teacher in Georgia said that her job was to do the "next need thing." People depended on her to "improve my soil, add my account at the commissary, feed my children, take me to the hospital, bury my mother, write my son, read this letter, mend my steps, find a minister or justice of the peace to get me married, show me how to build a sanitary privy."

All of these black teachers accepted leadership roles in their communities. Often this role involved caring for the poor and for those who suffered from unhygienic situations. It also involved helping the members of the community to improve their lot financially. Some teachers formed cooperatives to help buy land for individual families as well as for school buildings. Often the teacher, with her usually minimal education in health and hygiene, was the closest a town had to a doctor or nurse. In short, black women worked unbelievably long hours for very little money, taking on staggering responsibilities . . . and considered themselves blessed. But for all their efforts, the South remained a hostile place, infertile ground for growing young souls.

REVOLUTION OF THE HEART

Sometimes, I'm grieving from my hat down to my shoes./I'm a good-hearted woman that's a slave to the blues. Ma Rainey, "Slave to the Blues"

The year was 1902. A woman named Gertrude Rainey was traveling around the South with a musical troupe called the Rabbit Foot Minstrels. Somewhere in Missouri, she said later, she heard a song. It was a very sad song, about a man who went away, and it was being sung by a lone young woman. Rainey learned it and began to sing it on stage. Her audiences reacted to the song as strongly as she had. Something in them responded to the loneliness and the aching sorrow in the music. So "Ma" Rainey began to write other songs with the same feeling to them and called them the blues.

Train's at the station, I heard the whistle blow.
Train's at the station, I heard the whistle blow.
I done bought my ticket but I don't know where I'll go.

MA RAINEY, "TRAVELING BLUES"

Art has never been a luxury for black women. Much of what they created was immediately useful—pots and baskets and quilts, songs that kept the work moving. But even that which was not utilitarian was part of the art of survival. It provided a way to affirm identity, for oneself and for the community. It was a means of communication with other members of the black community and even with the white world. It was an outlet for apparently unbearable emotion and therefore a way of preserving psychological health.

You can send me up the river or send me to that mean old jail.
You can send me up the river or send me to that mean old jail.
I killed my man and I don't need no bail.

BESSIE SMITH, "SING SING PRISON BLUES"

Ironically, black women's art was also a source of pain, and this pain came directly from the white world's desire for the artistic expressions of black people. During slavery black singers were forced to perform for the occupants of the Big House. They had to provide, for the entertainment of the masters, the music they had conceived to soothe their own sorrows. This bittersweet aspect of black art continued after slavery when, in order to put food on the table, black artists sold their quilts or sang on street corners. Some black women artists were able to protect themselves in these situations. They sang to white people songs that mocked the white world. They dressed themselves in such dignity no one could touch them. They found fulfillment no one could take away. Others were destroyed by the contradictions. The black community valued both.

Of course, the blues were not born full-grown on that night in Missouri. They came out of the songs that had been sung on plantations and in black churches around the country. But no one has a better claim than Ma Rainey to having written and performed in public the first songs to be called "the blues." The music Rainey sang was earthy. It came out of the rural South and spoke about the experiences of country people. "Ma Rainey differed from most, if not all, the great women blues singers," writes Charles Edward Smith, "in that her style was directly influenced by rural Afro-American folk music, even while the content tended more and more to be that of urban blues—love misery, with its deep pathos and wry humor."

Within a few years after the crucial Missouri night, Rainey and the blues were enormously popular throughout the South. Then the first blues recording was made by Mamie Smith, in 1920, creating a prodigious demand for more records. When Rainey recorded "Moonshine Blues" for Paramount Records in 1923, her fame spread to the rest of the country. She made more than ninety records for Paramount in the next five years, later touring through the South and the Midwest on the black vaudeville circuit.

The next great name in blues singing was also a woman. The legendary Bessie Smith was born into a poor family in Tennessee. She began her career as a singer on the streets, singing for tips while her brother played the guitar. When she was eighteen, she got a job as a dancer with Moses Stokes's traveling minstrel troupe. At the time, the headliner for the troupe was Ma Rainey. The two women became, and remained, good friends. Within four years, Smith was a headliner herself. In another two years, she had her own troupe. In 1923, she was signed by Columbia Records, and her first Columbia album sold 780,000 copies in six months. Her stage appearances became even more successful. In such cities as Detroit and Chicago, where there were now large black populations, people lined up all the way around the block to hear her sing. According to Langston Hughes, her voice was so powerful that "When she sang in tent shows in the South, nobody needed to pay admission to *hear* her. But, of course, if they wanted to *see* her, they bought tickets."

Bessie Smith's music was, like Rainey's, connected to the rural tradition in African American music, but it became increasingly urban in content. Her songs dealt with her experiences as a black woman in the cities of the North, and those experiences were not pretty. Bessie Smith had a rough life and her music reflected it. She knew and sang about poverty and injustice, about crime and the slums of the cities. "Woman's Troubles Blues," for example, was about a young black woman unjustly put in prison. "Washerwoman's Blues" described, satirically, city life for migrant African Americans. "Poor Man's Blues" has been considered her greatest social protest song.

Smith also sang about sex in a way that must have made some of the respectable clubwomen shrink with shame. Her songs were filled with double entendres, risqué references, and thorough enjoyment of her sexuality. They were filled, too, with a woman's determination to protect herself and her self-respect. "I Ain't Gonna Play No Second Fiddle" and "I've Been Mistreated and I Don't Like It" set clear boundaries.

For a full decade, the blueswomen reigned as queens of the music business. They made the fortunes of a number of "race record" companies. And then, their time ended. With the end of the twenties, their enormous popularity waned. Some, like Bessie Smith, were overwhelmed by injustice, disappointment, and despair. Some continued their careers, much less spectacularly, for another five or six decades. To historians, the blueswomen represent an opportunity to hear from a part of the community of black women that is otherwise virtually silent. Working-class and working-poor women seldom wrote or spoke publicly about their lives. We do not have collections of letters from these women to their sisters. But we can hear their voices clearly when the blueswomen sing, and their voices give balance to the history now being uncovered.

The blueswomen were not the only black women who expressed the culture of black America through music. There was an entire world the respectable clubwomen never visited, where people drank and sang and danced away the sorrows of the day. It was a world of honky-tonks and brothels, filled with music that didn't die away until the sun came up. And black women were there, right beside the men, playing the stride piano and blowing their horns.

The very earliest reports of black dance music refer to women instrumentalists. Linda Dahl, in *Stormy Weather,* cites jazz historian Curtis D. Jerde's belief that "black women, especially among the lower classes, participated as instrumentalists in the music that prefigured jazz—particularly in the popular brass and marching bands—much more widely than has been recognized." Jerde theorizes that women instrumentalists were pushed out of black dance music when it entered the mainstream of American music, in part because of white prejudices against women and in part because there was now money to be made. However, at the end of the nineteenth century, they were still very much part of the scene.

Many of the names of these women have been lost, but there are some whose fame has endured. "Mama Lou," for example, was a brothel pianist and singer who is credited with writing the songs "Ta-ra-ra-boom-de-ay," "There'll Be a Hot Time in the Old Town Tonight," and "Frankie and Johnny." Then there were groups such as the Ladies Orchestra, which was formed by black women in Chelsea, Massachusetts, in 1884 and the Colored Female Brass Band, which toured Michigan in the late 1880s. Old jazz hands remembered Mamie Desdoumes of Storyville, the red-light district of New Orleans, who had only three fingers on her right hand and played only one tune but packed them in anywhere she played. Until white audiences began to discover jazz, there was apparently room for women in the band.

ANOTHER EXODUS

For almost half a millennium black people in the New World have been in motion. Much of it has been forced, and some of it voluntary and self-propelled. During the antebellum decades, thousands of enslaved people fled from the South, determined to escape. Many died trying. After the Civil War, many moved west to establish new black towns and settlements in Kansas and Oklahoma. At the same time, others attempted to return to Africa. But the Great Migration, the truly massive movement from the largely rural South to the urban areas of the North, came between 1910 and 1930. It changed life for black women in ways that are still causing confusion and concern at the end of the twentieth century.

"Moses, my servant is dead. Therefore arise and

go over Jordan." There are no deliverers.

They're all dead. We must arise and go over Jordan.

We can take the promised land.

NANNIE BURROUGHS, "UNLOAD YOUR

TOMS," *LOUISIANA WEEKLY,*

DECEMBER 23, 1933

THEY CARRIED THEIR
FREEDOM BAGS

CHAPTER NINE

STARTING IN ABOUT 1910, tens of thousands of black people left the Jim Crow South and settled in the northern states. What the North represented to them is difficult to define. For a century, it had been the land of freedom. After the Civil War, it became the land of refuge. In the early twentieth century, it was the land of opportunity. No matter what its reality, it held out the promise of a better life to many of those who lived in the oppressive South.

The North was also the land of cities. In the South, most black people lived in rural areas, but when they moved to the North they were leaving behind farms and fields. By 1920, almost 40 percent of Afro-Americans living in the North were concentrated in eight cities that contained only 20 percent of the total northern population. Five of these cities were in the Midwest—Chicago, Detroit, Cleveland, Cincinnati, and Columbus, Ohio. The other three were the northeastern cities of New York, Philadelphia, and Pittsburgh.

Traditionally, historians have focused, with good reason, on economic explanations for migration. Clearly the economic opportunities in midwestern cities drew black workers. The number of African Americans attracted by jobs available at the Ford, Dodge, Chrysler, Chevrolet, and Packard plants in Detroit increased from 5,741 in 1910 to 120,066 in 1930, accounting for the astounding 611.3 percent increase in the city's black population between 1910 and 1920. Chicago, meat packing center of the country, had a black population in 1910 of 44,103. By 1930, it was 233,903.

Making cars and slaughtering beef, however, were almost exclusively male activities. There were some factory jobs open to women, but most were not open to black women. The work they were able to get was the least desirable and least remunerative of all. Many black women were doomed to work in the same kinds of domestic service jobs they had held in the South. Of course, there was some economic difference. A maid earning $7 a week in Cleveland perceived herself to be much better off than her counterpart receiving $2.50 a week in Mobile, Alabama, regardless of the difference in cost of living. And those lucky enough to land jobs as factory workers believed themselves to be better off than domestic servants who endured the unrelenting scrutiny, interference, and complaints of household mistresses.

Still, it seems unlikely that so many women made the difficult journey north for no other reason than the slim possibility of a slightly better-paying job. Most had to save for long periods of time to accumulate the money to pay for a train ticket. Many left behind children, hoping to make enough to send for them later. Virtually all, like the black men who traveled north, had to say good-bye to parents and extended families, with far less hope of making a real change in their economic situation. There appear to have been other motives at work as well.

For black men, leaving the South meant leaving the constant fear of lynching, which had become horrifyingly commonplace in such states as Mississippi and Georgia. For black women, as we have seen, there was another, entirely compelling consideration. The need for sexual autonomy. The desire for sexual preservation. The fear of rape. In *Living In, Living Out,* Elizabeth Clark-Lewis records interviews with eighty-one domestic workers who traveled from the Deep South to Washington, D.C., in the early part of the century. They were quite frank about the dangers awaiting a young woman who went out to work in a white home. "Nobody was sent out before you was told to be careful of the white man or his sons. They'd tell you the stories of rape . . . hard too! No lies. You was to be told true, so you'd not get raped. Everyone warned you and told you 'be careful.' "

"You couldn't be out working," said another woman, "til you knew how people was raped. You'd know how to run, or always not be in the house with the white man or big sons. Just everyone told you something to keep you from being raped, 'cause it happened, and they told you."

Another woman told how her family tried to prepare her and her sisters to deal with this danger. "My mama told you first. Next was aunts and all. Now, then just before I was to leave with the family [I was to work for], my daddy just gave me a razor and he said it's for any man who tries to force himself on you. It's for the white man."

No white man had to fear prosecution for sexually attacking a black woman. And *all* black women, of whatever class or reputation, had to fear sexual assault, exploitation, and rape. The threat of rape was held over black women as the threat of beatings and lynching were held over black men. Escape from that climate of terror has to have been a primary motivation for black women to migrate.

Domestic violence entered the mix of motivations as well. The letters, diaries, and oral histories collected by the Black Women in the Middle West Project and deposited in the Indiana Historical Society contain descriptions of the domestic violence that inspired black women to leave their rural homes for uncertain futures in the city. Sara Brooks vividly described the events that led her to leave her husband for the third and final time. When she ran away from home the last time, she didn't stop running until she reached Cleveland almost a decade later. "When he hit me," she said, "I jumped outa the bed, and when I jumped outa the bed, I just ran. . . . I didn't have a gown to put on—I had on a slip and had on a short-sleeved sweater. I left the kids right there with him and I went all the way to his father's' house that night, barefeeted, with that on, on the twenty-fifth day of December. That was in the dark. It was two miles or more and it was raining. . . . I walked. And I didn't go back." While Brooks's experiences are hardly representative, they are nevertheless suggestive of the internal and personal reasons black women may have had for leaving the South.

Then too, a great many black "women" migrated because that is what they were told to do. These were the girls in their teens whose families arranged for them to leave their homes in the South to "help out" their families. Decades after the move that took her to care for her brother's children, one woman said, "The 'me' notion wasn't even thought about. My father's cousin came down home and her eyes fell on me for brother. That's all I know how to tell. My feelings wasn't one way or another. Who'd ask? . . . You had to help, and it'll be up here instead of down there."

There was considerable family ritual around the migration of these adolescents. The northern part of the family would choose a girl and negotiate with her mother and father, coming to terms about what she would be given in return for her "help," and what the family would be given to compensate them for losing her. The girl was not allowed to take part in or even hear this negotiation. What she did hear was what Clark-Lewis calls the "pleading process." In this ritual, the northern relative asked for the girl, and the southern family protested against losing her. "Mama brought me into the parlor with Daddy, Ma-Sis, and Brother," one woman explained. "Brother told Daddy he wanted me to go back north with him. Daddy hugged me and told Brother, 'No. She can't go. You got Lillie and Mary up there. This one here's my heart. She can't go.' They talked and talked. Then Ma-Sis started to cry when she was telling how she'd have to leave their two young ones alone if I didn't come. Finally Daddy broke down and said I could go." The next day she was given the dress that her parents had requested "a long time ago" for her to wear on the train.

After the negotiation and the pleading, there was the "traveling talk"—during which the girl became accustomed to the idea of leaving—as well as gifts and amulets for her to take on her journey, and finally the journey itself. In all of this, the black girl had little say. What her family wanted her to do, she did.

Another motivation for migration was simply the desire for freedom, for "something better," for some kind of personal fulfillment. This desire on the part of black women is difficult to define but easy to recognize. "At home you better not try to do no better," said one woman. "It wasn't for colored people to be much of nothing. But up here, I knew different." The yearning to be someone was not the least of the reasons black women moved north.

This focus on the sexual and personal impetus for black women's migration does not diminish the importance of economic motives. However, as historian Lawrence Levine puts it, "As indisputably important as the economic motive was, it is possible to overstress it so that black migration is converted into an inexorable force and Negroes are seen once again not as actors capable of affecting at least some part of their destinies, but primarily as beings who are acted upon—southern leaves blown North by the winds of destitution." It is reasonable to assume that many were indeed "southern leaves blown North." Many others, however, were self-propelled actors seeking respect, space in which to live, and a means by which to earn an adequate living.

THE JOURNEY NORTH

Black men and women migrated into the Midwest in different ways. Single men, for example, usually worked their way north, leaving farms for southern cities, doing odd jobs and sometimes staying in one location for a few years before proceeding to the next stop. This pattern has been called "secondary migration." A single black woman, on the other hand, usually traveled the entire distance in one trip. She often had a specific relative—or fictive kin—waiting for her at her destination. That person could have advanced her the fare, might be able to give or help her find a place to stay for a while, could be of help in the search for a job.

The different migratory patterns reflected the constraints on women in society at large. A woman traveling by herself was at greater risk than a man. After all, a man could and did, with less opprobrium and threat of bodily harm, spend nights outdoors. Men were usually better able to defend themselves against attackers. And, given the low esteem in which black women were held, even courts and law officers would have ridiculed and dismissed assault complaints from a black woman traveling alone, regardless of her social status. Yes, it was wise to make the trip all at once and better still to have company.

Although greater emphasis has been placed on men who left families behind, black women, too—many of whom were divorced, separated, or widowed—left loved ones in the South when they migrated. Like married men, single black women sent for their families after periods of time that ranged from months to years. It would be difficult, if not impossible, to estimate the number of women who had to leave their children with parents, friends, and other relatives in the South, but there is evidence in various places, such as this oral history of Elizabeth Burch of Fort Wayne, Indiana.

> I was born [December 20, 1926, in Chester, Georgia] out of wedlock to Arlena Burch and John Halt. My mother went north and that's where they—all of it began in a little town called Albion, Michigan, and she went back south to have me. . . . My mother decided, well, she go back up north. She married just to get away from home to go back north and this guy was working as a sharecropper and he had made enough money that year that he was willing to marry my mother and take her back up north. . . . So they left me with Miss Burch—Miss Mattie Elizabeth Burch, namesake which was my grandmother, and that's where I grew up, and years passed and years went through. I was just on the farm with my grandparents.

The difficulty of putting aside enough money to send for her children placed a tremendous strain on many a domestic's salary. It took Sara Brooks almost fifteen years to retrieve the three sons she had left behind in Orchard, Alabama. With obvious pride in her accomplishment, Brooks explained, "The first one to come home was Jerome. . . . Then Miles had to come because my father didn't wanna keep him down there no more because he wouldn't mind him. . . . Then Benjamin was the last to come." Brooks summed up her success. "So I come up to Cleveland with Vivian [her daughter], and after I came up, the rest of my kids came up here. I was glad—I was *very* glad because I had wanted them with me all the time, but I just wasn't able to support them, and then I didn't have no place for them, either, when I left and come to Cleveland 'cause I came here to my brother."

There were two very significant results of this kind of absentee mothering. First, the acculturation of these women into an urban lifestyle became a long, drawn-out, and often incomplete process. Second, as historians Peter Gottlieb and Jacqueline Jones persuasively maintain, black women served as critical links in the "migration chain." They proved most instrumental in persuading family members and friends to move north. It is precisely because women left children behind in the care of others that they contributed so much to the endurance and tenacity of the migration chain. Their attachment to the South was more than sentimental or even cultural. They left parts of themselves behind.

Family obligations encouraged many black women to return south for periodic visits. Burch recalled, "My mother would come maybe once a year—maybe Christmas to visit" her in Georgia from Ft. Wayne. Still other women returned to participate in community celebrations, family reunions, and religious revivals. Of course, such excursions southward had benefits beyond the most important one of maintaining bonds with family. They also allowed women to display new clothes and other accoutrements of success. Sara Brooks tells how, before she herself made the journey to Cleveland, she took delight in her sister-in-law's visits home. "I noticed she had some nice-looking little clothes when she come back to Orchard to visit. She had nice little dresses and brassieres and things, which I didn't have. . . . I didn't even have a brassiere, and she'd lend me hers and I'd wear it to church."

Unable, or unwilling, to sever ties to or abandon the South irrevocably, black women assimilated to northern life only patchily. It was this incompleteness of assimilation that was responsible for the southernization of the Midwest, where most of the migrants ended up. Vestiges of southern black culture were transplanted and continually renewed by these women in motion. The resiliency of this cultural transference is reflected in food preferences and preparation styles, reliance on folk remedies and superstitions, religious practices, speech patterns, games, family structures, social networks, and music, most notably the blues.

In short, although unattached black women may have traveled the initial distance to Chicago, Cleveland, Detroit, or Cincinnati in one trip, their cultural and emotional migration was a long process. And it was often one they undertook alone.

What I Wanted, I Worked for It

Black women who migrated north had fewer children than those who remained in the South, for a number of reasons. In urban settings, for one thing, children were not as economically important to the family as they were on the farm. Children were "hands" in the rural South, working in the fields from an early age to supplement the family income. In the North, they were mouths to feed. And even without knowledge of effective birth control, unattached black women could make a choice—sexual abstinence—that would limit the number of children they had. On August 23, 1921, Sarah D. Tyree wrote tellingly of her decision not to date. Tyree had a certificate from the Illinois College of Chiropracty but was, at the time, taking care of aged parents and her sister's children in Indianapolis.

> I have learned to stay at home lots. I firmly believe in a womanly in-
> dependence. Believe that a woman should be allowed to go and
> come where and when she pleases along if she wants to, and so long
> as she knows who is right, she should not have to worry about what
> others think. It is not every women who can turn for herself as I can,
> and the majority of women who have learned early to depend upon
> their male factors do not believe that their sister-woman can get on
> alone. So she becomes dangerously suspicious, and damagingly
> tongue-wagging. I have become conscious of the fact that because I
> am not married, I am watched with much interest. So I try to avoid
> the appearance of evil, for the sake of the weaker fellow. I do not
> therefore go out unaccompanied at night. There are some young
> men I would like to go out with occasionally if it could be under-
> stood that it was for the occasion and not for life that we go.

Black women may have had many reasons for practicing sexual abstinence, including deeply held religious convictions, disillusionment with black men, a history of unhappy and abusive marriages, experience with an earlier unplanned pregnancy, and adherence to Victorian ideals of morality. One of the most important—the desire to refute negative images of black women as a whole—leads us directly to a factor that has prevented serious consideration of the reality and extent of self-determined celibacy. In other words, there is one simple reason that historians and sociologists have not taken seriously the idea that black women had fewer children because they refrained from sex: they have not believed that black women would or could refrain from sex. Clearly, however, many did. "See, after Vivian was born," Sara Brooks reported, "I didn't have no boyfriend or nothing, and I went to Mobile, I didn't still have no boyfriend in a long time. Vivian was nine years old when Eric come. . . . But after Eric came along, I didn't have no boyfriend. I didn't want one because what I wanted, I worked for it, and that was that home."

As time passed and black women became more economically suffi-cient, better educated, and more involved in self-improvement efforts, in-cluding the flourishing black women's club movement, they began to have more access to birth control information. Then, too, as the black women's clubs, sororities, church groups, and charity organizations took hold within black communities, they gave rise to those values and attitudes traditionally associated with the middle classes. To black middle-class aspirants, the social stigma of having many children would, perhaps, have kept family size down.

Further, over time, the gradually evolving imbalance in the sex ratio meant that increasing numbers of black women in urban midwestern communities would never marry. And then there was the sad loss of babies before birth. Poor black women were overworked, undernourished, and inadequately housed. They suffered innumerable health problems, and these problems affected their pregnancies. In discussing the morbidity and mortality rates of black Chicagoans of the time, William Tuttle observes that "the statistics indicated that the death rate for Chicago's blacks was comparable to that of Bombay, India." Tuttle points out that the stillbirth rate was twice as high for black women as for white.

Here it is important to note the difference between black women who worked in middle-class occupations and those in working-class ones. Middle-class working women, regardless of color, had fewer children than those employed in blue-collar jobs. The professional and semi-professional occupations most accessible to black women during the years between world wars included teaching, nursing, and social work on the one hand, and hairdressing or dressmaking on the other. In some of the smaller midwestern communities and towns, married women teachers, race notwithstanding, were deprived of their jobs by school policy, especially if the marriage became public knowledge or the married teacher became pregnant. At least one black schoolteacher in Lafayette, Indiana, confided that she never married, although she had been asked, because in the 1930s and 1940s to have done so would have cost her the position. The pressure on all black professional women was considerable. The more educated they were, the greater the sense of being responsible, somehow, for the advancement of the race and the uplift of black womanhood. They held these expectations of themselves and found them reinforced by the demands of the black community and its institutions. Under conditions and pressure such as these, it would be wrong to argue that professional women practiced "voluntary" celibacy.

Nevertheless, the autonomy, so hard earned and enjoyed to varying degrees by both professional women and personal service workers, offered meaningful alternatives to the uncertainties of marriage and the demands of child rearing. The very economic diversity, whether real or imagined, that had attracted black women to the urban Midwest also held the promise of freedom to fashion socially useful and independent lives beyond family boundaries.

For most black women, the only one of the professions that seemed at all within reach was teaching. There were some, however, who managed to enter the fields of medicine, law, and journalism. Fortunately, it was dedication, not hope of wealth, that motivated these women, because dedication would be demanded of them and wealth almost always denied.

PROFESSIONAL WOMEN

In the post-Reconstruction South, several medical schools for African Americans were founded. By 1910, only two, Howard and Meharry, remained open, largely because by this time black men were being admitted to white medical schools. Black women, on the other hand, were not. Indeed, few women of any race were admitted to the vast majority of medical schools until the 1960s. As a result, the black schools were of great significance in the education of black women physicians, as was the Woman's Medical College of Pennsylvania. By 1900, Howard had produced 552 physicians, of whom 25 were black women. By 1900, the Woman's Medical College had sent forth a dozen black women. And by 1920, Meharry had produced 39 black women doctors.

For black women physicians, graduating from medical school was only the first problem. Establishing a practice was enormously difficult as well. Virtually no whites and only a handful of black men were willing to consult a black woman physician. That left black women and children—the poorest population in the country. And for those who can barely afford food and shelter, doctors are often considered a luxury. Moreover, black physicians were seldom allowed to treat their patients in white clinics, hospitals, and other health facilities. When allowance was made in these places for any black physician, that physician was male. As a result, black women often had to establish institutions in which to work.

Matilda Evans, the first black woman to practice in South Carolina, treated her patients in her home, no matter how ill they were, until her practice became large enough for her to rent a building and establish a hospital for thirty patients, with nurse training school attached. In all, she founded three hospitals between 1898 and 1916. She also created a free clinic for mothers and children in the basement of a black church in 1930 and organized the Negro Health Association of South Carolina. Lucy Brown, graduate of the Woman's Medical College, worked with eight black male physicians to found the Hospital and Nursing Training School in Charleston.

Another venue for black women physicians was historically black colleges and universities. The pay was tiny, but important work was done. In the early part of the twentieth century, the resident physicians at these schools included Halle Johnson, Ionia R. Whipper (daughter and niece of the famous Rollin sisters), Verina Jones, and Susan Steward. In addition to providing medical service, they taught classes and gave lectures on health and hygiene.

Discrimination against black women as doctors did not diminish significantly as the twentieth century progressed. It would be a long time before the world was ready to accept a woman—any woman—in that position of knowledge and authority. Describing her time at Tufts University Medical School in the early 1920s, Dorothy Ferebee wrote, "It was not easy. The medical school had five women out of 137 students. We women were always the last to get assignments in amphitheaters and clinics. And I? I was the last of the last because not only was I a woman, but a Negro, too." Ferebee persevered, and so did many other black women, but they faced another obstacle as states began to pass laws that required a hospital internship for licensing physicians. Now, graduating from medical school was not enough, and the few internships available to black physicians went to men. By the same token, the even fewer places for women went to white women. As the profession became more regulated, it became more difficult for black women to enter. And this was true not only of doctors, but of nurses as well.

For centuries in the American South, black women served as nurses to their own communities as well as to white families, sometimes handing down skills from generation to generation. But it was not until the Civil War that nursing became a trained profession and not until 1873 that the first American nurse training schools were established. These were relatively autonomous institutions at first, but soon hospitals took over the training of nurses. There were 15 hospital nurse training schools in 1880 and 431 schools twenty years later. As hospital nurse training schools mushroomed on the educational landscape, nurse leaders questioned the instructional quality and low admission standards. The inadequate, random instruction provided at the hospitals, the exploitation of student nurses, and the general low status accorded to even trained nurses motivated nurse leaders to organize what would be renamed, in 1911, the American Nurses' Association (ANA).

The professionalization of nursing had a negative impact on black nurses. As nursing became another way out of domestic service for thousands of European immigrant and poor white women, black women were increasingly denied the opportunity to acquire the needed training. Left with little alternative, African Americans founded their own network of nursing schools and hospitals. By 1920, there were thirty-six black nurse training schools. Alice Bacon, the white founder of one of these schools, Hampton Nurse Training School at Dixie Hospital, explained that the school was a means of retaining "in the hands of trained colored women a profession for which, even without training, the Negro women have always shown themselves especially adapted."

The women trained in these schools usually found work in black hospitals or in home nursing. They were denied work in white hospitals or were given the lowest, most menial work. This discrimination was often justified on the basis of the poor quality of education in the black hospital training schools. Black women were also barred from membership in most ANA affiliates. Since this organization was increasingly important in the move towards acceptance of nurses as professionals, exclusion was damaging.

The ANA's exclusionary practices motivated Martha Franklin, a black graduate of the Women's Hospital in Philadelphia, to launch a separate black nursing association. Beginning in 1906, Franklin mailed more than two thousand inquiries to black graduate nurses, superintendents of nursing schools, and nursing organizations to determine whether interest existed for a separate black society. In August 1908, fifty-two nurses convened at St. Mark's Episcopal Church in New York City to found the National Association of Colored Graduate Nurses (NACGN). In 1912, NACGN members numbered 125, and by 1920 the organization boasted a membership of 500.

Still, discrimination grew within the profession. A 1925 Rockefeller Foundation report concluded that "Negro nurses in every part of the country feel very keenly that they are debarred from qualifying themselves for leadership and it is true that most doors are closed to them." One of the doors that was firmly closed to black nurses was the one that led into service of their country. This was a particularly bitter irony, considering the origin of the U.S. Army Nurse Corps.

During the Spanish-American War much of the fighting was in Cuba and in the Philippines, and there were several all-black units involved. Although the war lasted only ten weeks, thousands of soldiers fell ill from tropical diseases. In July of 1898, the surgeon general of the United States called for a corps of black women to nurse black soldiers. Thirty-two black nurses went to Camp Thomas, Georgia, to care for black troops and were so successful that Congress created a permanent Army Nurse Corps in 1901.

Women were officially a part of the military for the first time. The Navy Nurse Corps was established seven years later, in 1908.

But black women were not included. The groups they had inspired were closed to them. Their only vehicle for working with the military was the Red Cross and even that would prove problematic.

When the United States entered World War I, the call went out for trained nurses. Although the first wave of black women nurses who attempted to enlist in the U.S. Army Corps expected to encounter racism, they were not prepared for the total rejection of their services during one of America's greatest crises. Disillusioned and hurt, black women nurses focused their anger initially on the American Red Cross. The Red Cross, an auxiliary of the U.S. Army Nurse Corps, recruited and enrolled nurses, then classified them as First Reserve nurses or Second Reserve nurses. The First Reserve was composed of nurses with the educational, moral, and professional qualifications required by the military nurse corps. The Second Reserve consisted of nurses available for critical civilian nursing but who were not eligible for the First Reserve.

Mabel K. Staupers and other black nurses demanded to know why so few of them were called or enrolled into either the First or Second Reserve. They were told by Jane Delano, head of the Red Cross Nursing Services, "We are enrolling colored nurses at the present time and shall continue to do so in order that they may be available *if at any time there is an opportunity to assign them to duty in military hospitals.*" (Italics ours) This, remember, was in the middle of a war. Black nurses continued to put pressure on both the Red Cross and the army. Finally, a month before the war's end, two dozen black nurses were called for service at three bases in the United States. In comparison, 21,000 white nurses had served.

After the war, the status of nursing as a profession skyrocketed. The courageous service of military nurses was applauded and even romanticized. But the prestige of black nurses plummeted. They had not served their country and therefore were given no share of nursing's newly earned public esteem. It was a painful and dispiriting setback. Integration of black women into the army and navy nurse corps would have to await another crisis, the coming of World War II.

Outside the field of medicine, black women entered the professions one by one. Since Charlotte Ray and Mary Ann Shadd Cary, there had been virtually no black women in the legal profession. Then, just after the Nineteenth Amendment was passed in 1920, giving women the vote, a handful of black women made their way in. In 1920, for example, Violette N. Anderson became the first black woman to practice law in Illinois. She later became the first woman prosecutor in Chicago and the first black woman lawyer to argue a case before the United States Supreme Court. In 1925, L. Marian Fleming Poe was admitted to the Virginia bar and became, so far as we know, the first black woman to practice law in a southern state. She opened a private practice in Newport News, where she practiced until the 1960s. In 1927, Sadie Tanner Mossell Alexander was the first black woman to be admitted to the bar and to practice law in Pennsylvania.

In journalism, black women were considerably more visible. At the turn of the century, there were almost fifty newspapers and forty magazines and journals published by African Americans. Women were involved in a significant way in most of them. In 1900, for example, novelist Pauline Hopkins became editor of the women's section of the *Colored American Magazine*, a Boston-based magazine. Within three years she was literary editor of the magazine. Margaret Murray Washington was editor of *National Note* until 1922.

Two black women's periodicals were founded during this time. *Women's World* began publication in Fort Worth, Texas, and *Colored Women's Magazine* appeared in Topeka, Kansas, in 1907. The latter was edited by two women, C. M. Hughes and Minnie Thomas, as a monthly family magazine and remained in publication until at least 1920. Women always had editorial control.

In periodicals for a general audience, black women also played a part. As the Baltimore *Afro-American,* the *Chicago Defender,* and the *New York Age* grew in influence and garnered larger and larger readerships, black women served as reporters, columnists, and editors. Alice Dunbar-Nelson, poet and short-story writer, worked as a journalist on both black and white newspapers, including the *Pittsburgh Courier,* the *Washington Eagle,* the *Chicago Daily News,* the *Chicago Record-Herald,* and the *New York Sun.* She also edited the Wilmington *Advocate* and served as an associate editor for the *AME Church Review.* Delilah Beasley began her career in journalism with a black newspaper, the Cleveland *Gazette.* She also contributed to white papers such as the Cincinnati *Enquirer.* From 1915 to 1925 in California, she wrote a column for the *Oakland Tribune.* That newspaper had, at the time, the largest circulation in the state.

California also became home to one of the most active and respected women in black journalism in the first half of the century. Charlotta Spears Bass was born in October 1880 in South Carolina. In 1900, at the age of twenty, she left South Carolina to live and work in Providence, Rhode Island. She moved in with her oldest brother and took a job working for the

Providence Watchman. Ten years later she was suffering from exhaustion and, at the suggestion of her doctor, moved to California to rest. It was to have been a two-year stay, but shortly after arriving she ignored her doctor's advice and took a part-time job at a newspaper, the *Eagle.* Before her two years in California were over, she had taken over the paper, renaming it the *California Eagle.* A new editor arrived—Joseph Bass, one of the founders of the *Topeka Plaindealer*—and soon the two were married. As managing editor and editor, respectively, Charlotta Spears Bass and her husband set their paper firmly on a course of social and political activism. They vehemently attacked the racial stereotypes and the glorification of the Ku Klux Klan in D. W. Griffith's film *The Birth of a Nation,* defended the black soldiers of the Twenty-fourth Infantry who were unjustly sentenced in the Houston riot of 1917, and supported the defendants in the Scottsboro trials.

In 1930, Charlotta Bass helped found the Industrial Business Council, which fought discrimination in hiring and employment practices and encouraged African Americans to go into business. She also formed a group to attack housing covenants that denied the right of black Americans to live wherever they chose. Bass became increasingly political in the two decades that followed and, in 1952, was the first black woman to run for vice president, on the Progressive party ticket.

All of these professional women faced obstacles that now seem to us almost insurmountable. In addition to the difficulties of getting training and finding work, they had family responsibilities that, in the tradition of black women, often went far beyond their immediate kin. For example, Mary Church Terrell, while serving as president of the NACW and traveling around the country to speak for the rights of black women and men, adopted both a niece and a nephew and raised them as her own. Often, unmarried schoolteachers reared the children of relatives when a mother died. Librarian Miriam Matthews moved in with her brother after his wife died to rear his two-year-old daughter. Amelia Perry Pride, in addition to her own three sons, reared four young girls from her neighborhood. Then, after one of her sons died, she brought up his three daughters. All this time she was working as a teacher, doing unpaid social work, and remaining active in her church.

Professionals also confronted the continuing struggle to gain recognition for their work. Stephanie Shaw gives a striking example of this from the life of a distinguished librarian, Sadie Delaney. Delaney received awards for her work with hospitalized veterans from such diverse groups as the Lions Club, the Veterans of Foreign Wars, and an influential physicians' association. Library journal editors and conference organizers invited her to contribute papers. She was commended for her work and consulted by library organizations around the world. Indeed, the warden of San Quentin asked her for help with bibliotherapy for his prisoners. The Rosenwald Foundation had her make up a booklist for the Rosenwald schools. Eleanor Roosevelt featured Delaney on one of her radio programs, and *Look* magazine singled her out for commendation. And she was still not allowed membership in the Alabama Library Association.

For artists, too, the obstacles remained formidable. Nonetheless, in the first decades of the twentieth century, two black women began a new trend in African American culture, breaking through European conventions to focus on Africa and the folklore of African America. Their leadership was particularly unusual because they worked in the visual arts.

GIVING COLOR TO THE WORLD

In the late nineteenth century, women began to be admitted to some American art schools—the National Academy of Design, the Pennsylvania Academy of the Fine Arts, the Art Institute of Chicago, the Cincinnati Art Academy, the Art Students League in New York City. A number of women were also able to gain access to some of the prestigious academies and studios of Europe. Meta Vaux Warrick Fuller, born in 1877 to a middle-class Philadelphia family, studied at the Pennsylvania Museum and School for Industrial Art (now the Philadelphia College of Art) and at the Ecole des Beaux-Arts and the Colarossi Academy in Paris. In the summer of 1901, after examining the clay model of her sculpture *Man Eating His Heart* (also called *The Secret Sorrow)*, Auguste Rodin proclaimed, *"Mon enfant, vous etes un sculpteur ne vous avez le sens de la forme!"* ("My child, you are a sculptor, you have the sense of form!")

Returning to Philadelphia in 1902, Fuller found an active black intellectual community and became a part of it. In 1910, a fire destroyed sixteen years of her work, including *Man Eating His Heart.* W. E. B. Du Bois asked Fuller to reproduce that work for the Emancipation Proclamation's fiftieth anniversary in New York in 1913. Instead she created *Spirit of Emancipation,* a three-figure group standing eight feet tall. Scholar Judith Kerr writes that it was "unlike any other of its genre. There were no discarded whips or chains, no grateful freedmen kneeling before a paternalistic Lincoln. Fuller had also not chosen to favor the female figure with Caucasian features, indicating her heightened race consciousness." Well into the 1960s, Fuller continued to create powerful political art, as well as work that expressed the African heritage of black Americans, receiving considerable recognition from the black community. Even the American art establishment acknowledged her work.

May Howard Jackson was not quite so fortunate but, like Fuller, she led the way for the African American consciousness of the Harlem Renaissance. Jackson studied at the Pennsylvania Academy of the Fine Arts, but did not go to Europe for additional training. From the beginning, she took as her subjects black and mixed-race people. Prominent figures such as Paul Laurence Dunbar, W. E. B. Du Bois, and Jean Toomer sat for her, but she also did figures of anonymous black people, as in *Mulatto Mother and Her Child.* Because of her sculptural portraits of African Americans, art historian Leslie King-Hammond writes that Jackson was "the founder of the first movement toward an Afrocentric aesthetic."

Jackson was, however, ahead of her time. Her realistic depiction of the physicality of African Americans was not palatable to the art establishment of the time, which was accustomed to black figures that were portrayed either sentimentally or humorously. These stereotypes were the only images acceptable or, probably, comprehensible to those who made decisions about the quality of art and artists. The rejection this prejudice occasioned made Jackson understandably bitter. In spite of a number of successful exhibitions and a short teaching career at Howard University, she paid for her position as a groundbreaker.

Still, Fuller and Jackson can be seen, at this distance, as significant forerunners to the male artists who would later respond to the call issued by philosopher Alain Locke in 1925 for a new era in African American art. Locke's book, *The New Negro,* had tremendous influence in the visual arts, as well as in literature and music. He acknowledged that some African American artists had been "notably successful," but he deplored their adherence to the European tradition. He went further to say African American artists should look to Africa, explore their "ancestral arts" more thoroughly, and develop the "Negro physiognomy" in their work. Fuller and Jackson had been doing both for two decades and continued to do so. They were clearly important precursors of the Harlem Renaissance whose recognition as such is long overdue.

But it may have been the developments in black theater that would act as a catalyst for that important movement in black art and culture, especially the black musical comedy, which put black women on the theatrical stage for the first time. Except in the productions of the Hyers sisters and Black Patti, women had been singularly absent from black theater. The minstrel show was first performed entirely by white men and then entirely by black men. The roles of black women were taken by men. With the birth of black musical comedy and the chorus line, that changed. Women still did not have actual roles, for the most part, but they were there, kicking away in the background. And people got used to seeing them.

Deriving from burlesque, vaudeville, and the minstrel show, black musical comedy appeared on the scene at virtually the same time as its white counterpart. The first was probably *The Creole Show,* produced in 1890, in which the chorus line brought black women onstage. In 1898, Sissieretta Jones's producer Bob Cole produced on his own the first all-black musical comedy created, directed, and managed by black theater professionals. In the tradition of the Hyers sisters, Cole created a show with consistent characters and a plot, making it one of the first genuine American musical comedies, black or white. *A Trip to Coontown* also had a chorus line. The chorus was a training ground and a launching pad for black women, where they learned to sing and dance and make the folks laugh. And occasionally, one of the chorus moved forward. The first of these was Aida Overton Walker.

Aida Overton Walker was a talented dancer and singer who had toured with Sissieretta Jones. She married George Walker in 1899, just as his act with Bert Williams was about to hit the big time. Williams and Walker recognized Aida's potential and gave her a featured role in their production *The Sons of Ham* in 1900. It was their biggest success up to that time. Two years later, Aida had her biggest success playing Rosetta Lightfoot in *In Dahomey.* It was while this show was touring Europe that she introduced the cakewalk to Britain and France. Overton Walker sang, danced, acted in, and even choreographed the Williams and Walker shows. When her husband became ill and had to leave the team in 1908, she dressed in men's clothes and performed his dances with Williams so that they would not have to default on their bookings. Later, she went on to perform in vaudeville and eventually became a producer.

Ten years would go by before another black woman took the spotlight on Broadway. In *On with the Show,* Robert C. Toll reports that, in these days of Jim Crow, the success of the black musicals aroused racist anger. When *In Dahomey* opened, there were fears of rioting. He goes on to say, however, "Violence did not drive Negroes off Broadway. . . . Bias, insidious invisible bias and middle-class financiers and producers did. Although the exclusion was not a single, sudden event, 1910 can be pinpointed as the critical date." For more than a decade, no black show would open on Broadway.

Away from the Great White Way, however, life was more eventful, especially in black dramatic theater. Very little had happened in this area since the 1870s, when the Hyers sisters formed the Coloured Dramatic and Operatic Company. In 1915, however, a young black woman named Anita Bush formed a company that would launch the black theater movement in New York. Bush was the daughter of a tailor who catered to performers. Because of this connection, she was able to watch, from backstage, an amount and variety of theater that was not accessible to most young black women. At sixteen, she persuaded her parents to allow her to join the Williams and Walker company. When it folded after Walker's death, she tried to get work as a dramatic actor, but there were no opportunities for black actors. Even the best and most experienced could hope for nothing but playing maids or handymen.

After seven years of getting by on roles in musicals, Anita Bush approached the manager of the Lincoln Theatre, in Harlem, with a proposal. Since the Lincoln was a leasing theater, it needed shows. Bush offered to produce them—legitimate plays with black actors. It was a startling idea, but the manager took her up on it and gave her two weeks to mount the first show. Bush made it and, within the year, the Anita Bush Players were successful enough to move to the larger Lafayette Theatre, where they became the Lafayette Players. For the next seventeen years, they produced quality drama with all-black casts. Most of the plays were those being done on Broadway with all-white casts—*The Count of Monte Cristo, Dr. Jekyll and Mr. Hyde,* and *Madame X.* They even performed the Jewish comedy *Potash and Perlmutter.*

Because of their work, said an article in *Billboard* magazine in August of 1921, "It is beginning to dawn on the American public that the Negro, in a none too distant future, is destined to command respectful attention and win favorable consideration in the realm of drama. In the past the theatregoer had visualized the Negro on the stage only in comedy, dance and song, and colored comedians have made enviable reputations as exponents of buffoonery; but today there is every indication that the Negro is soon to invade the legitimate field."

Others in the mainstream theater also had highly favorable things to say about the company, but the response that counted was that of the black community. Black audiences wanted and were willing to pay for serious theater. This so impressed some black businesspeople that they formed the Quality Amusement Corporation to sponsor the Lafayette Players and send them on tour. The reaction in other cities led QAC to form a string of theaters. These theaters were more than centers for community entertainment. They were places for black actors to work, learn, and perfect their skills. At the Lafayette in Harlem alone, the acting careers of Abbie Mitchell, Evelyn Ellis, Evelyn Preer, Edna Thomas, Laura Bowman, and Inez Clough were launched.

Young Anita Bush had changed the face of American theater. This became apparent when, in 1917, a trio of short plays by white poet Ridgely Torrence was given a major production at the Garden Theater. The plays attempted to portray black life with truthfulness and respect, and several members of the Lafayette Players were in the cast. Robert Benchley, critic for the *Tribune,* was beside himself with enthusiasm. George Jean Nathan, the leading critic of the day, put *two* of the actors—Opal Cooper and Inez Clough—on his list of the ten best performers on Broadway that year.

Following World War I, the black musical reappeared on Broadway, bringing its chorus lines with it. In 1920, vaudeville stars Noble Sissle and Eubie Blake teamed with another pair of vaudeville headliners, Flournoy E. Miller and Aubrey Lyles, to write *Shuffle Along,* the most influential musical production of the time. When it appeared on Broadway, New York was completely captivated. There had never been anything like it.

Shuffle Along had the usual stereotyped characters, and its plot wasn't anything to write home about, but it had the fabulous music of Eubie Blake and truly remarkable dancing. It also had a girl. Sissle and Blake, Flournoy and Lyles were the stars of the show, but they wrote in an ingenue role as well. At first it was played by Gertrude Sanders. But she was later replaced by the amazing Florence Mills, who was about to become the first real black superstar.

Florence Mills was only twenty-five, but she was not a novice. She had been in vaudeville as a child and then performed in cabarets. In *Shuffle Along,* she dazzled New York. According to historian Richard Newman, "The critics could never describe Mills's voice with its curious breaks, soft accents, sudden molten notes, and haunting undertones. Birdlike and flutelike were among the reviewers' frequently used adjectives. It was Mills's dancing, however, and the dancing in all the black shows spawned by *Shuffle Along* during the 1920s that completely stunned audiences." Overnight, Mills became as big a star as any black man who had ever performed on Broadway. Indeed, there were few performers of any color who could rival her success. One hit followed another, in New York, London, and Paris for seven years. And then, suddenly, she was dead. According to Newman, "Mills saw her work as a crusade on behalf of racial justice and understanding. She literally believed that every white person pleased by her performance was a friend won for the race. Her passion led her to drive herself without respite, and it broke her health." More than 150,000 people filled the streets of Harlem on the day of Mills's funeral. George Jean Nathan called her "America's foremost feminine player."

Mills was not the only black woman who found *Shuffle Along* a stepping stone to history. There was another young woman who tried out for the chorus and was turned down because she was too thin and too dark. She dusted on some face powder and went back, snaring a job as a dresser. But she didn't stop there. She learned all the songs and all the dances so that, when one of the chorines got pregnant, she was ready to step in. But Josephine Baker was not the sort to blend into a chorus line. From her first appearance on the Broadway stage, she mugged and shimmied and crossed her eyes and made the audience adore her. American audiences kept right on adoring her until the day she left them. When she appeared in Paris in *La Revue Negre,* she enthralled Europe. She saw no reason to return to America's race-conscious atmosphere.

Shuffle Along and the stars it launched made blackness suddenly fashionable in New York. Langston Hughes credited the show with inspiring the Harlem Renaissance, the decade when "the Negro was in vogue."

HARLEM RENAISSANCE

Writers and historians often speak of the Harlem Renaissance as though it were the one bright spot in the cultural history of black America. Women and men of African descent had for centuries, they seem to imply, been slaves and drudges. Then, for one decade, there emerged writers and painters and scholars who blossomed like Cinderella until the clock struck, not midnight, but 1935. They then returned to their rags and cinders, and American literature and culture returned to normal.

In truth, it was a glorious time, produced by a combination of factors—migration from the South, a coincidence of talent, the temporary lightening of the racism that occurs immediately after black soldiers give their lives in war. But the Harlem Renaissance was not a blip on the flat line of black culture. It was a flowering for which the seeds had been planted decades and even centuries before, and an amazing flowering it was. In a world where Jim Crow still ruled the South, where lynchings still occurred once or twice a week, where no black woman knew safety from insult, harassment, or rape, this is what was happening in New York.

The blues queens ruled over the recording business, selling records in unheard-of numbers. Musical comedy star Florence Mills was the toast of

Broadway, and word came back that Josephine Baker had conquered Europe. The Lafayette Players were producing serious theater starring black actors. The greatest white playwright of the time, Eugene O'Neill, was writing plays with important black roles, including *The Emperor Jones,* and *All God's Chillun Got Wings.* As the decade progressed, hundreds of black actors found work in DuBose and Dorothy Heyward's *Porgy* and Marc Connelly's *The Green Pastures.* Young black writers were addressing themselves to their African heritage and the oppression of their people, and instead of slamming the door in their faces, the literary establishment welcomed them. Langston Hughes, Countee Cullen, James Weldon Johnson, Arna Bontemps, Jean Toomer, and Claude McKay were on the A-list for New York's most prestigious literary parties.

For black women, unless they were entertainers, the moment was not quite so shining. Few managed to make either the A-list or the publishers' lists. In the eyes of white literati, they were simply not as glamorous as black men. But they were there and they were creating. And today they are being recognized for the quality and originality of their work. The woman who came closest to receiving significant recognition for her writing at the time was Zora Neale Hurston. Those whose names were almost lost for decades included Jessie Fauset, Nella Larsen, Dorothy West, Marita Bonner, Mercedes Gilbert, Gwendolyn Bennett, Georgia Douglas Johnson, May Miller, Regina Andrews, Anne Spencer, Helene Johnson, and others.

Zora Neale Hurston was a renegade. She wrote about the black experience, but not about "race relations." One reason she was not so enthusiastically received by the white establishment as some of the male writers may be that, in the world of her novels, white people were essentially irrelevant. Her characters were black and they lived almost entirely inside the black community. It has been said that Hurston's work did not concern itself with the black struggle for freedom. Actually, she was far ahead of her time in considering black love and courage and even violence *apart from* the mainstream white culture. As a result, her work seems much less dated than some that received more acclaim during the twenties and thirties.

Their Eyes Were Watching God, Hurston's best-known book, is now on high school reading lists along with George Eliot's *Silas Marner* and Thomas Hardy's *Tess of the D'Urbervilles.* Its main character, Janie, is light-skinned and lovely and, in the eyes of her community, destined to live as the wife of a prosperous black farmer. However, Janie insists on looking for passion, freedom, and a different kind of fulfillment. According to literary critic Alice Deck, "The novel insists on Janie's complete freedom to such an extent that she lives a feminist fantasy of expressing her sexual passion without facing its natural consequences of conception. This is a radical idea for the 1930s; that a beautiful black woman like Janie, left a widow living happily alone in her house at the end of the novel, can and should realize her fullest potential sexually and intellectually by and for herself."

Another novelist of the time, Nella Larsen, had none of Hurston's supreme self-confidence and disregard for the opinions of the white world. She had never experienced the nurturing atmosphere of the black community, from which Hurston took so much strength. Instead, she was brought up by her white mother and stepfather after the death of her West Indian father. She was surrounded by a white family, attended a white private school, and had her first real contact with the black world when she matriculated at Fisk University for one year. In her early twenties, Larsen made a clear commitment to her African American heritage. She married a black physicist and became part of New York's black social and literary scene. In 1928, she published her first novel, *Quicksand.* Both this and her second novel, *Passing,* deal with the lives of mixed-race people and their alienation from two worlds. They clearly draw on Larsen's own experiences and were important critical successes.

Two unfortunate experiences probably led to the ending of Larsen's promising career. In 1930, shortly after she became the first black woman to receive a creative writing award from the Guggenheim Foundation, Larsen was accused of plagiarizing a short story. She successfully defended herself against that charge. However, a few years later, her marriage ended in divorce and scandal. Rumors flew that Larsen's husband had been having an affair with a white woman and that Larsen had attempted to take her own life. Larsen never wrote again. She went back to her early training and spent the rest of her life as a nurse.

Georgia Douglas Johnson represents another aspect of the literary expression of black women. Also of mixed, middle-class ancestry, she had the gift of a lyric poet at a time when black poets were supposed to sound a note of militancy and racial pride. Her first volume, *The Heart of a Woman,* brought her severe criticism from those who felt she should address black issues. Her second, *Bronze: A Book of Verse,* did deal with those issues and was highly praised by leaders of both black and white literary communities. This was a continuing problem for Johnson. Her natural bent was toward the kind of lyrical verse that made Edna St. Vincent Millay America's most popular poet. But that sort of poetry was not yet acceptable from a black woman. Johnson was torn and her work suffered. In dramatic writing,

Johnson had no such problem. Her plays all had strong racial themes. *Blue Blood* concerned the rape of a black woman by a white man. *Plumes* dealt with a conflict within the black community between modern medicine and folk customs. *A Sunday Morning in the South* is about lynching.

Unfortunately for Johnson, American theater was not yet ready for black women to write plays. Many of hers were published, but they were not produced in the commercial theater. After the death of her husband in 1925, therefore, Johnson faced the problem of making a living for herself and her two children. The struggle, in a world indifferent or hostile to the productions of black women, led to increasing eccentricity in her behavior. According to Jocelyn Hazelwood Donlon, "During these later years, she developed into a local institution, widely known as 'the old woman with the headband and the tablet around her neck.' The tablet was for her to write down any idea that came to her." A year before she died in 1966, Johnson was given an honorary doctorate by Atlanta University. If she had lived a little longer, she might have experienced the reawakening of interest in the women of the Harlem Renaissance that occurred in the early 1970s. As it was, all the papers she left behind were thrown out.

Black women playwrights were essentially part of the literary rather than the theater scene in New York. Few plays about black people were produced, and most of those that were had been written by white men or, in rare cases, black men, but not black women. Indeed, had it not been for the two major black magazines of the time, it is doubtful that we would have heard of most of the women who make up the first generation of black women playwrights.

W. E. B. Du Bois believed that drama could be a tool for social change and cultural enrichment for black people. He called for "native drama," by which he meant plays about black people and by black people. He supported his call with a contest for one-act plays sponsored by the NAACP's *Crisis* magazine, of which he was editor. The contest was done in cooperation with the National Urban League's *Opportunity,* edited by Charles S. Johnson. The prizewinners won publication in one of the two magazines and a cash award. The first contest was held in 1925. Two of the three winning plays that appeared in *Crisis* were written by women. Four of the seven *Opportunity* winners were also by women.

In another move to encourage native drama, Du Bois founded the Krigwa Players, a theater company based in Harlem. Other Krigwa Players companies were formed in other cities, and many of the plays they performed were by black women. Mary P. Burrill's *Aftermath* was produced by the New York Krigwa Players. It also appeared in the David Belasco Little Theatre Tournament in 1928. Three of Eulalie Spence's plays were produced by the theater—*Foreign Mail, Fool's Errand,* and *Her.* The first two were also published by Samuel French. The Baltimore Krigwa Players produced plays by May Miller and Georgia Douglas Johnson. All of the Krigwa Players theaters disappeared by the thirties. While they existed, however, many other black women saw their plays produced.

Among visual artists, it was again sculptors who came to the fore. Nancy Elizabeth Prophet carved stark, naturalistic heads with a strong African influence. Augusta Savage created stunningly stylized works symbolic of black struggle and aspiration. Beulah Ecton Woodard, a prominent California sculptor, and Selma Burke, whose depiction of Franklin Roosevelt was adapted for the Roosevelt dime, both sculpted portrait busts. Virtually all of the first black women to gain recognition as artists were sculptors. There are a number of possible reasons. For one thing, the materials of sculpture were less expensive than paints and canvas, and most black women had limited resources. For another, according to art historian Tritobia Benjamin, "The tradition of art in West Africa, where most African Americans came from, emphasizes sculpture, rather than painting. Of course, you would then expect that black American artists of both sexes would be sculptors, and this isn't true. Most African American men were painters. There were only a few sculptors, primarily men who made their living as stonecarvers. The men, of course, had earlier access to training in European methods. Is it possible that, because they were denied that training, black women remained more closely connected to their African artistic heritage?"

At any rate, following in the footsteps of Fuller and Howard, Nancy Elizabeth Prophet, Augusta Savage, and the others formed what amounts to a school of black women sculptors during the Harlem Renaissance and beyond. But it may be the lives of Prophet and Savage that are most revealing to us. They were different in all but talent. Prophet was born into a middle-class family in the North, daughter of a Narragansett Indian father and a mother who described herself as a "mixed negro." Savage's family was southern working class and she was seventh of fourteen children of a carpenter-farmer-minister. Prophet was the only black student at the Rhode Island School of Design and married a black student at Brown University. Savage got married when she was fifteen, taught herself to sculpt, and sold her figures at the county fair.

Prophet refused to work at anything but fine art after graduation from college and, with the financial support of several socialite women, studied and exhibited in France for ten years. She came back to the United States and was disappointed to find that her European reputation did not translate into American success. She was forced to take teaching positions at Atlanta University and then at Spelman College, where she remained until 1944. She appears to have then suffered a nervous breakdown. She returned to Rhode Island, was unable to find a teaching position, and became a live-in maid. She died in poverty and obscurity in 1960. In the last year of her life she declared that she "had no use for the colored" and refused to be included in *American Negro Art,* by Cedric Dover, because she "was not a negro."

Savage, on the other hand, traveled to New York when she was twenty-nine years old, arriving in the city with $4.60 and a recommendation from the superintendent of the county fair. She attended Cooper Union, a tuition-free art school, and within a month had been advanced to the third year. With help from the black community, she was offered a scholarship to study in France. It was withdrawn when two white women from Alabama protested traveling or rooming with her. When the event was made public, she received an invitation to work with sculptor Hermon Mac-Neil. Eventually, she went to Paris to study on a Rosenwald Fellowship. When she returned, she opened the Savage Studio of Arts and Crafts in New York and taught some of the most important of a new group of young black artists. She also became an advocate for the rights of black artists.

Being a black woman virtually destroyed Elizabeth Prophet. It made Augusta Savage strong.

THE COLOR OF FREEDOM

Historian Elsa Barkley Brown has said that our political actions are shaped by the stories we tell about each other and ourselves. As the twentieth century moved forward, black Americans were moving toward a crisis of political action most could not even have conceived in 1910 or 1920, and black women were preparing for it. In the church and in the club movement, they were acquiring the skills of organizing, fund-raising, and communications that would be required for effective political action. But just as important, they were beginning to tell the right stories. They wrote plays attacking lynching and made images of racial pride. They sang songs about being strong and refusing to be exploited. As surely as a boxer trains for a fight both physically and psychologically, black women were training for a day when they would change the world.

But that day had not yet arrived. Instead, they faced almost two decades of digging in and hanging on, of basic survival and sheer endurance. In 1929, the stock market crashed and America was bewildered by poverty.

We cannot direct the wind,

but we can adjust the sails.

BERTHA CALLOWAY

THE GREAT
DEPRESSION

CHAPTER TEN

MARY MCLEOD BETHUNE told how she got the location on which she built the Daytona Institute, which she had founded in the early part of the century.

> Near by was a field, popularly called Hell's Hole, which was used as a dumping ground. I approached the owner, determined to buy it. The price was $250. In a daze, he finally agreed to take five dollars down, and the balance in two years. I promised to be back in a few days with the initial payment. He never knew it, but I didn't have five dollars. I raised this sum selling ice cream and sweet-potato pies to the workmen on construction jobs, and I took the owner his money in small change wrapped in my handkerchief.
>
> That's how the Bethune-Cookman college campus started.

This story, although it happened well before the Great Depression, says much about the experience of black women during that catastrophic period. To begin with, the woman telling the story, who raised five dollars selling pies, became a presidential advisor and the most influential black leader of the 1930s and 1940s. Then the story shows just how close to Depression-era conditions the lives of black women already were. Finally, it emphasizes the resources black women could bring to those conditions. All through their history, they had been in training to survive the worst, and now they were faced with it.

The Great Depression of the 1930s was one of the most catastrophic periods in American history. Americans in all walks of life suffered economic hardships, and African Americans were particularly hard hit. The thousands of black men and women who had left the South in the 1920s for northern cities and midwestern communities in search of a better future for themselves and their families now found themselves embroiled in a fierce struggle for jobs, housing, education, and first-class citizenship. As their economic status worsened, they also increasingly faced brutal violence, race riots, and blatant racial discrimination and segregation. But there was a great irony in the situation of black Americans at this time. Because of the measures taken by the Roosevelt administration to assist all Americans, some black people were able to break through barriers of prejudice they might never have breached otherwise. Black artists, from painters and sculptors to writers and actors, were able to find work in government-sponsored projects. Young people received training in specialized fields of labor. Though often discriminated against by locally controlled branches of the Works Progress Administration (WPA), tens of thousands of black workers were able to find work.

Independently of government programs, the Rose McClendon Players launched the modern black theater movement, and Ethel Waters became the first black dramatic star. In music, Billie Holiday, Pearl Bailey, and Ella Fitzgerald inaugurated the age of the great jazz vocalist, while Marian Anderson used her magnificent operatic voice in the service of freedom. And one of the great leaders of the modern Civil Rights movement, Ella Baker, began on the road that would eventually lead to the lunch counter sit-ins of the 1950s and 1960s.

The Depression was a time of suffering and want for the black community. Among the working poor, the situation often became desperate. But black women brought to this crisis the determination and ingenuity they had always displayed. And as grassroots organizer Frances Mary Albrier said many years later, "[T]he Depression brought people together better than anything else that I know of."

THE GRIM YEARS ARE UPON US

In the first decades of the century, a huge proportion of black women worked outside the home in jobs that were considered "unskilled labor" and were therefore highly vulnerable. In 1929, on the eve of the Great Depression, almost 40 percent of black women were in the labor force. Of these, 26.9 percent were agricultural workers and 35.8 percent were domestic workers. Only 5 percent of black women held jobs in manufacturing. Fewer than 5 percent worked in white-collar jobs. (At the same time, 69.6 percent of employed white women held jobs in manufacturing or white-collar work.) And then, suddenly, disaster struck. By January of 1931, *more than a quarter* of all black women who lived in any city with a significant black population had lost their jobs. The jobless rate for African American women was as high as 68.9 percent in Detroit, far higher than that of white women and the same as or higher than that of black men.

By 1934, the government had classed 38 percent of black Americans—more than one-third—as no longer capable of self-support. (The figure for white Americans was 17 percent.)

Wherever black and white women were in competition for getting and keeping jobs, black women were the first to be laid off. Those who did not lose their jobs altogether were the first to be subjected to shortened shifts or fewer days' work. In domestic work particularly, the financial problems of white employers translated into less money spent on household help. The bottom rung of the ladder was not a good place to be during the Depression. Unemployed people tended to be downwardly mobile. A woman who lost a job as a schoolteacher became a file clerk. A file clerk became a waitress. A waitress took a job cleaning house. And because of racial preferences, a white waitress with no experience cleaning house could take a cleaning job away from a black woman who had been doing that sort of work for years. The black domestic worker then fell off the bottom of the ladder. By 1940, there were 160,000 fewer black women in the workforce than at the beginning of the decade.

In the rural South, the situation for black women began to deteriorate much earlier. In the 1920s an invasion of boll weevils in the cotton fields and the decline of prices for agricultural products had wreaked havoc in the lives of black southerners. Conditions worsened during the Depression when landowners reduced crop size and fewer workers were needed. Agricultural employment for black women dropped 50 percent during the 1930s. (The figure for black men was 20 percent.) Sharecropping families found themselves working for nothing but the house in which they lived.

Black families were often desperate. Black women met the challenge by giving up some of what they had worked so hard for. They took lower pay and accepted worse conditions. Some returned to the despised live-in work. In some northern cities, they participated in "slave-markets" on street corners in white neighborhoods. On these corners, black women gathered each morning, and white housewives came to offer a day's work at an absurdly low wage. Sometimes domestic workers were paid in nothing more than food and cast-off clothing. "In 1929," recalls Emma Tiller, "me and my husband were sharecroppers. We made a crop that year, the owner takin' all of the crop. . . . I picked cotton. We weren't getting but thirty-five cents a hundred [pounds], but I was able to make it. 'Cause I also worked people's homes, where they give you old clothes and shoes." Tiller also remembers standing in line for government food in a small, mostly white Texas town. "Only five of us in that line were Negroes, the rest was white. We would stand all day and wait and wait and wait. And get nothin' or if you did, it was spoiled meat."

Some urban black women fell back on the skills that had sustained their grandmothers and great-grandmothers in the markets of the South. They became peddlers of whatever they could find or make, going from door to door. Others made or sold alcohol or ran the numbers game. In

Chicago during the 1930s, about five thousand people were employed by the policy business—illegal gambling.

The black community also used the survival skills they had developed during slavery and the post-Reconstruction era. When the rent was due, they threw a rent party. The women of a church would sponsor a chicken dinner that fed the people and raised money to take care of more. Black nightclub owners staged benefit concerts. Black actors and musicians performed without charge at fund-raising events. In Harlem, the Abyssinian Baptist Church organized its own relief organization. In the first quarter of 1931, the people of the church, primarily women, served 28,500 free meals, gave away 525 food baskets, and distributed 17,928 pieces of clothing and 2,564 pairs of shoes.

Community activist Willye Jeffries remembered, "Back in the Thirties, when it was really tough, and nobody was working, we divided whatever we had with each other. Being on relief, I'd get that little piece of check, pay off my rent. They were givin' you then a little surplus food, remember? You'd have to go to the station and pick up some meat and some beans and bread and stuff like that. We'd divide it with our friends."

This sense of community was often extended beyond the black community. Black women reached out with compassion to others who had been stricken by the economic devastation. When one of the thousands of hoboes who roamed the countryside came to the back door of a white kitchen, recalls Emma Tiller, he was often turned away by the lady of the house, but "the Negro woman who worked for the white woman would take food and wrap it in newspapers. Sometimes we would hurry down the alley and holler at 'im: 'Hey, mister, come here!' And we'd say, 'Come back by after a while and I'll put some food in a bag, and I'll set it down aside the garbage can so they won't see it.' . . . They would sit and talk and tell us their hard luck story. Whether it was true or not, we never questioned it. It's very important you learn people as people are."

White activist Peggy Terry had similar memories of the generosity of black Americans during the Depression. She and her husband were homeless, hitchhiking from one place to another looking for work. "I remember one night, we walked for a long time, and we were so tired and hungry, and a wagon came along. There was a Negro family going into town. Of course, they're not allowed to stop and eat in restaurants, so they'd cook their own food and brought it with 'em. They had the back of the wagon filled with hay. We asked them if we could lay down and sleep in the wagon, and they said yes. We woke up, and it was morning, and she invited us to eat with 'em. She had this box, and she had chicken and biscuits and sweet potatoes and everything in there. It was just really wonderful."

The greatest tools black women had at their disposal during the height of the Depression were the leadership and organizing skills they had cultivated during the previous four decades of involvement in club and church work. Black women's culture taught them how to identify issues needing to be addressed, how to mobilize their sisters, how to develop persuasive arguments, and how to fight for the survival and well-being of their families and communities. Grounded in a social welfare–oriented cultural tradition, they appreciated the necessity for collective action in a way that few white people could and were often responsible for organizing multiracial groups to fight against oppressive landlords or pool resources.

Black women in Detroit rose to the situation by creating an ingenious organization based on the principles of mutual aid, economic nationalism, and self-determination—the Housewives' League of Detroit. It was a crucial forerunner of the radical action of the 1950s and 1960s.

Housewives' League of Detroit

On June 10, 1930, a group of fifty black women responded to a call issued by Fannie B. Peck, wife of Reverend William H. Peck, pastor of the two-thousand-member Bethel African Methodist Episcopal Church and the president of the Booker T. Washington Trade Association. Out of this initial meeting emerged the Detroit Housewives' League. Peck had conceived the idea of creating an organization of housewives after hearing a lecture by M. A. L. Holsey, secretary of the National Negro Business League. Holsey had described the successful efforts of black housewives of Harlem to consolidate and exert their considerable economic power. Peck became convinced that if such an organization worked in Harlem, it would work in Detroit. As an admirer later recalled, Peck "focused the attention of women on the most essential, yet most unfamiliar factor in the building of homes, communities, and nations, namely—'The Spending Power of Women.' "

The Detroit organization grew with phenomenal speed. From the original fifty members, by 1934 its membership had increased to ten thousand black women, all banded together to fight for the economic well-being of their families and their community. According to Peck, the black woman had finally realized "that she has been traveling through a blind alley, making sacrifices to educate her children with no thought as to their obtaining employment after leaving school."

The Housewives' League combined economic nationalism and black women's self-determination to help black families and businesses survive the Depression. The only requirement for membership was a pledge to support black businesses, buy black products, and patronize black professionals, thereby keeping money in the community. Black women were the most strategically positioned group to preserve and expand the black internal economy, and they believed that "it is our duty as women controlling 85 percent of the family budget to unlock through concentrated spending closed doors that Negro youth may have the opportunity to develop and establish businesses in the fields closest to them." Each black neighborhood in Detroit had its own chapter of the Housewives' League, and the community leaders attended monthly meetings of the executive board. The organization took pains to make sure that all interested women had the opportunity to join and participate, lessening the development of class-based hierarchies within the organization.

Fulfilling the duties of membership in the league required considerable effort and commitment. Members of each chapter visited their neighborhood merchants, demanding that they sell black products and employ black children as clerks or stockpersons. If the managers refused, the women stopped buying from them. It was simple and effective. Chapter leaders organized campaigns to persuade their neighbors to patronize specific businesses owned by or employing African Americans. Across the city, league officers organized lectures, planned exhibits at state fairs, discussed picketing and boycotting strategies, and disseminated information concerning the economic self-help struggles of African Americans in other sections of the country. The Research Committee gathered data and made recommendations as to the types of businesses needed in various communities and neighborhoods and reported the results of "directed spending" tactics.

The league quickly spread to other cities. During the Great Depression, according to historian Jacqueline Jones, the Housewives' Leagues "in Chicago, Baltimore, Washington, Detroit, Harlem, and Cleveland relied on boycotts" to secure "an estimated 75,000 new jobs for blacks." Frances Albrier remembers what it was like in Chicago.

> I was in the Pullman service at that time. The maids' quarters were on the South Side. I wanted to go to Woolworths to get some manicuring material. As I went into Woolworths, I met this picket. He

had a sign "Don't Buy Where You Can't Work," so I questioned him. He said that . . . Woolworths would not hire any black clerks. "We're picketing this store on the South Side, and we're picketing the main store downtown. All black people are to stay out." So I said, "Fine, I'll go." That made quite an impression on me. They kept their campaign up about two months. The next time that I went to Chicago and went to Woolworths, I saw three black clerks.

Jones also notes that during the Depression these leagues *"had an economic impact comparable to that of the CIO in its organizing efforts, and second only to government jobs as a new source of openings."* (Italics ours) Her reference to the CIO is an important one. The formation of the Congress of Industrial Organizations was one of the few bright spots in the employment situation for African Americans during the first half of the century.

THE WORKING WOMAN

Almost half of all black women in America have worked outside their homes ever since Emancipation, while the percentage of white women in the labor force was usually 10 to 30 percent until the 1970s. This has been primarily an evidence of poverty, not conscious pursuit of liberation, but it has been true. And yet, the labor movement has, for most of its history, been singularly uninterested in this particular group of workers. Black women themselves, on the other hand, have shown no reluctance to organize. As early as 1862, black women fieldworkers went on strike. In 1881, a strike by the Washerwoman's Association of Atlanta involved three thousand black women. The American Federation of Labor (AFL) was formed that same year without black women.

For the most part, black women were outside the factories as well as the union. During World War I, when there were labor shortages, some inroads were made. But the end of the war meant an end to economic progress. Without the protection of unions, the gains black women had made disappeared. They went back to the fields and the white people's kitchens.

All of this began to change in 1935, when the Congress of Industrial Organizations (CIO) broke away from the AFL. The CIO focused on unskilled workers in the South and on black workers in general. One CIO affiliate in St. Louis, the Food Workers' Industrial Union, was organized by a black woman, Connie Smith. Its members were three thousand nut pickers, 85 percent of whom were black women, and they were able to organize a successful strike. According to historian Ruth Feldstein, "Manager 'Boss Funsten' failed to break the interracial strike by offering white women more money if they returned to work, marking a departure in management's traditionally successful manipulation of the racial caste system."

Black women were also deeply involved in the Southern Tenant Farmers Union (STFU), a group organized to protest federal agricultural policies that proved harmful to the rural poor of the South. Two of the union's spokespersons were black women. Carrie Dilworth and Henrietta McGee both worked to bring to national attention the plight of sharecroppers. However, it was in unionizing in the tobacco industry that black women were most apparent. Since the early nineteenth century, there had been a rigid hierarchy among tobacco workers. Jobs were assigned on the basis of race and gender, with black women receiving the most difficult and tedious job, that of stemmer. In 1938, stemmer Louise "Mamma" Harris instigated a series of walkouts at the I. N. Vaughn Company in Richmond. The walkouts led to strikes that were supported by other CIO affiliates, including the white women of the International Ladies Garment Workers Union, a fact that horrified Richmond police. The strikes led to the formation of the Tobacco Workers Organizing Committee, another CIO affiliate.

In 1943, a major strike against the R. J. Reynolds tobacco company would involve a number of black women leaders, including Theodosia Simpson and Miranda Smith. Because of this strike, Reynolds agreed to go to the negotiating table with Local No. 22 of the Food, Tobacco, Agricultural, and Allied Workers of America (FTA), and Miranda Smith later became southern regional director of the FTA. It was the highest position held by a black woman in the labor movement up to that time. During most of the thirties, however, the unions could accomplish little, simply because there were so few jobs of any kind to be had by anyone. In 1932, Franklin Delano Roosevelt had become president of the United States because he promised to change that.

THE ROOSEVELT ADMINISTRATION

Franklin Roosevelt won the 1932 presidential election without the support of black Americans. It was not that the African American community had any great love for his opponent, Herbert Hoover, nor any dislike for Roosevelt himself. However, intrigued as they might be by new ideas and stirring promises, black people simply could not bring themselves to vote for a Democrat. They had placed their faith for so long in the Republican party, the party of Abraham Lincoln, that turning away from it was difficult and a little frightening.

As soon as Roosevelt was in office, he began to rebuild the economy with the help of his "alphabet soup" of new government agencies. There were the NRA (National Recovery Administration), the AAA (Agricultural Adjustment Administration), the CCC (Civilian Conservation Corps), the NYA (National Youth Administration), and the WPA (Works Progress Administration). During Roosevelt's first term in office, none of these agencies worked to help black Americans specifically, and while some benefitted black people, others inadvertently hurt them.

The NRA, for example, established wage rates by region. Wages were usually set lower in the South because of lower living costs. However, since the lowest-level jobs were almost always held by black workers, the NRA ended up limiting the wages of black women and men. In some cases, the NRA set a minimum wage to cover workers of all races, but this usually meant that employers stopped hiring black workers. If they could not pay black workers less than white, they would hire all white workers. Another agency, the AAA, created a problem for black sharecroppers. It paid landowners in the South to take their land out of cultivation. Theoretically, the payment made was to be split with the sharecroppers on the land. In practice, however, landowners kept the payments and evicted the sharecroppers. In addition, virtually all New Deal programs were administered by local officials, as part of the "grassroots democracy" philosophy. In the South, this meant that white administrators were able to perpetuate racist policies. As an example, relief payments in Georgia were about 70 percent higher for white recipients than for black.

Still, these instances of discrimination were not intended or authorized by the administration. Dissatisfied as they were with Roosevelt's efforts on their behalf, most black Americans began to see him as a far better option than any of those who aspired to run against him. Frances Albrier told of the concern of her branch of the NAACP, in California, about Roosevelt's failure to get an antilynching bill passed. Roosevelt asked national NAACP president Walter White to go to California. "Walter White told us that the president wants you to know that he is still against lynching. It's terrible and he's humiliated, being president of the United States when black people are lynched. But there are any number of issues and things he would like to do for the people of the country . . . [t]hat would benefit the thousands of black people. . . . We were satisfied with that explanation. We went ahead and backed Roosevelt." In the 1936 election, 76 percent of African Americans voted for the Democratic party candidate for president.

Of course, it has been said that the Roosevelt they voted for was Eleanor. Eleanor Roosevelt was everything her husband did not dare to be when it came to racial politics. If he was afraid too much sympathy for African Americans would lose him congressional support for his economic programs, his wife had no such fears. Some of her best friends were black, and she made no bones about it. She had obvious sympathy for the plight of those who suffered injustice and discrimination, and she used every ounce of her influence to try to alleviate it. One of the First Lady's friends was a woman who would become perhaps the most significant contribution of the Roosevelt administration to racial justice in America.

Mary McLeod Bethune and the Black Cabinet

The most powerful black woman in American government to date never held an elected office. She was never even nominated to run. As with many other black women over the years, every position she held was one to which she was appointed. The black women's club movement was an unparalleled political training ground for its members. For Mary McLeod Bethune it was more than that. It was a power base. She used it, deliberately and with calculated effect, to gain the political influence she needed to accomplish great things for her people.

Bethune was born in South Carolina in 1875. After graduating from Scotia Seminary in North Carolina, she was rejected by the Presbyterian church's mission program because of her race. Instead, she became a teacher. In 1904, at the age of twenty-nine, she founded the Daytona Educational and Industrial Institute in Daytona, Florida. The school building was a rented house, and the student body consisted of four young women. Gradually, with the help of the community, it grew. Child-care advocate Lucy Miller Mitchell was a student at the school in those early years. "The colored families in that community supported Mrs. Bethune in many, perhaps unpretentious, ways," she remembered. "To help raise money, they would give chicken suppers. Many times, the money raised from these modest efforts helped to carry the grocery bills or to pay some of the teachers." Fourteen years later, Bethune's school was a four-year high school called the Daytona Normal and Industrial Institute. Among its missions was the training of African American teachers for Florida's public schools. In 1923, the Daytona Institute merged with Cookman Institute, a nearby men's school, and became Bethune-Cookman College.

While she was developing her school, Bethune was also working in the club movement. In 1917, she became president of the Florida Fellowship of Colored Women's Clubs, a position she held until 1924 when she became president of the National Association of Colored Women (NACW). At that point, Bethune held the highest position an African American woman could expect to hold. She proceeded to use it. Her first important move involved the National Council of Women (NCW), a council of thirty-eight women's organizations, thirty-seven of which were white. As part of the NCW, the NACW was eligible to attend an international conference of women that took place every five years and was meeting in Washington, D.C., in 1925. Groups from thirty-five countries would be attending. Bethune had plans for this conference and she set to work.

She made sure that her chief lieutenants would be at the conference. She had demanded and been granted desegregated seating at all conference events. At the conference, when that policy was violated, she and the other members of the NACW walked out. The press was waiting, and Bethune was brilliant. She made a direct appeal to American patriotism. It was humiliating to the United States, she declared, for its citizens to practice and suffer from segregation in the presence of all these other countries. Bethune won the confrontation inside the conference, but more important, she won the first battle in her campaign to become the acknowledged representative of America's black women.

In 1927, Bethune traveled to nine European countries, representing African American women. She worked to establish a national headquarters for the NACW in Washington, D.C., with a paid secretary. If the NACW had not had a term limit, she might have remained there, in spite of the organization's drawbacks. And the NACW did have drawbacks, at least for Bethune's purposes. As historian Elaine M. Smith points out, "Although NACW had always taken a stand on some public questions directly affecting its membership, it had been basically a decentralized organization responding to local and state self-help projects—maintaining the [Frederick] Douglass home and establishing a $50,000 scholarship fund. Bethune had attempted to mold it into a unitary body that could forcefully and consistently project itself into a myriad of public issues as the authoritative voice of Black women."

When the Great Depression battered the country, the NACW became even more conservative, despite Bethune's best attempts. It was time for a change. On December 5, 1935, Bethune was one of thirty representatives of black women's *national* voluntary organizations who voted into being the National Council of Negro Women (NCNW). She was elected president of the new council. For her purposes, the national nature of the organizations was crucial, because each woman on the council headed a group that represented dozens or even hundreds of other groups. Counting the full membership of each organization, Mary McLeod Bethune now officially represented five hundred thousand women. When she spoke publicly, she spoke for all those women. Without ever running for public office, she had a constituency of half a million people.

During her work in the club movement, Bethune had become close friends with Eleanor Roosevelt, who brought her in to work with the federal government. The year after Bethune founded the NCNW, Franklin Roosevelt acknowledged her new status by appointing her to a post in the National Youth Administration (NYA). She and Eleanor Roosevelt persuaded the president that the NYA needed a Negro Division to assure that benefits would be distributed equally, and Bethune was appointed director of the Negro Division of the NYA. The highest position in the federal government ever held by a black woman, it gave her considerable status in the Roosevelt administration. This, added to the influence she already enjoyed as one of the First Lady's closest friends, made her the "race leader" of the Roosevelt years.

In her new role Bethune needed help, and so she organized the Federal Council on Negro Affairs, an informal networking group that came to be known as the "Black Cabinet." It included twenty-seven men and three women who were working within the alphabet-soup agencies. Bethune and her group were directly or indirectly responsible for, among other things, the admission of black women into the Women's Army Corps (WAC), the training of black pilots in the Civilian Pilot Training Program, and the creation of the Fair Employment Practices Commission. After Roosevelt's death, Bethune continued her active role in government under the presidency of Harry Truman. In spite of the fact that she was never elected to any office, she was probably the most powerful black woman ever to serve in the United States government. So far.

THE BLACK ARTIST

The Works Progress Administration—later the Work Project Administration—had one clear goal. It was designed to put people to work. As might be expected, the jobs were not passed out with an even hand, but a great deal of good work was done. In the WPA's Federal Arts Project (FAP), thousands of artists were given work painting, sculpting, and teaching art. In the Federal Theatre Project (FTP), actors acted and directors directed. For black artists, however, WPA work had a huge significance. It offered exposure that most of them could only dream of without the support of the federal government. It offered collective work spaces where ideas could be shared in an entirely new way. In a sense, it was the patron black artists had never had.

This advantage fell more to black men than to black women. In the FAP, more black men were assigned to painting murals, and more black women taught children how to draw and paint. There were exceptions, including Georgette Seabrook Powell, who painted murals in Harlem Hospital and Queens General Hospital. However, most of the black women who gained jobs funded by the FAP worked in the community art centers. These women had a lasting effect on black art in America.

Augusta Savage was a strong voice for black artists. To get more African Americans involved in FAP work, she lobbied politicians and declared her cause to the press, but she also worked behind the scenes. She made hundreds of recommendations to the FAP and even searched out material to support the artists' applications. Prominent black artist Jacob Lawrence credited Savage with having played an important role in developing his very successful career. She also gained FAP support for the Harlem Community Art Center, of which she became director. More than fifteen hundred residents of Harlem took classes at the center, and a number went on to have important careers.

In 1938, Savage took a leave of absence from the center. She had been commissioned to create a sculpture that would symbolize the African American contribution to American music for the 1939 World's Fair. *The Harp,* inspired by James Weldon Johnson's lyrics to "Lift Every Voice and Sing," consisted of a line of elegantly stylized black singers grouped to suggest a harp. The sixteen-foot-tall plaster sculpture was widely publicized and came to be greatly loved in the black community. However, the New York Commission of the World's Fair declined to cast the sculpture into bronze, and Savage was unable to find private sponsors. *The Harp* was bulldozed at the end of the fair, leaving behind photographs and a few souvenirs cast in iron from the original maquette. Savage returned to her students in Harlem, saying, "If I can inspire one of the youngsters to develop the talent I know they possess, then my monument will be in their work. No one could ask more than that."

Sculptor Selma Burke worked with Savage at the Harlem Community Art Center. Like Savage, she was the daughter of a minister and had begun sculpting using clay dug out of the earth. She had an early African influence in her life because her missionary uncles brought back with them masks and religious figures. As noted earlier, a profile portrait Burke did of Franklin Roosevelt in 1944 became the basis of the image on the Franklin dime.

There were other community art centers in Cleveland, Chicago, Atlanta, Richmond, Oklahoma City, Memphis, and Jacksonville, Florida. In addition to classes, where black children had a place to learn to express themselves, there were studios and workshops where black artists could work and share with each other. It is not too much to say that the FAP centers, staffed largely by black women, produced a new generation of black visual artists.

Other talented black Americans still struggled to express themselves in their chosen fields. Film and theater were particularly resistant to new ideas and images, and their impregnability was a source of concern not only to actors but to the black community at large. By the 1930s, Hollywood was not just entertaining America. It was shaping the public mind, creating and reinforcing stereotypes, telling the stories about us as a people and as individuals that we would believe for generations to come. And, as Langston Hughes and Milton Meltzer wrote in the book *Black Magic,* "The silver screen was for many years Black America's daily betrayal before millions of people." At the outset, the stories told about black women allowed them three possible personas—the mammy, the maid, or the siren. During the 1930s another was added—the tragic mulatto.

The Mammy figure appeared as early as *The Birth of a Nation* in 1915. She was almost always fat, dark-skinned, and at least middle-aged. In terms of character, according to historian Catherine Clinton, "The myth of the Mammy revolves around two basic principles. First, that a slave woman within the white household devoted her maternal instincts and skills to the white family who owned her and that she took pleasure and pride in this service. Second, that she gained status from this role and was revered within the black community." This myth has persisted over more than a century in American theater and film. The three greatest Mammy figures were Hattie McDaniel, Louise Beavers, and, in the second half of her extraordinary career, Ethel Waters.

The first Academy Award ever presented to a black actor went to McDaniel for playing Mammy in *Gone with the Wind* in 1939. In all her Mammy roles, as Donald Bogle points out in *Brown Sugar,* "Boldly, she looked her white costars directly in the eye, never backing off from anyone. . . . Sometimes McDaniel seemed angry. Although the movies never explained it, her undercover hostility, even when coated with humor, was never lost on the audience." Louise Beavers played Mammy/maid roles hundreds of times, from a 1927 silent version of *Uncle Tom's Cabin* to the fifties television show *Beulah.* Her Mammy portrayals were kind, with an innate dignity and a sharp wit. In *Imitation of Life* in 1934, she and Fredi Washington breathed genuine life into a melodramatic script. The woman who utterly transcended the mammy roles she played, however, was Ethel Waters.

Ethel Waters had one of the most remarkable careers of anyone in American entertainment. She began in vaudeville as Sweet Mama Stringbean, a lanky blues singer. She moved on to the club scene in New York and recordings for Black Swan Records. In 1927, she began to appear in Broadway musicals such as *Africana, Blackbirds,* and *Rhapsody in Black.* Then, in 1933, Irving Berlin caught her act at the Cotton Club. He signed her for his musical *As Thousands Cheer,* and Waters became the first black star in an all-white Broadway hit. Before long, she was the highest-paid woman, black or white, on Broadway.

Waters's first dramatic role came in 1939, when she played the lead role of Hagar in *Mamba's Daughters,* by Dorothy and DuBose Heyward. Hagar was a black mother, not a mammy. Her important relationships were with her own black family. And Waters was magnificent in the role. The play opened on January 3, and her performance received the highest accolades from all of the critics except Brook Atkinson, the influential critic for the *New York Times.* He didn't like the play and he didn't like Waters in it.

His negative review provoked an unprecedented response. A group of theater professionals took out an advertisement in Atkinson's own paper the following Sunday which read, in part, "We the undersigned feel that Ethel Waters' superb performance in *Mamba's Daughters* . . . is a profound emotional experience which any playgoer would be the poorer for missing. It seems to be such a magnificent example of great acting, simple, deeply felt, moving on a plane of complete reality, that we are glad to pay for the privilege of saying so." This extraordinary tribute was signed by some of the brightest lights of American film and theater, including Judith Anderson, Tallulah Bankhead, and Burgess Meredith. It moved Atkinson to go back to see *Mamba's Daughters,* and he changed his mind.

Waters played Mammies for the rest of her dramatic career, but she did them brilliantly. She received an Oscar nomination for her role in the 1949 film *Pinky* and was a triumph in Carson McCuller's *Member of the Wedding* on Broadway and in the film. As Dulcy in the film version of William Faulkner's *The Sound and the Fury,* she symbolized endurance and moral strength. In these roles, she laid a foundation for the powerful black women who would follow her in American film.

America's denigration of the morality of black women was expressed in the stereotype of the black siren. But the film image was actually more than that. In it, the male fear of women—with its concomitant fascination—converged with white fears and fascination about black people. This made for a potent image of dangerous sexuality. Like the sirens of Greek myth, the sirens of the movies used their exotic wiles to lure men into peril. Nina Mae McKinney became the first black screen siren when she appeared in the King Vidor film *Hallelujah* in 1929. The critics described her character as "half woman, half child." Given that she was seventeen at the time, this was not surprising. McKinney was beautiful, light-skinned, and sexy. She set the pattern for future black sirens.

It was the siren role that brought Lena Horne to Hollywood, but her story had a twist. She played the "other woman" in the film version of the play *Cabin in the Sky* in 1943 and would almost certainly have inherited the screen siren mantle had it not been for her father. When Hollywood wooed his daughter, the elder Horne walked into Louis B. Mayer's office and informed him that Lena would not play stereotyped black roles. If Mayer wanted his daughter, her contract would be so drafted. Otherwise, she would simply go back to her successful career as a singer. Mayer agreed, and the result was that she didn't have any role at all in most of her films. Instead, she would appear, separate from her costars and the plot, sing a song, and disappear. This had the advantage that the studio could cut her from the film for southern distribution.

The tragic mulatto was a variation on the black siren. It was the role Fredi Washington played in *Imitation of Life* in 1934. Peola, a young woman who decides to pass for white, fascinated audiences, as did the "almost white" actor who played her. Washington did not remain in Hollywood to pander to this fascination but returned to Broadway and a triumph in *Mamba's Daughters*. She later retired from acting and became a political activist.

Even the women who remained active in show business made great efforts to escape from stereotyping. Louise Beavers appeared in a number of independently made black films and performed in New York in a one-woman show. Lena Horne fashioned an impressive career in music, where she could exercise control. Others appeared exclusively in all-black films. On the stage, black theater professionals were working to gain even more autonomy. At the center of this move was a black woman, the great Rose McClendon.

When the Federal Theatre Project (FTP) was organized, black units were organized in major cities. In New York, there were three factions in competition for administration of the unit, but they were all in agreement when Rose McClendon's name was put forward as director of the project. McClendon was thirty-six years old when she first appeared on a professional stage. But from the moment she walked down the stairs in Lawrence Stalling's *Deep River* in 1926, she became the Black First Lady of Theater. For the next seventeen years, she appeared in virtually every significant Broadway play about black life. She also worked untiringly to change the position of black actors and playwrights. She served on the board of the Theatre Union, directed plays for the Harlem Experimental Theatre, and organized the Negro People's Theatre. In her honor, the first important black theater in New York since the Lafayette Players was named the Rose McClendon Players.

Founded in 1937, that theater was the beginning of the modern black theater movement. The company included Ossie Davis and Ruby Dee, Jane White, Helen Martin, and several other important black actors. After five years, it folded, but a number of its members were involved in the founding of the American Negro Theatre (ANT). The ANT became a training ground and launching pad for Rosetta LeNoire, Alice Childress, Isabel Sanford, and Clarice Taylor, as well as for such male stars as Sidney Poitier and Harry Belafonte. Its biggest hit was *Anna Lucasta.*

In the end, it was not the New York Negro Unit of the FTP that made the biggest splash, but the Chicago group, which put together an all-black version of Gilbert and Sullivan's operetta *The Mikado,* calling it *Swing Mikado.* It was hugely successful and started a vogue for all-black versions of many white classics, including *Swingin' the Dream, Carmen Jones,* and even *My Darlin' Aida.*

One of the most important productions of the era was *Cabin in the Sky.* As with many other white-written plays, its significance lies primarily in the way it was developed by its black cast. In the original script, plain and patient Petunia is married to the likeable Little Joe Jackson, who has a tendency to fool around. Her rival for Little Joe's affections is the sultry Georgia Brown. Petunia and God get together to save Little Joe's soul. The producers cast Ethel Waters as Petunia and Katherine Dunham as Georgia Brown.

That was a little like making Shakespeare head writer for Saturday Night Live. Every character Waters played had at her core a strength that came from spirituality. She persuaded the producers that, as Petunia is God's collaborator, she should have a serious, genuine faith. This changed the whole focus of the play, for the better, and it was a great success. Waters went on to play in the film version, but Dunham was replaced by Lena Horne.

Fortunately for American theater and dance, Katherine Dunham's role in the theater production of *Cabin in the Sky* provided her with enough money to develop her dance company. She was thus able to continue a revolution in American dance that had started at the beginning of the decade.

Dance has always been an integral part of African American life, and the dances of black people have always been an important part of American theatrical life. But the first performances given within, and taken seriously by, the concert dance world began in the 1930s. What was called "the First Negro Dance Recital in America" took place in 1931. It was presented by the New Negro Art Theater Dance Company, cofounded by Edna Guy and Hemsley Winfield. In that same year, Katherine Dunham founded the Negro Dance Group in Chicago.

Dunham was a unique figure in modern dance. Trained in anthropology at the University of Chicago, she did her fieldwork in the Caribbean, where she studied African-based ritual dance. She received a Guggenheim fellowship to study in Haiti, Jamaica, Martinique, and Trinidad. She formed her own company after receiving her Ph.D. from Northwestern. Like so many other black artistic pursuits at the time, the company was supported in large part by the WPA. At their first important concert, in 1938, they stunned the audience with *L'Ag'Ya,* a dance choreographed by Dunham and inspired by the martial arts of Martinique.

In February of 1940, the Katherine Dunham Dance Company appeared at the Windsor Theater in New York. The audience and the critics were overwhelmed. The *New York Times* said, "With the arrival of Katherine Dunham on the scene the development of a substantial Negro dance art begins to look decidedly bright. Her performance with her group at the Windsor Theater may very well become a historic occasion, for certainly never before in all efforts of recent years to establish the Negro dance as a serious medium has there been so convincing and authoritative an approach." This tremendous success led to an offer by the producers of *Cabin in the Sky.* They hired the entire troupe to dance in the show and gave the feature role of Georgia Brown to Dunham herself. The money the dancers made in the show helped to support them for some time and to finance Dunham's continuing research. It also led to future Broadway appearances, in *Tropical*

Revue, Bal Negre, Blue Holiday, and *Caribbean Carnival.* Dunham choreographed and performed in *Carib Song.* And in 1943, Dunham opened the Katherine Dunham School of Arts and Research in New York, which became a training ground for artists not only in dance, but in theater arts, literature, and world culture. Eartha Kitt was one of the dancers who studied there, as were Talley Beatty and Archie Savage.

The bitter paradox of the black performer—using your art to entertain your oppressor—is nowhere so evident as it is among musicians, perhaps because it is so difficult to maintain detachment while singing or playing your heart out. One of the casualties of this paradox was the great Billie Holiday.

Billie Holiday, born Eleanora Fagan in 1915, grew up with poverty, pain, and music. By the time she started singing at a speakeasy when she was fifteen, she had been raped, locked away in a reformatory, forced into prostitution, and had served four months in prison. In the album notes to *Billie Holiday's Greatest Hits,* Timme Rosenkrantz and Inez Cavanaugh describe what it was like to see and hear her in her early years in the clubs. "Billie lifted a voice that was the embodiment of her strange beauty—the heaven, the hell, the joy, the pain of being a Negro. Out came the music from the depths of her soul as if in constant struggle to reconcile the love in her heart with the hell in her life." That painfully wonderful voice took Holiday to a huge success at the Apollo Theatre in 1935, the brutal experience of touring through Jim Crow country, and finally an unqualified success at New York's multiracial nightclub, Cafe Society, in 1939.

It was at Cafe Society that Holiday introduced the song "Strange Fruit," based on a poem by Lewis Allan. The lyrics graphically and bitterly described lynched bodies hanging from trees in the South.

> *Southern trees bear a strange fruit,*
> *Blood on the leaves and blood at the root,*
> *Black body swinging in the Southern breeze,*
> *Strange fruit hanging from the poplar trees.*
>
> *Pastoral scene of the gallant South,*
> *The bulging eyes and the twisted mouth,*
> *Scent of magnolia sweet and fresh,*
> *And the sudden smell of burning flesh!*
>
> *Here is a fruit for the crows to pluck*
> *For the rain to gather, for the wind to suck,*

For the sun to rot, for a tree to drop.
Here is a strange and bitter crop.

Holiday was severely criticized for singing the song, but she refused to back down. Like so many other black women, she found the pain of being part of a lynching community unbearable. Determined to make her voice heard in the most dramatic protest against racial violence she could make, she recorded "Strange Fruit" on the Commodore label. She alienated large parts of her audience, even risked her career because she felt so strongly the need to defend black men.

Holiday made another strong statement with the song she chose for the flip side of the record. The song was called "Fine and Mellow," and it began with the usual blues complaint that her man treated her badly. However, it progressed to a declaration that, if he didn't do better, she would go away, no matter how fine and mellow he was. In the juxtaposition of these two songs, Holiday summed up the profoundest feelings of many black women toward black men. "I will risk all I have to protect you from harm," she seems to be saying, "but if you mess with me, I'll leave you."

Billie Holiday was one of the greatest of all jazz musicians, but the horrors of her life led her to a heroin addiction that destroyed her. Her suffering was ended by death in an automobile accident in 1959.

Holiday was just one of the remarkable jazz vocalists whose careers began in the 1930s and 1940s. For a time, they seemed to spring up like daffodils all over Harlem. Pearl Bailey tells a wonderful story in her autobiography, *The Raw Pearl.* In 1934, a friend talked her into entering the amateur contest at a music hall called the Harlem Opera House. She got there too late and ended up down the street, where another theater—the legendary Apollo—was also having an amateur night. She entered that one instead. "I won . . . for 'In My Solitude,' arrangement homemade," she writes. "Maybe my nice appearance helped, too. I'm grateful I didn't go down the street to the Opera House. I doubt I would have made it there, for that night a young girl walked on stage, opened her mouth, and the audience that had started to snicker ended up cheering. The girl sang 'Judy.' Her name was Ella Fitzgerald. She won, and that voice will go down in history."

Lena Horne, Sarah Vaughan, Carmen McRae, Betty Carter, and Dinah Washington were among the other black women who began singing in the thirties and forties. Just reciting the names conjures the glamour, passion, and strength these women brought to the world of American music. But there was another, different sort of singer who emerged during this time, a woman who came to represent the pride of black people.

Marian Anderson's brilliant concert career began in Europe, where she did not have to face the racism that so plagued black artists in America. She sang and studied in England, Germany, France, and Italy. In Salzburg in 1935, Arturo Toscanini said after hearing her sing, "What I heard today one is privileged to hear only in a hundred years." Shortly thereafter, Anderson returned to the United States and began a series of concerts under the management of impresario Sol Hurok. Then, in 1939, the Daughters of the American Revolution (DAR) refused to book Anderson into their Constitution Hall in Washington, D.C. When the refusal was made public, Eleanor Roosevelt immediately resigned from the DAR and made a phone call to Secretary of the Interior Harold L. Ickes, who invited Anderson to give a concert on the steps of the Lincoln Memorial on Easter Sunday. More than seventy- five thousand people, black and white, filled the park and the surrounding streets.

A black woman artist became the symbol for a new spirit in America.

SOCIAL ACTION

During the 1930s the NAACP found the direction it would follow for the next half century. Under the leadership of powerful leader Walter White, it grew from seventy thousand members in 1931 to a quarter of a million before White left office in 1955. It also shifted focus from its earlier goals—an end to racial violence and discrimination in housing and public places and the securing of voting rights—to a single-minded dedication to desegregation of schools through legal challenges. It was an important goal and it would be a tremendous struggle. But since there were still only a handful of black women being admitted to and graduating from law school, it also put men squarely in the forefront of the NAACP. For some years, the court battles would be fought by men, and that simple fact reinforced a tendency that had existed in the organization from its founding to look for its leadership among men.

However, just as there had been important black women among the founders of the NAACP—including Mary Church Terrell and Ida B. Wells-Barnett—there were also important black women among its leadership in the decades before and immediately after the Second World War. The early women included Mary Burnett Talbert, who served as a vice president of the NAACP from 1918 until her death in 1923, organizing chapters in Louisiana and Texas. Later, there were Juanita Jackson Mitchell, leader of the youth program, and Daisy Adams Lampkin, who served as a regional field secretary and then national field secretary. Lampkin was the organization's primary fund-raiser and an extraordinary recruiter of new members. Then, at the end of the 1930s, the NAACP attracted one of the most dynamic organizers in black America, Ella Baker.

Ella Baker first became involved with radical politics in 1930 when, at the age of twenty-seven, she moved to New York. Within two years, she had cofounded the Young Negroes Cooperative League, in Harlem, and soon became its national director. The goal of the group was to encourage and organize consumer cooperatives. Its philosophy was one of collective decision making and outreach to all members of the community. Individualism was criticized, and charismatic leadership was not applauded. Baker also worked with the Harlem Housewives Cooperative and the Women's Day Workers and Industrial League, as well as the YWCA. In all of her work, according to historian Barbara Ransby, she "refused to be relegated to a separate 'women's sphere,' either personally or politically. She often participated, without reservation, in meetings where she was the only woman present, and many of her closest political allies over the years were men."

In 1940, Baker joined the NAACP. Already an experienced organizer, she saw the local chapters as the key to the effectiveness of the group. She started as an assistant field secretary and eventually became national field secretary. In her work of organizing and recruiting, she traveled throughout the South, making friendships and contacts that she would keep for a lifetime. In 1943, she became director of branches. Three years later, she decided to leave the national staff of the organization because of political differences. "In her organizational life," writes political scientist Dianne M. Pinderhughes, "she valued 'group-centered leadership rather than leader-centered groups'; and she argued that 'Strong people don't need strong leaders.' This put her at odds with the hierarchically structured NAACP, which used its large membership (which she had helped build in the 1940s) to finance its legal campaign but did not allow it to be activated for locally specific purposes." Although Baker resigned her national position, she remained active in the New York branch. And her position in the Civil Rights movement after the war would be a crucial one.

THE WAR

On December 8, 1941, the United States entered World War II. Black women, along with white, entered the workforce to replace men who had gone to fight. Within six months, they also entered the army itself.

In May of 1942, the Women's Army Auxiliary Corps (WAAC) was created. In 1943, it was incorporated into the U.S. Army as the Women's Army Corps (WAC). By the end of the war, more than four thousand black women had become WACs. The 688th Central Postal Battalion was the first all-black female unit overseas. The eight hundred women of the battalion served in England. The WACs also created a famous black band known as the 404th Army Service Band. It performed at military, civilian, and church functions, both black and white, all around the country. The first black woman to be commissioned as an officer was WAC Charity Adams Earley. She was the highest-ranking black woman during World War II.

The navy not only admitted black women during World War II, but they set a goal of raising black recruitment to 10 percent. In 1944, Bessie Garret became the first black woman accepted into the Women's Reserve of the United States Navy, commonly called the WAVES. Two black women, Frances Wills and Harriet Pickens, were among the first WAVES officer graduates from Smith College, but the navy fell far short of its 10 percent quota. As of 1945 there were only fifty-six black WAVES. However, the navy was the first branch of the armed services that incorporated women into its regular forces, in 1948. The Coast Guard admitted five black women during World War II.

Mabel K. Staupers led an aggressive fight to eliminate quotas established by the U.S. Army Nurse Corps. Although many black nurses volunteered their services during World War II, they were refused admittance into the navy, and the army allowed only a limited number to serve. In 1943, although the navy had notified Staupers that it had decided to place the induction of black nurses under consideration and the army had raised its quota of black nurses to 160, the situation had not greatly improved. In an effort to draw attention to the unfairness of quotas, Staupers requested a meeting with Eleanor Roosevelt. In November of 1944, the First Lady and Staupers met, and Staupers described in detail black nurses' troubled relationship with the armed forces. In January of 1945, when Norman T. Kirk announced the possibility of a draft to remedy a nursing shortage within the armed forces, Staupers made a well-publicized response. "If nurses are needed so desperately," she asked, "why isn't the army using colored nurses?"

Afterward she encouraged nursing groups of all races to write letters and send telegrams protesting the discrimination against black nurses in the army and navy Nurse Corps. There was an immediate groundswell of public support for the removal of quotas. Buried beneath an avalanche of telegrams from an inflamed public, Kirk and Rear Admiral W. J. W. Agnew, along with the War Department, declared an end to quotas and exclusion. On January 10, 1945, Kirk stated that nurses would be accepted into the army Nurse Corps without regard to race, and five days later Agnew announced that the navy Nurse Corps was open to black women. Within a few weeks, Phyllis Daley became the first black woman to break the color barrier and receive induction into the corps.

The end of discriminatory practices by a key American institution helped to erode entrenched beliefs about the alleged inferiority of black health-care professionals and paved the way for the integration of the American Nurses' Association. In 1948, the ANA opened the gates to black membership, appointed a black nurse as assistant executive secretary in its national headquarters, and elected Estelle Massey Osborne to the board of directors.

Nursing was not the only field in which the war hastened progress. There were also some advances for black women in the labor movement. As in World War I, black women during World War II entered the factories from which they were ordinarily excluded. According to Ruth Feldstein, the percentage of black women in the industrial labor force tripled. However, they were underpaid and they were "last hired, first fired." They were also often faced with antagonism from white workers, even to the extent of "hate strikes." The unions did not offer much support. Indeed, the unions were the first place black women had to fight both racial and gender discrimination.

Then, in 1943, the CIO formed the Committee to Abolish Racial Discrimination. The United Auto Workers in Detroit co-sponsored with the NAACP a rally in support of black women. Ten thousand workers turned out to demand that war industry jobs be opened to black women. Between 1940 and 1945, black membership in the unions went from 200,000 to 1.25 million.

SHAKING THE TREE OF LIBERTY

Black and white Americans had survived the Great Depression together. They had fought the Second World War together. In 1946, the soldiers started coming home together. Would the cooperation brought on by disaster have any lasting effects?

What white America did not know was that the experiences of the last two decades had already made their mark—on the hearts and minds of the African American people. The war itself had been presented as the great battle for democracy, a war to end tyranny and oppression. The people of America responded to President Franklin D. Roosevelt's plea that they fight for the "Four Freedoms"—freedom of speech, freedom of worship, freedom from want, and freedom from fear. Just as the idealism of the Revolutionary War had changed the atmosphere in America in the late eighteenth century, so now did the idealism of World War II fill the air in the late 1940s. The end of the war marked the beginning of a new era in the United States and the world. The next twenty-five years saw independence movements succeeding and new countries coming into being all over Africa and Asia, starting with India in 1947. The United Nations helped the cause when it was formed and, in 1948, adopted a declaration that said the organization would support human rights without regard to race, sex, language, or religion.

Prosperity had arrived. Opportunity was all around. Freedom was in the air. And black women, like everyone else in the country, had suffered and worked for this new day. They were not going to be denied.

As I see it, Blacks must become the active conscience of America, but conscience is a

drowsy thing. It stirs, it turns over, takes another nap and falls into a deep, deep sleep.

'Leave me alone,' conscience cries. 'Let me sleep, let me sleep,' conscience cries.

'Let time take care of it—time, time is the answer. Maybe ten years or maybe another

hundred years.' Oh, no, America, your conscience, like old Pharaoh's of old,

will not rest or sleep until we can eat here at John A. Brown's.

CLARA LUPER, *BEHOLD THE WALLS*

TOWARDS
FREEDOM

CHAPTER ELEVEN

DR. MARTIN LUTHER KING, JR. Thurgood Marshall. A. Philip Randolph. Adam Clayton Powell. Whitney Young, Jr. Medgar Evers. Roy Wilkins. Julian Bond. Stokely Carmichael. The names are a litany of the great and the almost great, of the martyred and the mundane. They are the leaders of the great black crusade, the Civil Rights movement. For decades history has been so dazzled by their commitment and charisma that it has not looked behind them to see the tens of thousands of black women standing there.

The historian Charles M. Payne puts the modern Civil Rights movement into a different perspective. He states that, in the years before 1964, there were considerably more women in the movement than men. Between the ages of thirty and fifty, women outnumbered men three or four to one, and they were not just raising funds and handing out flyers, according to Lawrence Guyot, a member of the Student Nonviolent Coordinating Committee (SNCC). "It's no secret that young people and women led *organizationally*," he has stated, and others who were active in the movement corroborate. This presents a puzzle to students of political history, who have always contended that women are less active in politics than men in virtually every situation. What made black women different?

One explanation could be that there were more women than men, numerically, in the South at the time. The Great Migration had taken more men to the North, as had the smaller migration after World War II. But Payne's statistics tell us something different. In families where both husband and wife were present, the wife was still far more likely to be an active participant in the movement than the husband.

What about reprisals? Were men more likely to be vulnerable to serious counterattacks? This was probably not a deciding factor. Reprisals often targeted whole families, regardless of which member of the family actively participated in political activity. Too, the danger for women was great enough that they were unlikely to be thinking in terms of degrees. They were jailed, clubbed, and beaten. Every adult woman activist Payne interviewed had lost her job.

The answer to the question of why black women were disproportionately involved in the day-to-day activities of the early civil rights struggle appears to lie, first, in the participation of black women in religious and community activities and, second, in their cultural preparation for resistance. Black women in the 1930s and 1960s knew how to organize, were accustomed to working together, and felt a strong kinship with members of the community beyond their immediate families. The church and community work in which they had been involved for two centuries—and especially in the sixty years before the Civil Rights movement—made them ideal political activists.

It was irrelevant that some of the churches opposed their political actions. They had also been disagreeing with the preacher, in the name of God, for a very long time. Inside the church or out, black women carried more than their share of the load and felt entitled to make up their own minds. When Jarena Lee went out to preach against the dictates of her church in the early nineteenth century, she called on God as her sanction. There was a higher power, she insisted, than the men of the church, and it was that power she acknowledged and obeyed. Her spiritual daughters said the same about civil rights. God had given them the right to freedom. They were going to fight for that right, in His name, no matter who spoke against them.

Interestingly, women were often inspired to join the movement by a son or niece or close friend. When they saw loved ones taking risks in a just cause, they believed they should offer support. The black woman's sense of community was a powerful force in this time of crisis. So, too, was her sense of the efficacy of even small actions. These were women who had founded schools and hospitals by running bake sales and quilting bees. They were in a direct line politically from Bethune, who bought the land for her school selling pies and ended up an advisor of presidents. They had fought to be seated at women's conventions in the face of powerful white opposition and had won. Others might view the early stirrings of the movement with cynicism or despair, but black women knew better. And if their names were not household names, that was no big surprise. They knew just how much you can get done if you don't care who gets the credit.

And so, while black women seldom spoke to the press or got their pictures in the paper, they were expert grassroots organizers. They had the skills that were needed at that moment in history. But how was it that they were prepared, psychologically and emotionally, to participate in this massive resistance effort? That is the other part of their story.

In the Kingdom of Culture

The cultural expressions of black women such as quilts and pottery and adornment have long been ways of affirming the identity of the individual and of the community. But there have been other forms of expression with a different content and purpose, specifically created to avow and to protest the oppression of black people. These can be traced back to the abolitionist writings of Charlotte Forten and the slave narratives of Harriet Jacobs and Elizabeth Keckley. They continued with the protest poetry of Frances Ellen Watkins Harper and the musical dramas of the Hyers sisters tracing the slavery, resistance, and freedom of black people. In the late nineteenth and early twentieth centuries, many of these cultural productions centered on lynching, including the first protest play to be produced in the modern era, *Rachel,* by Angelina Weld Grimké. In that play, produced by the NAACP in 1916, a young woman faces her fears of lynching, descends into madness, and decides to forswear motherhood rather than rear a child who might be lynched. Grimké returned to the theme in two stories and in some of her poetry. Grimké's close friend Mary Burrill also wrote about lynching, in her play *Aftermath,* as did other black women of the period. Lynching was not only a very real horror; it was a potent symbol for the oppression of black people.

In the 1940s, of course, there was Billie Holiday's performance of the song "Strange Fruit," which also spoke with great emotional intensity to black women and men. Indeed, many of the blues singers sang almost as often about the oppressive circumstances of their lives in America as they did about lost love and cheating men. They were entertainers, but they knew their audiences needed more than escape. It was part of their job to help create a collective consciousness, a social and *political* consciousness. And, as Angela Davis has said, "The consciousness of the social character of Black people's suffering is a precondition for the creation of a political protest movement."

In the dances of Katherine Dunham and Pearl Primus, too, black women helped to create an awareness of the political nature of black suffering in America. Primus, in fact, choreographed a dance to the song "Strange Fruit."

One last horrifying, courageous piece of theater was created by a woman named Mamie Bradley when her teenaged son, Emmett Till, was killed while visiting in the South in 1955. Before he left, she warned him, "If you have to get down on your knees and bow when a white person goes past, do it willingly." Young Emmett seems not to have heeded his mother's urgent warning. Mamie Bradley recalls how it was reported to her.

About three days into Mississippi, they went into a little country store. This was Money, Mississippi. They had games on the front porch and you could buy pop and candy, little junk. The boys were playing checkers and Emmett decided to go into the store and buy something. His young cousin went into the store with him. Emmett bought bubble gum and some candy.

As they came out of the store, according to the accounts I heard from some of the boys, someone asked Emmett, "How did you like the lady in the store?" They said Emmett whistled his approval.

The response of Roy Bryant, the "lady's" husband, and her brother, W. J. Milan, was predictable and violent. They drove Emmett Till to the Tallahatchie River, tied a seventy-pound cotton gin to him, and shot him in the head before throwing him into the river. A speedy trial resulted in a "not guilty" verdict.

The recovered body was sent back to Chicago, where Mamie Bradley opened the coffin and collapsed on the train platform crying, "Lord, take my soul." Of a reporter she demanded, "Have you ever sent a loved son on vacation and had him returned in a pine box, so horribly battered and waterlogged that someone needs to tell you that this sickening sight is your son—lynched?"

Bradley, unlike the fictional heroine of Angelina Grimké's 1920 play, did not descend into madness. Rather, she resolved to resist and place her suffering into the collective consciousness of the black community. Most mothers would have wanted to hide the horror of what happened, perhaps hoping that in silence and secrecy the pain and ugliness would go away. But Mamie Bradley chose another course. She allowed *Jet* magazine to publish photographs of the mutilated corpse. She delayed the burial for four days so that thousands of people could visit the funeral home, letting "the world see what they did to my boy."

This was a deliberate and enormously powerful preparation for resistance. Myrlie Evers Williams remembered, "I bled for Emmett Till's mother. I know when she came to Mississippi and appeared at mass meetings how everyone poured out their hearts to her, went into their pockets when people had only two or three pennies, and gave . . . some way to say that we bleed for you, hurt for you, we are so sorry about what happened to Emmett. And that this is just one thing that will be a frame of reference for us to move on to do more things, positively, *to eliminate this from happening ever again.*" (Italics ours)

Many other members of the generation that began fighting for justice in the years immediately following the murder of Emmett Till remember vividly seeing the photographs or hearing Mamie Bradley talk. They have written in their autobiographies or talked in interviews about the impact her powerful act of resistance had on them. By publicly expressing her rage and sorrow, Mamie Bradley made her son's death an impetus for rebellion. Mamie Bradley herself went back to school to become a teacher. "My burning thing," she said, "the thing that has come out of Emmett's death is to push education to the limit: you must learn all you can. Learn until your head swells." She also makes a very clear distinction between resistance and hatred. "I did not wish [my son's killers] dead. I did not wish them in jail. If I had to, I could take their four little children—they each had two—and I could raise those children as if they were my own and I could have loved them. . . . I haven't spent one night hating these people. I have not looked at a white person and saw an enemy. I look at people and I see people." She did not hate, but she certainly did not accept, and her attitude was one shared by millions of black women whose spiritual heritage gave them the strength to fight back in the decade to come.

The First Front

Black women knew that their freedom and that of their children was linked directly to education. But quality education, in the view of most black political leaders, meant desegregating the schools, from elementary to university level. At every stage of the battle were women who fought for the right to learn, from young Linda Brown to Charlayne Hunter-Gault. A remarkable number of test cases involved young women.

Pauli Murray began her battle for the entrance to law school in 1938. First, the University of North Carolina refused her admission because of her race, and then Harvard rejected her because she was a woman. She persisted and was finally accepted at the University of California at Berkeley, where she received an LL.M. degree in 1945. In 1965, she became the first African American to receive a Doctor of Juridical Science degree from Yale University Law School.

By the mid-1940s, women like Pauli Murray would no longer have to fight alone. The NAACP had put the desegregation of schools at the top of its agenda. In 1946, Constance Baker Motley joined the NAACP Legal Defense and Education Fund, headed by Thurgood Marshall. This outstanding lawyer would be involved with the most important civil rights suits of the day. One of Motley's first cases involved defending the constitutional rights of Ada Sipuel.

Under Oklahoma law, it was a misdemeanor—not a serious crime, but a crime nonetheless—for school officials to admit "colored" students to white schools or to teach classes of mixed races. The Oklahoma NAACP convention in 1945 decided to attack segregated education by trying to enroll black students in the graduate schools and professional schools at the University of Oklahoma and Oklahoma State University. Ada Lois Sipuel volunteered to be a test case, knowing that she might be delaying her education for years and that she would certainly be putting herself into a pressure-filled and possibly dangerous situation. In 1946, she applied to the University of Oklahoma School of Law, the only law school in the state at the time. The university rejected her application on the basis of her race. Motley represented Sipuel as two Oklahoma courts upheld the university's decision. (The university claimed that it was planning to open a "substantially equal" law school for Negroes.)

The NAACP took the case to the U.S. Supreme Court. Thurgood Marshall argued the case, with able assistance from Motley. In 1948, the court reversed the Oklahoma court decision and ordered the University of Oklahoma School of Law to admit Sipuel, open a separate school for her, or suspend the white law school. The state pretended to do the second, by roping off a small space in the state capitol, calling it a law school, and assigning three law professors to be the faculty. Sipuel and the NAACP, of course, did not stop fighting. Finally, in the summer of 1949, Sipuel was admitted to the University of Oklahoma Law School. By this time she was married and pregnant with her first child.

After the Sipuel case, states could not require African Americans to wait until they established separate graduate or professional schools. This was one of dozens of cases the NAACP sponsored that attacked the "separate but equal" doctrine. Another was *Davis v. County School Board of Prince Edward County.* In 1950, sixteen-year-old Barbara Johns organized a strike at her high school in Prince Edward County, Virginia, to protest the conditions at the school. The idea of school desegregation didn't occur to Johns and her friends; they just wanted Prince Edward County to live up to the "equal" in "separate but equal." The case was taken on by the NAACP on the condition that it become a desegregation case. In 1952 the case was lost, and the Virginia courts upheld "separate but equal." By the time the case came to trial, Barbara Johns had been forced to move to Montgomery, Alabama, for her own safety. She stayed with her uncle, Vernon Johns, who was the pastor of the Dexter Avenue Baptist Church. He retired in 1954 and was replaced by Martin Luther King, Jr.

The same year the Barbara Johns case went to the Virginia courts (1952), the NAACP went to the U.S. Supreme Court with its biggest case so far—a direct challenge to the "separate but equal" precedent set by *Plessy v.*

Ferguson. Marshall, Motley, and other NAACP lawyers presented a group of five cases, which were heard under the name of only one—*Brown v. The Board of Education of Topeka, Kansas*—because that particular case was outside the South. The years of legal challenges, the gradual chipping away at the wall of judicial conservatism finally paid off. In 1954, the court voted unanimously that, as Chief Justice Earl Warren wrote, "in the field of public education the doctrine of 'separate but equal' has no place. Separate educational facilities are inherently unequal."

That court ruling was only one step on the journey toward integrated schools, however. Most southern states began to exercise their ingenuity in attempts to avoid compliance with the ruling, and the Justice Department under the Eisenhower administration looked the other way. But the NAACP did not. In 1955 alone, the NAACP filed desegregation petitions with 170 school boards in seventeen states. All over the South, black women challenged the schools' noncompliance with the high court's ruling. In 1956, Autherine Juanita Lucy Foster fought to become the first African American to attend the University of Alabama. She was expelled a few days later, supposedly because of statements she made about the university's race relations. Charlayne Hunter-Gault risked her personal safety as one of the first two black students to enter the University of Georgia, Athens, in January 1961. None of these black women acted naively. They knew before they filled out their applications that they were enlisting in an army of civil rights soldiers. They knew that they faced harassment, delays in their education, and animosity from the people students need most—the faculty. They may not have known, however, to what lengths white supremacists would go to try to keep the schools to themselves.

What no one knew was that, in December of 1955, the entire civil rights struggle would change. This time, the battlefield would be neither university nor courtroom, and the event would not be controlled by lawyers. Organized by black women, it would mark the beginning of a new stage in the movement and bring forth a strong new leader.

MONTGOMERY

The image of Rosa Parks sitting, tired, on a bus in Montgomery, Alabama, is one that touched hearts across the country. In her pleasant, dignified face, Americans could read the story of black women who had been pushed around too much and pushed too far. But there was another story behind Parks's decision to remain seated. It began, officially, four days after the *Brown v. Board of Education* decision when Jo Ann Gibson Robinson of the Montgomery, Alabama, Women's Political Council (WPC) wrote a letter. The letter in question was addressed to Montgomery's mayor, W. A. Gayle, and in it Robinson reiterated the complaints of the black community concerning conditions on the city's buses. "Please consider this plea," she wrote, "for even now plans are being made to ride less, or not at all, on our buses." In other words, the WPC was prepared to declare a boycott.

On Montgomery's buses, black passengers were required to sit at the back, as they were in other cities in the South. They were also often required to pay their fare at the front of the bus, get off, and then get back on through the rear door. In addition, they sometimes had to stand while there were empty seats in the front area reserved for whites. In the middle section, which was supposedly open to anyone, black riders were often rudely ordered to give up their seats to white passengers who were just getting on. A great many more black women than men rode on the buses, and so they were subjected to these indignities more regularly. They had also been resisting them for some time before December of 1955. As early as 1944, Viola White was arrested, beaten, and jailed for refusing to abide by Jim Crow rules. She was released from jail but, when she died ten years later, her appeal had not been heard.

When Jo Ann Robinson became president of the WPC, she made bus desegregation its primary goal. In March of 1955, a fifteen-year-old girl, Claudette Colvin, was arrested for refusing to give up her seat in the middle section of a bus. The WPC was ready to declare the boycott, but they were dissuaded by male civil rights leader E. D. Nixon. He felt that Colvin, who was pregnant at the time, would not be an appropriate symbol around which to organize. In July of the same year, the U.S. Court of Appeals in Richmond, Virginia, declared in *Flemming v. South Carolina Electric and Gas Company* that bus segregation, even on buses that operated within one state, was unconstitutional.

It was not until December, however, that Rosa Parks refused to give up her seat in the unreserved section to a white man. She had not planned the protest, but she was prepared for it. She had long been a civil rights activist and, indeed, had been present at the meetings when it was decided not to mobilize around Colvin. Later she said she had "a life history of being rebellious against being mistreated because of my color," and that she had finally "been pushed as far as I could stand to be pushed. . . . I had decided that I would have to know once and for all what rights I had as a human being and a citizen."

The moment Robinson heard of Parks's arrest, she assured herself of Nixon's support and then wrote a flyer that said, "Another Negro woman has been arrested and thrown into jail, because she refused to get up out of her seat on the bus for a white person to sit down. . . . Negroes have rights, too, for if Negroes did not ride the buses, they could not operate. . . . The next time it may be you, or your daughter, or mother." It asked Montgomery's black citizens to refuse to ride the buses on the following Monday, the day Parks would go to court. Robinson then took the flyer to the Alabama State College campus, where she was a faculty member. She stayed up all night and, with the help of a colleague, mimeographed thirty thousand copies of the flyer. The WPC had planned distribution routes months earlier and, the next day, Robinson and two students delivered bundles of flyers to beauty parlors and schools, to factories and grocery stores, to taverns and barber shops.

Monday morning, the buses were almost bare of African American customers. Monday afternoon, civil rights leaders formed an organization— the Montgomery Improvement Association—to supervise the protest. A man, young Dr. Martin Luther King, Jr., was elected president. A number of women served on the MIA executive committee, including Robinson, Rosa Parks, Irene West, Euretta Adair, and Erna Dungee.

As the boycott continued, leadership passed more and more to King and other male leaders. The women who had originally planned and declared the boycott remained behind the scene. MIA financial secretary Erna Dungee Allen, looking back, said, "We really were the ones who carried out the actions." For example, women leaders organized the highly efficient carpool system for those who needed to get to work without buses, which has been credited with keeping the boycott alive for more than a year. In addition, the women, according to Allen, "were very vocal and articulate, especially in committee meetings." However, for a number of reasons, men played their traditional role of representatives to the white world. Robinson remained crucial to the action, serving as an organizer and negotiator and editing the monthly MIA newsletter.

Many other women supported the boycott in their own ways. Cook Georgia Gilmore created a club that sold baked goods and donated the proceeds to the MIA. Inez Ricks then formed another club, and every week the two groups competed to see which could donate more money. And then there were the women who refused to ride the buses. Some of them walked twelve miles a day so that they could work all day cleaning house. Others rode in carpools. Others had the support of their white women employers, who drove them. But they remained faithful to the boycott.

Rosa Parks's appeal was delayed in state court, so MIA and NAACP lawyers filed a suit in the names of Claudette Colvin, Mary Louise Smith, and two other women. That suit went to the U.S. Supreme Court in November of 1956, and Alabama's city and state segregation laws were ruled unconstitutional. When the ruling took effect in December, the black citizens of Montgomery called off the boycott, and thousands of black women lifted their bags and stepped back onto the buses—to sit wherever they liked.

One year after Montgomery, the scene shifted back to the schools and the city of Little Rock, Arkansas.

LITTLE ROCK NINE

The most famous battle to force integration of the schools occurred in Little Rock in 1957. Nine black students were scheduled to enter Central High School in Little Rock when Governor Orval Faubus decided that it would be good campaign strategy to oppose their admission. Faubus was facing reelection, and his strongest opponent was an avid segregationist. In a bid to prove his own antiblack credentials, he took a stand at the schoolhouse door, with the Arkansas National Guard as his muscle men. That night on the news the people of Arkansas saw nine black teenagers being barred from the high school by rows of armed soldiers.

What most of America didn't know was that those nine students, six of whom were girls, had been carefully chosen for their jobs. They had been selected for scholastic achievement, of course, but they had also been screened for emotional stability and supportive families. The person who picked them was Daisy Bates, president of the Arkansas NAACP.

Bates was one of the many black women who led civil rights battles in their own communities, including Gloria Richardson in Cambridge, Massachusetts; Clara Luper in Oklahoma City; Mary Fair Burkes and Jo Ann Robinson in Montgomery. Bates was also a journalist, co-owner with her husband of a newspaper called the *Arkansas State Press*. Since 1941, the Bateses had reported civil rights abuses and paid for it in advertising losses and harassment. Then, in 1952, the NAACP approached her about becoming president of the Arkansas state conference of NAACP branches. She agreed, and two years later she started going personally with black children as they tried to enroll in all-white schools. Bates made sure each rejection was duly noted by the news media.

Bates and the NAACP kept up a steady pressure on the Little Rock superintendent of schools to integrate Central High School, and Bates carefully coached her group of nine students to participate in the integration. They were prepared, and their parents were prepared, to deal with publicity, hostility, and opposition. No one could have prepared them for what happened.

The day after Faubus's grandstand play, Bates and a police escort took the students into Central High School in secret. However, the violence outside the school made it unsafe for them to stay and, for a second time, they left. For several weeks the students didn't attend any school while the NAACP and state and federal governments tried to work out an agreement. In the end, Eisenhower sent in the 101st Airborne Division, a crack combat troop, to ensure the children's safety. Soldiers were stationed both inside and outside the school, and each student had a soldier as bodyguard. The personal guard for each student lasted for two months, and members of the battalion or federalized National Guard troops remained on the campus of the school until January. Only one of the nine black students withdrew from Central High. All the others graduated. Persecution by white students continued to the end.

In *Cooper v. Aaron,* the court case that resulted from Little Rock, the Supreme Court made an important ruling. It declared that state governments must enforce the desegregation mandated by the *Brown* decision. Congress also passed the Civil Rights Act of 1957, which was the first modern attempt by the federal government to deal with the issue of civil rights. However, the act had no enforcement provisions. It wasn't until seven years later that Congress empowered the justice department to take legal action and use federal funds to uphold the *Brown* decision, with the Civil Rights Act of 1964. The NAACP, however, didn't wait for the government to back up its own laws, and in the years that followed the *Brown* decision, Constance Baker Motley was in the center of the organization's challenges to the system. She became the NAACP Legal Defense Fund's principal trial lawyer. In 1991, she summed up these years.

Among the better known cases I personally tried were those against the Universities of Mississippi, Georgia, and Alabama, and Clemson College in South Carolina. As a result, James Meredith, the plaintiff in the University of Mississippi case, became a national hero in 1962. Charlayne Hunter-Gault and Hamilton Holmes, the plaintiffs in the University of Georgia case, brought Georgia kicking and screaming into the twentieth century in 1961. George Wallace and

Alabama gave up massive resistance to desegregation in 1963. And now South Carolina brags about Harvey Gantt, the plaintiff in the Clemson College case in 1962, who became mayor of Charlotte.

Over the years, Motley argued ten civil rights cases in the Supreme Court, winning nine. During one of those cases, Ramsey Clark, who was then attorney general of the United States, was in court and heard her. Afterward, he went back to the White House and suggested to President Lyndon Johnson that he appoint Motley to the federal bench. Initially, Johnson submitted her name for a seat on the Court of Appeals for the Second Circuit, but, according to Motley, "the opposition to my appointment was so great, apparently because I was a woman, that Johnson had to withdraw my name. I remember how stunned both Johnson and [Thurgood] Marshall were at the strength and intensity of the opposition."

Motley was only one of several black women involved in civil rights law. The NAACP's first national youth director, Juanita Jackson Mitchell, went back to school in the 1940s to get her law degree and, in 1950, became the first black woman admitted to the bar in Maryland. She successfully tried a suit to desegregate Maryland's state and municipal swimming pools and beaches. Because of her work in a 1953 case, Baltimore became the first southern city to desegregate its public schools after the *Brown* ruling. She also defended student activists and, in 1966, won the "Veney raid" case on appeal. She was representing homeowners whose houses had been searched without warrants but with the authorization of Baltimore's commissioner of police.

Marian Wright Edelman was in school at Spelman College in Atlanta in 1960. When she participated in a sit-in, she was among fourteen students who were arrested. Soon she had decided to forego graduate studies in Russian and become a lawyer. She graduated as a valedictorian from Spelman and entered Yale University Law School as a John Hay Whitney Fellow. Her civil rights activities continued. She went to Mississippi to work on voter registration in 1953 and, after graduation, returned as one of the first two NAACP Legal Defense and Education interns. She opened a law office, became the first black woman to pass the bar in Mississippi, got demonstration students out of jail, and was put in jail herself. She also became involved in several school desegregation cases and served on the board of the Child Development Group of Mississippi, which represented one of the largest Head Start programs in the country. In the 1970s, she would found the Children's Defense Fund.

The NAACP would need all its lawyers in the next few years. In the late 1950s and early 1960s, the protest movement spread throughout the South, and the carefully orchestrated legal challenges of the NAACP were no longer the only weapons black people were willing to use in this battle. Thanks to the counsel of Dr. King and, probably, the overwhelming number of women involved, the demonstrations remained nonviolent. Increasingly, however, they were marked by the energy and anger of youth. And increasingly, the protesters ended up in jail.

Students from all over the country, black and white, threw their bodies into the fight. They sat down at lunch counters and were dragged away. They marched at amusement park gates and were thrown into police vans. They rode on buses and were clubbed and put in jail. They were young and filled with rage and willing to do whatever needed to be done. Many of these young people had come out of the NAACP youth clubs, but when they looked for an organization to coordinate their independent protests, they did not find what they wanted in that group. They tried to be a part of King's Southern Christian Leadership Conference, but it, too, was lacking, at least for them. The answer was Ella Baker.

In the Thick of the Fight

After Montgomery, Martin Luther King, Jr., and the Southern Christian Leadership Conference (SCLC) had approached Ella Baker to lead their Crusade for Citizenship. The veteran civil rights worker agreed, but she soon discovered that King's group was no more in line with her political philosophy than the NAACP had been. Again, too few people were making decisions for too many.

After the historical Greensboro sit-in, Baker resigned from the SCLC, determined to find a way to work with the student movement. In order to facilitate this, she took a job with the Young Women's Christian Association (YWCA). Then, in April of 1960, she organized a conference at Shaw University, to which she invited the young people who had been involved in the many independent student protests. The result of the conference was the founding of the Student Nonviolent Coordinating Committee (SNCC).

Ella Baker was SNCC's éminence grise. She imbued the student group with her own political principles, steering them away from the more conservative and hierarchical tendencies of the older civil rights groups. She spoke strongly for grassroots democracy and decision making by groups, rather than individual leaders. She also strongly recommended involving the community at large. As a result, SNCC leaders included poor people, young people, and women. Using Baker's longtime contacts in the Deep South, SNCC went into rural areas, working with farmers and sharecroppers, focusing largely on voters' registration.

Several SNCC women were involved in the Freedom Rides through the South. Diane Nash was one of eleven students jailed in Rock Hill, South Carolina, in the first jail-no-bail action. They remained incarcerated for a month. Nash became coordinator of the SNCC contingent of Freedom Riders. When a conflict in priorities evolved within SNCC, Ella Baker was able to head off a split by suggesting that the organization develop two separate branches and follow both agendas. Nash became head of the direct action wing while Charles Jones headed the voter registration drive. Nash, another critically important woman in the Civil Rights movement, became a field staff organizer with the SCLC, and was involved in organizing both the 1963 march on Washington and the 1964–65 Selma campaign.

In 1962, SNCC joined with the Congress of Racial Equality (CORE), the SCLC, and the NAACP and formed the Voter Education Project (VEP). Within two years VEP had registered at least five hundred thousand black voters in the South. In the meantime, one of the most important symbolic events of the movement took place in Washington, D.C., along with one of the most painful symbolic exclusions of black women. On August 28, 1963, in the midst of the battle, 250,000 people, black and white, marched on the capital in Washington to show their support for goals of the Civil Rights movement. The march was organized by a group of civil rights leaders that was headed by A. Philip Randolph. Anna Arnold Hedgeman, a longtime veteran of the movement, was the only woman on the organizing committee. As time for the march approached, she was forced to plead that the male organizers treat black women with the respect they deserved.

Anna Arnold Hedgeman began her work in the community in the 1920s when she became executive director of a black branch of the YWCA in Jersey City, New Jersey. In her memoir she recalls spending her days off in Harlem where she became acquainted with the culture of the Harlem Renaissance at a literary salon in the home of Madame C. J. Walker's daughter, A'Lelia. In 1927, she moved to Harlem, accepting the position of membership director of the Harlem YWCA. It is significant to note that, while working at the Harlem YWCA, Hedgeman sponsored a number of events that featured prominent black women intellectuals and political activists. In her memoir she confided, "the Harlem YWCA featured women of achievement because we knew that Negro women shared with all women a kind of second-class citizenship in American culture."

Throughout the 1930s, Hedgeman remained active in protest activities, her militancy resulting in a forced resignation from the directorship of the black branch of the Brooklyn YWCA. She had used that position to organize a citizen's coordinating committee to seek provisional appointments for black Americans to the Department of Welfare. They secured the first 150 appointments the city had ever given to the black community. She formed coalitions with white women on the race relations committee of the Federation of Protestant Churches to expand employment opportunities for black clerks in department stores. She was involved in the planning of the first march on Washington Randolph organized, in 1941. It was called off after Roosevelt issued Executive Order 8802, which banned racial and religious discrimination in war industries, government training programs, and government agencies. Through the 1940s and 1950s, Hedgeman continued to be deeply involved in working for the black community in both private and public sectors.

In 1963, as the day of the march grew near, Hedgeman realized that no black women were being scheduled to speak. On August 16, with all her impeccable credentials behind her, she sat down to write a memorandum to A. Philip Randolph. She did not ask to be allowed to speak herself, in spite of the fact that her efforts were responsible for bringing at least thirty thousand people to the march, but she did ask that one black woman be allowed to present a major address. Her first suggestion was Myrlie Evers, widow of murdered civil rights leader Medgar Evers. Her second was Diane Nash Bevel of SNCC, whom she called "the consummation of the quality of the past of Negro woman and part of the hope of all of us for the future."

Hedgeman's request was denied. She described the day of the march in her memoir.

> On the day of the March, the wives of the civil rights leaders and other Negro women were asked to sit on the dais and Daisy Bates was asked to say a few words. Mrs. Rosa Parks, the courageous woman who had refused to "move to the back of the bus" in Montgomery, was presented, but most casually. We grinned, some of us, as we recognized anew that Negro women are second-class citizens in the same way that white women are in our culture.

As she listened to Martin Luther King, Jr.'s, powerful "I Have a Dream" speech, Hedgeman wrote on her program, "I wished very much that Martin had said, 'We have a dream.' "

Meanwhile, in Mississippi, violence and the fear generated by it still kept black citizens from voting. During Freedom Summer hundreds of volunteers came from all over the United States to register Mississippi's black population. The group was mixed, in part because it was believed that violence against a mixed group would attract more attention than against an all-black group. This strategy proved all too painfully accurate. When white activists Andrew Goodman and Michael Schwerner and black activist James E. Chaney were found murdered, the press raised a huge outcry, and white sympathy in the country in general swung dramatically away from the white supremacists. The degree of violence the black people of Mississippi faced that summer of 1964 was horrifying. There were one thousand arrests. Thirty-five people were shot. There were eighty beatings, thirty buildings bombed, and three people, in addition to Goodman, Chaney, and Schwerner, were killed.

That same year, under the guidance of Ella Baker, SNCC members Annie Devine, Victoria Gray, and Fannie Lou Hamer helped to found the Mississippi Freedom Democratic Party (MFDP) in an attempt to contest the authority of the all-white Democratic party in the state. In one year, the MFDP had registered eighty thousand people in its Freedom Ballot campaign. The party elected a delegation to the 1964 Democratic convention and presented itself as a challenger to the regularly elected delegation. The MFDP argued that it was the only Mississippi delegation that had been chosen in an election run according to the U.S. Constitution and the policies of the Democratic party.

The Democrats did not, of course, simply see the error of their ways and seat the MFDP, but the action did cause considerable controversy and draw attention to the situation. Fannie Lou Hamer addressed the convention to talk about injustice in Mississippi, about disenfranchisement and violence. She described how she and five others had been arrested and beaten. That speech ranks among the most important of the civil rights movement. The MFDP delegation was not seated, but the Democratic party agreed that, at the 1968 convention, no delegation that had benefitted from discrimination in its election would be seated. In the following two years, legislation was passed that would help the Democrats keep that promise.

CIVIL RIGHTS ACT OF 1964

Between 1964 and 1968, registration of black voters in Mississippi went from 8 percent to 62 percent. In other words, in 1964, fewer than one out of every ten adult African Americans in Mississippi could legally cast a ballot, but four years later, six out of ten had registered and could have a say in the government of the nation. In some countries, armed revolutions have taken place that made less difference than that.

The years 1964 and 1965 were watershed years for the Civil Rights movement and for such women as Ella Baker, Rosa Parks, Daisy Bates, and Diane Nash Bevel, who had been fighting for so long to change the racist face of America. Through the years of effort on different fronts, in different organizations and with different tactics, these women and others had kept the issue at the forefront of the American consciousness and conscience. Finally, the federal government started to catch up, passing the Civil Rights Act of 1964 and the Voting Rights Act of 1965.

The Civil Rights Act of 1964 was written to guarantee that all Americans would have access to public accommodations such as restaurants and hotels. It also authorized the federal government to use the courts to force desegregation in schools. Finally, Title VII of the act forbade discrimination in employment on the basis of race.

At this point, the nineteenth-century controversy surrounding the Fifteenth Amendment repeated itself. Originally, Title VII did not cover gender, and there were women who felt that it should. Almost certainly one of those women would have tried to add the word "sex" to the bill, but none of them got the chance. They were beaten to it by Representative Howard Smith of Virginia, who added the word as an attempt to make the bill so completely outrageous that no one in Congress would vote for it. It was a miscalculation. As Paula Giddings relates it in *When and Where I Enter,* "There *was* much ribaldry in the Congress; the day Smith made his proposal was called 'Ladies Day' in the House. But evidently the good ol' boys were laughing so hard they missed a step. Some of their colleagues, particularly Representative Martha Griffiths of Michigan, were able to marshal forces sufficient to pass the bill—with the sex provision." The Equal Employment Opportunities Commission was created to enforce Title VII, and together they changed American business.

The Voting Rights Act was ushered in by a major civil rights demonstration when members of SNCC, the SCLC, and CORE set out on a march from Selma, Alabama, to Montgomery in March of 1965. At the very outset, the marchers were clubbed and teargassed by police on horseback.

"Bloody Sunday," as it was called, was nationally televised, and the country was horrified. After two weeks of tension and a nationally televised speech by President Lyndon Johnson in which he said the marchers had "awakened the conscience of this nation," they set out again. This time they were protected along the way by federal marshalls and the national guard. When the marchers, a previously agreed-upon three hundred people, arrived in Montgomery, the crowd grew to a total size of thirty thousand. Five months later, Lyndon Johnson signed the Voting Rights Act into law.

The new law gave the federal government power to oversee elections and address problems quickly. No longer tied to dragging cases through the court system, when government officials saw signs of discrimination, they now had the power to take over the process of registering voters and running election centers immediately. Most black Americans could now, for the first time since Reconstruction, actually participate in the electoral process, and not just as voters. Before the Voting Rights Act only about one hundred African Americans held political offices in the United States. Twenty-five years later the number had risen to nearly seven thousand.

BREAKING THROUGH

Until the passage of the Voting Rights Act, virtually all of the black women in public office had been appointed, not elected. Like Mary McLeod Bethune, they sometimes exercised considerable influence, but their tenure in office was dependent on the good graces of those who appointed them. Few black women even ran for office, although there were exceptions to that rule. As noted previously, in 1952, for example, newspaper editor Charlotta Spears Bass was nominated for the vice presidency of the United States on the Progressive party ticket.

Bass was one of the founders of the Progressive party. Its platform called for peace and an end to discrimination and segregation, unemployment, and government corruption. Bass believed that neither of the two traditional parties was committed to working for black people, so she supported Henry Wallace's candidacy for president in 1948. Although she was now approaching seventy, she began to travel extensively in the service of her growing political concerns. In Prague, she supported the Stockholm Appeal to ban the bomb at the peace committee of the World Congress. She traveled in the Soviet Union and praised its lack of racial discrimination.

In 1950, Bass ran on the Progressive party ticket for the congressional seat from the fourteenth legislative district in California. She was unsuccessful, but she brought attention to important political issues. In her 1952 run for the vice presidency, she campaigned fiercely, reserving her hardest attacks for Republican vice presidential candidate Richard Nixon. Her refrain during the campaign was, "Win or lose, we win by raising the issues." In addition to civil rights and peace, Bass stressed the issue of women's rights, encouraging women to run for political office.

There were other black women in elected office before 1965, including Crystal Bird Fauset, who was elected to the Pennsylvania House of Representatives in 1938, and Daisy Elliott, who served in the Michigan State Legislature from 1962 through 1978 and from 1980 through 1982. One of the first black women to run for office with the real expectation of winning was NAACP lawyer Constance Baker Motley. Motley had been appointed in 1963 to fill the unexpired term of a New York state senator. The following year, she was elected to that office, making her the first black woman in the New York Senate. She resigned not long thereafter to run for, and win, the presidency of the Borough of Manhattan. Later she became the first black woman on the federal bench when she was confirmed as a U.S. district court judge.

A number of other black women were elected to local and state office in the years that followed. In 1966, Barbara Jordan became the first black woman in the Texas Senate, from which she went on to the U.S. House of Representatives. That same year, Grace Towns Hamilton became the first black woman elected to the Georgia legislature. Mae Street Kidd was elected to the Kentucky legislature in 1967. Hannah Diggs Atkins was the first black woman in the Oklahoma legislature, elected in 1969 and serving through 1980 and then going on to become Oklahoma's secretary of state and a delegate to the United Nations.

Politics was not the only area where black women were making progress during these years. The Civil Rights movement was raising the American consciousness about race, and that new awareness helped black women move forward, if sometimes only in small steps, in virtually every field. The achievements ranged from the arts to sports to rock and roll. The number of "firsts" during the late 1940s through the 1960s is dazzling.

Black women and men virtually took over track and field. At the 1948 Olympics, Alice Coachman and Audrey Patterson became the first black women to win Olympic medals—gold for Coachman in the high jump, which also set an Olympic record, and a bronze for Patterson in the 200-meter dash. In 1960, Wilma Rudolph was the first U.S. woman to win three gold medals at the Olympics, and in 1968, Wyomia Tyus became the first person ever to win two consecutive gold medals in the 100-meter dash. Mae Faggs, Barbara Jones, Willye White, Earlene Brown, and Mildred McDaniel also broke barriers and continued the tradition of excellence for black women in track and field events. In 1956, Nell Jackson became the head coach of the U.S. Olympic track and field team. She was the first African American to hold a head coach position for an Olympic team. In 1969, she became the first African American to be on the U.S. Olympic Committee Board of Directors.

Black women weren't just sweeping up the medals at the Olympics. They were integrating sports that had always been considered purely white domains. In 1950, Althea Gibson was the first African American of either gender to play in the U.S. Open and in 1951 the first black American to play at Wimbledon. In 1957, she won the Wimbledon singles and doubles championships and became the first black woman to be on the cover of *Sports Illustrated*. "Big Mo" Aldridge became the first black woman to make the national Amateur Athletic Union (AAU) women's basketball team. In 1956, Ann Gregory integrated a women's amateur golf championship, and in 1967 Renee Powell joined the LPGA tour.

Black women began to appear in academia at all levels, although mostly in small numbers. At Columbia University in 1947, Marie M. Daly became the first black woman in America to earn a Ph.D. in chemistry. In 1949, at the University of Michigan and Yale University, respectively, Marjorie Lee Brown and Evelyn Boyd Granville became the first black women in America to earn Ph.D. degrees in mathematics. In 1951, Mildred Fay Jefferson became the first black woman to graduate from Harvard University's Medical School.

In 1946, Helen O. Dickens, the daughter of a former slave, received her certification from the American Board of Obstetrics and Gynecology. Four years later, she was the first black woman admitted to the American College of Surgeons. In 1958, Edith Irby Jones broke through the racial barriers of southern medical schools when she became the first African American, male or female, to be admitted to the University of Arkansas School of Medicine. Later, in 1985, Jones was the first woman president of the National Medical Association, a predominantly black medical society. The American Board of Surgery certified its first black woman, Hughenna L. Gauntlett, in 1968.

In 1948, the African Methodist Episcopal (AME) Church agreed to ordain women. The United Methodist Church had approved ordination for women in 1924, but it was limited.

Black dancer Mary Hinkson joined the Martha Graham Dance Company in 1951, and Sara Yarborough joined the Harkness Ballet in 1958.

Ernesta G. Procope founded E. G. Bowman Co. Inc. in the 1950s. It was the first minority-owned insurance brokerage firm on Wall Street. With more than two thousand large corporations and government entities on its client roster, it is still the largest.

In the mid-1960s, Ethel L. Payne spent ten weeks in Vietnam covering the war. She became one of the first black women in broadcasting when she provided commentary to CBS News. In 1954, Norma Merrick Sklarek became the first black woman to be licensed as an architect.

Fashion model Naomi Sims made history as the first black woman to appear on the covers of *Ladies' Home Journal,* in 1968, and *Life,* in 1969.

All of these women made their mark, and their achievements were both facilitated by and inspiring to the black political scene. But nowhere is the relationship between politics and life more intimate than in the arts. Because artists deal in images and stories, they help shape the way we think about the world. From the postwar years to the late 1960s, the shape changed significantly.

THE DEATH OF AUNT JEMIMA

In 1959, the face of American theater changed. *A Raisin in the Sun,* by Lorraine Hansberry, was produced on Broadway. For the first time, American mainstream theater saw a black play that wasn't a musical, a comedy, or a social problem play. Instead, it was a straightforward, naturalistic story about a working-class family whose goals were a nice place to live and a little hope for the future.

A Raisin in the Sun was more than a play. It was a very clear statement of just exactly what white supremacist America had been trying to deny for centuries—that black people are *people.* And it was a hit. Not only was Hansberry famous, but virtually every member of the cast would soon be as well. Sidney Poitier became the biggest black male star in movie history and kept that title for almost two decades. Ruby Dee went on to a distinguished career on stage, in films, and on television. Claudia McNeil was recognized at once as a great stage actor. Diana Sands became a Broadway star and the first black woman to be given the opportunity to play great nonblack roles. From that moment, in spite of setbacks, the black theater movement has been a powerful force in American theater.

The situation in films could not have been more different. It helps to understand Hollywood in the fifties if you think of it as King Kong. It wasn't just an eight-hundred-pound gorilla; it was an eight-hundred-*ton* gorilla clutching the Empire State Building and batting off tiny fighter planes with a big hairy paw. King Kong Hollywood was racist and sexist and scared to death of the Hayes office (censors) and Joe McCarthy (the House Un-American Activities Committee) and southern theater owners and its own shadow. So how did a black woman with talent and a yen to be in the movies approach the gorilla?

Pearl Bailey walked up and said, "Now, looka here, honey." Then she started joshing and fooling and having a good time. She talked straight, but never too mean. She made a few movies—*Isn't It Romantic?, Carmen Jones, That Certain Feeling, Porgy and Bess,* and others—and then became television's first black woman star. She didn't have her own show until the seventies, but she had her nightclub success, and she was on everybody else's show. King Kong pulled up a chair, sat back and relaxed, charmed down to his big, hairy toes.

Eartha Kitt walked up to the gorilla and said, "Meowwwwwww." She batted the big gorilla on the nose with her paw, teased it, tickled it, scratched it, and then moved fast. She was as independent as a kitten and as appealing. Fresh from captivating Broadway audiences in *New Faces of 1952, Mrs. Patterson, Shinbone Alley* (in which she played a cat), and *Jolly's Progress,* she came to Hollywood to be Anna Lucasta in the film version of the play and to appear as the bad girl in *St. Louis Blues.* Her updated, sophisticated version of the screen siren was just right for the time.

(Later the kitten would scratch too hard when she was invited by Lady Bird Johnson to a genteel White House gathering of notable women where the question was raised, "Why is there so much juvenile delinquency in the streets of America?" Kitt's answer involved poverty, racism, and an unjust war in Vietnam. King Kong put his big paw down on the kitten and left it there for more than a decade.)

And then there was Dorothy Dandridge, who did exactly what the gorilla wanted her to do until her life ended in tragedy. Dandridge was very ambitious and she approached her goal of stardom methodically. Besides taking classes and going to auditions, she worked with Lena Horne's singing coach and did not avoid comparisons with Horne. She was so successful in her singing career that she saved one New York nightclub from bankruptcy. For Dandridge, it was all preparation. She wanted to be a movie star. And finally Hollywood called. After a series of forgettable films, she was cast opposite Harry Belafonte in the 1953 film *Bright Road.* Playing a southern schoolteacher, she impressed critics and audiences with her honest performance and her personal dignity. She was accepted as a serious and skilled actor.

Dandridge's performance in the film *Carmen Jones,* an adaptation of Bizet's opera *Carmen,* was dazzling. *Life* put her on its cover, and the critics went wild. *Time* said she "holds the eye—like a match burning steadily in a tornado." Comparing her role with the one she played in *Bright Road,* *Newsweek* said, "The range between the two parts suggests that she is one of the outstanding dramatic actresses of the screen. She won an Academy Award nomination, the first for a Black woman in the category of Best Actress, and she was suddenly an international star."

She would not make another film for three years.

When Dandridge finally appeared in front of a camera again, it was in the first of a series of films in which she played opposite white actors. A 1966 article in *Ebony* summed up the situation. Dandridge was a leading lady, it pointed out, and that was the problem. "Except for Harry Belafonte and the quietly but brilliantly rising Sidney Poitier, there were no prominent Negro romantic leads about. Besides, a Negro male can be made a star without becoming a leading man. He may play a variety of roles not involving romance. *But a leading lady such as Dorothy had to set male hormones sizzling."* (Italics ours)

The situation was reminiscent of the career of Chinese actor Anna May Wong, who, in order to avoid an interracial happy ending, died in every single one of her films. Dandridge played a hot-blooded, passionate woman who never kissed her leading man. In 1959, she was cast as Bess in the film version of *Porgy and Bess.* The only real improvement over her past few films was that now she was tempting black men instead of white men. Dandridge rose above her material. She won the Golden Globe Award for best actress in a musical.

Dandridge made two more films, but her career was over. When Rouben Mamoulian was selected to direct *Cleopatra,* he told Dandridge that he wanted her for the part. "You won't have the guts to go through with it," she said. "They are going to talk you out of it." Of course, they did. The role of the greatest black temptress in history went to violet-eyed Elizabeth Taylor. Dandridge died in September of 1965 of an overdose of antidepressants.

In television in the 1950s, as in the movies, the world was very, very white, and all black women worked as maids. First, there was *Beulah.* It started as a radio show starring Hattie McDaniel but came to television with Ethel Waters in the title role of the wisecracking maid. She was followed by McDaniel and then Louise Beavers. Then there was Amanda Randolph's

Louise on Danny Thomas's *Make Room for Daddy,* from 1953 to 1964. Even Nichelle Nichols, though no maid, found herself doing little more than pushing buttons for Captain Kirk as Lieutenant Uhura in *Star Trek* from 1966 to 1969.

The influence of the Civil Rights movement was apparent in 1963 when *East Side/West Side* debuted. Featuring Cicely Tyson, the show explored inner-city problems and sometimes used important black actors as guest stars. In one guest appearance, Diana Sands won an Emmy. Unfortunately, *East Side/West Side* lasted only one season.

The role of the sixties on television was Julia, in Diahann Carroll's show of that name. Television executives decided to eliminate all traces of the black stereotype in creating the character. To begin with, Julia was not a maid. She was also not sexy, poor, ignorant, foolish, afraid of the dark, submissive, smart-alecky, or anything else that had ever been cited as part of the stereotyping of black women. Along with everything else, they got rid of her ethnicity. She was, in every way, a nice middle-class young woman. It was all thoroughly inoffensive and all wrong. They had made her not more human, but less. But the show was successful, and black women watched, happy to see any progress made. *Julia* was clearly a transitional show. Later and more authentic portrayals of black women probably would not have reached the small screen without it. It did not, however, produce a rash of successors.

SONG FROM THE SOUL

Film and television were trying to ignore or whitewash black women in the 1950s and early 1960s, but the music industry had a better idea, at least economically. It decided to exploit them. As in the 1920s, the migration of African Americans to the large cities during and just after World War II meant that there was a concentrated market in urban areas for black products and black culture. In the 1950s, a number of small black record companies started up. These companies produced the kind of music that was once called "race music," but they had to find a new name, one more appropriate to the spirit of the time. So they called it rhythm and blues. It sounded like the blues, or sometimes like a jazzy version of the blues, or sometimes even like the blues with a little country thrown in, and some of its major figures were black women. In the 1950s, Dinah Washington was known as "Queen of the Blues" and Ruth Brown as "Miss Rhythm."

It soon became obvious that rhythm and blues was appealing not only to black listeners. R & B songs were making it to the Top 40 charts. A *Rolling Stone* interviewer once asked Ruth Brown, "At what point did rhythm and blues start becoming rock and roll?" She answered, "When the white kids started to dance to it." And when the white kids started to dance to black music in the early 1950s, many adults in white America got nervous. Their nervousness boiled over when Frankie Lymon, of Frankie and the Teenagers, danced with a white girl on Alan Freed's television show. The show was canceled.

But that did not solve the problem. Rhythm and blues/rock and roll might be racial dynamite, but it was also highly profitable. So the record companies came up with a compromise reminiscent of the minstrel show. White performers began "covering" black hits. Some recorded their own versions of black songs because they loved the music, but a great many had more mercenary motives. If white radio stations were uncomfortable with black artists, the record companies would give them white artists singing black music. Some black men survived the sweep—Chuck Berry, Sam Cooke, Fats Domino—but in the early years of rock and roll there were no black women at the top of the pop charts, except Zola Taylor, a member of The Platters.

Some rhythm and blues artists—LaVern Baker, Ruth Brown, and Etta James—had crossover hits in the Top 40, but black women really found a way into rock and roll in the late fifties. That way was doo-wop, the poor kids' music. Girls liked it because, to sing close harmony a capella, they didn't need expensive equipment, and they didn't need to know how to play a musical instrument, something that gender roles discouraged. The black "girl groups" created what music historian Gillian G. Garr called "the first major rock style associated with women." The Bobbettes reached the pop charts with "Mr. Lee" and then disappeared. The Chantels, in 1958, had two hits, "Every Night (I Pray)" and "I Love You So." Then, in 1961, a girl group hit the top of the pop charts for the first time. The group was the Shirelles and the song was "Will You Love Me Tomorrow," by Carole King and Gerry Goffin. The group had ten more hits in the Top 40 over the next two years, five of them in the Top 10. The first record from Motown Records to hit the top of the charts was the Marvelettes' "Please Mr. Postman." Motown also produced Martha (Reeves) and the Vandellas, whose hits included "Dancing in the Streets" and "Nowhere to Run."

But the biggest girl group of all time came out of Detroit in 1964 with "Where Did Our Love Go." In the five years the group remained together, The Supremes had twelve number-one singles. They became the most successful American rock and roll group of the sixties, black or white, and one of the most successful of all time. But as solo performers in rock and roll, black women still faced apparently unsurmountable obstacles. Until the mid-1970s the number of black women who had number-one singles on the pop charts can be counted on far fewer than the fingers of one hand. Very much the same can be said of white women.

Rock and roll was dominated by men, most of them white. But there were other areas of music where black women made an indelible mark. Mahalia Jackson brought gospel to white America. In 1946, she signed with Apollo Records and by 1954 was so popular that she had television and radio shows. Her recording of "Move On Up a Little Higher" sold more than a million copies, the first gospel recording to do so.

Few black women were on the concert stage or in opera. The popular perception was that classical music was still very much a white domain— purer, better, and requiring more skill than "black" music such as R & B, gospel, or rock and roll. Not until 1946 did a black woman, Camilla Williams, sign a contract with a major American opera company. The Metropolitan Opera Company did not hire a black singer until 1955, when Marian Anderson performed in Verdi's *Un Ballo in Maschera*. The Metropolitan presented Mattiwilda Dobbs the next year.

The world of dance was different, perhaps because it has been a field where women have frequently had more influence or because it is not a mass-media art form or because, like small theaters, small dance companies have always had to operate with virtually nonexistent budgets. At any rate, black women in dance during the civil rights era created fine and powerful art and made strong statements. As in opera, some black women broke through the barriers into classical ballet. Janet Collins became the first black prima ballerina in the Metropolitan Opera ballet in 1951. Carmen DeLavallade was with the Met from 1956 through 1958. But the most exciting and dramatic changes took place in the world of modern dance.

Katherine Dunham remained a force, of course, and she was joined by Pearl Primus. They both created powerful protest dances, expressing in physical movement the outrage of black people. Like Dunham, Primus traveled to uncover the sources of African American dance and inspired white choreographers to explore them as well. These two women were among the black dancers who made African American dance a strong influence on American theatrical performance.

In literature, there were few publications by black women. Three poets, however, stand out in these years. Gwendolyn Brooks, Margaret Walker, and Margaret Danner were bridges on which later black women writers crossed to success.

Gwendolyn Brooks's first book of poetry, *A Street in Bronzeville,* was published in 1945, when she was twenty-eight years old. She took the literary world by the proverbial storm. The reviews were highly favorable, and the book brought Brooks to the attention of other black writers. She also received a Guggenheim fellowship in 1946 and 1947 and grants from the American Academy of Arts and Letters and the National Institute of Arts and Letters. Her next book, *Annie Allen,* won the Pulitzer Prize for poetry in 1950. She was the first black person, man or woman, to receive the award in any category.

The Bean Eaters, a collection of poetry that appeared in 1960, speaks in powerful, moving, and sometimes bitterly ironic language of the lives of black people. In the late 1960s, the change in black consciousness carried Brooks farther along her poetic path. Her 1968 book, *In the Mecca,* contains a long narrative poem interrupted by ballads and balladlike interpolations. Set in the old Mecca Building in Chicago, it details a mother's search for a lost child among the crowded, violent, hate-and-anger-filled inhabitants of the building. Hortense Spillers calls the Brooks who wrote this book "Gwendolyn the Terrible." In 1968, Brooks was named Poet Laureate of Illinois, succeeding Carl Sandburg.

Gwendolyn Brooks was, for many years, *the* black woman in literature. Calvin Hernton, in his article "The Sexual Mountain and Black Women Writers," writes, "Except for Gwendolyn Brooks, and perhaps Margaret Walker, the name of not one black woman writer and not one female protagonist was accorded a worthy status in the black literary world prior to the 1970s. Gwendolyn Brooks was *the* exception. Her age, her numerous prizes and awards and honors from the white literary world, the prestige she *already* had, plus her unquestionable genius, made her, *per force,* the acceptable exception."

Margaret Walker's first book of poetry, *For My People,* was published in 1942. Its publication has been called one of the most important events in black literary history. Not since Georgia Douglas Johnson had a black woman published a book of poetry, and Walker was the first black poet to be chosen for Yale University's Series of Younger Poets. *For My People* is a powerful work of poetic excellence. Written with strong rhythm and imagery, it presents a world of emotions that are both personal and mythic. Her next book, *Jubilee,* did not come out until 1966, twenty-four years later. A fictionalized reconstruction of the life of Walker's great-grandmother, the book describes a woman who maintains her own spirituality in the face of tremendous oppression.

The third poet, Margaret Danner, published her first book, *Impressions of African Art Forms,* in 1960. In 1961, she accepted the post of poet-in-residence at Wayne State University in Detroit and began the community arts work that would be so satisfying to her. She and the center helped to make Detroit a focus of the black arts movement in the 1960s. In 1963, *To Flower Poems* was published, and in 1966 Danner and Dudley Randall collaborated on a volume called *Poem Counterpoem. Iron Lace* appeared in 1968.

These three poets, along with the two novelists Ann Petry and Paule Marshall, presaged a renaissance in black women's literature that would begin, roughly, when *Jubilee* was published in 1966. To put this explosion of black women's literature in perspective, it is only necessary to point out that from 1942 to 1966—the twenty-four years that separated Margaret Walker's first book from her second—there were twelve significant novels or books of poetry published by black women. In the *five* years between 1967 and 1972 there were at least sixteen.

In 1967, Nikki Giovanni's first book of poetry and Virginia Hamilton's first children's book were published. The year 1968 saw the first books of poetry by Alice Walker and Audre Lorde, and Kristin Hunter's children's book *The Soul Brothers and Sister Lou* sold a million copies. In 1969, Maya Angelou published *I Know Why the Caged Bird Sings,* and first books appeared from poets Sonia Sanchez, June Jordan, and Lucille Clifton. Toni Morrison wrote *The Bluest Eye,* published in 1970. And the list goes on.

The books of these and other black women writers, published during and after this short five-year period, have entered the canon of classic American literature. And they have not only won prizes and critical acclaim. They have sold at the bookstores and hit the bestseller lists. The story of America was suddenly no longer white and it was no longer male. The importance of these artistic expressions goes far beyond their literary value. How they affected American society in general and the black community in particular is probably the most crucial aspect of the story of black women in the 1970s and 1980s.

1. The spirit that served black women well throughout the Great Depression is obvious in the faces of these women out for a stroll on Seventh Avenue in New York on a Sunday afternoon in 1938. *(Photograph by Austin Hansen, Austin Hansen Collection, Photographs and Prints Division, Schomburg Center for Research in Black Culture, The New York Public Library, Astor, Lenox, and Tilden Foundations)*

2. This sharecropper was one of thousands pushed off the land they had farmed for decades during the Depression. *(Farm Security Administration (FSA) photograph by Arthur Rothstein, 1939, Prints and Photographs Division, Library of Congress)*

The Great Depression

World War II

1

2

1. The first black WACS assigned to overseas duty were the seven hundred women sent to England to handle the Army Postal Directory Service for the entire European theater of operations. (*Visual Materials from the NAACP Records, Prints and Photographs Division, Library of Congress*)

2. The Office of War Information distributed this photograph of a young black woman sewing flags in the quartermaster corps depot in Philadelphia. Many other women replaced male workers in industry for the duration. (*Photograph by Howard Liberman, OMI photo, Prints and Photographs Division, Library of Congress*)

3. Through the untiring efforts of Mabel K. Staupers and the National Association of Colored Graduate Nurses (NACGN), black nurses won the right to serve their country in World War II. These nurses are in Australia for training in 1944. (*Photograph by Frank Prist, Corbis–Bettman*)

3

4. The International Sweethearts of Rhythm, a primarily black women's swing band, broke attendance records at Chicago's Regal Theatre, Los Angeles's Plantation Club, and Detroit's Paradise Theatre in the late 1930s and 1940s. When nonblack musicians joined the band after 1943, they sometimes had to pass for black in the South to avoid Jim Crow arrests of the entire band. *(Prints and Photographs Division, Moorland-Spingarn Research Center, Howard University)*

4

5

5. These black Catholics on the South Side of Chicago in 1942 were among the millions of women who created community within the church. *(FSA photo, Prints and Photographs Division, Library of Congress)*

Decades of Protest

2

1. This young Howard University student wears a symbolic noose and the name of a murdered black American at a 1934 demonstration protesting the omission of lynching from the agenda of a national conference on crime. *(Corbis-Bettman)*

I

2. Although not as turbulent as the late 1950s and early 1960s, the 1940s were marked by a growing unwillingness to accept the unjust status quo. *(Visual Materials from the NAACP Records, Prints and Photographs Division, Library of Congress)*

3. Black women protest against a store whose owner was accused of, admitted, and at the time of the photograph, was under indictment for assaulting preadolescent girls. The picketers succeeded in closing the store. *(Visual Materials from the NAACP Records, Prints and Photographs Division, Library of Congress)*

3

4. The spirit of the Civil Rights movement is caught in the face of this woman demonstrating in Monroe, North Carolina, on August 26, 1961. *(Photograph by Declan Haun, Estate of Declan Haun)*

5. When the voting rights act went into effect in 1965, thousands of black women took the opportunity to vote for the first time, like this woman with her son registering in Canton, Mississippi. *(Photograph by Matt Herron, © 1976, Matt Herron, Take Stock)*

6. This young woman illustrates the changes in the Civil Rights movement and black identity as she participates in the march led by Martin Luther King, Jr., through Cicero, Illinois, in 1968. *(Photograph by Declan Haun, Estate of Declan Haun)*

4

5

6

I

1. Veteran civil rights leader Ella Baker inspired the founding of the Student Nonviolent Coordinating Committee and guided it with her philosophy of grassroots organizing. This photograph was taken in 1980. *(Photograph by Salimah Ali, ©Salimah Ali/Photo Legends 1980, Courtesy of the photographer)*

2. In 1995, women protested a threatened California law that would abolish the state's affirmative action programs. A few months later, the law passed. *(Photograph by Gerry Gropp, SIPA Press)*

2

Today's Black Woman

See Freedom in Her Face

3

4

5

6

7

3. As she ran her victory lap at the 1992 Summer Olympics, white Olympic star Bruce Jenner called Jackie Joyner-Kersee "the greatest athlete in the world. Man or woman, the greatest athlete in the world." Here she celebrates at the 1996 Olympics. (*Photograph by Gary Hershorn, Reuters, Archive Photos*)

4. Gwendolyn Brooks, seen here at seventy, was the first African American to win a Pulitzer Prize and was for many years *the* black woman in American literature. (*Photograph by Bill Tague, Courtesy of The Contemporary Forum*)

5. A founder of the black theater movement in America, Ruby Dee remains a powerful and exciting actor in the 1990s. (*Archive Photos/fotos international*)

6. Marva Collins showed the practicality and resourcefulness that are traditional among black women when she founded her small school in Chicago. Her innovative methods at Westside Prep have proved so successful that she has been awarded education's highest honors. (*Courtesy Westside Preparatory School*)

7. When she refused to give up her seat on a Montgomery bus in 1955, Rosa Parks ignited one of the earliest and most important protests of the Civil Rights movement. (*Photographs and Prints Division, Schomburg Center for Research in Black Culture, The New York Public Library, Astor, Lenox, and Tilden Foundations*)

1. Sherrie Knight of Talking Drums expresses exuberance and power, the future and the past, in this 1986 portrait. (*Photograph by Lydia Ann Douglas/Peazey Head Productions, Courtesy of the photographer*)

2. A young mother at a Salvation Army center in Chicago faces an uncertain future with dignity. (*Photograph by Ron Seymour, Courtesy of the photographer*)

Two Faces of Hope

Our lives preserved. How it was; and how it be.

Passing it along in the relay. That is what I work

to do: to produce stories that save our lives.

TONI MORRISON,

"SALVATION IS THE ISSUE"

THE CAGED BIRD
SINGS

CHAPTER TWELVE

I T   W A S   O N L Y   a matter of time. Black women were bound to come into their own in American society. They had the strength, the courage, the creativity. The barriers in their way were high and wide, but they were not infinite. Title VII of the Civil Rights Act of 1964 and the subsequent development of affirmative action programs helped to knock down some part of the stone wall a racist and sexist society had created. So, too, did the political movements that developed out of the civil rights struggles of the 1950s and 1960s. But progress was not always direct, and it did not move in expected channels. A time came when black women had to reevaluate the survival skills that had served them over more than three centuries, take firm hold of their own political and social destinies, and create their own successes.

The successes came in business, politics, the professions, and the arts, and they had implications for every area of American life. They also brought to the fore some issues in the black community that had been on the back burner for two centuries and did it in a complex and often painful way. In the 1970s and 1980s, black women searched for their place in the politics of race and gender. Angela Davis became a countercultural icon, and Aretha Franklin sang out for respect for black women. Oprah Winfrey transformed their public image. The wall began to come tumbling down.

BLACK POWER

While black people in the South battled two of African America's traditional enemies—law and violence—black people in the North watched. Young black women and men in Detroit, Chicago, Los Angeles, and New York saw dogs let loose on peaceful demonstrators and firehoses turned on children. They witnessed, on their televisions, the deaths of black leaders and white sympathizers. Never having stood at a "colored only" water fountain, many of them could not accurately evaluate the progress that was made during the Civil Rights movement, but the hatred and violence directed toward black people was manifest. It had a tremendous impact on those silent watchers.

These same young black people were, in their own lives, constantly confronted by the third of the enemies—custom. This intangible foe was in many ways more difficult to fight and far more frustrating than the others. Discrimination in the North, precisely because of its lack of legal sanction, was insidious, eroding self-esteem and attacking black dignity. "Youth looked at their parents and the older ones," recalls Frances Albrier, "and they developed an impatience. They felt that they had taken too long and they had been too patient, and why wait? They felt the time is *right now* to strike. They should fight for their change right now." By the middle 1960s, many northern African Americans were filled with rage and looking for a way to affirm themselves. They found it first in the Nation of Islam and its most powerful spokesman, Malcolm X, and later in the Black Power movement he inspired.

Malcolm X, before and after his break with the Nation of Islam, spoke of black pride. He proposed, not patience and quiet dignity, but violence and anger. He spoke not of the need and right to enter the white world, but of the beauty of the African heritage. He spoke impolite truths about white hypocrisy, and young northern blacks loved him. When he was murdered, in 1965, African Americans lost an important voice. But Malcolm's message had been heard and was being echoed, increasingly, by diverse voices across the United States. SNCC, always more radical and less patient than other civil rights organizations, was one of the first to pursue openly the "Black Power" philosophy. In fact, Stokely Carmichael, elected as SNCC chairman in 1966, is given credit for coining the term. CORE adopted the philosophy soon after, while the SCLC and the NAACP both rejected it.

The same year that SNCC and CORE were becoming more openly militant, the Black Panther Party was founded, promoting black pride, black militancy, black self-protection, and black self-reliance. It started community programs that provided everything from free breakfasts to free movies, legal advice, and clothes. But the image of the new black movement, cultivated by the media, was of young black men with guns. As with Malcolm X, white America didn't know what to do. Neither, for that matter, did many veterans of the Civil Rights movement. Activist Pauli Murray recalls her first days teaching at Brandeis University in 1967: "From the moment I arrived on campus, I was thrown into fundamental philosophical and moral conflict with the advocates of a black ideology as alien to my nature and as difficult for me to accept as white ethnocentrism. This emerging racial rhetoric smacked of an ethnic 'party line' and made absolutely no sense to me; in turn, some of my most deeply held values about universal human dignity were considered obsolete by young black radicals."

Every year from 1965 through 1970, race riots took place in major cities across the United States. No longer did black activists focus on nonviolent demonstrations in the South. Black anger had exploded everywhere. Even Martin Luther King began speaking out about northern injustice and criticizing the U.S. government sharply about the Vietnam War. His murder in 1968 was proof, to many black Americans, of the end of the dream. That is certainly the way it felt to welfare rights activist Little Dovie Thurman.

> When Dr. King was assassinated, that changed things. . . . I got so angry. What was King saying? What was he talking about? Here he is so nonviolent, always praying, and they beat him up and they put him in jail and now they killed him. I was saying, "Give me a gun, give me a gun, give me something." . . .
>
> I just broke loose from all my white friends. I didn't want to see them. I didn't want to talk to them. All I wanted to do was get the one who killed Dr. King.

Many black women joined Black Power movements, worked very hard, and remained largely unrecognized and unheard of. The cult of black manhood worked against them, as it had in the nineteenth century. Under Jim Crow, as under slavery, black men had been deprived of the traditional American male privileges. White society met black male aggression, or even dignity, with violence and demanded, instead, submission. Black men could not protect their families and often could not support them. The Black Power movement reacted to this reality with an extreme emphasis on masculinity and an expectation that women would assume traditional female roles as a way of supporting black manhood. And yet, women in these organizations actually managed to make greater progress in some ways than they had in more traditional civil rights groups. Black Panther leaders took a radical approach to American society, calling into question everything that the mainstream culture held sacred. And that included the treatment of women.

Three women operated within the top echelons of the Black Panther Party (BPP). They were Kathleen Neal Cleaver, Elaine Brown, and Ericka Huggins. In addition, Angela Davis, who was very much involved in the BPP prison inmate program, gained national notoriety as the first woman to become a national countercultural hero. In 1969, these women and others started to make their voices heard in the Black Panther newspaper and at BPP meetings. Then, when Huey Newton went into exile in Cuba, Elaine Brown became chairperson of the party.

Still, the position of women in the struggle for black rights, whether in the older Civil Rights movement or in the younger Black Power movement, left a great deal to be desired. So, too, did the position of women in all the leftist political activity of the 1960s and 1970s, which was intense. White American society was changing radically. Not since the Civil War and Reconstruction had black issues so profoundly influenced American public and private life. Influenced by the nonviolent protests of the Civil Rights movement, the white youth of America began to protest the Vietnam War and by association the values that had made that war possible. In part because of the success of the Civil Rights movement and the addition of the word "sex" into Title VII of the Civil Rights Act of 1964 and in part because of the sexism in movement politics, both black and white women began to question the inequity of their position in society.

HALF THE SKY

The gender discrimination of the black rights movement had its parallel in the racial discrimination of the women's movement, yet there were fewer black women who were willing to participate in the feminist movement in spite of the fact that *both* movements discriminated. Those who did, however, affected the future development of black feminism, or "womanism," in ways that are still difficult to assess.

Florynce "Flo" Kennedy was a lawyer and activist who first made her mark when the organizers of a Montreal antiwar meeting refused to let BPP leader Bobby Seale speak. They insisted that his talk of racism went beyond their antiwar agenda. Kennedy stormed the platform and, in her words, "started yelling and hollering." It was the beginning of her new career as a spokesperson for black, gay, and women's rights. She often spoke on the same platform as white feminist Gloria Steinem, and comparisons were sometimes made to the alliance between Susan B. Anthony and Sojourner Truth.

Kennedy was a strong supporter of Shirley Chisholm's 1972 bid for the presidency, an event that has not yet received the attention it deserves in the history of feminist politics. The real story lies not in how the electorate reacted to her, but in the fact that she ran at all. It is difficult to imagine any white woman of that time—or this, for that matter—making the attempt. What made Chisholm able to make the decision to run was, quite simply, the fact of her blackness.

While black and white women share many concerns, they do not always have the same demons. Ask the average white woman what "liberation" means and she will probably talk about working outside the home because to her that means "meaningful" work. She may also mention developing confidence and self-esteem, especially when dealing with men. But those are simply not the goals of the average black woman. She almost certainly *must* work outside the home to support her family, as did her mother and her grandmother. And all too often their work has been anything but meaningful. She also has a confidence with regard to men that derives from her relative economic autonomy and from the history of male-female relationships in the black community.

Black women want and need "liberation," but they are more likely to define that word in terms of power and rights, drawing much more direct parallels to other Civil Rights movements. This was the case with Shirley Chisholm. Her political slogan, "Unbought and Unbossed," reflected her attitude. The first black woman to be elected to the U.S. House of Representatives, in 1968, she served in Congress for fourteen years. During that time, she spoke up unhesitatingly for progress in human rights. An early member of the National Organization for Women (NOW) and a founder of the National Women's Political Caucus (NWPC), she also became a spokesperson for the National Abortion Rights Action League (NARAL).

When Chisholm decided to campaign for the presidential nomination of the Democratic party in 1972, there were many people who saw her bid as quixotic or symbolic. It was neither. She ran because she felt qualified for the office and because she *had a right to run*. And in spite of the fact that the media refused to take her seriously and her campaign chest was only lightly filled, she made it all the way to the convention, where she received 150 votes on the first ballot.

Flo Kennedy organized the Feminist party to advance Chisholm's campaign, but others she had counted on did not come through. She was disappointed in both white feminists and black men for their lack of support. What she failed to understand is that both those groups had more concern for the approval of the white male establishment than she did and were therefore more likely to be cowed by its disapproval.

Another black woman who worked alongside white feminists was Pauli Murray, a civil rights activist who had confronted both racism and sexism in her struggle to get various advanced law degrees. She was one of the founders of the National Organization for Women, and her commitment to the feminist struggle never flagged. There were other black women, however, who found that NOW did not represent them. In 1973, they formed the National Black Feminist Organization (NBFO). Other women, who felt the NBFO was not sufficiently concerned with poor and lesbian women, formed the Combahee River Collective. And outside the organizations, individual black women fought one of the most significant battles of the modern feminist movement, that against sexual harassment.

Black women have been subjected to sexual harassment throughout their history in America. Until sexual discrimination in the workplace was made illegal, however, there was no way to attack the problem in the courts. In the eyes of the law, it did not exist. A woman who was raped by a co-worker could charge him with rape and try to take him to court. A woman who was subjected to forced touching and fondling by her boss could make an attempt to charge him with sexual assault, though that would almost certainly be a fruitless act. A woman who, day in and day out, was constrained to listen to sexual innuendo and humiliating remarks could do nothing at all.

Then, in 1976, things began to change. Within a very short time, a number of women brought suit charging that sexual harassment was sex discrimination. Black women brought several of these earliest cases, which were usually based on a woman's being fired after refusing sexual advances. Within a few years, the courts had ruled that sexual harassment on the job was in fact a violation of the Civil Rights Act of 1964.

Black women have been in the forefront of the struggle to define and treat sexual harassment as a crime. Catharine MacKinnon has outlined several probable reasons for this. First, the white apologist's myth of black women's sexuality may make them more vulnerable to harassment. Second, the scarcity of job opportunities for most black women might make men believe that they would be less likely to complain about harassment, again increasing the probability of its occurring. Third, that same abysmal job situation may actually make black women as a whole *more* likely to protest, because they must use any means to protect the little they have against a threat of loss, including a threat brought by a sexual harasser.

However, if sexual harassment is seen primarily in terms of power, the most important reasons for the place of black women at the forefront of this struggle probably relates to their position in the hierarchy of power. A man who resists giving up power to a woman, or who takes out his anger and frustration on a woman because she is less powerful, may be more likely to try to victimize a black woman than a white one. Black women, because of their historical position in American society, are likely to have fewer resources outside the courts for resisting this victimization. For better or worse, many black Americans have come to see the law as their most dependable ally in the struggle for justice and equality, and many black women in the past two decades have seen no more effective defender of their honor.

In the end, however, the strongest reaction among black women to the questions raised by feminism came not so much in the political or legal arenas as in the arts, especially with regard to the question of violence towards women. Once again, black women used cultural expression to enunciate their strongest concerns.

THE ARTS

The issue of women's rights was a difficult one for the black community. It carried with it all sorts of racial and historical baggage. Living within American society, black men felt the need to fulfill the traditional American masculine role, especially since they had been denied the right to do so for centuries. At the same time, black women were accustomed to a greater degree of independence than the traditional American feminine role allowed for. That was the first conflict.

The second conflict was, if anything, more serious. The lynching of black men was a powerful issue, symbolically and in reality, for the entire black community. It was so powerful, in fact, that, in the struggle for black rights, it thoroughly overshadowed the violence black women endured. They too were lynched, though in much smaller numbers. In addition, because they were women, they were raped, beaten, and killed in the thousands by men. And the men who committed this violence against them were both white and black.

To talk about their suffering at the hands of white men, because it so often involved sexuality, was difficult enough for black women. The time came, however, when they were ready to air that oppression as a part of the confrontation with white supremacy. The terrible reality of their oppression by men of their own color, on the other hand, was personal and political dynamite. No one wanted to light the fuse. Black women anticipated, correctly, that exposing their private pain and the sexism in their community would be seen as a betrayal of black men and would intensify the fragility of the black family. On a broader level, they believed that disclosure would erode the moral authority their men held in relations with dominant white power. The tendency to close ranks, to keep silence in order to protect the community, was strong, too strong for most black women to oppose. Dissemblance had proved a very positive survival skill in the past, and it was difficult for most women to recognize that it might have outlived its usefulness.

Artists were different. They saw it as their role to give voice to what they experienced in their daily lives. To a degree, their creations could be both illuminating and politically nonthreatening. Black women writers, after all, did not put their work forward as representing any political faction, and offended parties could put the book down or leave the theater. So, in order to move forward the quest for social justice and racial and sexual equality, some of black women's most dangerous issues were first aired in the "safe" space of the arts. The artistic vanguard moved forward to draw the fire that follows when and wherever the actions and voice of black women threaten male status and white power.

For the first time, black women writers talked about incest, domestic violence, and rape within the community. Several of the writers paid for their daring. Playwright Ntozake Shange was vilified for her revelation of the violence of black men in *For Colored Girls,* as was Alice Walker when, in 1985, her novel *The Color Purple* was made into a film by Steven Spielberg. All the fears other black women had about speaking out were confirmed, and these crucial issues did not move to the forefront of black political activity. But artists continued their exploration.

Visual artists, in the meantime, influenced by a feminist reexamination of the nature of art itself, discarded many of the restrictions of the fine arts. Following in the traditions of Africa and of their African American ancestors, black women shaped art into quilts and dolls and woven forms, often with expressly African inspirations. No one is a better example of this thrust than Faith Ringgold, who began to work as an artist in the early 1960s as the Civil Rights movement was reaching its peak. As black voices throughout the South were speaking up for their rights, Ringgold was realizing that the European artistic tradition couldn't accurately reflect her voice. She explored the flatter, more abstract African style of portraying figures, while the content of her paintings reflected the racial conflicts engulfing the country.

Then, as feminism grew in the 1970s, the issues brought forward by that movement were reflected in Ringgold's work. She began making masks, quilts, and soft sculptures. The "Family of Woman" masks and "Slave Rape" painting series expressed her growing consciousness about issues of importance to black women. Today, her quilts tell stories, using the traditional feminine craft to make statements about the lives of women, coming full circle from Harriet Powers and her symbolic quilts of the nineteenth century. The cloth, fabric, and fiber employed by Powers and Ringgold have also been used by such artists as Senga Nengudi, Viola Burley Leak, Januwa Moja, Joyce Scott, Xenobia Bailey, Julee Dickerson-Thompson, Elizabeth Catlett, and Betye and Alison Saar, among others.

Black women who were more clearly a part of popular culture also expressed the new consciousness. Again, while avoiding overtly political statements, they were able to assert their determination to claim their place in the world. Aretha Franklin was not the first and would not be the last, but she was the Queen. She was perfect for the new age of black women. Following in the tradition of Ma Rainey, Bessie Smith, and Billie Holiday, the former gospel singer gave notice in her music that she would be treated with "Respect." That song was written by Otis Redding, but Franklin chose it for her first Atlantic Records album and made it a feminist anthem. She then had six consecutive Top 10 singles on Atlantic. By 1970, she was one of the most important recording artists in the country, the "Queen of Soul."

The strong black women musicians who emerged from the late 1960s to the present were a powerful indication of the new spirit in the community. Tina Turner proved that she could out-James-Brown James Brown. Patti LaBelle with her group LaBelle, showed that she could out-glam-rock the glam rockers. And the Pointer Sisters brought new meaning to the words "girl group." Donna Summer practically defined disco. In the male-dominated genre of rap, Salt-N-Pepa and Queen Latifah led the pack of female rap stars who answered the men. In the white-dominated world of folk rock, Tracy Chapman showed that a black woman could express the black reality in that genre as well as in any other.

In addition, these women often became embodiments of the changes black women wanted and needed to make in their lives. Tina Turner's escape from an abusive marriage was public, as were her successful endeavors to rebuild her life. Queen Latifah used her success as a rap singer to build a production company and a career in television and films, both behind and in front of the camera. She also articulated a powerfully affirmative view of the dignity of black women.

One black woman, Oprah Winfrey, actually transformed popular culture. She first came to prominence in 1984 when she took over *A.M. Chicago,* a television talk show that was in serious trouble in the ratings. It aired opposite Phil Donahue, a Chicago favorite, and not one of its many hosts had been able to make a dent in his audience. It took a month for Winfrey to equal Donahue's ratings. This was in a city notorious for its racial problems—not the ideal milieu for a black woman. It took Winfrey three months to surpass Donahue in the ratings. A year and a half after she arrived in Chicago, the new *Oprah Winfrey Show* expanded to an hour. It became one of the most popular, and certainly one of the most influential, television programs in history. In 1989, Winfrey bought her own television and movie production studio. In 1996, she changed the direction of her show from confessional—some said voyeuristic—talk to a more positive, in-

spirational format. Her "Oprah's Book Club" recommended serious literature to her watchers and became a powerful influence on book sales.

Oprah Winfrey's success marked a difference in the image of black
women in American culture that was unmistakable and of great importance. She epitomized what might have been another stereotype but was
undeniably a positive one—the successful black woman.

THE SUCCESSFUL BLACK WOMAN

The new black woman was attractive without being blatantly sexual.
She was intelligent, well educated, well dressed and, of course, successful in
her chosen field. In virtually every case, success came to her through re-
lentless hard work—"working like a slave"—the acquisition of education
and social skills, and the cultivation of a strong sense of self-worth. As slavery had been for Booker T. Washington, poverty was to the Successful Black
Woman an enemy to be mastered and overcome. While the stories of these
women challenged patriarchy, they inherently reinforced the efficacy of
American values, beliefs, and customs, and despite their determination and
industry, they could not have succeeded without Title VII.

"Affirmative action" is one of the most emotionally loaded phrases to
enter the language in a very long time, but it began as a very simple concept. Title VII of the Civil Rights Act of 1964 was written to prevent discrimination in employment. Its provisions were concerned with "negative"
action, that is, *not* doing discriminatory things. Then, a series of presidential directives supplemented the negative with the positive. They stated that
businesses and other agencies should actively work to correct discriminatory situations.

Through the actions of Title VII's enforcement arm, the Equal Employment Opportunity Commission, affirmative action changed the face of
American employment. In the first decade of its existence, 850,000 black
workers found jobs in social services for local, state, and federal government
alone. During the 1970s and 1980s, the number of African Americans in the
work force had risen by *one-half.* Black women were important beneficiaries
of these changes, but their position remained far behind black and white
men and, in most cases, white women. In 1988, for example, the magazine
Black Enterprise published a list of the "25 Hottest Black Managers." There
were no women on the list. When challenged, the magazine explained its

process of selection, and it seems that, out of 125 final candidates, there was only one woman. She met the qualification of heading a major division or department "directly impacting the fiscal health and overall direction" of her company, but she did not have a compensation package "including salary, bonuses, stock options, and pension plans of at least $250,000." She had enough clout, in other words, but she didn't make enough money.

Two years later, *Fortune* magazine published a study of the 4,000 highest-paid officers and directors employed by the 799 largest public corporations. Of these, 19 were women. To be in sync with the number of women in the population, that number would have to be 2,000. To represent the number of women in the workforce, it would be 1,500. None of the women was black.

In 1993, *Black Enterprise* presented its readers with a list of "America's Most Powerful Black Executives." Four women made the group of forty. Four years later, Ann M. Fudge was named president of Maxwell House Coffee. Although corporate power remained largely a male preserve, progress was being made. In 1994, there were twelve black women on the boards of directors of Fortune 500 companies, and the numbers were growing. And in 1995, a list of the four hundred richest people in America included the name of a black woman—Oprah Winfrey.

By the mid-1990s, there were more than four hundred thousand black women in the United States who owned their own businesses, often because they had been rejected or discriminated against in the business mainstream. In deciding to take control of their own destinies, they also increased the black community's self-reliance. Madame C. J. Walker would be proud.

Black women also began to take their place in the political arena. In 1973, Lelia K. Smith Foley was elected mayor of Taft, Oklahoma. Eight years after the Voting Rights Act of 1965, the continental United States had its first black woman mayor. Three years later, Unita Blackwell became mayor of Mayersville, Mississippi, where she had once been denied the right to vote. And by 1988, there were so many black women mayors that they formed the Black Women Mayors' Caucus (BWMC) at the National Conference of Black Mayors. In 1973, there was a total of 337 black women in public office in the United States. By 1989, there were 1,814—more than five times as many. They included state and federal legislators, among whom were Barbara Jordan, Cardiss Collins, Yvonne Braithwaite, and Maxine Waters.

There continued to be important political appointments as well. In 1977, Patricia Roberts Harris became secretary of Housing and Urban Development (HUD), making her the first black woman in a U.S. cabinet; Eleanor Holmes Norton became the first woman chair of the Equal Employment Opportunity Commission (EEOC); and Mary Frances Berry was appointed assistant secretary for education in the Department of Health, Education, and Welfare (HEW). In 1979, Harris became secretary of HEW and Berry was appointed to the U.S. Commission on Civil Rights. In 1988, Juanita Kidd Stout became the first black woman to serve on a state supreme court when she was appointed in Pennsylvania. In 1993, Hazel O'Leary became the first woman and the first African American to serve as secretary of the Department of Energy, and Joycelyn Elders was confirmed as surgeon general of the United States. And, astonishingly, between *50 and 60 percent* of all Democratic party state officials were African American women.

The Successful Black Woman is not the end result of black women's history. She is just one more part of the story. And important as she was, she was not the most compelling part of it. In many ways, the fundamental values of the community of black women were even better expressed by women whose names were far less familiar, women like Osceola McCarty, Regina Benjamin, and Carol Porter.

Osceola McCarty was a laundress in Hattiesburg, Mississippi, for better than seventy years. Because she had to leave elementary school to take care of her aunt, who was ill, she didn't have much education. Some time in the late 1940s, after her price for doing a bundle of laundry—a week's wash for a family of four—went up to ten dollars, she began to put a little away every week, at compound interest. Fifty years later, she had a great deal of money to do with as she pleased. What pleased Osceola McCarty was educating black young people, so she donated $150,000 to the University of Southern Mississippi in Hattiesburg to establish a scholarship fund.

Regina Benjamin is the town doctor in Bayou La Batre, Alabama. The 2,500 African American, Laotian, Vietnamese, and white citizens of the town make their living from the sea and are, consequently, very poor. When Dr. Benjamin first came to the town, she moonlighted in emergency rooms in the city, some distance away, so that she could treat patients who couldn't pay her. Then, determined to find a better way, she went back to school to get an MBA. Through her studies, she discovered how to get federal funds to help support her practice and spread this newfound knowledge to other practitioners and clinics around the country. In 1995, she was asked to join the board of the American Medical Association and was chosen as one of *Time* magazine's "Fifty for the Future."

In 1985, when a child Carol Porter had helped deliver a few months earlier died of malnutrition, the registered nurse from Houston, Texas, knew she had to do something. Using only their own money, she and her husband began loading their car every Saturday afternoon with pots of hot chicken, rice, and gravy and drove around the city looking for hungry kids. As their awareness of the need grew, so did their activities. By 1995, the Porters and their organization, Kid-Care, were serving twenty thousand meals to children every month and were providing preschool, daycare, tuition, and summer camp. Their $500,000 budget was being met by donations, with no help from any government agencies.

In the mythology of the American mainstream, strength and self-reliance belong to the rugged individualist, the one who stands alone. But among black women, strength comes from being part of a community, and service to the community is the act not of a do-gooder, but of a leader. Difficult as it may be, service is not sacrifice, but part of the fullness of life. The busiest, most successful woman is expected to take in her brother's child, and her cousin's too, if necessary. The most powerful, respected woman is the one who finds a way to feed, clothe, and educate others. The history of black women teaches that every life belongs to the community, and to throw away a life is to cheat the community, just as to allow any member to lose her life is a negligence the community must not allow.

Black women's history teaches us that, unless we fulfill our duty to family and community, there is no satisfaction and no possibility for peace. However, it also reveals that each individual's sense of self-worth must come from inside. The child on a southern plantation who was whipped into calling a white baby "Marster," but who kept inside herself the knowledge that it was foolishness, had a powerful survival skill. No one can rob you of your dignity; you have to hand it over. Anger that controls you is dangerous. The value another person puts on you is of no importance, unless that person is one whom *you* value and respect.

Looking back on the stories that fill the chapters of this book, it is tempting to think that black women are somehow "naturally" stronger and wiser than the rest of the population, that they are born with more courage and resourcefulness and, perhaps, compassion. But that's no more true than any other stereotype. The values that have helped black women survive are entirely communicable. And at a time when the problems of our society seem insoluble and the obstacles to peace and freedom insurmountable, all Americans have a great deal to learn from the history of black women in America.

Sometimes I can see the future stretched out in

front of me—just as plain as day. The future

hanging over there at the edge of my days.

Just waiting for me.

LORRAINE HANSBERRY,

A RAISIN IN THE SUN

A NEW ERA FOR BLACK WOMEN

EPILOGUE

TODAY AND TOMORROW are not the usual subjects of a book of history. It is too soon to draw conclusions about today, and no one knows what tomorrow will be. But preserving voices is also historical work, and black women are speaking as they never have before. The world they are living in is complex in the extreme, and the paradoxes of their lives are both exciting and intensely painful.

In the decade of the 1990s, Carol Moseley Braun was elected to the United States Senate, the first black woman to be so chosen. Ann Fudge became CEO of Maxwell House. Toni Morrison won the Nobel Prize for Literature. Rita Dove became poet laureate of the United States. Ruth Simmons was chosen president of Smith College, making her the first African American president of an Ivy League school. Mae Jemison went into space. Oprah Winfrey was on her way to being America's first black billionaire.

According to the 1993 U.S. Census, college-educated black women had a higher median income than college-educated white women. And the median income for all black women was now only $1,500 less than for white women. Between 1984 and 1994, the number of black women executives more than doubled.

More black women served in the Clinton Administration than in any previous administration, including Dr. Mary Frances Berry as chairman of the U.S. Commission for Civil Rights, Dr. M. Joycelyn Elders as surgeon general, Hazel O'Leary as secretary of the U.S. Department of Energy, and Alexis Herman as secretary of labor.

There were black women pilots, construction workers, entrepreneurs, and neurosurgeons. Black women made films, produced television shows, and headed record companies. Each woman faced her own individual difficulties, and all black women faced some of the same.

> *They have a problem dealing with me because I am Black. And they don't have a problem telling me how they feel because I'm a woman.*
>
> EDWINA HOLDEN, CONSTRUCTION WORKER

For a black woman, making her mark in the world still meant working harder than anyone else and being better than anyone else. It required an extraordinary degree of determination and willingness to take risks, but fortunately that was a part of the legacy of black women.

> *I'm aggressive. I don't stand back. And I like to think that I do my job pretty well. I don't do a lot of moaning, groaning or complaining. I just do what I've got to do—that's how you're successful in the military.*
>
> STAFF SERGEANT ALLISON SMITH

I started talking to God and I said, "God, you've got to help me find
something else, something I'm going to really enjoy and not mind getting up
and doing every morning. . . . I just can't take it anymore.
                            BESSIE M. PENDER, TEACHER AND FORMER CUSTODIAN

Here and there, the contributions of black women to America and the world
were beginning to be recognized. High school literature anthologies had a
different look. History texts began to mention some black women besides
Sojourner Truth and Harriet Tubman. Toni Morrison's Pulitzer Prize was a
stunning example, but there were more modest ones as well.

What took you so long?
                            SHIRLEY OWENS ALSTON, SINGER, BEING INDUCTED INTO THE
                    ROCK AND ROLL HALL OF FAME IN 1996 AS A MEMBER OF THE SHIRELLES

But there was another side to the picture. The census revealed that almost
half of all black families were headed by single mothers, and 46.1 percent
of those families headed by black women were under the federal poverty
line. (The same is true of only 24.8 percent of single white mothers.) As if
they were not sufficiently burdened by the fact of their poverty, these
women were often blamed for the problems of black youth. If they remained at home, they were "welfare queens" who set a bad example for
their children. If they worked, they were said to have abandoned their responsibilities as mothers.

We may no longer issue scarlet letters, but from the way we talk we might
as well: W for welfare, S for Single, B for black, CC for children having
children, WT for white trash.   PATRICIA J. WILLIAMS

There are children out there who have their mother and their father at
home and then they still go out there and do something wrong. You can't
say it's because you're a single parent and you went to work.
                            SARAH BUTLER, COIN LAUNDRY MANAGER

Black women had the highest rate of HIV infection of any women in the
country. Their unemployment rate was almost twice that of the national average. And their lives were often marked with violence.

On a warm spring night nearly two years ago, I watched a little girl run
with her family to a crime scene, where two Black men had been found

shot to death. One of the men was her uncle. She was half-running, half-walking, her small round face distorted by terror and tears. "I don't have any more uncles left. I don't have any more uncles left," she screamed, stomping her feet near the yellow police tape. "That was the last one. That was the last one."   MARCIA D. DAVIS, WRITER

The effects of black male violence and of violence against black men and boys reached far into the lives of black women. Their husbands, lovers, sons, and nephews were all in peril. Almost half a million black men were in prison. Homicide was the leading cause of death of young black men. A popular poster referred to them as an endangered species; and the lives of black women remained, of necessity and by choice, entwined with theirs.

If Black men are an endangered species, then we are sitting ducks.
                              BONNIE HONORA-HAMMONS, COLLEGE STUDENT

Black women came to the forefront in the struggle to make young black men—and the entire black community—safer. In Chicago, the Reverend Willie Barrow was leading Operation PUSH to get guns out of the neighborhoods, as well as to fight domestic violence, take care of untended children, and work for higher education. Elaine Jones was heading the NAACP Legal Defense and Educational Fund. The Children's Defense Fund, which was watching out for the health and welfare of the children, was the work of Marian Wright Edelman.

We as mothers are a very powerful, powerful group of people. They came from us, they lived inside us, and because of that we have to make sure the violence, the senselessness that took them away, not be in vain.
                DEE SUMPTER, FOUNDER OF MOTHERS OF MURDERED OFFSPRING

Romona H. Edelin was leading the National Urban Coalition, and even the NAACP had turned for its leadership to a woman. Myrlie Evers Williams had been active in the movement since the 1960s, when her husband, civil rights worker Medgar Evers, was murdered. She came into her new position as chairwoman of the NAACP sounding much like such women as Ella Baker and Anna Arnold Hedgeman. "The NAACP must vigorously pursue and make welcome members from alienated segments of society," she said at her inauguration.

The violence in the black community was not directed only against men. Following the disclosures of black women artists of the 1970s and

1980s, others began to speak out about domestic violence and rape. It was difficult for black women to talk publicly about these issues because of their feelings of loyalty to the community. And they were often criticized when they did. Old patterns, based on putting racial considerations above any others, often left black women without the support they should have received. When a black woman accused Mike Tyson of rape, several prominent black ministers strongly supported the boxer before any evidence was heard and continued to do so.

> *Rape is not a serious offense within the Black community. It's a horrible thing to say, but it's not. . . . The assumption is that Mike Tyson was mistreated by the White jury.*
> BEVERLY GUY-SHEFTALL, FEMINIST WRITER AND EDITOR

Generally, relations between black women and black men were facing a moment of truth. As black women progressed economically, narrowing the gap between themselves and black men, there were two options for the male part of the black community. They could feel justifiably proud because African Americans were considerably ahead of white America in terms of gender equality, or they could feel threatened because they were no longer as far ahead of their women as white men were of theirs. There were signs of both emotions.

Black women, on the other hand, were becoming less apologetic for their autonomy and their achievements. Having long stood behind black men, they were now ready to stand beside them. Life and history had made most black women *de facto* feminists. Interestingly, they were able to show, probably better than white feminists were ever able to, that equality can exist side-by-side with love and joy.

> *I've gotten a lot of ribbing about a quote I made recently in a magazine article where I said that living with a man is like driving a car with the air conditioning on—it still works, it just puts more strain on the engine. Well, for all those people who took the time to comment on that statement, please don't misunderstand me. I do enjoy my cars with air conditioning.*
> VANESSA GILMORE, FEDERAL JUDGE

Finally, black women in the 1990s taught America new lessons in what it meant to be American. The motto of the nineteenth-century black clubwomen—"Lifting as We Climb"—took on new meaning.

White feminist Gloria Steinem told audiences in the 1970s that women's liberation was not just about getting a bigger piece of the pie. It meant changing the world to reflect values that have traditionally been associated with women—compassion, nurturing, understanding. Many white feminists have tried to do just that, but they have been hampered by the fact that, with sufficient luck and determination, some white women can actually grab that bigger piece of pie and run with it. It is possible for white women to assimilate into the mainstream almost without a ripple, if they really try.

Black women are in a different situation. Their history and their position in the black family and the black community make them different. When ambitious, educated black women step into the mainstream, they take along with them sons or nephews who are being shot at in the neighborhoods. They stir up the waters when they turn to beckon a fellow church member who is caring for her drug-addicted daughter's child. They bring a history so different from any that America has ever dealt with in her senators and CEOs that it is impossible to ignore.

> *I don't want the story of my life to be about racism, though it has played a major role. I want my story to be about attainment, love of family, art, helping others, courage, values, dreams coming true.*
>
> FAITH RINGGOLD, ARTIST

And America would do well not to ignore it. Black women are survivors. They have developed values over almost four centuries that actually seem to work. At a time when the problems of our society often seem insoluble and the obstacles to peace and freedom seem insurmountable, all Americans have a great deal to learn from black women.

> *Use me as an example. When the walls are closing in, when someone doesn't know where to turn, tell people I was there. I kept going. So can others.*
>
> GAIL DEVERS, OLYMPIC ATHLETE

The Collaboration

WE BEGAN WORKING together, in a distant sort of way, in 1990, on the encyclopedia *Black Women in America*. Darlene, with publisher Ralph Carlson, originated the project and then co-edited it with Rosalyn Terborg-Penn and Elsa Barkley Brown. Kathleen, unofficial house writer for Carlson Publishing, was a major contributor. The encyclopedia was two volumes of biographies and topical essays put together by a virtual army of people. Most of them were black women, but there were also a fair number who fell outside that category, including Kathleen and Ralph Carlson himself. We worked together more closely on Facts on File's *Encyclopedia of Black Women in America*, a twelve-volume set geared toward young people. Darlene was editor of the encyclopedia and Kathleen was editor-in-chief.

It was during the research for that second encyclopedia that it became painfully clear to Kathleen that there was a huge hole in the material available on black women. Paula Giddings's *When and Where I Enter* was a powerful analysis of the role black women have played in the legal and political arena in America, and other historians had written enormously valuable books about other specific areas and time periods. There was Deborah Gray White's research into black women in the plantation South and Wilma King's look at the lives of enslaved children, Brenda E. Stevenson's inquiries into enslaved families and Elizabeth Clark-Lewis's study of domestic workers in Washington, D.C. Elsa Barkley Brown has shed new light on the political activities of black women during Reconstruction, and Rosalyn Terborg-Penn has reshaped our thinking about the suffrage movement. Jacqueline Jones and Tera Hunter have looked into the role of black women as workers. Stephanie Shaw has investigated black professional women at the end of the nineteenth century, and Evelyn Higginbotham has made an insightful study of black women's religious activism.

But no one had written a history of African American women. No one had told that story, separate from any other. Kathleen, at the urging of Ralph Carlson, approached Darlene with the idea of a collaboration to fill this gap. She was emboldened to do so by Darlene's essay "Black Women's History, White Women's History: The Juncture of Race and Class," which ended with these words:

> I believe that at this particular historical conjuncture it is imperative
> that some black women historians treat white women as a means to
> enrich understanding of African American women. Likewise white

women scholars need to study black women and other women of color to a far greater extent than has been the case. In any event the time for cussing is past, now let's get busy.

In making her argument, Kathleen pointed out that anything she wrote on the history of black women was and always would be informed by Darlene's ideas and insights and attitudes. Might as well make the collaboration official. Darlene agreed.

We both knew that the story of black women was a remarkable one. We also knew that a great many people, over the centuries and even over the last few decades, have not wanted it told. Some have dismissed it, saying it wasn't worth telling. Others have actively suppressed it, afraid of what it would reveal. Still others have tried to deny that there was any story particular to black women. They have insisted that, after you've told the story of African Americans and the story of women, you're finished. Black women are included in those narratives.

But no matter what anyone may say to the contrary, black women are different. They're different from black men and they're different from white women. It is true that much of what they have experienced derives from racism and much from sexism. At the same time, however, much of what black women have experienced and still experience today—both bad and *good*—involves the blending of their separate identities in a way that chemists would call a combination, not just a mixture. Both race and gender are transformed when they are present together, and class is often present as a catalyst.

Unfortunately, both black men and white feminists have sometimes seen this separate identity as threatening. Many members of both groups want to put their arms metaphorically around the black woman's shoulder and say, "She's with us." Black women are sought after by black historians and white feminist historians, by black political leaders and by white feminist political leaders. But their inclusion is provisionary. They will be valued for their difference so long as they do not mention it too often. It just makes people feel nervous and guilty.

This is a sad situation for everyone, and it is an unnecessary one. Unity and loyalty do not depend on absolute homogeneity. Maybe it's the American obsession with race that makes it so difficult for us as a nation to get rid of our fear that difference implies, even guarantees, animosity and opposition. But denial of difference is not the road to harmony. It is the road only to a kind of false unity that is so fragile it will splinter at a touch.

In a landmark article, "What Has Happened Here," Elsa Barkley Brown compares history to a Louisiana conversational style called "gumbo ya ya," in which everyone talks at once and all the stories told interrelate and play off each other. "History," says Barkley Brown, "also is everybody talking at once, multiple rhythms being played simultaneously. The events and people we write about did not occur in isolation but in dialogue with a myriad of other people and events. In fact, at any given moment millions of people are all talking at once." Listening to all these voices at once can be confusing, but silencing any of them puts in danger the very meaning of the historical pursuit. We were sure it was time for the voice of black women to be heard loud and clear.

Fortunately for us, so was Broadway Books. They accepted our proposal in record time and with great enthusiasm. Roosevelt University and Northwestern University coincidentally cooperated by bringing Darlene to Chicago on visiting professorships for the 1996–97 school year. Michigan State University cooperated by funding some of the research.

And thus began the countless—sometimes it seemed *endless*—conversations, the stacks of books arriving in Kathleen's mail from Darlene's office, the discovery that we were on the same wavelength *most* of the time. When we started, we actually thought that Darlene's twenty-five years of research and thought about black women's history, combined with Kathleen's half a dozen years in that area, would make further investigation minimal. One and a half intense years later, we know how wrong we were. Books about black women are coming out at a phenomenal rate. Every month brought new information about black professional women in the nineteenth century or labor struggles in the early twentieth. We're both suffering from eyestrain but exhilarated by the tremendous efforts of historians of black women in the last five or six years.

Towards the end of the project, we gained another member of the team, Hilary MacAustin, who did our photographic research for us. She found us hundreds of excellent photographs of black women and discovered that there were literally thousands more available. Our problem was not to unearth fine images but to make very difficult choices among the ones we had. In the end, we put to one side pictures of some of the most famous women—from Mary McLeod Bethune to Whoopi Goldberg—in order to include women we believed our readers would be unfamiliar with and would want to see.

We have crossed many boundaries to collaborate on this book. Darlene is a historian. Kathleen is a writer. Darlene is a scholar, a member of the academy. The only part of a university Kathleen really likes is the library. Darlene grew up in Chicago and Kathleen in Oklahoma City. Darlene is black and Kathleen is white. But we have a great many things in common, including certain crucial values and ways of approaching our work. We are also the same age and grew up during the same period in history. More important, it was our experience of the history of our time—the Civil Rights movement, the war in Vietnam, the Black Power movement, Kent State, the 1968 Democratic convention, the early feminist movement—that made Darlene a historian and Kathleen a writer. Both of us turned to our chosen professions in an effort to understand and possibly even to have some impact on a world troubled by conflicts of race, class, and gender.

For Kathleen, having spent most of her adult life working on women's issues, the work on *A Shining Thread of Hope* came as a revelation. All the painful things were there, in distilled form—injustice, waste, violence, sexual abuse—but there was a new note. There was an autonomy of feeling and action that commanded attention. Beyond that, resistance and affirmation were made *explicit* in a way that illuminated the lives of all women. Kathleen came to believe that the history of black women was not just another small part of the history of women in America. It was not on the margins, but at the center of American women's history. This was her very personal place to work from to gain a new understanding of the whole thing.

For Darlene, the experience was less surprising but no less profound. She found that collective conversations and reflections, combined with collaborative writing and teaching, eased the production of new knowledge. She was fascinated by the project of writing for a broader audience outside the academy and delighted by the collaborative process. We share similar vocabularies and rhythmic patterns of expression. We laugh at the same kinds of things and even learned how to communicate without words. We criticized each other without rancor and offered support during difficult times. Through collaboration we were able to write a book much better than either of us could have done alone.

Another important collaboration, Darlene's teaching experience at Northwestern University, also aided in the development of this book during the spring semester of 1997. While serving as the Avalon Professor at Northwestern University, Darlene benefitted enormously from the intellectual exchange with the following professors: Adam Green, Michael Hanschard, Michael Harris, Nancy McLean, Aldon Morris, Fran Paden, Charles Payne, Sandra Richards, and Diane Slaughter-DeFoe. The course she taught was entitled, "Black Women's History and Autobiography." Darlene also appreciated working with Professors Lynn Wiener and Christopher Reed at Roosevelt University, where she served as the Harold Washington Distinguished Professor during the fall 1996 semester.

Too often in today's world, we talk as though empathy were the only form of understanding, as though if you can't know, really know, another person's thoughts and feelings, you cannot comprehend anything about her. This reinforces the belief that if we are different, we must be at odds. Writers and historians believe in a different kind of understanding, one that comes from work and study and commitment. Empathy enters into it, as does imagination, but *learning* is at its basis. We believe in this kind of understanding and hope that this book, while it nourishes the pride and self-knowledge of the black women of America, will also give people of all kinds a chance to experience the enrichment and understanding that the knowledge of black women's history has already brought to us.

Acknowledgments

IN A VERY real way, this collaboration involved all of the following people. Michael Nowak, Kathleen's life partner and best editor, read every chapter as it was completed and usually sent it back to us with the words, "It doesn't sing yet." Linda Werbish, Darlene's able administrative assistant, made sure the lines of communication remained open and that everyone had what she needed to keep working. Darlene's daughter, Robbie Davine Clark, offered constant support and encouragement. William C. Hine, Darlene's best friend and companion, made valuable comments on several chapters that helped us to "get it right."

Our manuscript readers were Jim Schulz, Tracy Moncure, Nicholas Patricca, Wilma King, Leslie Moch, Julia Robinson, Erin Moncure, Earnestine Jenkins, and Jacqueline McLeod. Several scholars offered encouragement and/or read chapters and made suggestions that strengthened the book and contributed to its completion. They are Professors James D. Anderson, Betty Brandon, David Barry Gaspar, Thavolia Glymph, Valinda Littlefield, Daniel Littlefield, Aldon Morris, Susan Reverby, and Deborah Gray White. Their insights were invaluable.

We were helped greatly by the staffs of the Northwestern University Library and the Chicago Public Library and by Kathy Clayton and Karen Creviston of the Amanda Park Branch of the Timberland Library System of Washington State. Howard University's Moorland-Spingarn Research Center provided many of the photographs. William Loren Katz of New York also shared photographic images in his possession.

Others who helped in many ways include Sara Thompson, Karen Konecky, Barbara Ann Clark, Alma Jean McIntosh, Les and Frances Thompson, Ralph Carlson, Diane Epstein, Maplean Thompson King, Fannie Venerable Thompson, Fannie Perry, Clotine Mason, Cherrie Foster, Joan Catapano, our enormously supportive agent Geri Thoma, and our editor Janet Goldstein.

Endnotes

Prologue

page 3 "He was rejected": George Sheldon, as cited in *The Black Presence in the Era of the American Revolution,* by Sidney Kaplan and Emma Nogrady Kaplan (Amherst: University of Massachusetts Press, 1989), p. 240.

3 "our Lucy argued the case": Kaplan, p. 241.

3 "In this remarkable woman": Kaplan, p. 240.

Chapter One: A New and Alien World

11 "[We] have no historical record": Claire Robertson, "Africa into the Americas?" *More Than Chattel,* edited by David Barry Gaspar and Darlene Clark Hine (Bloomington: Indiana University Press, 1996), p. 10.

17 During the 1600s and early 1700s: Lerone Bennett, Jr., *Before the Mayflower: A History of Black America*, 6th ed. (New York: Penguin Books, 1993).

19 Also, African women were accustomed: Joan Rezner Gundersen, "The Double Bonds of Race and Sex," in *We Specialize in the Wholly Impossible: A Reader in Black Women's History*, edited by Darlene Clark Hine, Wilma King, and Linda Reed (Brooklyn: Carlson Publishing, 1995), p. 195.

19 When Thomas Addison died: Herbert G. Gutman, *The Black Family in Slavery and Freedom, 1750–1925* (New York: Pantheon Books, 1976), p. 342.

20 "Of the 36 slaves": Brenda E. Stevenson, *Life in Black and White: Family and Community in the Slave South* (New York: Oxford University Press, 1996), p. 211.

20 In a study of 589 advertisements: Gutman, p. 344.

20 "she has a practice of goeing": Gutman, p. 345.

20 By the late 1600s in Philadelphia: Gary B. Nash, *Forging Freedom: The Formation of Philadelphia's Black Community, 1720–1840* (Cambridge: Harvard University Press, 1988), p. 9.

22 "Free blacks virtually invented": Stephen Birmingham, *Certain People: America's Black Elite* (Boston: Little, Brown, 1977), p. 115.

22 Nancy Lenox Remond, whose family: Dorothy Sterling, editor, *We Are Your Sisters: Black Women in the Nineteenth Century* (New York: Norton, 1984), p. 96.

23 "No MAN would ever have been treated": Frances Greene, *Memoirs of Eleanor Eldridge,* excerpted in *Black Women in 19th Century American Life,* edited by Bert Loewenberg and Ruth Bogin (University Park: Pennsylvania State University Press, 1976), p. 88.

25 "singular genius and accomplishments": Benjamin Rush, as cited in *The Black Presence in the Era of the American Revolution,* by Sidney Kaplan and Emma Nogrady Kaplan (Amherst: University of Massachusetts Press, 1989), p. 175.

27 "The root of jazz is Africa uprooted": Linda Dahl, *Stormy Weather* (New York: Limelight Editions, 1989), p. 3.

28 The average number of slaves: Brenda E. Stevenson, "Slavery," *Black Women in America: An Historical Encyclopedia,* edited by Darlene Clark

Hine, Elsa Barkley Brown, and Rosalyn Terborg-Penn (Brooklyn: Carlson Publishing, 1992), pp. 1051–1052.

28 "Mr. Mavericks Negro woman": John Josselyn, *An Account of Two Voyages to New England Made During the Years 1638, 1663,* as cited in Gutman, p. 352.

29 "Whereas some doubts have arisen": Don Nardo, *Braving the New World* (New York: Chelsea House, 1995), p. 32.

29 By 1670, free black men: Sharon Harley, editor, *The Timetables of African American History* (New York: Simon and Schuster, 1995).

Chapter Two: A Tale of Three Cities

38 "very lady-like in manners and conversation": Sallie Holley, in a personal letter, as cited in *We Are Your Sisters: Black Women in the Nineteenth Century,* edited by Dorothy Sterling (New York: Norton, 1984), p. 121.

38 "a stunning, signed painting": Tritobia Hayes Benjamin, Introduction to Visual Arts Volume, *Facts on File Encyclopedia of Black Women in America* (New York: Facts on File, 1997), p. 150.

39 "the first evidence which history affords": Charles Wesley, as cited in *The Black Presence in the Era of the American Revolution,* by Sidney Kaplan and Emma Nogrady Kaplan (Amherst: University of Massachusetts Press, 1989), p. 100.

40 "held many glorious prayer meetings": cited by Jualynne E. Dodson in "African Methodist Episcopal Preaching Women of the Nineteenth Century," *Black Women in America: An Historical Encyclopedia,* edited by Darlene Clark Hine, Elsa Barkley Brown, and Rosalyn Terborg-Penn (Brooklyn: Carlson Publishing, 1992), p. 12.

43 "Ostentatious in their dress": Walter J. Fraser, Jr., *Charleston! Charleston!* (Columbia: University of South Carolina Press, 1989), p. 5.

43 "it was by a woman that Rice": cited by Peter H. Wood in *Black Majority: Negroes in Colonial South Carolina from 1670 through the Stono Rebellion* (New York: W. W. Norton, 1974), pp. 35–36.

43 When New World slaves planted rice: Wood, p. 61.

44 An 1852 slave inventory: Stevenson, "Slavery," *Black Women in America,* p. 1052.

44 "Carolina looks more like a negro country": Wood, p. 132.

45 In 1740, the Assembly passed: Fraser, p. 67.

47 [Their masters] give them all: cited by Robert Olwell in "Loose, Idle and Disorderly," *More Than Chattel: Black Women and Slavery in the Americas,* edited by Barry Gaspar and Darlene Clark Hine (Bloomington: Indiana University Press, 1996), p. 10.

49 It was the custom in Charleston: Bernard E. Powers, Jr., *Black Charlestonians: A Social History, 1822–1885* (Fayetteville: University of Arkansas Press, 1994), pp. 19–21.

49 When nineteenth-century visitor John Lambert: All three citations in this paragraph are from Powers, p. 22.

50 "Like the patriarchs of old": cited by Elisabeth Muhlenfeld in *Mary Boykin Chestnut: A Biography* (Baton Rouge: Louisiana State University Press, 1981), p. 110.

51 In 1708, almost a decade after France: Gwendolyn Midlo Hall, *Africans in Colonial Louisiana* (Baton Rouge: Louisiana State University Press, 1992), p. 3. The population statistics in the next few paragraphs are from Hall.

52 a flock of our *negresses:* Journal du Bord, *l'Annibal,* voyage of 1729–1730, entry for July 13, 1729, cited by Hall, p. 91.

53 One man, Jacques Charpentier: Hall, pp. 150–152.

54 The Bambara were probably: Hall, p. 106.

55 "The Bambara came to Louisiana": Hall, p. 52.

58 there were 988 slaves freed: Kimberly S. Hanger, "Origins of New Orleans's Free Creoles of Color," *Creoles of Color of the Gulf South,* edited by James H. Dormon (Knoxville: University of Tennessee Press, 1996), p. 8.

59 To begin with, most of these "women": Mary Gehman, *The Free People of Color of New Orleans: An Introduction* (New Orleans: Margaret Media, Inc., 1994), pp. 36–38.

60 Hinard was born free: Virginia Gould, "Eufrosina Hinard," *Black Women in America,* pp. 562–563.

60 Marie Bernard Couvent was born: Florence Borders, "Marie Bernard Couvent," *Black Women in America,* pp. 287–288.

61 Marie Laveau was born free: Virginia Gould, "Marie Laveau," *Black Women in America,* p. 701.

61 "defiance, pride, posturing": Linda Dahl, *Stormy Weather* (New York: Limelight Editions, 1989), pp. 6–7.

63 In 1809 in South Carolina: William L. Katz, *Breaking the Chains: African American Slave Resistance* (New York: Atheneum, 1990), pp. 22, 33.

Chapter Three: Survival and Other Forms of Resistance

66 *I can sit on the gallery:* All of the italicized selections in this chapter are from the Federal Writers Project interviews, unless otherwise noted. The books from which they are quoted are Charles L. Perdue, Jr., Thomas E. Barden, and Robert K. Phillips, ed. *Weevils in the Wheat* (Charlottesville: University Press of Virginia, 1976); James Mellon, ed. *Bullwhip Days: The Slaves Remember* (New York: Weidenfeld & Nicolson, 1988); and Belinda Hurmence, ed. *Before Freedom: 48 Oral Histories of Former North and South Carolina Slaves* (New York: Mentor, 1990). Books and page numbers are noted below:

    Katie Rowe, *Bullwhip Days,* p. 24.

    Silvia Chisolm, *Before Freedom,* pp. 162–163.

    Rebecca Jane Grant, *Before Freedom,* pp. 138–142.

    Lulu Wilson, *Bullwhip Days,* pp. 322–327.

    Ellen Betts, *Bullwhip Days,* pp. 381–388.

    Sarah Debro, *Before Freedom,* pp. 46–51.

    Hannah Crasson, *Before Freedom,* pp. 15–18.

    Sylvia Cannon, *Before Freedom,* pp. 191–198.

    Adeline Jackson, *Before Freedom,* pp. 119–121.

    Mildred Graves, *Weevils in the Wheat,* pp. 120–121.

    Henry James Trentham, *Before Freedom,* pp. 5–7.

    Katie Blackwell Johnson, *Weevils in the Wheat,* pp. 160–163.

    Hilliard Yellerday, *Bullwhip Days,* p. 147.

    Caroline Hunter, *Weevils in the Wheat,* pp. 149–151.

    Martha Haskins, *Weevils in the Wheat,* pp. 135–136.

    Mary Reynolds, *Bullwhip Days,* pp. 15–23.

    Virginia Hayes Shepherd, *Weevils in the Wheat,* pp. 255–264.

    Annie Wallace, *Weevils in the Wheat,* pp. 292–296.

    Fannie Berry, *Weevils in the Wheat,* pp. 30–50.

Mattie Curtis, *Before Freedom,* pp. 30–33.

Savilla Burrell, *Before Freedom,* pp. 199–201.

Josephine Smith, *Before Freedom,* pp. 28–29.

69 Girls usually began working: Richard Steckel, "Women, Work, and Health Under Plantation Slavery in the South," *More Than Chattel: Black Women and Slavery in the Americas,* edited by Barry Gaspar and Darlene Clark Hine (Bloomington: Indiana University Press, 1996), p. 44.

72 "Slave women have often": Deborah Gray White, *Ar'n't I a Woman? Female Slaves in the Plantation South* (New York: Norton, 1985), p. 119.

75 "Seeing a wench ploughing": cited by Charles Sackett Syndor in *Slavery in Mississippi,* quoted in Stevenson, "Slavery," *Black Women in America: An Historical Encyclopedia,* edited by Darlene Clark Hine, Elsa Barkley Brown, and Rosalyn Terborg-Penn (Brooklyn: Carlson Publishing, 1992), p. 1053.

75 "human hoeing machines": Jacqueline Jones, *Labor of Love, Labor of Sorrow: Black Women, Work and the Family from Slavery to the Present* (New York: Basic, 1985), p. 18.

78 "To say that women did housework": Claire Robertson, "Africa into the Americas?" in Gaspar and Hine, p. 21.

79 This was the case with the woman: Stevenson, *Black Women in America,* p. 1061.

80 "probably passed down": Brenda E. Stevenson, *Life in Black and White: Family and Community in the Slave South* (New York: Oxford University Press, 1996), p. 229.

81 "I thinks about Massa": Mellon, pp. 129–132.

82 "preferring to stay with her mistress": White, p. 150.

82 There were, for example, twenty thousand slaves: Herbert G. Gutman, *The Black Family in Slavery and Freedom, 1750–1925* (New York: Pantheon Books, 1976), p. 14.

83 *I remember well my mother:* Moses Grandy, cited in Katz, p. 33.

85 There . . . is very little evidence: Stevenson, p. 160.

86 "Around the quiet campfires": Katz, *Breaking the Chains,* p. 29.

88 *"any* refrain to *any* hymn": Eileen Southern, *The Music of Black Americans: A History* (New York: W. W. Norton, 1971).

91 "When Douglass was resisting": James Oliver Horton, *Free People of Color: Inside the African American Community* (Washington: Smithsonian Institution Press, 1993), p. 94.

92 How many times I spit: Katz, p. 30.

96 "My wife was torn": William and Ellen Craft, "Running a Thousand Miles for Freedom," in Arna Bontemps, editor, *Great Slave Narratives* (New York: Beacon Press, 1969), p. 285.

98 "Women knew what was": Horton, p. 106.

98 Herbert Gutman offers evidence: Herman G. Gutman, *The Black Family in Slavery and Freedom, 1750–1925* (New York: Pantheon Books, 1976), pp. 80–81.

99 "slave abortions, much less infanticide": Eugene Genovese, *Roll, Jordan, Roll: The World the Slaves Made* (New York: Pantheon, 1974), p. 497.

Chapter Four: Resistance Becomes Rebellion

103 "During these years she consulted": James Oliver Horton, *Free People of Color: Inside the African American Community* (Washington: Smithsonian Institution Press, 1993), p. 63.

104 It "officially" began with white sympathizers: Benjamin Quarles, *Black Abolitionists* (New York: Oxford University Press, 1969).

106 "O, ye daughters of Africa, awake!": Maria W. Stewart, *Religion and the Pure Principles of Morality, the Sure Foundation on Which We Must Build,* excerpted in *Words of Fire: An Anthology of African American Feminist Thought,* edited by Beverly Guy-Sheftall (New York: The New Press, 1995), p. 27.

106 "By nineteenth-century norms": Carolyn Calloway-Thomas, "Mary Ann Shadd Cary," *Black Women in America: An Historical Encyclopedia,* edited by Darlene Clark Hine, Elsa Barkley Brown, and Rosalyn Terborg-Penn (Brooklyn: Carlson Publishing, 1992), p. 225.

107 "The symbol of Sojourner Truth": Nell Irvin Painter, "Sojourner Truth," *Black Women in America,* p. 1172.

107 And a'n't I a woman?: Frances W. Titus, editor, *Narrative of Sojourner Truth,* 1878.

108 "Faced with a hostile audience": Painter, *Black Women in America,* p. 1173.

109 "We have attended": Dorothy Sterling, editor, *We Are Your Sisters: Black Women in the Nineteenth Century* (New York: Norton, 1984), p. 176.

109 "When the Constitution of the A.": Lewis Tappan, in a letter to Theodore Dwight Weld, May 26, 1840, *Letters of Dwight Weld,* cited by Shirley Yee in *Black Women Abolitionists: A Study in Activism, 1828–1860* (Knoxville: University of Tennessee Press, 1992), p. 93.

110 I have delayed replying": Sterling, p. 123.

111 "This raised such a storm": Elizabeth Buffum Chace, *Two Quaker Sisters,* edited by Lovell, cited by Yee, p. 93.

112 "Everlasting shame and remorse": Sterling, p. 220.

112 "Do you ask the disposition": Maria W. Stewart, *Religion and the Pure Principles of Morality,* in *Maria W. Stewart, America's First Black Woman Political Writer: Essays and Speeches,* edited by Marilyn Richardson (Bloomington: Indiana University Press, 1987), p. 39.

112 "as moral and responsible beings": cited in *African American Women and the Vote, 1837–1965,* edited by Ann D. Gordon, Bettye Collier-Thomas, John H. Bracey, Arlene Voski Avakian, Joyce Avrech Berkman (Amherst: University of Massachusetts Press, 1997), p. 3.

114 One day between eleven: Sterling, p. 222.

114 An elderly New York woman: Suzanne Lebsock, *The Free Women of Petersburg: Status and Culture in a Southern Town, 1784–1860* (New York: W. W. Norton, 1984), pp. 96–98.

121 [T]his remarkable accomplishment: Henry Louis Gates, Jr. "Harriet E. Wilson," *Black Women in America: An Historical Encyclopedia,* edited by Darlene Clark Hine, Elsa Barkley Brown, and Rosalyn Terborg-Penn (Brooklyn: Carlson Publishing, 1992), p. 1271.

Chapter Five: The War for Freedom

126 Outside of the Fort were many skulls: Susie Baker King Taylor, *Reminiscences of My Life in Camp with the 33rd U.S. Colored Troops, Late 1st South Carolina Volunteers,* 1902. Published as *A Black Woman's Civil War Memoirs,* edited by Patricia W. Romero with an introduction by Willie Lee Rose (New York: Markus Wiener Publishing, 1988), p. 87.

128 "when William Tecumseh Sherman": Noralee Frankel, "The Southern Side of 'Glory'" *We Specialize in the Wholly Impossible: A Reader in Black Women's*

History, edited by Darlene Clark Hine, Wilma King, and Linda Reed (Brooklyn: Carlson Publishing, 1995), pp. 335–336.

129 "Of this fight I can only say": *Break Those Chains at Last*, p. 33.

130 "My great-great-grandmother": Romero, p. 27.

130 My brother and I being the two eldest: Romero, p. 29.

131 "About four o'clock, July 2": Romero, p. 90.

134 "Mrs. Carey [sic] raised recruits": Dorothy Sterling, editor, *We Are Your Sisters: Black Women in the Nineteenth Century* (New York: Norton, 1984), p. 258.

135 "I suggested the object of my mission": Sterling, pp. 249–250.

135 I went to Duff Green's Row: Sterling, p. 245.

136 "After this discussion": Sterling, p. 248.

138 "The women came up in a body": Leon F. Litwack, *Been in the Storm So Long: The Aftermath of Slavery* (New York: Knopf, 1979), p. 394.

139 "Thursday, Nov. 13 . . . Talked to the children": Gerda Lerner, editor, *Black Women in White America: A Documentary History* (New York: Pantheon, 1972), p. 96.

142 "[O]ne day I was in the field": Charles L. Perdue, Jr., Thomas E. Barden, and Robert K. Phillips, editors, *Weevils in the Wheat* (Charlottesville: University Press of Virginia, 1976), p. 121.

142 Eliza Sparks remembered Yankee: Catherine Clinton, "Civil War and Reconstruction," *Black Women in America: An Historical Encyclopedia,* edited by Darlene Clark Hine, Elsa Barkley Brown, and Rosalyn Terborg-Penn (Brooklyn: Carlson Publishing, 1992), p. 243.

142 "Most slaves stayed behind": Clinton, *Black Women in America*, p. 244.

143 "thousands of infuriated creatures": cited in Christopher E. Henry, *Forever Free* (New York: Chelsea House, 1995), p. 37.

144 On the afternoon of July [13th]: Sterling, pp. 232–233.

Chapter Six: Free Women in Search of Freedom

149 They even enacted laws, called Black Codes: Christopher E. Henry, *Forever Free* (New York: Chelsea House, 1995), pp. 70–71.

149 "If you see him plowing": cited by Lerone Bennett, Jr., *Before the Mayflower: A History of the Negro in America: 1619–1964* (Baltimore: Penguin Books, 1964), p. 217.

150 "They had a passion": Dorothy Sterling, editor, *We Are Your Sisters: Black Women in the Nineteenth Century* (New York: Norton, 1984), p. 311.

150 My mother came for us: excerpted in *Black Women in 19th Century American Life*, edited by Bert Loewenberg and Ruth Bogin (University Park: Pennsylvania State University Press, 1976), p. 101.

151 In Kent County, Maryland, alone: Sterling, p. 313n.

153 "Who'd tell them Cooks Mill people": Elizabeth Clark-Lewis, *Living In, Living Out: African American Domestics and the Great Migration* (New York: Kodansha International, 1996), pp. 12–14.

154 When elections were held: Henry, pp. 76–77.

155 "[In] periods of transition": cited by Lerone Bennett, Jr., in *Black Power U.S.A.: The Human Side of Reconstruction, 1867–1877* (Chicago: Johnson Publishing, 1967), p. 318.

156 We have lived to see: In our search for the voices of black women, we found this one and lost the source.

158 The Republican convention in Virginia: For this discussion of black women and the vote we relied on Elsa Barkley Brown's "To Catch the Vision of Freedom," *African American Women and the Vote, 1837–1965,* edited by Ann D. Gordon, Bettye Collier-Thomas, John H. Bracey, Arlene Voski Avakian, Joyce Avrech Berkman (Amherst: University of Massachusetts Press, 1997), pp. 66–99.

160 "I am in the most convenient": Sterling, p. 271.

161 "There has been much opposition": Sterling, p. 299.

161 "This is hard work": Sterling, p. 286.

161 Rev. Kimball rose and said: Sterling, p. 288.

162 Crumpler was born in Richmond: Allison Jolly, "Rebecca Lee Crumpler," *Black Women in America: An Historical Encyclopedia,* edited by Darlene Clark Hine, Elsa Barkley Brown, and Rosalyn Terborg-Penn (Brooklyn: Carlson Publishing, 1992), pp. 290–291.

162 Rebecca Cole was a student: Brenda Galloway-Wright, "Rebecca J. Cole," *Black Women in America,* pp. 261–262.

163 Susan Smith McKinney Steward: William Seraile, "Susan McKinney Steward," *Black Women in America,* pp. 1109–1112.

163 Between about 1855 and 1890: Darlene Clark Hine, "Physicians, Nineteenth-Century," *Black Women in America,* p. 923.

163 Charlotte E. Ray became an officer: Dorothy Thomas, "Charlotte E. Ray," *Black Women in America,* pp. 965–966.

164 In 1883, activist Mary Ann Shadd: Carolyn Calloway-Thomas, "Mary Ann Shadd Cary," *Black Women in America,* p. 225.

Chapter Seven: Blossoming in Hard Soil

167 "Every Democrat must feel": Lerone Bennett, Jr., *Before the Mayflower: A History of Black America,* 6th ed. (New York: Penguin Books, 1993), p. 247.

168 In one parish in Louisiana: Bennett, *Before the Mayflower,* pp. 247–248.

169 "The object of the [Fourteenth] Amendment": cited in Bennett, *Before the Mayflower,* p. 267.

169 "in view of the Constitution": cited in Bennett, *Before the Mayflower,* pp. 267–268.

170 The institutionalized rape of black women: Hazel V. Carby, *Reconstructing Womanhood: The Emergence of the Afro-American Woman Novelist* (New York: Oxford University Press), 1987, p. 37.

173 people of African descent: William Loren Katz, *Black Women of the Old West* (New York: Atheneum, 1995), p. 4.

174 "I expect to have a Negro population": Katz, p. 61.

174 Langston "boasted a literacy rate": Katz, p. 63.

175 Josephine Allensworth and her husband: Lonnie Bunch, "Josephine Leavell Allensworth," *Black Women in America: An Historical Encyclopedia,* edited by Darlene Clark Hine, Elsa Barkley Brown, and Rosalyn Terborg-Penn (Brooklyn: Carlson Publishing, 1992), pp. 22–23.

180 "to teach an ignorant and suspicious": Elizabeth Fortson Arroyo, "Josephine St. Pierre Ruffin," *Black Women in America,* p. 995.

181 The state association of black women's clubs: Lynda F. Dickson, "Denver, Colorado, Club Movement," *Black Women in America,* pp. 321–322.

181 There were dozens of Phyllis: Adrienne Lash Jones, "Phyllis (Phillis) Wheatley Clubs and Homes," *Black Women in America,* pp. 920–922.

182 In some cases, professional women: Stephanie J. Shaw, *What a Woman Ought to Be and to Do* (Chicago: University of Chicago Press, 1996), pp. 187–188.

182 I assured her [that] I had been careful: cited in Shaw, p. 22.

185 The men tried to force male officers: Evelyn Higginbotham, "Baptist Church," *Black Women in America,* p. 87.

186 "And so . . . our mothers and grandmothers": Alice Walker, *In Search of Our Mothers' Gardens: Womanist Prose* (San Diego: Harcourt Brace Jovanovich, 1983).

187 Last year I sent her word": cited in *Anonymous Was a Woman,* edited by Mirra Bank (New York: St. Martin's Griffin, 1995), p. 118.

188 Annie E. Anderson Walker was a case: Tritobia Hayes Benjamin, Introduction to Visual Arts Volume, *Facts on File Encyclopedia of Black Women in America* (New York: Facts on File, 1997), pp. 153–154.

189 "By the late 1870s the Hyers": Eileen Southern, *The Music of Black Americans,* 2nd ed. (New York: Norton, 1983), p. 240.

190 "Art is of great value": Dorothy Winbush Riley, editor, *My Soul Looks Back, Less I Forget: A Collection of Quotations by People of Color* (New York: Harper Perennial, 1991), p. 21.

191 "If in our homes there is implanted": Evelyn Higginbotham, "Baptist Church," *Black Women in America,* p. 205.

Chapter Eight: No Mountain Too High

193 "exercising all his tremendous influence": Alex Chadwick, *Illustrated History of Baseball* (New York: Portland House, 1988), p. 23.

195 "save our money and leave": cited in Wanda Hendricks, "Ida Bell Wells-Barnett," *Black Women in America: An Historical Encyclopedia,* edited by Darlene Clark Hine, Elsa Barkley Brown, and Rosalyn Terborg-Penn (Brooklyn: Carlson Publishing, 1992), pp. 1243–1244; originally from *Crusade for Justice: The Autobiography of Ida B. Wells* (Chicago: University of Chicago Press, 1970).

198 "Nine negroes massacred outright": cited in Lerone Bennett, Jr., *Before the Mayflower: A History of the Negro in America: 1619–1964* (Baltimore: Penguin Books, 1964), p. 277.

201 Maggie Walker, the woman who would: Gertrude Marlowe, "Maggie Walker," *Black Women in America,* pp. 1214–1219.

202 "And the great all absorbing interest": *Addresses—Maggie Walker,* 1909, cited in Margaret Duckworth, "Maggie L. Walker," *Notable Black American Women,* edited by Jessie Carney Smith (Detroit: Gale Research, 1992), pp. 1189–1190.

203 "I am a woman who came from:" cited in A'Lelia Perry Bundles, "Madame C. J. (Sarah Breedlove) Walker," *Black Women in America,* p. 1209; originally from "Report of the 13th Annual Convention," National Negro Business League, Chicago, 1912.

204 "crisscrossed the country": *Black Women in America,* p. 1212.

204 "The girls and women": *Black Women in America,* p. 1212; originally from "Report of the 14th Annual Convention," National Negro Business League, Philadelphia, 1914.

206 "When I say I built a school": Stephanie J. Shaw, *What a Woman Ought to Be and to Do* (Chicago: University of Chicago Press, 1996), p. 176.

207 "They deliberately concealed": Valinda Littlefield, Introduction to Education volume, *Facts on File Encyclopedia of Black Women in America* (New York: Facts on File, 1997), p. 18.

208 One Jeanes teacher in Georgia": Littlefield, p. 18.

210 "When she sang in tent shows": Langston Hughes and Milton Meltzer, *Black Magic: A Pictorial History of the African American in the Performing Arts* (New York: Da Capo Press, 1990), p. 80.

Chapter Nine: They Carried Their Freedom Bags

215 "Nobody was sent out": Elizabeth Clark-Lewis, *Living In, Living Out: African American Domestics and the Great Migration* (New York: Kodansha International, 1996), p. 48.

215 "You couldn't be out working": Clark-Lewis, p. 48.

215 "My mama told you first": Clark-Lewis, p. 49.

215 "When he hit me": Sara Brooks, *You May Plow Here: The Narrative of Sara Brooks,* edited by Thordis Simonsen (New York: Touchstone Edition, Simon and Schuster, 1987), p. 219.

216 "The 'me' notion wasn't even thought about": Clark-Lewis, p. 54.

216 "Mama brought me into the parlor": Clark-Lewis, pp. 64–65.

216 "At home you better not try": Clark-Lewis, p. 159.

217 "As indisputably important": Lawrence W. Levine, *Black Culture and Black Consciousness: Afro-American Folk Thought from Slavery to Freedom* (New York: Oxford University Press, 1977), p. 274.

218 I was born . . . out of wedlock": The Maddy Bruce Story, May 18, 1984, transcript, Deborah Starks Collection, box 1, folder 4, oral histories, Black Women in the Middle West Project (BWMW), Fort Wayne, Indiana (Indiana Historical Society, Indianapolis).

218 "The first one to come home": Brooks, pp. 211–214, pp. 216–217.

219 "My mother would come": Burch, BWMW Project.

219 "I noticed she had some": Brooks, p. 195.

220 I have learned to stay: Sarah Darthulin Tyree to Jennie P. Fowlkes, August 23, 1921, Frances Patterson Papers, box 1, folder 2, BWMW Project (Indiana Historical Society, Indianapolis).

220 "See, after Vivian was born": Brooks, p. 206.

221 "the statistics indicated that": William M. Tuttle, Jr., *Race Riot: Chicago in the Red Summer of 1919* (New York: Atheneum, 1982), p. 164.

223 "It was not easy": cited by Vanessa Gamble, "Physicians, Twentieth Century," *Black Women in America,* p. 926; originally from Susan Lynn Smith, "Sick and Tired of Being Sick and Tired: Black Women and the National Negro Health Movement, 1915–1950," dissertation, 1991.

224 "in the hands of trained": Alice Bacon, "The Hampton Training School for Nurses," *Fourth Annual Report of the Training School for Nurses and Dixie Hospital* (Hampton, Virginia, 1895–96), p. 16.

224 "Negro nurses in every part": Ethel Johns, "A Study of the Present Status of the Negro Woman in Nursing, 1925, p. 40. Copy found in Rockefeller Foundation papers, Box 122.

225 "We are enrolling colored nurses": Adah B. Thoms, *Pathfinders: A History of the Progress of Colored Graduate Nurses* (New York: McKay Co., 1929), p. 156.

227 All of these professional women: Stephanie J. Shaw, *What a Woman Ought to Be and to Do* (Chicago: University of Chicago Press, 1996), p. 132.

228 *"Mon enfant, vous etes":* Tritobia Hayes Benjamin, Introduction to Visual

Art Volume, *Facts on File Encyclopedia of Black Women in America* (New York: Facts on File, 1997), p. 158.

229 "unlike any other of its genre": Judith Kerr, "Meta Vaux Warrick Fuller," *Black Women in America,* p. 472.

229 "the founder of the first movement": cited by Benjamin, p. 159.

232 "The critics could never describe": Richard Newman, "Florence Mills," *Notable Black American Women,* edited by Jessie Carney Smith (Detroit: Gale Research, 1992), pp. 755–756.

233 "America's foremost feminine player": George Jean Nathan, *New York Telegram,* April 16, 1927.

234 "The novel insists": Alice Deck, *"Zora Neale Hurston,"* Notable Black American Women, p. 545.

236 "During these later years": Jocelyn Hazelwood Donlon, "Georgia Douglas Johnson," *Black Women in America: An Historical Encyclopedia,* edited by Darlene Clark Hine, Elsa Barkley Brown, and Rosalyn Terborg-Penn (Brooklyn: Carlson Publishing, 1992), p. 642.

237 "The tradition of art in West Africa": Tritobia Hayes Benjamin, Introduction to Visual Arts Volume, *Facts on File Encyclopedia of Black Women in America* (New York: Facts on File, 1997), p. 155.

Chapter Ten: The Great Depression

241 Near by was a field: Gerda Lerner, editor, *Black Women in White America: A Documentary History* (New York: Pantheon, 1972), p. 139.

242 By January of 1931, *more than a quarter*: Statistics in the following paragraphs are from Lois Rita Helmbold, "The Depression," *Black Women in America: An Historical Encyclopedia,* edited by Darlene Clark Hine, Elsa Barkley Brown, and Rosalyn Terborg-Penn (Brooklyn: Carlson Publishing, 1992), p. 323.

243 "In 1929 . . . me and my husband": Studs Terkel, *Hard Times: An Oral History of the Great Depression* (New York: Pantheon Books, 1986), pp. 261–262.

244 "Back in the Thirties": Terkel, *Hard Times,* p. 459.

244 "The Negro Woman who worked": Terkel, *Hard Times,* p. 48.

244 "I remember one night": Terkel, *Hard Times,* p. 53.

245 "focused the attention of women": Christine M. Fuqua, President, National Housewives' League of America, "Declaration of May 18, 1948 as Fannie B. Peck Day," Housewives League of Detroit Collection, box 4, Burton Historical Collection, Detroit Public Library.

245 "that she has been traveling": Fannie B. Peck, "History and Purpose of Housewives' League," May 2, 1934, Housewives League of Detroit Collection, box 1.

246 "it is our duty as women": Constitution of Housewives' League of Detroit and Declaration of Principles," Housewives League of Detroit Collection, box 1.

246 "in Chicago, Baltimore, Washington": Jacqueline Jones, *Labor of Love, Labor of Sorrow: Black Women, Work and the Family from Slavery to the Present* (New York: Basic, 1985), p. 215.

246 I was in the Pullman service: Ruth Edmonds Hill, *The Black Women Oral History Project from The Arthur and Elizabeth Schlesinger Library on the History of Women in America,* Volume 1 (Westport: Meckler, 1991), p. 319.

247 *"had an economic impact":* Jones, p. 215.

248 "Manager 'Boss Funsten' failed": Ruth Feldstein, "Labor Movement," *Black Women in America,* p. 686.
249 "Walter White told us": Hill, Volume 1, p. 394.
250 "The colored families in that community": Hill, Volume 8, p. 18.
251 "Although NACW had always": Elaine Smith, "Mary McLeod Bethune," *Black Women in America,* p. 119.
258 "With the arrival of Katherine Dunham": John Martin, *New York Times,* cited in Terry Harnan, *African Rhythm-American Dance* (New York: Knopf, 1974), p. 106.
261 "What I heard today": Kosti Vehanen, *Marian Anderson: A Portrait* (New York: Whittlesey House, 1941), p. 130.
262 "refused to be relegated": Barbara Ransby, "Ella Baker," *Black Women in America,* p. 72.
262 "In her organizational life": Dianne M. Pinderhughes, "Civil Rights Movement," *Black Women in America,* pp. 240–241.
263 "If nurses are needed so desperately": Mabel K. Staupers, reported in *The People's Voice,* January 13, 1945.

Chapter Eleven: Towards Freedom

269 "The consciousness of the social character": Angela Davis, "Black Women and Music: A Historical Legacy of Struggle," *African Intellectual Heritage: A Book of Sources,* edited by Molefe Asante and Abu S. Barry (Philadelphia: Temple University Press, 1996), p. 773.
269 "About three days into Mississippi": Studs Terkel, *Race: What Blacks and Whites Think and Feel about the American Obsession* (New York: New Press, 1992), p. 20.
270 "Have you ever sent a loved son": cited by Juan Williams, *Eyes on the Prize: America's Civil Rights Years, 1954–1965* (Boston: Blackside), pp. 43–44.
270 "I bled for Emmett Till's mother": Juan Williams, editor, *Eyes on the Prize: America's Civil Rights Years, 1954–1965* (New York: Viking, 1987), p. 47.
271 "My burning thing, the thing that has": Terkel, *Race,* p. 22.
274 "a life history of being rebellious": cited by Stewart Burns in "Montgomery Bus Boycott," *Black Women in America: An Historical Encyclopedia,* edited by Darlene Clark Hine, Elsa Barkley Brown, and Rosalyn Terborg-Penn (Brooklyn: Carlson Publishing, 1992), p. 808; interviewed by Sidney Rogers, 1956.
275 "Another Negro woman:" Jo Ann Gibson Robinson, *The Montgomery Bus Boycott and the Women Who Started It: The Memoir of Jo Ann Gibson Robinson,* edited by David J. Garrow (Knoxville: University of Tennessee Press, 1987), cited by Burns, p. 808.
275 "We really were the ones:" quoted by Steven M. Millner, "The Montgomery Bus Boycott": A Case Study in the Emergence and Career of a Social Movement," *The Walking City: The Montgomery Bus Boycott, 1955–1956,* edited by David J. Garrow, cited by Burns, pp. 808–809.
277 Among the better known cases: Constance Baker Motley, "My Personal Debt to Thurgood Marshall," *Yale Law Journal,* November 1991.
278 "the opposition to my appointment was so great": Motley, *Yale Law Journal.*
280 "the Harlem YWCA featured women": Anna Arnold Hedgeman, *The Trumpet Sounds: A Memoir of Negro Leadership* (New York: Holt, Rinehart, and Winston, 1964), p. 41.
281 "the consummation of the quality": Hedgeman, 180.

281 On the day of the March: Hedgeman, 180.

289 "Except for Harry Belafonte": "Ill-fated Star Defies Scrutiny Even in Death," *Ebony,* March 1966.

293 "Except for Gwendolyn Brooks": Calvin Hernton, "The Sexual Mountain and Black Women Writers," *Wild Women in the Whirlwind: Afra-American Culture and the Contemporary Literary Renaissance,* edited by Joanne M. Braxton and Andrée Nicola McLaughlin (New Brunswick: Rutgers University Press, 1990), p. 196.

Chapter Twelve: The Caged Bird Sings

296 "Youth looked at their parents": Ruth Edmonds Hill, *The Black Women Oral History Project,* Volume 1 (Westport: Meckler, 1991), p. 500.

298 When Dr. King was assassinated: Studs Terkel, *Race: What Blacks and Whites Think and Feel about the American Obsession* (New York: New Press, 1992), p. 61.

300 This was the case with Shirley Chisholm: Lisa Woznica, "Shirley Chisholm," *Black Women in America: An Historical Encyclopedia,* edited by Darlene Clark Hine, Elsa Barkley Brown, and Rosalyn Terborg-Penn (Brooklyn: Carlson Publishing, 1992), pp. 236–238.

301 Catharine MacKinnon has outlined: Catharine A. MacKinnon, *Sexual Harassment of Working Women: A Case of Sex Discrimination* (New Haven: Yale University Press, 1979).

303 No one is a better example: Emily Cousins, "Faith Ringgold," *Black Women in America,* pp. 982–984.

307 between *50 and 60 percent:* Joint Center for Political Studies, cited in "Candidates of Color," *about . . . time,* October 1992.

307 Osceola McCarty was a laundress: Rick Bragg, *New York Times,* November 12, 1996.

307 Regina Benjamin is the town doctor: Andra Medea, "Regina Benjamin," *Facts on File Encylopedia of Black Women in America,* (New York: Facts on File, 1997), pp. 38–40.

307 In 1985, when a child Carol Porter: Gary Houston, "Carol Doe Porter," *Facts on File Encyclopedia of Black Women in America,* pp. 150–151.

Epilogue: A New Era for Black Women

310 Most of the quotations in the epilogue are from the March 1997 issues of *Ebony* and *Emerge.* Those that are not are noted.

311 *What took you so long?:* India Cooper, "The Shirelles," *Facts on File Encyclopedia of Black Women in America,* p. 229.

311 *We may no longer issue scarlet letters:* Patricia J. Williams, "Notes from a Small World," *New Yorker,* April 29 and May 6, 1996.

314 *I don't want the story of my life:* Faith Ringgold, *We Flew Over the Bridge: The Memoirs of Faith Ringgold* (Boston: Little, Brown, 1995), p. 270.

Bibliography

T H E   H I S T O R I A N S   W H O S E   work has made this book possible number in the hundreds. Most of their research has been done in the last two decades, although the foundation was being laid at the turn of the last century. To credit all of these workers in the field would be impossible, but an attempt must be made to indicate the sources to which we turned most often.

Throughout the book there is material from two landmark collections of the words and writings of black women: Gerda Lerner's *Black Women in White America* and Dorothy Sterling's *We Are Your Sisters*. The general histories of African American people that we found most useful for reference were John Hope Franklin's *From Slavery to Freedom* and Lerone Bennett, Jr.'s *Before the Mayflower*. The work of the many dedicated historians who contributed to *Black Women in America* (BWIA), edited by Darlene Clark Hine, Elsa Barkley Brown, and Rosalyn Terborg-Penn, was extremely useful. Particular debts to these historians are noted in the paragraphs that follow. Two collections of significant articles in the field were also important sources. These are *We Specialize in the Wholly Impossible,* edited by Darlene Clark Hine, Wilma King, and Linda Reed, and *More Than Chattel,* edited by David Barry Gaspar and Darlene Clark Hine.

Bibliographical information about all of the sources mentioned follows this essay.

The two major sources for information concerning Lucy Terry Prince were the entry written by Jan Furman in *Black Women in America* and Sidney and Emma Nogrady Kaplan's *The Black Presence in the Era of the American Revolution.*

The principle sources for "Chapter One: A New and Alien World" were Claire Robertson's article "Africa into the Americas?" in *More Than Chattel;* Joan Rezner Gundersen's "The Double Bonds of Race and Sex: Black and White Women in a Colonial Virginia Parish" from *We Specialize in the Wholly Impossible;* and Paula Gidding's *When and Where I Enter.*

A great deal of the information in the section on Philadelphia in "Chapter Two: A Tale of Three Cities" had as its source Gary B. Nash's *Forging Freedom.* This was augmented by Kaplan's *The Black Presence in the American Revolution,* Debra L. Newman's article "Black Women in the Era of the American Revolution in Pennsylvania," and Loren Schweninger's "Property Owning Free African American Women in the South," both from *We Specialize in the Wholly Impossible.* For the information in the section on Charleston, we relied on Walter J. Fraser, Jr.'s *Charleston! Charleston!,* Bernard Powers's *Black*

Charlestonians, and Robert Olwell's article "Loose, Idle and Disorderly" in *More Than Chattel.* Gwendolyn Midlo Hall's *Africans in Colonial Louisiana* was the source of much of the information on New Orleans, as were the articles in *Creoles of Color of the Gulf South,* edited by James H. Dormon.

With the exception of a few that are noted in the text, the quotations from formerly enslaved people in "Chapter Three: Survival and Other Forms of Resistance" are from the Federal Writers Project narratives. The primary sources for information about antebellum slavery were Deborah Gray White's *Ar'n't I a Woman?;* Brenda E. Stevenson's "Slavery" entry in *Black Women in America,* her article "Gender Conventions, Ideals, and Identity among Antebellum Virginia Slave Women" in *More Than Chattel,* and her book *Life in Black and White;* Herbert Gutman's *The Black Family in Slavery and Freedom;* and Wilma King's *Stolen Childhood.* An important source for the section "The Making of a Culture" was Eileen Southern's *The Music of Black Americans.*

Much of the information about abolition and the free community in "Chapter Four: Resistance Becomes Rebellion" was found in James O. Horton's *Free People of Color,* Shirley Yee's *Black Women Abolitionists,* Suzanne Lebsock's *The Free Women of Petersburg,* and three entries from *Black Women in America:* Brenda Stevenson's "Abolition Movement," James O. Horton's "Free Women in the Antebellum North," and "Free Women in the Antebellum South," by Adele Logan Alexander and Virginia Gould. Additional information was found in Whittington B. Johnson's "Free African American Women in Savannah, 1800–1860" and Loren Schweninger's "Property Owning Free African American Women in the South, 1800–1870," both from *We Specialize in the Wholly Impossible.*

Not a great deal has been written on the role of black women in the Civil War, but Noralee Frankel's "The Southern Side of 'Glory': Mississippi African American Women During the Civil War" from *We Specialize in the Wholly Impossible* was very useful in the research for "Chapter Five: The War for Freedom," as was Catherine Clinton's entry "Civil War and Reconstruction" in *Black Women in America.*

The discussion on black women and the vote in "Chapter Six: Free Women in Search of Freedom" was based on Elsa Barkley Brown's "To Catch the Vision of Freedom," from *African American Women and the Vote, 1837–1965.*

Sources for "Chapter Seven: Blossoming in Hard Soil" included William Loren Katz's *Black Women of the Old West,* which, although it was written for a young adult audience, contains valuable and carefully presented material about the subject; and Stephanie Shaw's *What a Woman Ought to Be and to Do.*

In "Chapter Eight: No Mountain Too High" the material on teachers relied on Valinda Littlefield's introductory essay in the *Education* volume of *Facts on File Encyclopedia of Black Women in America.* Information about the two Walkers came largely from the entries "Madame C. J. (Sarah Breedlove) Walker," by A'Lelia Perry Bundles and "Maggie Lena Walker," by Gertrude W. Marlowe, both in *Black Women in America.*

Portions of "Chapter Nine: They Carried Their Freedom Bags" were adapted from the article "Black Migration to the Urban Midwest: The Gender Dimension," originally published in *The Great Migration in Historical Perspectives* and later modified for *Hine Sight.* Much important material came from Elizabeth Clark-Lewis's *Living In, Living Out* and, again, from Shaw's *What a Woman Ought to Be and to Do.*

Rita Lois Helmbold's "The Depression," in *Black Women in America* was very helpful in the writing of "Chapter Ten: The Great Depression." The material on the Detroit Housewives' League was adapted from "The Housewives' League of Detroit: Black Women and Economic Nationalism," originally published in *Visible Women: New Essays on American Activism* and later modified for *Hine Sight.*

Charles Payne's *I've Got the Light of Freedom* provided valuable insight for "Chapter Eleven: Towards Freedom," as did Barbara Ransby's "Ella Baker" and Stewart Burn's "Montgomery Bus Boycott" in *Black Women in America.*

Bibliography of Materials Used in Research

Aptheker, Bettina. *Woman's Legacy: Essays on Race, Sex, and Class in American History.* Amherst: University of Massachusetts Press, 1982.

Bennett, Lerone, Jr. *Before the Mayflower: A History of Black America,* 6th edition. New York: Penguin Books, 1993.

Bernhard, Virginia, Betty Brandon, Elizabeth Fox-Genovese, and Theda Perdue, editors. *Southern Women: Histories and Identities.* Columbia: University of Missouri Press, 1992.

Bogin, Ruth, and Bert James Loewenberg. *Black Women in Nineteenth Century American Life.* University Park: Pennsylvania State University Press, 1976.

Bogle, Donald. *Brown Sugar.* New York: Da Capo Books, 1990.

Braxton, Joanne M., and Andrée Nicola McLaughlin. *Wild Women in the Whirlwind: Afro-American Culture and the Contemporary Literary Renaissance.* New Brunswick: Rutgers University Press, 1990.

Carby, Hazel V. *Reconstructing Womanhood: The Emergence of the Afro-American Woman Novelist.* New York: Oxford University Press, 1987.

Clark-Lewis, Elizabeth. *Living In, Living Out: African American Domestics and the Great Migration.* New York: Kodansha International, 1996.

Dormon, James H., ed. *Creoles of Color of the Gulf South.* Knoxville: University of Tennessee Press, 1996.

Ferguson, Leland. *Uncommon Ground: Archaeology and Early African America, 1650–1800.* Washington, D.C.: Smithsonian Institution Press, 1992.

Foster, Frances Smith. *Written by Herself: Literary Production by African American Women, 1746–1892.* Bloomington: Indiana University Press, 1993.

Fox-Genovese, Elizabeth. *Within the Plantation Household: Black and White Women of the Old South.* Chapel Hill: University of North Carolina Press, 1988.

Franklin, John Hope. *From Slavery to Freedom: A History of Negro Americans.* New York: Knopf, 1980.

Fraser, Walter J., Jr., *Charleston! Charleston!* Columbia: University of South Carolina Press, 1989.

Gaspar, David Barry, and Darlene Clark Hine, eds. *More Than Chattel: Black Women and Slavery in the Americas.* Bloomington: Indiana University Press, 1996.

Genovese, Eugene. *Roll, Jordan, Roll: The World the Slaves Made.* New York: Pantheon, 1974.

Giddings, Paula. *When and Where I Enter: The Impact of Black Women on Race and Sex in America.* New York: Morrow, 1984.

Gordon, Ann D., Bettye Collier-Thomas, John H. Bracey, Arlene Voski Avakian, Joyce Avrech Berkman, eds. *African American Women and the Vote, 1837–1965,* Amherst: University of Massachusetts Press, 1997.

Gutman, Herbert G. *The Black Family in Slavery and Freedom, 1750–1925.* New York: Pantheon Books, 1976.

Guy-Sheftall, Beverly. *Words of Fire: An Anthology of African American Feminist Thought.* New York: The New Press, 1995.

Hall, Gwendolyn Midlo. *Africans in Colonial Louisiana.* Baton Rouge: Louisiana State University Press, 1992.

Hedgeman, Anna Arnold. *The Trumpet Sounds: A Memoir of Negro Leadership.* New York: Holt, Rinehart, and Winston, 1964.

Hine, Darlene Clark, ed. *Black Women in United States History.* Brooklyn: Carlson Publishing, 1990.

———, Elsa Barkley Brown, and Rosalyn Terborg-Penn, eds. *Black Women in America: An Historical Encyclopedia.* Brooklyn: Carlson Publishing, 1992.

———, Wilma King, and Linda Reed, eds. *We Specialize in the Wholly Impossible: A Reader in Black Women's History.* Brooklyn: Carlson Publishing, 1995.

———, ed. *Facts on File Encyclopedia of Black Women in America.* New York: Facts on File, 1997.

Horton, James Oliver. *Free People of Color: Inside the African American Community.* Washington: Smithsonian Institution Press, 1993.

Hurmence, Belinda, ed. *Before Freedom: 48 Oral Histories of Former North and South Carolina Slaves.* New York: Mentor, 1990.

Jones, Jacqueline. *Labor of Love, Labor of Sorrow: Black Women, Work and the Family from Slavery to the Present.* New York: Basic Books, 1985.

Kaplan, Sidney, and Emma Nogrady. *The Black Presence in the Era of the American Revolution,* rev. ed. Amherst, University of Massachusetts Press, 1989.

Katz, William Loren. *The Black West.* Garden City: Doubleday, 1971.

———. *Breaking the Chains: African American Slave Resistance.* New York: Atheneum, 1990.

———. *Black Women of the Old West.* New York: Atheneum, 1995.

Lebsock, Suzanne. *The Free Women of Petersburg: Status and Culture in a Southern Town, 1784–1860.* New York: W. W. Norton, 1984.

Lerner, Gerda, ed. *Black Women in White America: A Documentary History.* New York: Pantheon, 1972.

Levine, Lawrence. *Black Culture and Black Consciousness: Afro-American Folk Thought from Slavery to Freedom.* New York: Oxford University Press, 1977.

Litwack, Leon F. *Been in the Storm So Long: The Aftermath of Slavery.* New York: Knopf, 1979.

Loewenberg, Bert, and Ruth Bogin, eds. *Black Women in 19th Century American Life.* University Park: Pennsylvania State University Press, 1976.

Medea, Andra, and Kathleen Thompson. *Against Rape.* New York: Farrar Straus & Giroux, 1974.

Mellon, James, ed. *Bullwhip Days: The Slaves Remember.* New York: Weidenfeld & Nicolson, 1988.

Mumford, Esther. *Seattle's Black Victorians.* Seattle: Ananse, 1980.

Murray, Pauli. *Proud Shoes: The Story of an American Family.* New York: Harper and Row, 1978.

———, *Pauli Murray.* Knoxville: The University of Tennessee Press, 1987.

Nash, Gary B. *Forging Freedom: The Formation of Philadelphia's Black Community, 1720–1840.* Cambridge: Harvard University Press, 1988.

Neverdon-Morton, Cynthia. *Afro-American Women of the South and the Advancement of the Race, 1895–1925.* Knoxville: University of Tennessee Press, 1989.

Payne, Charles. *I've Got the Light of Freedom: The Organizing Tradition and the Mississippi Freedom Struggle.* Berkeley: University of California Press, 1995.

Perdue, Charles L., Jr., Thomas E. Barden, and Robert K. Phillips, eds. *Weevils in the Wheat.* Charlottesville: University Press of Virginia, 1976.

Powers, Bernard E., Jr. *Black Charlestonians: A Social History, 1822–1885.* Fayetteville: University of Arkansas Press, 1994.

Quarles, Benjamin. *The Negro in the Making of America.* New York: Macmillan, 1964.

———, *Black Abolitionists.* New York: Oxford University Press, 1969.

Shaw, Stephanie J. *What a Woman Ought to Be and to Do.* Chicago: University of Chicago Press, 1996.

Smith, Jessie Carney. *Notable Black American Women.* Detroit: Gale Research, 1992.

Southern, Eileen. *The Music of Black Americans.* 2nd ed. New York: Norton, 1983.

Sterling, Dorothy, ed. *We Are Your Sisters: Black Women in the Nineteenth Century.* New York: Norton, 1984.

Stevenson, Brenda E. *Life in Black and White: Family and Community in the Slave South.* New York: Oxford University Press, 1996.

Taylor, Arnold H. *Travail and Triumph: Black Life and Culture in the South Since the Civil War.* Westport, Connecticut: Greenwood Press, 1976.

Terkel, Studs. *Hard Times: An Oral History of the Great Depression.* New York: Pantheon Books, 1986.

———. *Race: What Blacks and Whites Think and Feel About the American Obsession.* New York: New Press, 1992.

Toll, Robert C. *On with the Show: The First Century of Show Business in America.* New York: Oxford University Press, 1976.

White, Deborah Gray. *Ar'n't I a Woman? Female Slaves in the Plantation South.* New York: Norton, 1985.

Wood, Peter H. *Black Majority: Negroes in Colonial South Carolina from 1670 through the Stono Rebellion.* New York: W. W. Norton, 1974.

Yee, Shirley. *Black Women Abolitionists: A Study in Activism, 1828–1860.* Knoxville: University of Tennessee Press, 1992.

Narratives and Other Writings by Black Women

Andrews, William L., ed. *Sisters of the Spirit.* Bloomington: Indiana University Press, 1986.

Jacobs, Harriet A. *Incidents in the Life of a Slave Girl, Written by Herself.* Edited and with an introduction by Jean Fagan Yellin. Cambridge: Harvard University Press, 1987. (First published in 1861 under the pseudonym Linda Brent).

Keckley, Elizabeth. *Behind the Scenes; Thirty Years a Slave and Four Years in the White House.* New York: Oxford University Press, 1988.

Richardson, Marilyn, ed. *Maria W. Stewart, America's First Black Woman Political Writer: Essays and Speeches.* Bloomington: Indiana University Press, 1979.

Taylor, Susie Baker King. *Reminiscences of My Life in Camp with the 33rd U.S. Colored Troops, Late 1st South Carolina Volunteers,* 1902. Published as *A Black Woman's Civil War Memoirs,* edited by Patricia W. Romero with an introduction by Willie Lee Rose. New York: Markus Wiener Publishing, 1988.

Wilson, Harriet E. *Our Nig; or, Sketches from the Life of a Free Black.* Introduction and notes by Henry Louis Gates, Jr. New York: Vintage, 1983. (First published in 1859.)

Other Recommended Books About Black Women

Fleischner, Jennifer. *Mastering Slavery: Memory, Family, and Identity in Women's Slave Narratives.* New York: New York University Press, 1996.

Gilmore, Glenda Elizabeth. *Gender and Jim Crow: Women and the Politics of White Supremacy in North Carolina, 1896–1920.* Chapel Hill: University of North Carolina Press, 1996.

Guy-Sheftall, Beverly. *Words of Fire: An Anthology of African American Feminist Thought.* New York: New Press, 1995.

Harley, Sharon, and Rosalyn Terborg-Penn, eds. *The Afro-American Woman: Struggles and Images.* Port Washington, New York: Kennikat, 1978.

Hine, Darlene Clark. *Black Women in White: Racial Conflict and Cooperation in the Nursing Profession, 1890–1950.* Bloomington: Indiana University Press, 1989.

Hull, Gloria T., Patricia Bell Scott and Barbara Smith, eds. *But Some of Us Are Brave.* Old Westbury, New York: Feminist Press, 1982.

Hunter, Tera W. *To 'Joy My Freedom: Southern Black Women's Lives and Labors After the Civil War.* Cambridge, Massachusetts: Harvard University Press, 1997.

Knupfer, Anne Meis. *Toward a Tenderer Humanity and a Nobler Womanhood: African American Women's Clubs in Turn-of-the-Century Chicago.* New York: New York University Press, 1996.

Morton, Patricia. *Disfigured Images: The Historical Assault on Afro-American Women.* New York: Greenwood Press, 1991.

Painter, Nell. *Sojourner Truth: A Life, a Symbol.* New York: W. W. Norton, 1996.

Peterson, Carla L. *"Doers of the Word": African American Women Speakers and Writers in the North, 1830–1880.* New York: Oxford University Press, 1995.

Rouse, Jacqueline Anne. *Lugenia Burns Hope: Black Southern Reformer.* Athens: University of Georgia Press, 1989.

Saville, Julie. *The Work of Reconstruction: From Slave to Wage Laborer in South Carolina, 1860–1870.* New York: Cambridge University Press, 1994.

Schwalm, Leslie Ann. *A Hard Fight for We: Women's Transition from Slavery to Freedom.* Champaign: University of Illinois Press, 1997.

Smith, Barbara, ed., *Home Girls: A Black Feminist Anthology.* New York: Kitchen Table: Women of Color Press, 1983.

Index

Female Benezet, 39
Feminism, 299–302, 313–14, 316
Feminist Party, 300
Ferebee, Dorothy, 223
Ferguson, Catherine Williams, 23–24
Fields, Mary (Stagecoach Mary), 175–76
Film, 254–57, 288
Firsts. *See* Accomplishments of black
   women
Fitzgerald, Ella, 242, 260
*Fleming v. South Carolina Electric and Gas
   Company*, 274
Fletcher, Francis, 173
Florida Fellowship of Colored Women's
   Clubs, 251
Foley, Lelia K. Smith, 306
Food, Tobacco, Agricultural, and Allied
   Workers of America (FTA), 248
Food Workers' Industrial Union, 247
Forten, Charlotte, 127, 138–39, 269
Forten, Charlotte Vandine, 37–38
Forten, James, 37, 138
Forten, Margaretta, 38, 113
Forten, Sarah, 110
Fortune, T. Thomas, 197
Foster, Autherine Juanita Lucy, 273
France, Louisiana as colony of, 50–57
Frankel, Noralee, 334
Franklin, Aretha, 296, 304
Franklin, Benjamin, 25
Franklin, John Hope, 333
Franklin, Martha, 224
Fraser, Walter J., Jr., 333
Free Africa Society, 39
Free black(s)
   in colonial America, 9, 17, 20, 21–26,
      29, 49–50, 58
   discrimination against, after Civil War,
      149
   land distribution to, 174
   traditional gender roles among 19th-
      century, 109
Free black women
   as antislavery activists, 105–13
   during colonial period, 21–26, 37–39,
      49–50, 58, 59–62
   freedom of individual slaves attained
      by, 111–12, 114–18, 135
   in Reconstruction era, 147–64
Freedmen's Bureau, 150, 151, 161
Freedom Rides, 280
Freedom Summer, 282
Freeman, Eleanor, 4

Froumountaine, Julian, 123
Fudge, Ann M., 306, 310
Fugitive Slave Law, 114, 116
Fuller, Meta Vaux Warrick, 228–29
Furman, Jan, 333

Gantt, Harvey, 278
Garrett, Bessie, 263
Garrett, Thomas, 116
Garrison, William Lloyd, 105, 109, 135
Gary, M. W., 167
Gaspar, David Barry, 333
Gender. *See also* Sexism; Women's rights
   black and women's suffrage and,
      157–60
   colonial America and roles based on,
      16–19
   contemporary discussion on, 313–14
   discrimination based on, in black rights
      movement, 299–302
   resistance to slavery and, 92–93
   slave labor of antebellum South and
      roles based on, 75–79
   traditional roles of, among 19th-
      century free blacks, 109
   values of white middle-class toward,
      adopted by black club women,
      182–83
Genovese, Eugene D., 99, 108
Gibbins, Isabella, 156
Gibson, Althea, 286
Giddings, Paula, 283, 315
Gilmore, Georgia, 275
Gilmore, Vanessa, 313
Giovanni, Nikki, 294
Gloucester, Elizabeth, 113–14
Goodman, Andrew, 282
Gould, Virginia, 334
Grandy, Moses, 83
Granson, Milla, 74
Grant, Rebecca Jane, 69
Graves, Mildred, 77, 78, 142
Gray, Victoria, 282
Great Depression, 240–65
   black arts and cultural expression in,
      253–61
   black economic self-determination and
      Housewives League of Detroit during,
      245–47
   black education during, 241, 250–51
   black unemployment during, 242–45
   black working women during,
      247–48